Lewis Mumford

ROOTS OF CONTEMPORARY AMERICAN ARCHITECTURE

a series of thirty-seven essays
dating from the mid-nineteenth century to the present

This book, collected and edited by Lewis Mumford, contains an introductory essay and biographies of the twenty-nine writers whose work appears herein.

DOVER PUBLICATIONS, INC.
NEW YORK

Published in Canada by General Publishing Company, Ltd., 30 Lesmill Road, Don Mills, Toronto, Ontario.
Published in the United Kingdom by Constable and Company, Ltd., 10 Orange Street, London WC 2.

This Dover edition, first published in 1972, is an unabridged republication of the second (1959) edition of the work originally published in 1952. The Biographical Sketches have been updated especially for this edition, and the illustrations appear for the first time.

International Standard Book Number: 0-486-22072-9
Library of Congress Catalog Card Number: 75-171490

Manufactured in the United States of America
Dover Publications, Inc.
180 Varick Street
New York, N. Y. 10014

Preface to the Dover Edition

Roots of Contemporary American Architecture was first published in 1952 by Reinhold Publishing Corporation. In the present edition the original Prefatory Note has been replaced by the Preface to the Second Edition, prepared for the Grove Press reprint in 1959. The Acknowledgments have been omitted, and the Biographical Sketches updated within the limitations of space. The illustrations are all new and have been selected especially for the present edition.

L.M.

October, 1971

Preface to the Second Edition

When this book was first published in 1952, it filled a gap that was a disgrace to American scholarship in architectural history. Largely by the use of original documents, it revealed the long period of intellectual germination that had preceded the emergence of indigenous modern forms in the eighteen-eighties, and their re-emergence, partly by importation from abroad, at the end of the nineteen-twenties. Though no one would try to write a history of Renaissance architecture without doing justice to the treatises on classic architecture that preceded it and accompanied it—Alberti, Palladio, Vitruvius—the long development of modern forms in our country had been minimized, and the role of a few original talents, like Louis Sullivan's, had been exaggerated, precisely because the ideological preparation had been neglected.

What this anthology sought to show was that modern architecture, in our own day a broad busy highway linking up every part of the country, could first be identified by old wagon tracks traced by the original pioneers. So far from being a mere revolt against academicism and historicism, it had a continuous history of its own, in thought and constructive experiment: indeed, it was nothing less than an attempt, in the words of the great English scholar, W. R. Lethaby, to give form to our new civilization. In creating that tradition, Greenough and Emerson, Thoreau and Jarves, Olmsted and Downing, were as well worth considering as the masters of early skyscraper architecture in Chicago; and these in turn had something to say about their basic beliefs and purposes that powerfully supplemented, if it did not go beyond, what they had concretely expressed in their buildings. If this book had done nothing more than call attention to the architectural reflections of John Wellborn Root and Joseph Warren Yost, it might well have justified its existence; while in bringing forth specimens of the robust architectural criticisms of Montgomery Schuyler, it not merely revealed the kind of intellectual encouragement that great pioneers like Richardson, Sullivan, and Wright had met with, but demolished the notion that original works of architecture were doomed to languish in the cultural desert of the genteel eighteen-nineties, withered by indifference, misunderstanding, and lack of patronage.

The notion that modern architecture emerged from a long foreground in our American past doubtless comes as a surprise to many laymen whose historical perspective scarcely spans more than a decade; and this would apply to many architectural students coming out of professional schools where courses in architectural history were ruthlessly wiped out, in the revolt against academic clichés, instead of being re-thought and re-cast so as to establish the living continuity between past, present, and the emerging future. The notion that modern architecture had not existed in America until the so-called "International Style" was transported here was almost too silly to be worth refutation; for it rested purely on the debater's trick of defining the modern as just that particular set of geometric abstractions and restrictive formulae that the leading architectural figures in Europe had derived from Mondrian and Ozenfant. This made no sense as history either in Europe or America; for the roots of contemporary form strike just as deep there as in our country, if not deeper, since the constructive audacity of modern architects and engineers had its earliest exemplars in the Gothic cathedral builders, and in their lineal successors, the more exuberant among the Baroque masters. Though each cultural period has a tendency to emphasize its discontinuity with the ideas and forms of its predecessor, no one can understand Eric Mendelsohn without taking into account Hans Poelzig, or Le Corbusier without reckoning with Auguste Perret, or Gropius without remembering van de Velde, who had built an earlier Bauhaus. If this is true for even the limited span of a generation or two, it is even more true for the larger movements of architecture: without Morris in England and Richardson in America the inchoate modern forms that were already in existence would have waited longer to find their effective esthetic expression. The "International Style" was only an eddy, in some ways a regressive backwater, in the development of contemporary form; for, under the increasingly perverse leadership of various leaders, it turned more and more into an external imitation of the outward forms of a mechanically functional architecture, with a sedulous disregard of human needs, functions, and purposes.

What the cult of the "International Style" did most to reveal in America was the incurable inferiority complex of many Americans, especially those who have made themselves at home in Europe without having had the good fortune to strike any deep roots in their own country. From colonial days on, this had led many people to prefer imported products, even if inferior, to home-grown ones, even if excellent. That attitude deserves no more respect than the opposite one of assuming that the local and the home grown are, by that fact alone, blessed with some ineffable superiority that transcends their all too visible and notorious limitations. Americans who belong to either of these camps are incapable of forming a just judgment about either their own native products or those of other countries. To be embarrassed over the genius of Frank Lloyd Wright, because it had no esthetic resemblance to the glib mannerisms of Le Corbusier, as more than one advocate of modern architecture was embarrassed a generation ago, was to identify a spinsterly meagerness of appreciation with good taste.

This book should be an aid in making a break with both forms of provincialism: with the isolationism that turns its back on the work of other nations or on the work of able European and Asiatic architects practicing in America, and with the "internationalism" that is open to every foreign innovation but excludes the contributions made by our own country. For THE ROOTS OF CONTEMPORARY AMERICAN ARCHITECTURE rests on two main assumptions. The first is that modern architecture is a continuation of the great traditions of historic architecture, not a break with or a rejection of them, merely because it does not pay more ancient modes the base flattery of outward imitation or mechanical revival. When modern architecture departs from the past, it does so for good reasons, either because the conditions of life generally have changed, or because fresh technological facilities offer fresh incentives for their imaginative use, or because new feelings and values demand a fresh form of esthetic expression, or for all these reasons together. In these departures, modern architecture is no further away from the architecture of the Renaissance than the forms of those times were distant from those of the Gothic period. Only those who would depart from the human norm entirely, to lay the foundations for that dehumanized creature, Post-Historic Man, preconditioned for comatose rocket flights into space, have any reason to conceive modern architecture as a complete break from the main trunk of tradition. But for such people, architecture has already ceased to exist: neither their underground shelters nor their launching platforms nor their universal crematoria have need of the architect.

The second assumption that governed the selection of these essays is that what we properly call modern architecture in America is part of a larger movement, now visible over the whole world. This is not, as many of the exponents of the "International Style," or of mechanical functionalism, hold—or at least once held—a uniform movement, utilizing the machine to produce mechanically identical forms all over the planet, without regard for historic tradition, for climatic differences, for accessible materials, for varied technical capabilities, for the individuality of the landscape or the urban form, and, above all, for the unique expression of the individual spirit, the architect himself, whose very manner of handling the common, the repetitive, the modular, the standardized reveals his personal mastery, and may open the way for even more positive expressions of his imagination, through the new use of traditional arts and modes.

There is no reason to confuse uniformity with universality: those who have made this mistake have committed many architectural blunders, like the glass wall under a subtropical summer climate, that would be laughable if they were not so lamentable in their results. An emphasis on the American contribution to the universal forms of modern architecture indicates that our contemporary mode of building is the repository of many regional and national traditions, each of which has contributed something of value to the universal movement, and, without forfeiting its national or regional characteristics, can absorb something in return. Thus the modern interior, from Frank Lloyd Wright on, owes a debt to the Japanese print and the Japanese house; thus, too, America took over the veranda from India, and may once more, under certain limited conditions, embrace with profit the screened wall also—*pace* Le Corbusier!—an Indian invention.

With these assumptions accepted, it is plain that one might compile a similar group of papers, embodying parallel ideas and architectural formulations, from British, French, German, or Italian sources. Certainly, it would be foolish for any one country to claim exclusive intellectual leadership or pre-eminence in achievement. Architecture, like all the other goods of our time, is a common enterprise, in which all mankind will eventually share in a continuous round of give and take: not by accident are some of the brightest names in American architecture today of Japanese or Chinese origin. I have no apologies, therefore, for having left out classic European statements on the same theme. If I have restricted myself to American publications, it is only because, in the first instance, each country must develop its own resources and build on its own tradition, in order to have a body of ideas to contribute to the common stock.

But on looking back over my selection, I am conscious of much that I might have added, of equal or greater interest: so though this is a reasonably full selection, it still leaves an opening for other similar works, based perhaps on different criteria. My chief regret is that I have left out a few brave native items, most of all Henry James's observations on both the virtues and the limitations of modern domestic architecture, as already practiced half a century ago. For in THE GREAT GOOD PLACE, that healing parable, he expressed in a few sentences, and to perfection, the ultimate human rationale of all the simplifications that the best modern architects have introduced, anticipating Mies van der Rohe by describing an architecture "all beautified with omissions." And again in an essay on New York in THE AMERICAN SCENE, he made a perceptively devastating analysis of the open type of plan, often taken as a definite hallmark of modern form. This judgment was not on the basis of Frank Lloyd Wright's departures, but on his experience of ordinary houses in the conservative and traditional East, where the open plan had already transformed the interior without yet achieving any equivalent exterior expression. James pointed out that this sort of domestic architecture produced the public atmosphere of a hotel lobby; and he observed, with remarkable prescience, that this demolition of privacy would grow worse before the need for privacy, indeed the right to privacy, was understood and restored.

Today, in giving this book a wider means of circulation I find fresh reasons for its existence. For during the last few years the impression has grown up, in certain quarters, that modern architecture, which began suddenly to flower in the Thirties all over the world, has gone suddenly to seed. Certainly there are many signs among contemporary architects of inner disturbance, of a loss of conviction and direction, of a failure to orient their course by the cardinal points, of a growing lack of coherence and order. On one hand, some of the architects whose work seemed full of promise only twenty years ago, have shown a greater talent for publicity than for building: their designs seem based on no other principle than "I'll try anything once," though they depart from the old popular song by adding, not "If I like it I'll do it again," but "If anyone likes it I'll never do it again." This attitude is as productive of real originality and cumulative development as the Detroit practice of changing the superficial characteristics of motor cars every year is a contribution to improved locomotion. On the other hand, there are supposedly modern architects, some of them originally most dogmatic about its forms and methods, who have made a complete about-face, and who have gleefully proclaimed a return to eclecticism. But these evidences of retreat and confusion bear witness to the inadequacy of the "International Style" formula, and even more to the ambivalent nature of modern technology.

Many unanticipated miscarriages and regressions have taken place in modern civilization, and it would be surprising if they did not make an appearance in modern architecture. Perhaps the greatest weakness of those who have attempted to formulate the conditions for an adequate expression of modern art, is that they tended, out of an innocent optimism that was understandable in the nineteenth century, to identify "modern" with "good," "progressive," "humane," "democratic," and to imagine that in embracing solely the new, particularly all those aspects of the new created by a machine technology and the physical sciences, we were also embracing the highest possibilities that opened to mankind. That attitude was naive; and by now it is damnably out of date. Modern civilization has produced the totalitarian state, the extermination camp, and nuclear weapons capable of wiping mankind off the face of the earth. No small part of the modern is brutally contrary to all that our Victorian ancestors lauded; it must be identified with the regressive and the anti-human. Even in countries like the United States, with a long tradition of freedom and self-respect, new varieties of compulsions and conformities, expressed in business as well as government, overpower our rational purposes and make mock of them: witness the American motor car, that rolling neurosis. Modern architecture, therefore, not merely gives expression to the best aspects of modern civilization: it also gives full representation to its worst elements—its purposeless materialism, its lubricious desire for publicity, its denial of the organic and the personal, its deference of human needs to those of the ever-growing, ever-expanding machine. Insofar as architecture is the expression of society, all these hideous contradictions will find an outlet in modern architecture, and have already found an outlet. This situation would not be notably different if the entire architectural profession had been hypnotized by Sir Albert Richardson and Mr. Henry Hope Reed: for there is no salvation from our dehumanized and irrational purposes by clothing ourselves in the motheaten fancy dress costumes of another age. That effort at grace and salvation would only add to the domain of the irrational.

All these weaknesses, now increasingly visible, must be granted: the modern is in fact a two-faced Janus; and unless our civilization returns to a more rational and humane base, in both its politics and its technology, there is no way of bringing to further fruition all the hopes and promises that underlay the development of modern form in every department. This is somewhat dismaying, and if modern architecture were a mere annual, flowering with the season, to be replaced by a different plant next year, we might have even more reason to be disheartened, and to join the panicky crowd that follows the annual fashion, even though it is now a fashion for the incoherent, the dehumanized, the irrational, and the absurd. But if modern architecture, like modern civilization, is part of a continuous human tradition, it can still, while preserving all that is life-promoting in our own age, draw on even deeper sources in the past; for its roots are planted in the soil of history, and if anything human survives the Age of Extermination, the age in which we now live, modern architecture will survive, too. It was not born yesterday; and it will not die tomorrow, unless all that is precious and human dies with it, too.

LEWIS MUMFORD

Amenia, New York
1959

Contents

List of Illustrations

A Backward Glance

by

Lewis Mumford

What the American Tradition Is Not

What is the American tradition in architecture? It is the modern tradition in architecture, as it has been shaped by the conditions and needs and opportunities of life in the United States. Viewed broadly, it is part of a world-wide change that is reshaping man's environment and laying the foundations for a new civilization. What we in America have contributed to this tradition is important, not because our efforts were self-enclosed or self-sufficient, but because they brought together a larger number of forces and ideals and, in so doing, made the modern movement more truly universal. The roots of contemporary architecture, as the following essays will show, strike deep.

At the outset, I range the American tradition with a world-wide movement toward shaping new architectural forms. By this I would distinguish the interests and purposes of this book from more restricted interpretations of "American tradition." When most people use this term, they conjure up precisely those elements that are not American. If they think of our earliest provincial architecture, they think of forms that were not yet definitely modified by New World needs or values, except perhaps in the farmhouses of seventeenth century New England where, by constant accretions and adaptations, an organic form began to take shape. So, too, people who mean by the "American tradition" our Georgian buildings betray by the very name the fact that they are referring to patterns and designs that were not in the least native: they forget that these same forms were typical of colonial architecture from Samarkand to South Africa.

Our Greek revival architecture itself, though it perhaps antedated similar work in Europe and had wider currency, derived, as the European examples did, from Stuart and Revett's Antiquities of Athens. If here this mode was seized upon passionately and gained wide ascendancy, that was mainly because the image of Greece, as the very pattern of democratic culture, was uppermost in the minds of the cultivated classes at a time when even ordinary schoolboys might read their Plutarch and recite their Demosthenes. Latrobe's effort to acclimate the classic forms more fully, in the Capitol, by substituting maize for acanthus leaves, did honor to his love for his adopted land, but contributed nothing to the new forms that were finally to make their appearance here. Even a primitive kind of building like the log cabin was not as native as we once liked to think: Shurtleff has proved that the log cabin, a true native of the northern woodlands of Europe, was brought over by the Swedes to Delaware in the eighteenth century. Though later the log cabin proved highly useful on the frontier, before sawmills became common or trees scarce, it is hardly an American contribution; just the contrary, this "typically indigenous" form turns out in fact to be a universal one.

The Birth of a New World

The American tradition, as the following writings will define it, is a mode of thinking and feeling, of planning and organizing and building, that Americans became conscious of only after they had established their political independence, had thrown off their colonial ways, and had begun to create a new mold for their life, in which past habits were modified by new processes, new activities, new purposes.

The first architectural writings on this tradition antedated any new building forms: the architects spelt the new ideas out in words long before they learned the art of translating them into sticks and stones and steel. The new possibilities that had first disclosed themselves in America were first plumbed by the writers of the Golden Day, by Emerson, Hawthorne, and Thoreau, by Whitman and Melville. These writers were no longer in the imitative colonial tradition in literature: after three hundred years of settlement, the culture that formed them had not merely established roots, but had sent forth new shoots, and produced new sports that were as indigenous and as unexpected, in this soil, as the Concord grape or the greening apple tree.

Though our country of course remained an integral part of Western Civilization as a whole and shared many European traits and interests the American landscape and the new way of life gave it special qualities, a tang and perfume, a texture and a color, that were as distinctively its own as the strong bouquet of a New York State wine, even when pressed from some grape long acclimated to the Garonne or the Rhine. While the imitation of Europe continued unabated, in both architecture and literature, this tendency was the work of the *nouveaux riches*, of poetasters and mediocrities in the arts; for the original minds of the period would have none of it. *Leaves of Grass*, *Moby Dick*, *Walden* revealed new experiences, a new way of looking at the world; and the forms of these works were as original as their contents. When in the eighties, in New England and the Middle West, this same spirit touched architecture, it is no accident that the architects who led this movement, Louis Sullivan and Frank Lloyd Wright, had in their youth turned for spiritual sustenance to Emerson and Whitman.

The great American writers of The Golden Day were touched by new experiences: the struggle with the wilderness, the adventurous efforts of the pioneer both to break fresh earth and stake out new spiritual claims, the exploration of remote seas by clipper-ships and whalers, and the multiplying contacts that were taking place with non-western cultures in Africa, Asia, and the South Seas. The disaffection from Europe, which characterized the patriotic American of this period wearied of a doomed feudalism and properly frightened by the savage new industrialism of Manchester and Birmingham—this disaffection opened the American mind to other cultures than the European. For Emerson, the Persian classics were as close as the Greek and Roman myths, just as for Frank Lloyd Wright, fifty years later, the clean exquisite lines of a Japanese print were even closer than the traditional image and line of the Renaissance.

With the same openness and readiness, the best minds of the Golden Day accepted the new triumphs of science and the machine: Emerson was more receptive to the doctrine of evolution than his Swiss-born contemporary, Agassiz, and even Thoreau, that dedicated lover of the primitive, found the music of the new telegraph wires in the wind as quickening as the more traditional Aeolian harp. In his search for cultural elements that were missing in the new world, the pious American might trudge over Europe, ransacking its castles and palaces and art galleries and museums; but the writer of *Self-Reliance,* in a sturdier spirit, would sing: "Give to pots and trays and pans, grace and glimmer of romance."

The new American saw the possibility of a fresh integration in culture, which would carry into the modern age the spirit that had created the great cultural epochs of the past. Sometimes the rejection of Europe and the past was over-harsh, in proportion perhaps to the attraction they still exercised on spirits not yet quite sure of themselves: hence Holgrave's extravagant diatribe, in *The House of the Seven Gables,* against seeing with dead men's eyes, a spirit that was later carried forward in Frank Lloyd Wright's pronouncements. But as in the rejection of the parent during adolescence, this attitude was an essential step in achieving independence: the right, as it were, to grow along one's own natural lines. If the revolt came earlier in literature than in architecture, that is only because architecture deals with more refractory materials. The writer can afford to wait for his audience, as Thoreau, Whitman, and Melville did in fact wait for a response to their best works: but the architect must remain impotent until his client has caught up with him. If the architect is too far in advance of his times to have the opportunity to build, he will be an architect in name only. This essential relation of agreement and cooperation between architect and client has, however, another side to it that is too frequently overlooked: namely, that the great periods of architecture are those in which the client has, by his sympathy and understanding, brought forth the architect's utmost powers, as the clients of Richardson, Sullivan, Root, Holabird, and Wright brought forth theirs. And that is why architecture is perhaps a better indication of the general vitality of a society than any other art.

As long as the American was content to imitate, without fresh adaptations, the modes of planning and building native to Europe, particularly to England, there was a certain coherence in our building; but it was gained at the price of any independence or originality, or fitness to the time, the place, and the purpose. What was truly vital in Jefferson's design for the University of Virginia was not his zealously studied classic forms but his layout of the university buildings in parallel rows, with connecting arcades separated by lawns open at both ends, instead of forming the more typical medieval quadrangle. In general, the courage to break loose from the stereotypes of the past did not come till after the Civil War. When it came, it was associated with the rise of mechanical industry; and its first outcome was disorder, confusion, vulgarity, and downright barbarism. The new pioneers of industrialism, as innocently unconscious of the foulness they were creating as a baby is of his bowel movements, were exerting an effect upon western civilization at large even more devastating than that of the land pioneer in America, who plowed the soils and opened the land to erosion and moved on. Yet industrialism, however vile at first appearance, was a formative element in the new culture that was coming forth; and the best buildings of the period were the industrial primitives—the cotton factories, the iron and glass market halls, the hothouses—whose forthright pragmatism was itself a symbol of the growing dominance of the machine, not merely in industry itself, but in the ordering of men's minds. When Schinkel beheld the cotton factories of Manchester, he properly hailed them as the source of a new architecture.

Unfortunately, most of Schinkel's contemporaries in architecture, even in America, lacked his insight or his powers of imaginative assimilation. To soften the obvious barbarism of the new industrial towns, the genteel architects of the nineteenth century took refuge in the dead forms of earlier cultures. If they were reluctant to change the old systems of construction, so as to use more fully new materials and technical processes, they were even more reluctant to abandon the old masks, hallowed by long use in church and palace. To cover the nakedness of the new utilitarian structure, they cut a Greek peplum, a Roman toga, a Medieval suit of armor, or a brocaded Renascence coat and ruff, to hide that dark Caliban. Such advances as were made in the use of style-forms as surface decoration were advances, usually, in historical correctness and mechanical versimilitude. Archaeological research and the photograph deprived the architect of the inspiration of ignorance or the self-confidence of fresh invention, which made so many "imitative" buildings of the Baroque period truly fresh creations, in everything except residual details.

By the middle of the nineteenth century, this studied resurrection of the dead had turned every big city into a cemetery of eclecticism: even Egyptian tombs, as in the famous prison in New York, or in many minor fraternity houses in college towns, would be added to Chinese pagodas and Roman temples. By that time a single building, like Colonel Colt's Armsmear near Hartford, might even boast, in addition to all its other styles, Turkish features: every city was in effect an architectural whatnot. Though an occasional architect, like the powerful, masculine Frank Furness in Philadelphia, would sometimes create a basically fresh and vigorous building like the library at the University of Pennsylvania, whose virtues sprang out of their defiance of correctness, it was difficult for those who wished to pass beyond eclecticism to avoid pious submission to the dead. So it was that the inventive James Bogardus, that pioneer in the use of the cast-iron building, designed his columns with classic forms; so, too, Henry Hobson Richardson did not arrive at a nonhistoric, and therefore contemporary, style till the last half dozen years of his life.

But long before the 'eighties, a new approach to both architecture and life began to take form in the American mind. It is important to grasp this sequence; for a fear of ideas is one of the marks of our present cultural self-stultification; and nothing could be more misleading than a history of American architecture concerned solely with technical processes and building forms, without any reference to the ideal framework in which all these changes took place. Even the belief in the machine, the desire to use the new processes and express them in building, is itself a formative idea. The first hint of a change comes forth in the earliest essays I have presented, those of Thoreau and Downing and Vaux though the latter two, particularly Downing who died in 1852 at far too early an age, were partly fettered by the now obsolete forms. Yet, just as Downing discovered new values in American plants and trees, I have little doubt that, had he lived, he would have developed, along the lines that Olmsted and Richardson actually followed, into an original creative artist.

But the great precursor of modern form, or at least the great philosopher, was Horatio Greenough. In his actual works of art he was still, like Downing, tied to the past, though he had courage enough to break with contemporary prudery in modelling the naked torso of George Washington in the fashion of the Roman emperors. But in his search for new principles of form, fitted to the modern age, this original mind laid the groundwork for a new esthetic doctrine, a doctrine capable of dealing with the new forces and values that science and mechanization were producing. Technical audacity and scientific originality provided at least a partial framework for a new scheme of life; and Greenough had the insight to see that this must likewise affect our esthetics. Emerson had at once recognized the penetration of Greenough's clean, first-hand evaluation of the new arts; but the essays in which this Yankee Stone Cutter set forth his philosophy, though republished in a Memoir in the eighteen-seventies, never had a wide popular success, comparable to that which greeted Le Corbusier some two generations later when he put forth ideas of the same order in *Vers une Architecture*. Nevertheless it is possible that Greenough's ideas continued to work under the surface; and this may even help to explain the fact that their next expositor was another young New Englander, Louis Sullivan.

Actually, the architectural demonstration of Greenough's ideas about function and form did not achieve anything like Greenough's clarity until John and Washington Roebling designed the Brooklyn Bridge. Even then, the architects were slow to follow this lead or, even when they followed it, to recognize what they were doing for what it actually was. Indeed, Le Baron Jenney, one of the major technical innovators, seems to have gone about his work absentmindedly—often instinctively doing the right thing but never conscious enough of it to give a rational account of his purpose. From the eighteen-forties to the eighteen-eighties, the new practices that were to invigorate American architecture were confined mainly to the shipyards and the factory. James Jackson Jarves turned to the Yankee clipper to exemplify the new form, indeed the new method of thought, that would presently affect architecture. Yes, the clipper ship, or even the new Yankee clocks, the American ax, most shapely and delicately poised of the new forms, made the sensitive see that the new was not necessarily the ugly, nor were the products of the machine less beautiful in their own fashion than the more intricate forms of handicraft. Here the new style, shapely, naked, clean, was actually in process of formation. We will follow its results in the section on the machine.

Domestic Forms and Regional Adaptations

Though the United States was a focal point for the invention of modern forms and for the new tradition, I must emphasize that it was part of a larger movement and that a similar tale could be told, with appropriate modifications, for other countries within the same orbit of civilization.

The new tradition rested on a fivefold foundation: the domestic, the regional, the mechanical, the social, the universal all entered into it. The decisive point of departure was a break with the conception of an architectural absolute, an archetypal perfection established for all time by the Greeks and the Romans—that brittle error of the Renascence. This error had been taken over even by the opponents of the Renascence modes, like Pugin and Ruskin; for these men sought to give to some moment in the development of Gothic architecture, such as the style of Thirteenth Century Lombardy which Ruskin favored, the same stereotyped authority that Palladianism had claimed for the classic. Behind this conception, supposedly based on history, was actually the conviction that history does not count: that time does not make a difference: that it is possible, by some formula for proportion, some fixation on special forms, to possess an eternal quality in art without doing justice to the time-bound, the local, the living and the subjective, and therefore the unique and finally incalculable. The sort of mind that accepted this formula—it is the same sort that now seeks salvation in the Golden Section—supposes that ours is a static world of Platonic form: so that the same elements may be transported anywhere and used by anyone willing to master the formula. That was a viable doctrine for the conquistadors and homesick colonial settlers: if they carried the "classic" with them, they would always find themselves at home.

But when architecture is so considered it loses the qualities of a living art; it is at best a mask or a form of scenic decoration; sometimes a comely mask, but nevertheless a mask. The renunciation of this false historicism brought about a return to real history, and restored continuity with a living tradition. One of the first steps in innovation, both in England and in America, was to return to the simple elemental forms of the seventeenth century farmhouse, to a vernacular that was continuous with the whole tradition of building in the ages before it, and had reached a fresh level of fitness and comely form derived from the new taste for privacy and from a sense of family life. In the 1850's, William Morris and Phillip Webb had returned to this tradition in the Red House, a building which, despite its occasional ogive arched windows, was in no sense a Gothic revival house; and a generation later, the same impulse led to the creation of a new kind of stained shingled cottage by Henry Hobson Richardson and his many followers, McKim and White (as in the adventurous Low House at Bristol, R. I.) Bruce Price, Clarence Luce and, not least, W. R. Emerson: indeed Emerson's house for L. Greenough in Jamaica Plain (1879) had the qualities Richardson brought to perfection even before the latter's best work.

Here was a true picking up of the thread of historic continuity in a type of building, the dwelling house, whose form was still to be affected, in any large degree, by mechanical inventions. The sources for this new architecture were many; and one of them, surely, was a growing sense of the qualities of the natural landscape, interpreted by Andrew Jackson Downing and carried even further by one of the greatest artists and citizens America has yet produced, Frederick Law Olmsted. One of the leading principles of this new naturalism in architecture and landscape design was that the building and landscape should form a harmonious whole. Sometimes this was taken in a too primly limited manner to mean that, say, pointed gables and fir trees should go together. But, as the curious will find if they examine Bruce Price's essay in *Homes in City and Country*, edited by Russell Sturgis, it involved much more than this: the proper placing of the building, to command a view, to court summer breezes, to get the maximum amount of winter sunlight. Our domestic architects of the eighteen-eighties were as conscious of "orientation" as the boldest experimenters today; and nothing that Mr. Richard Neutra has written about "the mystery and realities of the site" would have seemed in the least strange to them.

In this very matter of orientation, indeed, one discovers what a serious hiatus has occurred, particularly in America, through the lack of a conscious tradition, critically re-examined and passed on from generation to generation. The correct principles of orientation were long ago demonstrated by Vitruvius in his famous treatise; though that seems to have been the last lesson the pious followers of Vitruvius in the Renascence were ready to learn, unless Professor Anthony Garvan is right in thinking it dictated the plan of New Haven. So, too, the interest in Chinese art and thought in the eighteenth century did not apparently bring about any insight into the similar Chinese principles of orientation. In Brackenbridge's *Modern Chivalry*, at the beginning of the nineteenth century, he observed of the houses in a back country settlement: "There was still a defect of judgment in the construction of their houses, for the summer as well as the winter seasons. They were placed, in most cases, as they ought to be, *fronting the south*, but without perforations or passages for the air, by means of windows from the west to the east." That insight became universal. While the architects of the eighties arrived by themselves at the correct principle, of making the main rooms of the house face the south or southeast, that principle was presently buried once more; so that when it was first recovered by town planners, a generation later, they at first took for granted that an east-west exposure was the best one. Like every other choice made by the architect, orientation for sunlight is only one of the factors that must be taken into account; but the principle that utility rooms and rooms for nocturnal use should be on the north side, and living rooms, children's rooms, and the kitchen should be on the south side should remain a paramount factor in design in the northern hemisphere.

The principles of solar orientation was re-established on a scientific basis by a Boston architect, William Atkinson, who in turn drew upon various contemporary experiments. By building sunboxes, with a glass front open to the south, solar experimenters discovered that a temperature of 100 degrees Fahrenheit could often be obtained indoors when the outside temperature was zero or lower; and even more important, Atkinson demonstrated that a southern exposure in a temperate latitude is the most favorable one, since it gives a minimum amount of sunlight in summer and a maximum amount in winter. The first edition of Atkinson's book consisted of a thousand copies; and to judge by the effect it had on American architecture, very few of that thousand were sold, or at least read to any purpose. When Henry Wright, Sr. and George Keck in the nineteen-thirties once more sought independently to establish the correct principles of orientation, they worked, apparently, without knowledge of Atkinson's treatise. One wonders how many times "orientation" will have to be rediscovered before it becomes an integral part of the architect's equipment.

The new domestic tradition in America had still another source, a new love of color and texture, a new feeling for the natural, unmodified use of wood and stone. Perhaps, even as early as the eighties, some of this was derived from contact with the Japanese; but it was likewise part of a general revolt against the de-natured, the artificial or the over-artful. In the autumnal colors of the new shingled houses of the eighties, the butternut greens and russet browns and sumach reds of Richardson's later cottages and those of his followers, soon to be plunged deep into a foliage that would completely overwhelm them, at least in the summer, there was a deep harmony with the New England landscape: only the white and grey of the earlier shingled Cape Cod house, white gulls' wings against grey sea and sky, could match them for fitness. But Richardson also taught, in his exuberant Ames Lodge, for instance, or in his variegated libraries, that there was a special richness of texture in the rough countrystone and an equal richness of color in the contrast of sandstones and granites.

Unpainted woods were used in interiors, as John Burroughs fancied them in his ideal house, before Wright and Maybeck employed them: indeed redwood was a favored interior wood in the East at least twenty years before the new redwood houses, with their picture windows, were built by Maybeck and John Galen Howard in Berkeley, or by the brothers Greene in Pasadena. In that period happily the best architects of California, untouched by the Eastern reversion to the forms of colonialism and imperialism, carried on the domestic tradition of the eighties, which passed unbroken—though with fresh innovations—into the work of William Wurster and his colleagues. The growing taste for country life itself supported these architectural innovations; and in the new suburbs, like Short Hills and Summit,

New Jersey, where Halsey Wood practiced, like Roland Park in Baltimore and Oak Park near Chicago, some of the happiest individual buildings of the period arose. All had the characteristic signs of the new domestic feeling: simple entrance halls with fireplaces at the center, to give a feeling of inner snugness and security, with numerous nooks and hiding places, dear to children, in the living rooms and rounded stair towers: nooks that were to be later rationalized out of existence, though they gave the young places for quiet dreaming or mischievous eavesdropping on their elders which less romantic elevations have perhaps too ruthlessly eliminated.

But along with this went a new informality in living, which manifested itself in a peculiarly American type of open plan for the common living quarters. John Wellborn Root, writing on the domestic dwellings of the Middle West, observed: "One feature in the plans of Western city dwellings must be very clearly defined. This is their openness. Not only are windows upon the average larger than in the East but they are more frequent, as are also bay windows, oriels, etc., while in the general plan rooms are more closely related, openings between rooms wider, and single swinging-doors less frequent. Several dwellings in Chicago—and there are many in other western cities —have no doors whatever in the first story, except those at the entrance between the dining room and the butler's pantry, curtains being exclusively used." Root was in error only in thinking that this was a contrast between West and East: it was mainly a contrast between the old and the new, for many eastern plans show the same kind of openness: in both cases well before Frank Lloyd Wright had pushed the open plan to its logical conclusion by a thorough reorganization of space—rather than merely leaving a wall open on an otherwise conventional layout of rooms.

One thing is plain: the movement toward utilizing the indigenous, the natural, the regional, in the dwelling house resulted in the first buildings in the United States that could properly be called either original or truly contemporary or consciously wedded to their soil. Here again there is a close comparison with what happened in Britain a little later, under Voysey and Mackintosh, Ashbee, Baillie Scott, Unwin, Parker, and Lutyens; and in both cases the achievement of a true contemporary form was interrupted—though in America not completely choked off—by a fashionable reaction in favor of a genteel revivalism, safe and correct, based on picture-book precedents and doting tourists' memories. In America, between 1900 and 1930, a pious eclecticism, which denied both the facts of history and the requirements of modern life, broke the thread of tradition: the backwash of that new fashion was especially visible in the suburbs where Georgian country houses, Norman manors, Italian Renaissance villas, more correct than those of the eighteen-fifties but for that reason even more lifeless, were surrounded, near the city, with even gaudier lower middle class debasements. But one must not exaggerate the extent of this retreat during the first three decades of the twentieth century: it was not quite as overwhelming and as universal as it is sometimes made out to be.

The Architecture of the Interregnum

In his *Autobiography of an Idea,* Louis Sullivan, seeing the whole country through the dark spectacles of his own disintegration and defeat, caused many people to believe that all fresh design came to a standstill after the Chicago World's Fair of 1893 when the white cloud of classicism hung poisonously over the whole country and made McKim, Mead and White, Graham Anderson Probst and White, D. H. Burnham and Company, and Carrère and Hastings, the leading firms. That is far from the whole truth. The fact is that from 1895 to 1915 American architecture still had many vigorous moments: this was the period of Sullivan's own most original buildings, including the Schlesinger and Mayer department store (Carson, Pirie, Scott & Co.), of Wright's bold and characteristic development of his Prairie Houses, to say nothing of his Larkin Building and Midway Gardens; it was the period that on the Pacific Coast gave to Bernard Maybeck, to Irving Gill, to the Brothers Greene, the opportunity for many happy experiments with indigenous forms. In Chicago, Dwight Perkins designed his schools and park buildings, Sullivan's assistant Elmslie designed the Sullivanesque courthouse for Sioux City, Iowa, while Barry Byrne, coming out of Wright's office, created a fresh idiom for such traditional buildings as churches; if Irving Pond was a more modest innovator, he was far from being a reactionary.

Even in the less pretentious buildings of the time, the influence of the arts and crafts movement in purifying and simplifying public taste was a healthy one, and it had widespread effect. The mission furniture of this period, sound if ponderous, often survived generations of misuse in college dormitories and fraternity houses; while the new bungalows popularized by The Craftsman magazine, if often crude in design, introduced many substantial innovations in housekeeping—not only rationalized kitchens but the very idea of giving a house the convenience of an apartment by confining it to one floor. This, too, was the period of regional differentiation: a movement that is only now being carried far enough to introduce those subtle variations in adaptation to setting or to climate, that will give further grace and variety to our standardized procedures. But at least the beginnings were made—with increasingly marked distinctions, as between the low-lying prairie house of the Middle West, the shingled cottages with steep pitched roofs of New England, and the redwood house of the Bay Area in San Francisco, or the brilliant white stucco houses, sometimes with flat roofs, but no longer "Spanish colonial," which Irving Gill built in Southern California. As late as 1914, The Architectural Record published an article on a striking hillside home in Los Angeles, designed by E. B. Rust, done in redwood with low pitched gable roofs with wide overhangs. Such houses one finds scattered all over California: homely yet homey.

Nor was the influence of the current magazines, whether architectural or popular, wholly on the side of the Genteel Reaction; far from it. The pages of the Architectural Record, the Western Architect, and not least, Gustav Stickley's handsomely designed magazine, The Craftsman, gave modern architecture an impetus, by publicizing its good buildings and subjecting them to critical appreciation. All this should not be underrated. The innovators of this period were not in fact ostracized, still less deprived of the opportunity to work. Even the women's magazines, which came to exert such a retarding influence in abetting the reaction that took place after 1915, were on the side of the innovators. Did not the Ladies Home Journal early in the century specially sponsor Frank Lloyd Wright's design of two houses?

Actually, a sturdy sense of self-confidence was widespread during this period; so that Mr. Van Wyck Brooks, in the final volume of his literary history, has truly called this period The Confident Years. Montgomery Schuyler, whose architectural criticisms continued to appear in The Architectural Record, never hauled down the flag: he, who had been such an eager and searching exponent of the new architecture when he did a classic monograph on the work of Adler and Sullivan, almost at the end of his career in 1912, published an article on Frank Lloyd Wright—"an architectural pioneer." Perhaps here is the place to quote his judgment, in that article, on the works of Sullivan and Wright. "It is hard to see," he said, "how an unprejudiced inquirer can deny that such designers as Mr. Sullivan or Mr. Wright have the root of the matter, and that their works are of good hope, in contrast with the rehandling and rehashing of admired historical forms, in which there is no future nor any possibility of progress."

This is not to discount the forces of reaction. The blight of the World's Fair did in fact fall heavily upon the big cities, as the old-fashioned enterprisers of the eighties, brusque, exuberant, and vulgar, the men who built the steelworks and sank the oil wells and girdled the continent with railroads, gave way to a less attractive type, the slick financiers and manipulators, whose methods were more devious and whose vulgarity, though just as conspicuous, sought to mask itself in the hand-me-downs of culture, revarnished and framed, at fabulous prices, by equally adroit financial manipulators, like Joseph Duveen. These men were no longer creators but gaping and goggle-eyed connoisseurs: no longer builders but buyers; and their values, being based on the counters of finance, were as derivative as they were abstract. They pictured themselves as the Caesars and the Borgias and Napoleons of their era; and instead of taking chances in buying original works of art or financing contemporary buildings, they wanted only gilt-edged esthetic securities whose value was already well established in the market place.

The influence of metropolitan financiers was an unhappy one on American architectural taste: it stood like a wall against the adventurous, against the contemporary, against new values and new significances. Their animus was mordantly described by Thorstein Veblen, with scarcely more than an occasional touch of exaggeration, in his *Theory of Business Enterprise;* and though their almost childlike munificence brought to America many precious works of art of the past, their very insecurity of taste, which made them dependent upon the charlatans and confidence men of the esthetic world, set them in opposition to new departures in architecture. Like Duveen himself, buying up Monets and putting them in his cellar lest his clients acquire a taste for modern art, these ambivalent benefactors were perhaps afraid that the creative forces in America might devaluate all their lush ancestral investments, and their own false status as well.

After 1910 the Genteel Reaction prevailed almost unchallenged, for more than a decade, piling up ill-fitting masks of reminiscent beauty that covered the structural reality these architects dared not reveal, and disclosing an enervating emptiness of spirit. Its products ranged from the Roman Baths that became the Pennsylvania Railroad Station in New York to the elongated Guild Hall tower, laced with gold, that was the Woolworth Building. Whether the masks were classic or Gothic made little difference, though occasionally the organic structure itself would be so solidly conceived, like the Grand Central Terminal in New York, that it almost nullified, by its own inherent power, the triviality of the architectural detail. With Frank Lloyd Wright preoccupied in Japan with the Imperial Hotel from 1914 onward, with Sullivan passing into joblessness and destitution and some of their weaker brethren gradually fading from originality and conviction into eclecticism and cynicism, American architecture faltered in its development. It is significant that Bertram Grosvenor Goodhue, in his own career, almost completely retraced like a sleepwalker the course taken by Richardson, without any sense of being able to build on foundations already soundly laid; so that it was only with the McCoy house in Honolulu that he began to break away from historic modes, in plan as well as in elevation, to produce a fresh design that had, most charmingly, some relevance to its tropical environment.

This strange interregnum lasted longer than it should have because of an impoverishment of ideas, an exaggerated respect for the historically accredited, gentility itself. A similar recession took place in England, where the successful architects reacted from the fresh domestic designs of Voysey, Parker, and even Lutyens, to archaic Georgian modes with their anemic historic correctness, and in their inability to handle structures that were not in accord with the simple spatial and mechanical requirements of Georgian building. Why had this change come about? I once put this question to Sir Raymond Unwin, one of the leaders of the vernacular renascence, and found to my surprise that he had never even posed it to himself as a problem. Partly, perhaps, the reaction was due to a consciousness that originality, if undisciplined, might produce monstrosities; but partly it was because pecuniary canons of taste began to exercise an undue influence: to be correct was more important than to be alive. Even Gustav Stickley, who had almost singlehanded invigorated the Arts and Crafts movement in America, abandoned this effort around 1915 and took to reproducing older types of American furniture: not having the strength to assimilate the past, after his first youthful effort with modern forms, he copied old models without changing a line. Some of these forms, like the sprung Windsor chair, were so elemental in their conception as to be universal, as universal as, say, a barrel, another type of the sprung construction; but unfortunately sometimes the models imitated were as antiquated and body-defying as the ladder-back chair.

If, however, the situation for architecture became increasingly dismal in New York and Chicago, the provincial backwaters did not altogether lose the lesson of the great innovators of the eighties. Did not the bankers of Iowa, with sturdier taste than the Morgans and Mellons, remember Louis Sullivan and summon him to do a succession of small country banks despite his difficult personality and his disreputable habits? This element of regional self-respect and love, associated mainly with the more domestic aspects of life, is one of the permanent bequests, surely, of the American tradition, as it must be of any other living tradition that builds on native ground and on the ways and habits of the people.

But in no age are regional needs the sole constituents of architecture; for every region is part of a larger community, the nation and the civilization of which it is a part; and it draws many of its best elements, as it draws coffee or rubber or tung oil, from distant lands. This applies equally to the dwelling house: as we shall see presently, the esthetic sense, the technical processes, and the climatic adaptations characteristic of other parts of the world helped us, in various parts of our continent, to come closer to fulfilling our own needs.

The Contribution of the Machine

If it was out of a fresh sense of the soil and the landscape and the region that one part of the living American tradition has come—and must still come—it is through the challenge of the machine that another part has manifested itself. Here the American had a special advantage over the European. Raw materials existed here in abundance, but labor, except in the days of the most copious immigrations, was relatively scarce. This situation put a premium on American ingenuity, not in the least limited to the Yankee, for inventing labor-saving devices; it kept him from wasting precious time on embellishing, with irrelevant images, utilitarian objects otherwise complete without such ornamentation.

Now, clean mechanical forms, well-adapted to the function they served, did not of course originate with the power loom or the steam engine; indeed, the steam engine, for a long time, was a far from clean form. Even simple handicraft ages enjoyed such organic forms, in barns and haystacks, in walls and fortifications and warehouses. The mission of the machine was to universalize that simplicity and cleanliness in the interest of efficiency, or labor saving. All this was part of a heritage that the American shared with the new European; and during the early days of the paleotechnic revolution, our country lagged behind the superb constructions of Rennie and Telford and Brunel; though Ithiel Towne, with his wooden truss bridge, was no mean engineer.

By the third quarter of the nineteenth century we had almost come abreast of the British; and thanks to another British invention, the Bessemer process for making steel, the engineers and architects of Chicago suddenly leaped ahead. This story is by now a fairly familiar one; and I need not retell the evolution of the skyscraper in Chicago, all the more because I have marshalled together, in these essays, a series of firsthand accounts of the whole swift process. The habit of frame construction was first worked out in wood, for whose detailed story we must thank the Swiss historian, Sigfried Giedion; the enclosure of iron and steel in fire-resistant materials; the invention of the high speed elevator—all this resulted in the crystallization of a new form.

The evolution of the skyscraper, from the Home Insurance Building and the Tacoma Building onward, was the work of many hands and minds: for this reason one discovers such contradictory expressions as Root's Reliance Building and Sullivan's Insurance Buildings in St. Louis and in Buffalo, though each in its way had broken firmly with the past. Some of the purest expressions of the skyscraper, such as the Great Northern Hotel, had the façades accentuated with swelling bays, first so used in the Tacoma Building—though their original use in America doubtless goes back to Boston town dwellings. For a time these projecting bays seemed about to become a hallmark of the Chicago School. In the logical expression of steel and glass, it was scarcely possible to go farther than the Reliance Building, which in effect anticipated by a whole generation Mies van der Rohe's all-glass façade. But if the Reliance Building's form was not copied, this was perhaps due to no perversity of traditionalism, but to the fact that such a building had no defenses against extremes of heat and cold such as prevail all too uncomfortably in Chicago: so that Sullivan was on a sounder track when he designed his Stock Exchange Building and his Gage Building.

Within a brief decade, the formal possibilities of steel cage construction for office buildings had been explored—and practically exhausted. What was needed for further development was an organic approach, which would arrive at the appropriate shape and dimensions of the plot, would further the economic evolution of the plan, and would arrive at the correct height for economy and civic convenience. In brief, the next stage in the improvement of the business building was toward the reorganization and interrelation of the individual unit in terms of the planning of a whole urban quarter.

Unfortunately, the skyscraper, as Montgomery Schuyler pointed out, was an almost automatic response to land speculation: mechanization was subservient to the desire to achieve profitable congestion; and the architects as a profession did not oppose with any conception of public interests the private and shortsighted rapacity of the businessman—although that shortsightedness was, in time, to impose wastes, inefficiencies, and increased taxes upon every inhabitant of the city, in a vain attempt to correct a paralyzing congestion that should never have been allowed to come into existence in the first place. The architects of Chicago were technically adventurous, but socially timid: since they cheerfully accepted land speculation and congestion as if they were laws of nature, it was only by a happy accident that their site plans would turn out to be sound.

What we unfortunately are not conscious of in the history of the mechanization of architecture is the relation to the new mechanical methods and mechanical utilities to the other components of good building. In this, criticism has long been as backward as the architects themselves, who accepted their clients' limited programs with affable docility. So it happens that in plan one of the few office buildings that fully met the needs for light, air, circulation, and the economic use of space was the last of the old-fashioned masonry buildings: Burnham and Root's Monadnock Building. In other words, the whole movement toward steel-frame construction in tall buildings was pushed to its conclusion without any systematic attempt, at any point, to rationalize the plan itself and to create an efficient, flexible, well-lighted and well-aired quarters for the new bureaucracy.

As far as the plan goes, the Monadnock Building had more to teach than the Home Insurance Building or, for that matter, almost any other office building till the Airlines Building was designed for Rockefeller Center. For the Monadnock Building was a shallow oblong building, placed on an "island" surrounded on four sides by streets, so that its air and light were protected. Such a plan provides the maximum amount of live space and the minimum waste on corridors and dead space, fit only for storage. If that form had been translated into steel skeleton construction and had become one of the standard ground plans for business buildings, the commercial centers of our cities would have escaped the baffling congestion and disorder that have attended the attempt to hog cubic space, in order to increase speculative land values, at the expense of efficient transportation and the economic, healthy despatch of business.

Actually the skyscraper, from first to last, has been largely an obstacle to intelligent city planning or architectural progress. Its chief use was to overcrowd the land for private financial advantage, at no matter what cost to the municipality, and to provide, in the form of the meretricious towers that graced successive boom periods, a costly means of publicity and advertisement, conceived without any prudent calculation of the return on the investment. So the lesson of collective order was never learned; and the precedent it set was not even feebly recovered until Rockefeller Center was laid out. This gives to most of the discussions of the proper form of the skyscraper, even to Louis Sullivan's, an air of studied irrelevance. Though Sullivan recognized that, in the form it had taken, the skyscraper was an antisocial conception, his own analysis did not overcome this, nor did his own examples correct anything except the servile eclecticism of some, but by no means all, of his Chicago contemporaries. Esthetically, Sullivan reduced the problem of the expression of the skyscraper to that of a conventional base for shops and services, a shaft for offices, and a capital to screen the elevator machinery. In the Wainwright or the Prudential buildings the result was outwardly comely; but, not being related to a new plan which would secure the essentials of light and air, it was not really a radical departure.

In his preoccupation with the face of the skyscraper, Sullivan contributed little to the plan; it is indeed symptomatic of this that he regarded the Bayard Building in New York (so Claude Bragdon reported) as his most satisfactory skyscraper: for architecturally speaking, the Bayard Building is only a façade. So hobbled were American architects by the prevailing dominance of the profit motive in exploiting land and financing building investments, so uncritically did they accept the businessman's limited purposes and naive solutions, even when they robbed him of a sound long-term investment, that no essential improvement was made in skyscraper architecture from between

1885 and 1935: if anything, most later architects had fallen short of the bold achievements of the Chicago masters.

If the Monadnock building waited for half a century before its lessons were in any degree followed up, Wright's Larkin Building, which dates back to 1904, has waited even longer. Mr. Henry-Russell Hitchcock has characterized this building as a demonstration of the inherent monumentalism of industrial building; but that is almost the last thing I should be tempted to say of it. For one thing, the Larkin Building is not an industrial but a commercial structure, originally dedicated to the assorting of soap coupons and to higher branches of administrative work; for another, because of its external features, this building is in its esthetic and symbolic effect far more of a temple than the Unity Temple Wright was to design two years later. Consider the very plan of the building, with its shallow floors arranged around a quadrangular well, with only the ground floor utilizing the space in the center, getting its overhead light through the glass covered roof as in an old-fashioned department store. This interior had the effect of a great nave; and its acoustic properties were excellent: a fact made use of by the Larkin Company, which was one of the first companies to introduce music as a means of increasing the efficiency of its staff. Apart from this irrelevant monumentality, the functional requirements were admirably met by the shallow floor plan and by the windows, which were placed sufficiently above the heads of the workers to give a maximum light and a maximum flexibility in the use of unbroken wall space, with a minimum of unpleasant drafts.

This building had much to teach the architect about the design of efficient business quarters, though the shallow wings did not need the over-all enclosure. Here the lack of sound critical appreciation has been a handicap to further development. As for the monumentality, it lacked only one thing: a religious cult fit to be housed on that imposing scale, in such an original structure.

But the machine had other contributions to make to architecture than the creation of the skyscraper and the spanning of great spaces in auditoriums and factories. The new processes of mass production affected every part of construction: beginning with the piping and plumbing, with the prefabricated windows and doors: indeed by the nineties, both Gustavino acoustic tiles and plasterboard were being advertised; while prefabricated houses, beginning with the iron sheds that were shipped to California during the Gold Rush days, count as the oldest, if still the least successful effort at making mechanization take command: even Frank Lloyd Wright had his hand at designing them. Why the prefabrication of the dwelling house was in fact a mirage—although prefabrication itself steadily became a more important element in architecture—was first revealed by Henry Wright, Sr. In the form of new mechanical utilities, the machine had altered the internal balance of the building by decreasing the relative importance, economically, of the external shell and demanding an ever larger share of the building budget for the mechanical means of supplying water, gas, electricity, sewage outlets, heat, sanitary devices, to say nothing of paved roads and connections thereto. This analysis, exquisitely simple yet conclusive, deserves, I believe to be resurrected; for architects, builders, and clients have as a whole not sufficiently understood what was taking place, nor have they understood the constant choice that must be made between mechanical gadgets and space, since even the rich cannot afford both in unlimited amounts.

Yet with all these qualifications about the mechanical development of modern architecture, we must remember that the new problems of building, and the new forms made possible by industry, roused the imagination of the best architects. What is more, they will continue to do so even when machine-worship, that contemporary form of fetishism, becomes disreputable. Richardson, whom people still too patly associate with his earlier traditional forms, declared before he died that some of the structures he most wanted to design were a grain elevator and the interior of a river steamboat, then still a great popular mode of transportation; and if he did neither, he did create railroad stations, public libraries, warehouses, and business buildings including the admirable Pray Building in Boston, his last effort, which embodied the spirit of the age with utmost vigor and confidence.

Where Richardson left off in the Marshall Field Building and the Brattle Street house, Sullivan and Wright both began. But some of the best buildings of the next fifty years were examples of anonymous architecture: warehouses, factories, grain elevators, whose elemental shapes would in time affect the imagination of a Le Corbusier, a Gropius, a Mendelsohn. Sometimes these buildings were in fact the work of architects: Even during the Genteel Reaction, firms like Schmidt Garden and Martin in Chicago, or Albert Kahn in Detroit, produced factories and warehouses of great merit; and the interior of the Hill Auditorium at Ann Arbor (by Albert Kahn with Ernest Wilby as designer) stands next to Adler and Sullivan's Auditorium Building as one of the finest solutions for the problem.

But in the interpretation of the new possibilities of the Machine, Frank Lloyd Wright took the lead. The series of lectures he gave in Chicago at the beginning of the century, reaching their climax in his famous Hull House lecture reprinted here, showed a capacity for assimilating the new methods and forms that antedated Le Corbusier's brilliant polemics by almost a generation though it had its accompaniments, naturally, among a few of the European leaders, like Horta, Van de Velde, and, at the most rigorous rationalist extreme, Adolph Loos. In interpreting these new possibilities in America, the critics did not lag behind the architects: in particular, Montgomery Schuyler, the best equipped, the most discriminating, the most helpful critic of architecture—I might even say the only one fully worthy of the name—that America had yet produced. Schuyler's criticism of the Brooklyn Bridge was the bugle call of the new architectural criticism: an essay worthy in its way to stand beside the bridge itself—indeed it almost made further criticism superfluous. Schuyler not merely could recognize an original work when he saw it, as distinguished from the current feeble imitations and masks, but he understood the conditions under which, in his time, such works were produced. I only wish space permitted me to publish in its entirety his admirable essay on the work of Adler and Sullivan. Some day, I trust, an age more conscious of the need for tradition, and an America more heedful of its living past, more respectful of its own best achievements, will bring together in a single volume a representative group of Schuyler's essays. He could be tart as well as just. Did he not say that Richardson's overheavy masonry buildings were not defensible except in a military sense?

Like orientation, the machine has been rediscovered, as a source of form, from generation to generation: first in the fifties with Greenough, then in the eighties with the Chicago architects; and once more, thanks largely to Le Corbusier, in the nineteen-twenties. If at this last point I republish a little essay of my own, otherwise unimportant, it is only to show that, though the tradition did not persist here, neither did the recognition of the Machine's significance altogether vanish.

The Social Conception of Architecture

One further thread in the modern tradition must now be followed: the conception of architecture as a social art. In a broad way, this conception unites Ruskin and Greenough; for they both were conscious of the way in which the collective habits and purposes of the community are determinants of form. But the social conception came, through the teachings of William Morris and his followers, to mean something more than this: namely, that the architect has a social responsibility and that the individual building must be related to its site, to its landscape, to the neighborhood and city of which it is a part. The last stage in design is the expression of this relationship.

This conception did not develop solely out of a sociological understanding of the process of building, although it began there with Ruskin's pioneer analysis of *The Stones of Venice*, and was carried into contemporary life by Louis Sullivan, particularly in the *Kindergarten Chats*. But it came about likewise in a negative way, through the attempts by housing reformers and architects to correct the evils and disorders of an antisocial mode of building, in the cities that were being newly built or extended throughout the Western World. The lessons in collective design, that were first learned under the pressure of producing modern housing estates with very limited means, turned out to have an important bearing upon architectural composition. Under this new conception the community as a whole, not the individual building, becomes the center of our concern. The architect must visualize wholes and design wholes for a simple reason: we live in wholes, not as individual atoms moving at random, but as purposive beings, creating orderly patterns of related activities, made coherent by an orderly environment.

Viewed in this fashion, the beauty of the individual building cannot be self-contained: the handsomest building may be defaced by its surroundings, while the simplest of vernacular structures, if properly grouped and gardened, may have a charm out of all proportion to the quality of the individual units. So it follows that streets, courts, gardens, arcades of trees, parks, parkways, must be treated as an integral part of the building: not introduced as a belated afterthought, to be fitted into an irrelevant plan. To achieve social architecture is something, therefore, beyond the scope of the individual owner or architect: it demands a revision of current methods of land-subdivision and sale, and an effort by a cooperative group or a public authority to promote a collective design, based on a recognition of the interdependence of the structures and institutions that constitute a community. Even when buildings are created for private owners, the architect must become a representative and a spokesman for the whole community. In accord with this conception, the building and the town plan must be conceived and developed together. Under such planning, if a great building appears, it will have a worthy frame—as it usually did in the civic-minded towns of the Middle Ages.

This social conception of architecture is not, it goes without saying, a panacea. Where modern social purposes have been sound, handsome communities have come into existence: witness Chatham Village in Pittsburgh and Baldwin Hills Village in Los Angeles. But in the public housing of the nineteen-thirties, and still more the nineteen-forties, capable, socially minded architects, with apparently great opportunities, succeeded only in producing overstandardized plans, drab, segregated quarters, and grossly overcrowded sites, with people again housed at slum densities: buildings and site plans that could not be justified on either social or esthetic grounds. This proved, if proof were needed, that social architecture cannot lift itself above the level of its society; it must therefore remain impoverished and insignificant until society itself undergoes a profound renewal. If the slums of the nineteenth century proclaimed disorder and social fragmentation, the "model" superslums of the twentieth century tell a story of ideological sterility and bureaucratic regimentation that are equally hostile to human values and purposes.

In practice, the architects and planners in the United States who approached architecture most consciously from the social side were the group that Charles Harris Whitaker drew around the Journal of the American Institute of Architects, headed by Clarence Stein and Henry Wright. In the introduction to Stein's *New Towns in America* I have told the story of this whole movement; and this is not the place to tell it again—all the more because those concerned speak for themselves in the present book. As was so often true before, the American architects were not alone in this movement: they had their forerunners, particularly in Tony Garnier in France, and Raymond Unwin and Barry Parker in England, and the latter architects, who planned Letchworth Garden City and the Hampstead Garden suburban had a direct effect upon our own tradition, perhaps as early as the design of Forest Hills for the Russell Sage Foundation.

As the result of Whitaker's initiative during the First World War, the new ideas in housing and planning were put in circulation in time to influence powerfully the war housing work done by the United States Shipping Board and the War Housing Board. This was, I believe, the first positive example of public initiative, not to correct bad conditions but to create good ones, in America—at least since the early building of the New England towns.

The Impact of the Universal

One would not do justice to the American tradition in architecture if one neglected the part played in our own development by forces originating outside our country. Our very modern means of communication and transportation have made us conscious, as no other age before, of the existence of other regional traditions and cultures. One element of this universal tradition, the Machine, I have treated by itself. Obviously, the Machine, as a complex of methods and processes and products is no mere American contrivance, any more than it is a Russian one: indeed, it is not even a property of Western Civilization for, though it took form there, it drew upon distant cultures all over the world—from Korea for printing with movable metal types and from China in porcelain manufacture, from the Arabs in the magnetic compass.

But other universal elements, beside the machine, have had an influence on the American tradition; and, just because they have been so little noted in architectural histories, should have at least a passing notice here. One important influence was that of tropical architecture. Robert Louis Stevenson's house in Samoa was widely reproduced in photographs in the heyday of his popularity; a house with wide window spaces and porches, adapted to the climate; and from India about the same time came the similar concept of the bungalow, with all the rooms on one floor, that swept the United States in the first decade of this century. The Japanese house was likewise, in its elements, a tropical form, ill-adapted to the rigors of the Japanese climate; and superficially it had an effect on California architects like the Brothers Greene, though the Japanese flexibility of inner space was an innovation they were slow to carry further.

More important, however, than the house itself were the elements of standardization, module design, and extreme purity and simplicity, partly derived from the house, partly from the Japanese prints introduced into this country by John La Farge in the seventies and having an important influence, no doubt, on the culture and imagination of Frank Lloyd Wright. Purity, simplicity, standardization were universal elements available for use in any region, or any kind of building, once their significance was grasped. Another new factor in the new will-to-simplify was a pervasive but little noticed influence: the photograph. The simple mounting of photographs, in contrast to the ornate frames of current paintings in the nineties, had an effect in making people ready to abandon traditional forms of ornamentation and to seek esthetic satisfaction in proportion and tone and texture. It was in the early nineteen-hundreds in America that the walls of living rooms and dining rooms, often even bedrooms as well, ceased to be hung with a multitude of discordant reproductions, like an old-fashioned picture gallery, and were left mainly blank, to bring out the effect of an isolated picture or two.

Both Japanese painting and western photography probably had a hand in this new selectivity; but there was also a moral influence at work: that of Morris and Tolstoy, with their doctrine of returning to the elements: "Possess nothing that you do not know to be useful or believe to be beautiful." That dictum of Morris resulted in the general cleanings of form that characterized this period, and was promoted by the more advanced architects. Tolstoy's bedroom, with its plain white-washed walls, Florence Nightingale's living room, also in pure white and without that green Victorian emblem of respectability, the curtain, to say nothing of the new hospitals and the early Child's lunchrooms, also emblems of the now triumphant cult of hygiene and sanitation, all had their contributions to make to architectural form. And here, as elsewhere in the simplification of manners, the principles of the Society of Friends have long played a silent but effective part.

The American architect who went farthest in this simplification was, perhaps, Irving Gill, a bold pioneer on the West Coast—well in advance of the purism of Le Corbusier and Ozenfant—whose work still awaits a proper monograph. One further universal element, topping all these though perhaps ultimately drawing nourishment from the same roots, was Cubism. Cubism had, in fact, nothing to teach Frank Lloyd Wright; but the pleasure of translating organic forms into crystalline geometric ones, of renouncing the wavy line of L'Art Nouveau in favor of the right angle and the cube disclosed certain new aspects of the environment to which traditional art had been indifferent. One may say that Cubism released the architectural mind so that it felt free to deal with the machine and its products as esthetic forms in their own right. This was precisely how Root, Jenney, and Sullivan, in their best moments, had acted, almost instinctively, and as Frank Lloyd Wright had done consciously.

That a real break in the American tradition had taken place between 1910 and 1925, aggravated by the First World War with its slowing down of contacts by travel and commercial interchange, is proved by the fact that the new doctrines of architecture, derived from the Machine and from Cubism, came back to America in the mid-twenties without most people noting that they were only returning to the country of their origin. Even such a good historical student as Henry-Russell Hitchcock could treat Wright's early work, which was esthetically far more developed than Le Corbusier's, as if it were by then a back-number; a fact that made his early (1929) monograph on Wright's work irritatingly patronizing, though in time he amply rectified his judgment. From the perspective of a whole generation one can now see that Le Corbusier, in his historical innocence, sought to substitute a mannerism for the genuine organic style, visible in our grain elevators and our factories, that was in fact still in existence in America, though temporarily under eclipse in dwelling houses, public buildings, and skyscrapers.

Here Catherine Bauer's essay on a New Physical World and Walter Curt Behrendt's essay on Frank Lloyd Wright complement each other. The first essay emphasizes the fact that in our time the millennial search for One World, in which the latent brotherhood of man would become active and purposeful, has come to a provisional terminus which is also a new starting point. In no matter what medium the artist works, it is important that he should use those forms and develop those processes which will, in fact, create unity among men: hence a certain taming down of idiom and idiosyncrasy is called for, in order to make the physical background more intelligible and usable by other men. Even at some inevitable loss of intimacy, spontaneity, indigenousness, this effort to establish a common foundation is urgent. The kind of universality that the nineteenth century developed in sleeping cars and ocean steamers now has a much wider application, so that in our comings and goings over the earth it shall be possible to travel thousands of miles within a few hours, without undue discomfort or bewildering shock. Yet this underlying unity of design would become oppressive if it imposed any rigorous uniformity of pattern. Hence the significance of Frank Lloyd Wright's work, as interpreted by Behrendt; for Wright's designs are universal both in their origin and in their destination, without for a moment losing esthetic contact with the place, the climate, the people for whom most immediately the building was created.

It is fitting that the last essay in this book should come from Matthew Nowicki, a mind of universal range and a spirit of rare beauty. A Pole by nationality, born by chance in remotest Siberia near the China border, his own education had the broadest sort of European background: it had taken him, not merely to France, but to Italy and Greece and Egypt, where he absorbed at first hand the great forms of the past. Even before coming to America to serve as a consultant to the United Nations, he knew both the United States, where he had lived for a while as a youth when his father was Polish consul in Chicago, and Brazil. His architectural development was as comprehensive as his personal background: functionalism, cubism, and even—during the darkness of the German occupation—national traditionalism had claimed him. But by the time he came to America in 1947 he was already pushing through to an expression more richly universal than any of these schools. Though his work was hardly influenced by Wright, though it developed, indeed, partly out of an antipathy to Wright's more ostentatious moments, he was perhaps the only younger architect with anything like Wright's fertility of imagination or his intuitive ability to think and design, from first to last, in three dimensions, with interior and exterior developing together.

Nowicki's was a truly universal personality; and it is a happy accident that his last written work should be devoted to the same problem of Form and Function as that with which Horatio Greenough introduced the essential conceptions of modern architecture to America. These essays complement and correct each other. On such foundations, the modern tradition in American architecture can never be reduced to any of the current forms of know-nothingism or isolationism; for though the roots of an organic architecture will lie deep in our soil, our occupations, our people, our institutions, the atmosphere that surrounds it will, by the mere turning of the earth, carry freshening currents from every other country on earth, and in turn spread further what is universal and viable in our own tradition. Our inner strength and our potential service to humanity rest on this fact. We are most deeply ourselves, we Americans who have come together from every other land, when we are most actively part of a world-wide community. That, too, is one of the lessons of the American tradition in architecture. If we understand that lesson, and apply it resolutely in every sphere, we may again be at the beginning of good days.

I

Sources of Form

Form and Function

by

Horatio Greenough

American Architecture

We have heard the learned in matters relating to art express the opinion that these United States are destined to form a new style of architecture. Remembering that a vast population, rich in material and guided by the experience, the precepts, and the models of the Old World, was about to erect durable structures for every function of civilized life, we also cherished the hope that such a combination would speedily be formed.

We forgot that, though the country was young, yet the people were old; that as Americans we have no childhood, no half-fabulous, legendary wealth, no misty, cloud-enveloped background. We forgot that we had not unity of religious belief, nor unity of origin; that our territory, extending from the white bear to the alligator, made our occupations dissimilar, our character and tastes various. We forgot that the Republic had leaped full-grown and armed to the teeth from the brain of her parent, and that a hammer had been the instrument of delivery. We forgot that reason had been the dry nurse of the giant offspring, and had fed her from the beginning with the strong bread and meat of fact; that every wry face the bantling ever made had been daguerreotyped, and all her words and deeds printed and labeled away in the pigeonholes of official bureaus.

Reason can dissect, but cannot originate; she can adopt, but cannot create; she can modify, but cannot find. Give her but a cockboat, and she will elaborate a line-of-battle ship; give her but a beam with its wooden tooth, and she turns out the patent plow. She is not young; and when her friends insist upon the phenomena of youth, then is she least attractive. She can imitate the flush of the young cheek, but where is the flash of the young eye? She buys the teeth—alas! she cannot buy the breath of childhood. The puny cathedral of Broadway, like an elephant dwindled to the size of a dog, measures her yearning for Gothic sublimity, while the roar of the Astor House, and the mammoth vase of the great reservoir, shows how she works when she feels at home and is in earnest.

The mind of this country has never been seriously applied to the subject of building. Intently engaged in matters of more pressing importance, we have been content to receive our notions of architecture as we have received the fashion of our garments and the form of our entertainments, from Europe. In our eagerness to appropriate, we have neglected to adapt, to distinguish,—nay, to understand. We have built small Gothic temples of wood and have omitted all ornaments for economy, unmindful that size, material, and ornament are the elements of effect in that style of building. Captivated by the classic symmetry of the Athenian models, we have sought to bring the Parthenon into our streets, to make the temple of Theseus work in our towns. We have shorn them of their lateral colonnades, let them down from their dignified platform, pierced their walls for light, and, instead of the storied relief and the eloquent statue which enriched the frieze and graced the pediment, we have made our chimneytops to peer over the broken profile and tell, by their rising smoke, of the traffic and desecration of the interior. Still the model may be recognized, some of the architectural features are entire; like the captive king, stripped alike of arms and purple and drudging amid the Helots of a capital, the Greek temple, as seen among us, claims pity for its degraded majesty, and attests the barbarian force which has abused its nature and been blind to its qualities.

If we trace architecture from its perfection in the days of Pericles to its manifest decay in the reign of Constantine, we shall find that one of the surest symptoms of decline was the adoption of admired forms and models for purposes not contemplated in their invention. The forum became a temple; the tribunal became a temple; the theater was turned into a church; nay, the column, that organized member, that subordinate part, set up for itself, usurped unity, and was a monument! The great principles of architecture being once abandoned, correctness gave way to novelty, economy and vainglory associated produced meanness and pretension. Sculpture, too, had waned. The degenerate workmen could no longer match the fragments they sought to mingle, nor copy the originals they only hoped to repeat. The moldering remains of better days frowned contempt upon such impotent efforts, till, in the gradual coming of darkness, ignorance became contempt, and insensibility ceased to compare.

We say that the mind of this country has never been seriously applied to architecture. True it is that the commonwealth, with that desire of public magnificence which has ever been a leading feature of democracy, has called from the vasty deep of the past the spirits of the Greek, the Roman, and the Gothic styles; but they would not come when she did call to them! The vast cathedral, with its ever-open portals, towering high above the courts of kings, inviting all men to its cool and fragrant twilight, where the voice of the organ stirs the blood, and the dim-seen visions of saints and martyrs bleed and die upon the canvas amid the echoes of hymning voices and the clouds of frankincense—this architectural embodying of the divine and blessed words, "Come to me, ye who labor and are heavy laden, and I will give you rest!" demands a sacrifice of what we hold dearest. Its cornerstone must be laid upon the right to judge the claims of the church. The style of Greek architecture, as seen in the Greek temple, demands the aid of sculpture, insists upon every feature of its original organization, loses its harmony if a note be dropped in the execution, and when so modified as to serve for a customhouse or bank, departs from its original beauty and propriety as widely as the crippled gelding of a hackney coach differs from the bounding and neighing wild horse of the desert. Even where, in the fervor of our faith in shapes, we have sternly adhered to the dictum of another age, and have actually succeeded in securing the entire exterior which echoes the forms of Athens, the pile stands a stranger among us, and receives a respect akin to what we should feel for a fellow citizen in the garb of Greece. It is a make-believe. It is not the real thing. We see the marble capitals; we trace the acanthus leaves of a celebrated model—incredulous; it is not a temple.

The number and variety of our experiments in building show the dissatisfaction of the public taste with what has been hitherto achieved; the expense at which they have been made proves how strong is the yearning after excellence; the talents and acquirements of the artists whose services have been engaged in them are such as to convince us that the fault lies in the system, not in the men. Is it possible that out of this chaos order can arise?—that of these conflicting dialects and jargons a language can be born? When shall we have done with experiments? What refuge is there from the absurdities that have successively usurped the name and functions of architecture? Is it not better to go on with consistency and uniformity, in imitation of an admired model, than incur the disgrace of other failures? In answering these questions let us remember with humility that all salutary changes are the work of many and of time; but let us encourage experiment at the risk of license, rather than submit to an iron rule that begins by sacrificing reason, dignity, and comfort. Let us consult nature, and in the assurance that she will disclose a mine richer than was ever dreamed of by the Greeks, in art as well as in philosophy. Let us regard as ingratitude to the author of nature the despondent idleness that sits down while one want is unprovided for, one worthy object unattained.

If, as the first step in our search after the great principles of construction, we but observe the skeletons and skins of animals, through all the varieties of beast and bird, of fish and insect, are we not as forcibly struck by their variety as by their beauty? There is no arbitrary law of proportion, no unbending model of form. There is scarce a part of the animal organization which we do not find elongated or shortened, increased, diminished, or suppressed, as the wants of the genus or species dictate, as their exposure or their work may require. The neck of the swan and that of the eagle, however different in character and proportion, equally charm the eye and satisfy the reason. We approve the length of the same member in grazing animals, its shortness in beasts of prey. The horse's shanks are thin, and we admire them; the greyhound's chest is deep, and we cry, beautiful! It is neither the presence nor the absence of this or that part, or shape, or color, that wins our eye in natural objects; it is the consistency and harmony of the parts juxtaposed, the subordination of details to masses, and of masses to the whole.

The law of adaptation is the fundamental law of nature in all structure. So unflinchingly does she modify a type in accordance with a new position, that some philosophers have declared a variety of appearance to be the object aimed at; so entirely does she limit the modification to the demands of necessity, that adherence to one original plan seems, to limited intelligence, to be carried to the very verge of caprice. The domination of arbitrary rules of taste has produced the very counterpart of the wisdom thus displayed in every object around us; we tie up the camelopard to the rack; we shave the lion, and call him a dog; we strive to bind the unicorn with his band in the furrow, and make him harrow the valleys after us!

When the savage of the South Sea islands shapes his war club, his first thought is of its use. His first efforts pare the long shaft, and mold the convenient handle; then the heavier end takes gradually the edge that cuts, while it retains the weight that stuns. His idler hour divides its surface by lines and curves, or embosses it with figures that have pleased his eye or are linked with his superstition. We admire its effective shape, its Etruscan-like quaintness, its graceful form and subtle outline, yet we neglect the lesson it might teach. If we compare the form of a newly invented machine with the perfected type of the same instrument, we observe, as we trace it through the phases of improvement, how weight is shaken off where strength is less needed, how functions are made to approach without impeding each other, how straight becomes curved, and the curve is straightened, till the straggling and cumbersome machine becomes the compact, effective, and beautiful engine.

So instinctive is the perception of organic beauty in the human eye, that we cannot withhold our admiration even from the organs of destruction. There is majesty in the royal paw of the lion, music in the motion of the brindled tiger; we accord our praise to the sword and the dagger, and shudder our approval of the frightful aptitude of the ghastly guillotine.

Conceiving destruction to be a normal element of the system of nature equally with production, we have used the word beauty in connection with it. We have no objection to exchange it for the word character, as indicating the mere adaptation of forms to functions, and would gladly substitute the actual pretensions of our architecture to the former, could we hope to secure the latter.

Let us now turn to a structure of our own, one which, from its nature and uses, commands us to reject authority, and we shall find the result of the manly use of plain good sense, so like that of taste, and genius too, as scarce to require a distinctive title. Observe a ship at sea! Mark the majestic form of her hull as she rushes through the water, observe the graceful bend of her body, the gentle transition from round to flat, the grasp of her keel, the leap of her bows, the symmetry and rich tracery of her spars and rigging, and those grand wind muscles, her sails. Behold an organization second only to that of an animal, obedient as the horse, swift as the stag, and bearing the burden of a thousand camels from pole to pole! What academy of design, what research of connoisseurship, what imitation of the Greeks produced this marvel of construction? Here is the result of the study of man upon the great deep, where Nature spake of the laws of building, not in the feather and in the flower, but in winds and waves, and he bent all his mind to hear and to obey. Could we carry into our civil architecture the responsibilities that weigh upon our shipbuilding, we should ere long have edifices as superior to the Parthenon, for the purposes that we require, as the *Constitution* or the *Pennsylvania* is to the galley of the Argonauts. Could our blunders on terra firma be put to the same dread test that those of shipbuilders are, little would be now left to say on this subject.

Instead of forcing the functions of every sort of building into one general form, adopting an outward shape for the sake of the eye or of association, without reference to the inner distribution, let us begin from the heart as the nucleus, and work outward. The most convenient size and arrangement of the rooms that are to constitute the building being fixed, the access of the light that may, of the air that must be wanted, being provided for, we have the skeleton of our building. Nay, we have all excepting the dress. The connection and order of parts, juxtaposed for convenience, cannot fail to speak of their relation and uses. As a group of idlers on the quay, if they grasp a rope to haul a vessel to the pier, are united in harmonious action by the cord they seize, as the slowly yielding mass forms a thorough bass to their livelier movement, so the unflinching adaptation of a building to its position and use gives, as a sure product of that adaptation, character and expression.

What a field of study would be opened by the adoption in civil architecture of those laws of apportionment, distribution, and connection which we have thus hinted at? No longer could the mere tyro huddle together a crowd of ill-arranged, ill-lighted, and stifled rooms and, masking the chaos with the sneaking copy of a Greek façade, usurp the name of architect. If this anatomic connection and proportion has been attained in ships, in machines, and, in spite of false principles, in such buildings as made a departure from it fatal, as in bridges and in scaffolding, why should we fear its immediate use in all construction? As its first result, the bank would have the physiognomy of a bank, the church would be recognized as such, nor would the billiard room and the chapel wear the same uniform of columns and pediment. The African king, standing in mock majesty with his legs and feet bare, and his body clothed in a cast coat of the Prince Regent, is an object whose ridiculous effect defies all power of face. Is not the Greek temple jammed in between the brick shops of Wall Street or

Cornhill, covered with lettered signs, and occupied by groups of money-changers and applewomen, a parallel even for his African majesty?

We have before us a letter in which Mr. Jefferson recommends the model of the Maison Carrée for the State House at Richmond. Was he aware that the Maison Carrée is but a fragment, and that, too, of a Roman temple? He was; it is beautiful—is the answer. An English society erected in Hyde Park a cast in bronze of the colossal Achilles of the Quirinal, and, changing the head, transformed it into a monument to Wellington. But where is the distinction between the personal prowess, the invulnerable body, the heaven-shielded safety of the hero of the Iliad and the complex of qualities which makes the modern general? The statue is beautiful—is the answer. If such reasoning is to hold, why not translate one of Pindar's odes in memory of Washington, or set up in Carolina a colossal Osiris in honor of General Greene?

The monuments of Egypt and of Greece are sublime as expressions of their power and their feeling. The modern nation that appropriates them displays only wealth in so doing. The possession of means, not accompanied by the sense of propriety or feeling for the true, can do no more for a nation than it can do for an individual. The want of an illustrious ancestry may be compensated, fully compensated; but the purloining of the coat-of-arms of a defunct family is intolerable. That such a monument as we have described should have been erected in London while Chantrey flourished, when Flaxman's fame was cherished by the few, and Baily and Behnes were already known, is an instructive fact. That the illustrator of the Greek poets and of the Lord's Prayer should in the meanwhile have been preparing designs for George the Fourth's silversmiths, is not less so.

The edifices in whose construction the principles of architecture are developed may be classed as organic, formed to meet the wants of their occupants, or monumental, addressed to the sympathies, the faith, or the taste of a people. These two great classes of buildings, embracing almost every variety of structure, though occasionally joined and mixed in the same edifice, have their separate rules, as they have a distinct abstract nature. In the former class the laws of structure and apportionment, depending on definite wants, obey a demonstrable rule. They may be called machines each individual of which must be formed with reference to the abstract type of its species. The individuals of the latter class, bound by no other laws than those of the sentiment which inspires them, and the sympathies to which they are addressed, occupy the positions and assume the forms best calculated to render their parent feeling. No limits can be put to their variety; their size and richness have always been proportioned to the means of the people who have erected them.

If, from what has been thus far said, it shall have appeared that we regard the Greek masters as aught less than the true apostles of correct taste in building, we have been misunderstood. We believe firmly and fully that they can teach us; but let us learn principles, not copy shapes; let us imitate them like men, and not ape them like monkeys. Remembering what a school of art it was that perfected their system of ornament, let us rather adhere to that system in enriching what we invent than substitute novelty for propriety. After observing the innovations of the ancient Romans, and of the modern Italian masters in this department, we cannot but recur to the Horatian precept—

exemplaria Graeca
Nocturna versate manu, versate diurna!

To conclude: The fundamental laws of building found at the basis of every style of architecture must be the basis of ours. The adaptation of the forms and magnitude of structures to the climate they are exposed to, and the offices for which they are intended, teaches us to study our own varied wants in these respects. The harmony of their ornaments with the nature that they embellished, and the institutions from which they sprang, calls on us to do the like justice to our country, our government, and our faith. As a Christian preacher may give weight to truth, and add persuasion to proof, by studying the models of pagan writers, so the American builder by a truly philosophic investigation of ancient art will learn of the Greeks to be American.

The system of building we have hinted at cannot be formed in a day. It requires all the science of any country to ascertain and fix the proportions and arrangements of the members of a great building, to plant it safely on the soil, to defend it from the elements, to add the grace and poetry of ornament to its frame. Each of these requisites to a good building requires a special study and a lifetime. Whether we are destined soon to see so noble a fruit may be doubtful; but we can, at least, break the ground and throw in the seed.

We are fully aware that many regard all matters of taste as matters of pure caprice and fashion. We are aware that many think our architecture already perfect; but we have chosen, during this sultry weather, to exercise a truly American right—the right of talking. This privilege, thank God, is unquestioned—from Miller, who, robbing Béranger, translates into fanatical prose, "Finissons-en! le monde est assez vieux!" to Brisbane, who declares that the same world has yet to begin, and waits a subscription of two hundred thousand dollars in order to start. Each man is free to present his notions on any subject. We have also talked, firm in the belief that the development of a nation's taste in art depends on a thousand deep-seated influences beyond the ken of the ignorant present; firm in the belief that freedom and knowledge will bear the fruit of refinement and beauty, we have yet dared to utter a few words of discontent, a few crude thoughts of what might be, and we feel the better for it. We promised ourselves nothing more than that satisfaction which Major Downing attributes to every man "who has had his say, and then cleared out," and we already have a pleasant consciousness of what he meant by it.

Relative and Independent Beauty

There are threads of relation which lead me from my specialty to the specialties of other men. Following this *commune quodam vinculum,* I lay my artistic dogma at the feet of science; I test it by the traditional lore of handicraft; I seek a confirmation of these my inductions, or a contradiction and refutation of them; I utter these inductions as they occur to myself; I illustrate them by what they spontaneously suggest; I let them lead me as a child.

Persons whose light I have sought have been worried and fretted at the form, the body of my utterance. Since this soul, if soul it be, took the form of this body, I have received it as it came. If I seek another form, another dress than that with which my thought was born, shall I not disjoin that which is one? Shall I not disguise what I seek to decorate? I have seen that there is in the body and the dress an indication of the quantum and quality of the mind, and therefore doth it seem honest that I seek no other dress than mine own. I also know by heart some lines and proportions of the work of able penmen. The *lucidus ordo* of another mind is not displayed before me as pearls before swine. I love to bear in my bosom a nosegay plucked in classic ground: it sweetens me to myself. I respect too much the glory of Schiller and Winckelmann, of Goethe and Hegel, to dare purloin their vesture for my crudities. The partial development of my mind makes the dress and garb of imperfection proper for me. My notion of art is not a somewhat set forth for sale, that I should show it to advantage, or a soldier in uniform, anxious to pass muster, but rather a poor babe, whom I strip before the faculty, that they may counsel and advise—peradventure bid me despair.

Bodies are so varied by climate, and so changed by work, that it is rash to condemn them until impotence is demonstrated. The camelopard was long declared a monster, born of fancy, a nightmare of traveler's brain; but when the giraffe stood browsing in the treetops before us, we felt that we had been hasty. God's law is as far away from our taste as his ways are beyond our ways.

I know full well that, without dress and ornament, there are places whence one is expelled. I am too proud to seek admittance in disguise. I had rather remain in the street than get in by virtue of a borrowed coat. That which is partial and fractional may yet be sound and good as far as it goes.

In the hope that some persons, studious of art, may be curious to see how I develop the formula I have set up, I proceed. When I define Beauty as the promise of Function; Action as the presence of Function; Character as the record of Function, I arbitrarily divide that which is essentially one. I consider the phases through which organized intention passes to completeness, as if they were distinct entities. Beauty, being the promise of function, must be mainly present before the phase of action; but so long as there is yet a promise of function there is beauty, proportioned to its relation with action or with character. There is somewhat of character at the close of the first epoch of the organic life, as there is somewhat of beauty at the commencement of the last, but they are less apparent, and present rather to the reason than to sensuous tests.

If the normal development of organized life be from beauty to action, from action to character, the progress is a progress upward as well as forward; and action will be higher than beauty, even as the summer is higher than the spring; and character will be higher than action, even as autumn is the résumé and result of spring and summer. If this be true, the attempt to prolong the phase of beauty into the epoch of action can only be made through nonperformance; and false beauty or embellishment must be the result.

Why is the promise of function made sensuously pleasing? Because the inchoate organic life needs a care and protection beyond its present means of payment. In order that we may respect instinctive action, which is divine, are our eyes charmed by the aspect of infancy, and our hearts obedient to the command of a visible yet impotent volition.

The sensuous charm of promise is so great that the unripe reason seeks to make life a perennial promise; but promise, in the phase of action, receives a new name—that of nonperformance, and is visited with contempt.

The dignity of character is so great that the unripe reason seeks to mark the phase of action with the sensuous livery of character. The ivy is trained up the green wall, and while the promise is still fresh on evey line of the building, its function is invaded by the ambition *to seem* to have lived.

Not to promise forever, or to boast at the outset, not to shine and to seem, but to be and to act, is the glory of any coordination of parts for an object.

I have spoken of embellishment as false beauty. I will briefly develop this view of embellishment. Man is an ideal being; standing, himself inchoate and incomplete, amid the concrete manifestations of nature, his first observation recognizes defect; his first action is an effort to complete his being. Not gifted, as the brutes, with an instinctive sense of completeness, he stands alone as capable of conative action. He studies himself; he disciplines himself. Now, his best efforts at organization falling short of the need that is in his heart, and therefore infinite, he has sought to compensate for the defect in his plan by a charm of execution. Tasting sensuously the effect of a rhythm and harmony in God's world, beyond any adaptation of means to ends that his reason could measure and approve, he has sought to perfect his own approximation to the essential by crowning it with a wreath of measured and musical, yet nondemonstrable, adjunct. Now, I affirm that, from the ground whereon I stand and whence I think I see him operate, he thus mirrors, but darkly, God's world. By the sense of incompleteness in his plan, he shows the divine yearning that is in him; by the effort to compensate for defect in plan by any makeshift whatever, he forbids, or at least checks, further effort. I understand, therefore, by embellishment, *the instinctive effort of infant civilization to disguise its incompleteness, even as God's completeness is to infant science disguised*. The many-sided and full and rich harmony of nature is a many-sided response to the call for many functions; not an aesthetical utterance of the Godhead. In the tree and in the bird, in the shell and in the insect, we see the utterance of him who sayeth Yea, Yea, and Nay, Nay; and, therefore, whatever is assumed as neutral ground, or margin around the essential, will be found to come of evil, or in other words, to be incomplete.

I base my opinion of embellishment upon the hypothesis that there is not one truth in religion, another in mathematics, and a third in physics and in art; but that there is one truth, even as one God, and that organization is his utterance. Now, organization obeys his law. It obeys his law by an approximation to the essential, and then there is what we term life; or it obeys his law by falling short of the essential, and then there is disorganization. I have not seen the inorganic attached to the organized but as a symptom of imperfect plan, or of impeded function, or of extinct action.

The normal development of beauty is through action to completeness. The invariable development of embellishment and decoration is more embellishment and more decoration. The *reductio ad absurdum* is palpable enough at last; but where was the first downward step? I maintain that the first downward step was *the introduction of the first inorganic, nonfunctional element, whether of shape or color.* If I be told that such a system of mine would produce *nakedness*, I accept the omen. In nakedness I behold the majesty of the essential instead of the trappings of pretension. The agendum is not diminished; it is infinitely extended. We shall have grasped with tiny hands the standard of Christ, and borne it into the academy, when we shall call upon the architect, and sculptor, and painter to seek to be perfect even as our Father is perfect. The assertion that the human body is other than a fit exponent and symbol of the human being is a falsehood, I believe. I believe it to be false on account of the numerous palpable falsehoods which have been necessary in order to clinch it.

Beauty is the promise of Function. Solomon in all his glory is, therefore, not arrayed as the lily of the field. Solomon's array is the result of the instinctive effort of incompleteness to pass itself for complete. It is pretension. When Solomon shall have appreciated nature and himself, he will reduce his household, and adapt his harness, not for pretension, but for performance. The lily is arrayed in heavenly beauty because it is organized, both in shape and color, to dose the germ of future lilies with atmospheric and solar influence.

We now approach the grand conservative trap, the basis of independent beauty. Finding in God's world a sensuous beauty not organically demonstrated to us, the hierarchies call on us to shut our eyes and kneel to an aesthetical utterance of the divinity. I refuse. Finding here an apparent embellishment, I consider the appearance of embellishment an accusation of ignorance and incompleteness in my science. I confirm my refusal after recalling the fact that science has thus far done nothing else than resolve the lovely on the one hand, the hateful on the other, into utterances of the Godhead—the former being yea, the latter nay. As the good citizen obeys the good law because it is good, and the bad law that its incompleteness be manifest, so does every wrong result from divine elements, accuse the organization, and by pain and woe represent *X*, or the desired solution. To assert that this or that form or color is beautiful *per se* is to formulate prematurely; it is to arrogate godship; and once that false step is taken, human-godship or tyranny is inevitable without a change of creed.

The first lispings of science declared that nature abhors a vacuum; there we see humanity expressing its ignorance by transferring a dark passion to the Godhead which is light and love. This formula could not outlive experiment, which has demonstrated that God's care upholds us with so many pounds to the square inch of pressure on every side, and that the support is variable. The ancients knew somewhat of steam. They formulated steam as a devil. The vessels at Pompeii all speak one language—look out for steam! The moderns have looked into steam, and, by wrestling with him, have forced him to own himself an angel—an utterance of love and care.

We are told that we shall know trees by their fruits: even because of the fruits of refusing to kneel, and of worshiping with the eyes open, do I proceed to seek that I may find.

Mr. Garbett, in his learned and able treatise on the principles of design in architecture, has dissected the English house and found with the light of two words, fallen from Mr. Emerson, the secret of the inherent ugliness of that structure. It is the *cruelty* and *selfishness* of a London house, he says (and I think he proves it, too), which affects us so disagreeably as we look upon it. Now, these qualities in a house, like the blear-eyed stolidity of a habitual sot, are symptoms, not diseases. Mr. Garbett should see herein the marvelous expression of which bricks and mortar can be made the vehicles. In vain will he attempt to get by embellishment a denial of selfishness, so long as selfishness reigns. To medicate symptoms will never, at best, do more than effect a metastasis—suppress an eruption; let us believe, rather, that the Englishman's love of home has expelled the selfishness from the boudoir, the kitchen, and the parlor, nobler organs, and thrown it out on the skin, the exterior, where it less threatens life, and stands only for *X*, or a desired solution. If I have been clear in what I have said, it will be apparent that the intention, the soul of an organization, will get utterance in the organization in proportion to the means at its disposal: in vain shall you drill the most supple body of him that hates me into a manifestation of love for me; while my blind and deaf cousin will soon make me feel, and pleasingly feel, that I was the man in all the world that he wished to meet.

In seeking, through artistic analysis, a confirmation of my belief in one God, I offend such hierarchies as maintain that there be two Gods; the one good and all-powerful, the other evil and somewhat powerful. It is only necessary, in order to demolish the entire structure I have raised, that some advocate of independent beauty and believer in the devil—for they go and come together—demonstrate embellishment for the sake of beauty in a work of the divine hand. Let me be understood; I cannot accept as a demonstration of embellishment a sensuous beauty not yet organically explained. I throw the *onus probandi* on him who commands me to kneel. I learned this trick in Italy, where the disappointed picture dealer often defied me, denying his daub to be a Raphael, to say, then, what it was. No, my friend, I care not whose it is; when I say certainly not a Raphael, I merely mean that I will none of it.

If there be in religion any truth, in morals any beauty, in art any charm, but through fruits, then let them be demonstrated; and the demonstration, in regard to morals and faith, will work backward and enlighten art.

I have diligently sought, with scalpel and pencil, an embellishment for the sake of beauty, a sacrifice of function to other than destruction. I have not found it. When I, therefore, defy the believer in the devil to show me such an embellishment, I do so humbly. I want help.

It seems to me that a word of caution is necessary before seeking independent beauty. Beauty may be present, yet not be recognized as such. If we lack the sense of the promise of function, beauty for us will not exist. The inhabitants of certain Swiss valleys regard a goiter as ornamental. It is somewhat superadded to the essential, and they see it under the charm of association. The courtiers of Louis XIV admired the *talon rouge* and the enormous *perruque*. They were somewhat superadded to the essential, and they saw them under the charm of association. But the educated anatomist in Switzerland sees the goiter as we see it. The educated artist of Louis XIV's time saw the maiming pretension of his dress as we see it.

The aim of the artist, therefore, should be first to seek the essential; when the essential hath been found, then, if ever, will be the time to commence embellishment.* I will venture to predict that the essential, when found, will be complete. I will venture to predict that completeness will instantly throw off all that is not itself, and will thus command: "Thou shalt have no other Gods beside me." In a word, completeness is the absolute utterance of the Godhead; not the completeness of the Catholic bigot, or of the Quaker, which is a pretended one, obtained by negation of God-given tendencies; but the completeness of the sea, which hath a smile as unspeakable as the darkness of its wrath; the completeness of the earth, whose every atom is a microcosm; the completeness of the human body, where all relations are resumed at once and dominated. As the monarch rises out of savage manhood a plumed czar, embellishing his shortcomings with the sensuous livery of promise, yet, entering the phase of developed thought and conscious vigor, stands the eagle-eyed and gray-coated Bonaparte, so will every development of real humanity pass through the phase of nondemonstrable embellishment, which is a false completeness, to the multiform organization which responds to every call.

I hold the human body, therefore, to be a multiform command. Its capacities are the law and gauge of manhood as connected with earth. I hold the blessings attendant upon obedience to this command to be the yea, yea; the woe consequent upon disobedience, the nay, nay, of the Godhead. These God daily speaketh to him whose eyes and ears

* As any book is entitled to a digression, let one be made here. Boswell's *Johnson* supplies the matter: "We then fell into a disquisition whether there is any beauty independent of utility. The General (Paoli) maintained there was not. Dr. Johnson maintained that there was; and he instanced a coffee cup which he held in his hand, the painting of which was of no real use, as the cup would hold the coffee equally well if plain; yet the painting was beautiful." The Great Cham's logic was tangential, that time, and the "disquisition" never did return to the point; but later he veered a little nearer to what Greenough was to get at: "Johnson expressed his disapprobation of ornamental architecture . . . 'because it consumes labor disproportionate to its utility.' For the same reason he satirised statuary. . . . 'What, sir' (said Mr. Gwyn, the architect), 'will you allow no value to beauty in architecture or in statuary? Why should we allow it, then, in writing? Why do you take the trouble to give us so many fine allusions, and bright images, and elegant phrases? You might convey all your instruction without these ornaments.' Johnson smiled with complacency; but said, 'Why, sir, all these ornaments are useful, because they obtain an easier reception for truth; but a building is not at all more convenient for being decorated with superfluous carved work.' "

are open. Other than these I have not heard. When, therefore, the life of man shall have been made to respond to the command which is in his being, giving the catholic result of a sound collective mind in a sound aggregate body, he will organize his human instrument or art for its human purpose, even as he shall have adapted his human life to the divine instrument which was given him. I wish to be clear; the instrument or body being of divine origin, we formulate rashly when we forego it before thoroughly responding to its requirement. That it is in itself no final or complete entity is herein manifest, that it changes. The significance of yesterday, today, and tomorrow is this, that we are in a state of development. Now, the idea of development necessarily supposes incompleteness; now, completeness can know no change. The instrument of body is no haphazard datum, given as an approximation, whose shortcomings we are to correct by convention, arbitrium, and whim, but an absolute requirement, and only then responding to the divine intention when its higher nature shall be unfolded by high function, even as the completeness of the brute responds to the requirement of his lower nature.

Internecine war is the law of brute existence. War! The lion lives not by food alone. Behold, how he pines and dwindles as he growls over his butcher's meat! It is in the stealthy march, the ferocious bound, and deadly grapple, tearing palpitating flesh from writhing bone—a halo of red rain around his head—that he finds the completion of his being, in obedience to a word that proceeded out of the mouth of God. Now, the law of brute life is the law of human life, in so far as the brute man is undeveloped in his higher tendencies. They, therefore, who, having formulated a credo for infant intelligence, and finding domination thereby secured, proceed to organize a *perennial infancy*, that they may enjoy an eternal dominion, will sooner or later see their sheep transformed to tigers; for the law of development, being a divine law, can only be withstood by perishing. If what I have said be true, collective manhood will never allow exceptional development to slumber at the helm or to abuse the whip. Collective manhood calls for development. If exceptional development answer—Lo! ye are but wolves, manhood will reply—Then, have at you! He who cannot guide must come down. We feel that we cannot remain where we are.

I have followed the train of remark whither it led me. Let us resume. Organization being the passage of intention through function to completeness, the expressions of its phases are symptoms only. The same philosophy which has cloaked, and crippled, and smothered the human body as rebelling against its Creator, yet always in vain, because the human body, like the Greek hero, says, Strike! but learn—that philosophy has set up a theory of beauty by authority, of beauty independent of other things than its own mysterious harmony with the human soul. Thus, we remark that the human soul, so inclined to evil in the moral world, according to the same philosophy, is sovereign arbiter of beauty in the aesthetical world. The Creator, who formed man's soul with a thirst for sin, and his body as a temple of shame, has, therefore, made his taste infallible! Let us seek through the whole history of arbitrary embellishment to find a resting-place. We shall look in vain; for the introduction of the inorganic into the organized is destruction; its development has ever been a *reductio ad absurdum*.

There is no conceivable function which does not obey an absolute law. The approximation to that law in material, in parts, in their form, color, and relations, is the measure of freedom or obedience to God, in life. The attempt to stamp the green fruit, the dawning science, the inchoate life, as final, by such exceptional minds and social achievements as have produced a wish to remain here, and a call for a tabernacle, *these are attempts to divide manhood, which is one;* they are attempts to swim away from brute man, sinking in the sea of fate. They will ever be put to shame; for the ignorance of the ignorant confounds the wise; for the filth of the filthy befouls the clean; for the poverty of the poor poisons the quiet of the possessor. The brute man clings to the higher man; he loves him even as himself; he cannot be shaken off; he must be assimilated and absorbed.

I call therefore upon science in all its branches to arrest the tide of sensuous and arbitrary embellishment, so far as it can do it, not negatively by criticism thereof alone, but positively by making the instrument a many-sided response to the multiform demands of life. The craving for completeness will then obtain its normal food in results, not the opiate and deadening stimulus of decoration. Then will structure and its dependent sister arts emerge from the standstill of *ipse dixit* and, like the ship, the team, the steam engine, proceed through phases of development toward a response to need.

The truth of such doctrine, if truth be in it, must share the fate of other truth, and offend him whose creed is identified with the false; it must meet the indifference of the many who believe that a new truth is born every week for him who can afford to advertise. But it must earn a place in the heart of him who has sought partial truths with success; for truths are all related.

Structure and Organization

It is useless to regret that discussions of principle involve, to a certain extent, persons also. If this were not, on the whole, a good arrangement, principles would have been furnished with a better lodging. I take it that passions and interests are the great movers and steadiers of the social world, and that principles, like the bread on Sir John Falstaff's score, are an unconscionably small item.

The working forces and restraints are, like the furnaces and engines, the lock up and lock out of the mint at Philadelphia, all very effective for their objects. A showy front masks all these things and adorns Chestnut Street by the maimed quotation of a passage of Greek eloquence relating to something else. A huge brick chimney rising in the rear talks English and warns you that the façade is to be taken with some grains of allowance.

The domain of taste is eminently one of free discussion. In most civilized countries the individual is restrained by the magistracy from offending the public eye by unsightly or ill-timed exhibitions of any very peculiar dogma of his own, because it is thought that the harm thus done to the public is not compensated by the gratification of the unit. Still, he is allowed to maintain his theory by any means short of an invasion of the public sense of propriety.

One unaccustomed to trace the influence of associated ideas, of example, and of authority, would naturally suppose that each climate, each creed and form of government, would stamp its character readily and indelibly upon the structures of a thinking population. It is not so. It is only by degrees that leisure and wealth find means to adapt forms, elsewhere invented, to new situations and new wants.

When civilization gradually develops an indigenous type, the complex result still carries the visible germ whence it sprang. The harmony of the Chinese structures indicates a oneness of origin and modification. The sign manual of the Sultan is but the old mark pompously flourished. There is a blood relationship between the pipe of the North American savage and the temples of Central America.

In the architecture of Greece, of Italy, and of the more recent civilizations, on the other hand, we remark a struggle between an indigenous type, born of the soil and of the earlier wants of a people, and an imported theory which, standing upon a higher artistic ground, captivates the eye and wins the approval of dawning taste. If my limits permitted, it were not amiss to trace this conquest of refinement, and to follow it out also in relation to literature, and to dress, and amusements. The least effort of memory will suggest numerous invasions of artistic theory upon primitive expedients, conflicts between the home-grown habit which has possession and exotic theory which seeks it.

There is one feature in all the great developments of architecture which is worthy to occupy us for a moment. They are all fruits of a dominating creed. If we consider how vast was the outlay they required, we shall not wonder that religion alone has thus far been able to unite, in a manner to wield them, the motives and the means for grand and consistent systems of structure. The magnificence of the Romans, the splendor of Venice and Genoa, like the ambitious efforts of France, England, and Germany in more recent days, had a certain taint of dilettantism in their origin, which, aiming to combine inconsistent qualities, and that for a comparatively low motive, carried through all their happiest combinations the original sin of impotence, and gave, as a result, bombast instead of eloquence, fritter instead of richness, boldness for simplicity, carving in lieu of sculpture. The laws of expression are such that the various combinations which have sought to lodge modern functions in buildings composed of ancient elements, developed and perfected for other objects, betray, in spite of all the skill that has been brought to bear upon them, their bastard origin. In literature the same struggle between the ancient form so dear to scholars and the modern thought which was outgrowing it was long and obstinate. In literature the battle has been won by the modern thought. The models of Greece are not less prized for this. We seek them diligently, we ponder them with delight and instruction. We assimilate all of their principles that are true and beautiful, and we learn of them to belong to our day and to our nation, as they to theirs.

In all structure that from its nature is purely scientific—in fortifications, in bridges, in shipbuilding—we have been emancipated from authority by the stern organic requirements of the works. The modern wants spurned the traditional formula in these structures, as the modern life outgrew the literary molds of Athens. In all these structures character has taken the place of dilettantism, and if we have yet to fight for sound doctrine in all structure, it is only because a doctrine which has possession must be expelled, inch by inch, however unsound its foundation.

The developments of structure in the animal kingdom are worthy of all our attention if we would arrive at sound principles in building. The most striking feature in the higher animal organizations is the adherence to one abstract type. The forms of the fish and the lizard, the shape of the horse, and the lion, and the camelopard, are so nearly framed after one type that the adherence thereto seems carried to the verge of risk. The next most striking feature is the modification of the parts, which, if contemplated independently of the exposure and functions whose demands are thus met, seems carried to the verge of caprice. I believe few persons not conversant with natural history ever looked through a collection of birds, or fish, or insects, without feeling that they were the result of Omnipotence at play for mere variety's sake.

If there be any principle of structure more plainly inculcated in the works of the Creator than all others, it is the principle of unflinching adaptation of forms to functions. I believe that colors also, so far as we have discovered their chemical causes and affinities, are not less organic in relation to the forms they invest than are those forms themselves.

If I find the length of the vertebrae of the neck in grazing quadrupeds increased, so as to bring the incisors to the grass; if I find the vertebrae shortened in beasts of prey, in order to enable the brute to bear away his victims; if I find the wading birds on stilts, the strictly aquatic birds with paddles; if, in pushing still further the investigation, I find color arrayed either for disguise or aggression, I feel justified in taking the ground that organization is the primal law of structure, and I suppose it, even where my imperfect light cannot trace it, unless embellishment can be demonstrated. Since the tints as well as the forms of plants and flowers are shown to have an organic significance and value, I take it for granted that tints have a like character in the mysteriously clouded and pearly shell, where they mock my ken. I cannot believe that the myriads are furnished, at the depths of the ocean, with the complicated glands and absorbents to nourish those dyes, in order that the hundreds may charm my idle eye as they are tossed in disorganized ruin upon the beach.

Let us dwell for a moment upon the forms of several of the higher types of animal structure. Behold the eagle as he sits on the lonely cliff, towering high in the air; carry in your mind the proportions and lines of the dove and mark how the finger of God has, by the mere variation of diameters, converted the type of meekness into the most expressive symbol of majesty. His eye, instead of rushing as it were out of his head, to see the danger behind him, looks steadfastly forward from its deep cavern, knowing no danger but that which it pilots. The structure of his brow allows him to fly upward with his eyes in shade. In his beak and his talons we see at once the belligerent, in the vast expanse of his sailing pinions the patent of his prerogative. *Dei Gratia Raptor!* Whence the beauty and majesty of the bird? It is the oneness of his function that gives him his grandeur, it is transcendental mechanism alone that begets his beauty. Observe the lion as he stands! Mark the ponderous predominance of his anterior extremities, his lithe loins, the lever of his hock, the awful breadth of his jaws, and the depth of his chest. His mane is a cuirass, and when the thunder of his voice is added to the glitter of his snarling jaws, man alone with all his means of defense stands self-possessed before him. In this structure again are beheld, as in that of the eagle, the most terrible expression of power and dominion, and we find that it is here also the result of transcendental mechanism. The form of the hare might well be the type of swiftness for him who never saw the greyhound. The greyhound overtakes him, and it is not possible in organization that this result should obtain, without the promise and announcement of it, in the lengths and diameters of this breed.

Let us now turn to the human frame, the most beautiful organization of earth, the exponent and minister of the highest being we immediately know. This stupendous form, towering as a lighthouse, commanding by its posture a wide horizon, standing in relation to the lowly colonnades of Greece and Egypt, touching earth with only one-half the soles of its feet—it tells of majesty and dominion by that upreared spine, of duty by those unencumbered hands. Where is the ornament of this frame? It is all beauty, its motion is grace, no combination of harmony ever equaled, for expression and variety, its poised and stately gait; its voice is music, no cunning mixture of wood and metal ever did more than feebly imitate its tone of command or its warble of love. The savage who envies or admires the special attributes of beasts maims unconsciously his own perfection to assume their tints, their feathers, or their claws; we turn from him with horror, and gaze with joy on the naked Apollo.

I have dwelt a moment on these examples of expression and of beauty that I may draw from them a principle in art, a principle which, if it has been often illustrated by brilliant results, we constantly see neglected, overlooked, forgotten—a principle which I hope the examples I have given have prepared you to accept at once and unhesitatingly. It is this: in art, as in nature, the soul, the purpose of a work will never fail to be proclaimed in that work in proportion to the subordination of the parts to the whole, of the whole to the function. If you will trace the ship through its various stages of improvement, from the dugout canoe and the old galley to the latest type of the sloop-of-war, you will remark that every advance in performance has been an advance in expression, in grace, in beauty, or grandeur, according to the functions of the craft. This artistic gain, effected by pure science in some respects, in others by mere empirical watching of functions where the elements of the structure were put to severe tests, calls loudly upon the artist to watch keenly traditional dogmas and to see how far analogous rules may guide his own operations. You will remark, also, that after mechanical power had triumphed over the earlier obstacles, embellishment began to encumber and hamper ships, and that their actual approximation to beauty has been effected, first, by strict adaptation of forms to functions, second, by the gradual elimination of all that is irrelevant and impertinent. The old chairs were formidable by their weight, puzzled you by their carving, and often contained too much else to contain convenience and comfort. The most beautiful chairs invite you by a promise of ease, and they keep that promise; they bear neither flowers nor dragons, nor idle displays of the turner's caprice. By keeping within their province they are able to fill it well. Organization has a language of its own, and so expressive is that language that a makeshift or make-believe can scarce fail of detection. The swan, the goose, the duck, when they walk toward the water are awkward, when they hasten toward it are ludicrous. Their feet are paddles, and their legs are organized mainly to move those paddles in the water; they, therefore, paddle on land, or as we say, waddle. It is only when their breasts are launched into the pond that their necks assume the expression of ease and grace. A serpent upon a smooth hard road has a similar awkward expression of impotence; the grass, or pebbles, or water, as he meets either, afford him his *sine qua non,* and he is instantly confident, alert, effective.

If I err not, we should learn from these and the like examples, which will meet us wherever we look for them, that God's world has a distinct formula for every function, and that we shall seek in vain to borrow shapes; we must make the shapes, and can only effect this by mastering the principles.

It is a confirmation of the doctrine of strict adaptation that I find in the purer Doric temple. The sculptures which adorned certain spaces in those temples had an organic relation to the functions of the edifice; they took possession of the worshiper as he approached, lifted him out of everyday life, and prepared him for the presence of the divinity within. The world has never seen plastic art developed so highly as by the men who translated into marble, in the tympanum and the metope, the theogony and the exploits of the heroes. Why, then, those columns uncarved? Why, then, those lines of cornice unbroken by foliages, unadorned by flowers? Why that matchless symmetry of every member, that music of gradation, without the tracery of the Gothic detail, without the endless caprices of arabesque? Because those sculptures *spake,* and speech asks a groundwork of silence and not of babble, though it were of green fields.

I am not about to deny the special beauties and value of any of the great types of building. Each has its meaning and expression. I am desirous now of analyzing that majestic and eloquent simplicity of the Greek temple, because, though I truly believe that it is hopeless to transplant its forms with any other result than an expression of impotent dilettantism, still I believe that its principles will be found to be those of all structures of the highest order.

When I gaze upon the stately and beautiful Parthenon, I do not wonder at the greediness of the moderns to appropriate it. I do wonder at the obtuseness which allowed them to persevere in trying to make it work in the towns. It seems like the enthusiasm of him who should squander much money to transfer an Arabian stallion from his desert home, that, as a blindfolded gelding, he might turn his mill. The lines in which Byron paints the fate of the butterfly that has fallen into the clutches of its childish admirer would apply not inaptly to the Greek temple at the mercy of a sensible building committee, wisely determined to have their money's worth.

When high art declined, carving and embellishment invaded the simple organization. As the South Sea Islanders have added a variety to the human form by tattooing, so the cunning artisans of Greece undertook to go beyond perfection. Many rhetoricians and skilled grammarians refined upon the elements of the language of structure. They all spake: and demigods, and heroes, and the gods themselves, went away and were silent.

If we compare the simpler form of the Greek temple with the ornate and carved specimens which followed it, we shall be convinced, whatever the subtlety, however exquisite the taste that long presided over those refinements, that they were the beginning of the end, and that the turning-point was the first introduction of a fanciful, not demonstrable, embellishment, and for this simple reason, that, embellishment being arbitrary, there is no check upon it; you begin with acanthus leaves, but the appetite for sauces, or rather the need of them, increases as the palate gets jaded. You want jasper, and porphyry, and serpentine, and giallo antico, at last. Nay, you are tired of Aristides the Just, and of straight columns; they must be spiral, and by degrees you find yourself in the midst of a barbaric pomp whose means must be slavery—nothing less will supply its waste—whose enjoyment is satiety, whose result is corruption.

It was a day of danger for the development of taste in this land, the day when Englishmen perceived that France was laying them under contribution by her artistic skill in manufacture. They organized reprisals upon ourselves, and, in lieu of truly artistic combinations, they have overwhelmed us with embellishment, arbitrary, capricious, setting at defiance all principle, meretricious dyes and tints, catchpenny novelties of form, steam-woven fineries and plastic ornaments, struck with the die or pressed into molds. In even an ordinary house we look around in vain for a quiet and sober resting-place for the eye; we see naught but flowers, flourishes—the renaissance of Louis Quatorze gingerbread embellishment. We seek in vain for aught else. Our own manufacturers have caught the furor, and our foundries pour forth a mass of ill-digested and crowded embellishment which one would suppose addressed to the sympathies of savages. . . .

I do not suppose it is possible to check such a tide as that which sets all this corruption toward our shores. I am aware of the economical sagacity of the English, and how fully they understand the market; but I hope that we are not so thoroughly asphyxiated by the atmosphere they have created as to follow their lead in our own creation of a higher order. I remark with joy that almost all the more important efforts of this land tend, with an instinct and a vigor born of the institutions, toward simple and effective organization; and they never fail whenever they toss overboard the English dictum and work from their own inspirations to surpass the British, and there, too, where the world thought them safe from competition.

I would fain beg any architect who allows fashion to invade the domain of principles to compare the American vehicles and ships with those of England, and he will see that the mechanics of the United States have already outstripped the artists, and have, by the results of their bold and unflinching adaptation, entered the true track, and hold up the light for all who operate for American wants, be they what they will.

In the American trotting wagon I see the old-fashioned and pompous coach dealt with as the old-fashioned palatial display must yet be dealt with in this land. In vain shall we endeavor to hug the associations connected with the old form. The redundant must be pared down, the superfluous dropped, the necessary itself reduced to its simplest expression, and then we shall find, whatever the organization may be, that beauty was waiting for us, though perhaps veiled, until our task was fully accomplished.

Far be it from me to pretend that the style pointed out by our mechanics is what is sometimes miscalled an economical, a cheap style. No! It is the dearest of all styles! It costs the thought of men, much, very much thought, untiring investigation, ceaseless experiment. Its simplicity is not the simplicity of emptiness or of poverty; its simplicity is that of justness, I had almost said, of justice. Your steam artisan would fill your town with crude plagiarisms, *calqués* upon the thefts from Pompeii or modern Venice, while the true student is determining the form and proportions of one article.

Far be it from me to promise any man that when he has perfected the type of any artistic product he shall reap the fruit of his labor in fame or money. He must not hope it. Fame and money are to be had in plenty; not in going against the current, but in going with it. It is not difficult to conceive that the same state of the popular taste which makes the corrupted style please will render the reformed style tasteless. It is not possible to put artistic products to a test analogous to that which tries the ship and the carriage but by a lapse of time. True it is that society always reserves a certain number of minds and of eyes unpoisoned by the vogue of the hour, and in the sympathy of these must the artist often find his chief reward in life.

From: *A Memorial of Horatio Greenough*, by Henry T. Tuckerman. New York: 1853, pages 117–130, 131–143, 170–183.

A New Scale of Values

by

Calvert Vaux

Although there is a cheering prospect for American architecture in the good time coming, its present appearance is in many ways far from satisfactory. Over the length and breadth of this country are scattered cities and villages by thousands, and public and private edifices innumerable; and yet we may fairly say, There are the buildings, but where is the architecture? There is the matter, but where is the manner? There is the opportunity, but where is the agreeable result? Is it in the churches? A few really creditable specimens may be pointed out, but the large majority are unquestionably deficient in truthful dignity and artistic beauty. Is it the public buildings? Several fine works of art may at once occur to the mind, and although a floating doubt somewhat questions the Americanism of their expression, still, as they are nobly conceived and do not shrink from the ordeal of the artist's pencil, it is granted that they are successful. Then comes the question of the great majority again. Does the memory linger with pleasure over the reminiscences of a provincial tour, and delight to recall the pleasant impression left on the mind by each elm-shaded town, with its tasteful hall, schoolhouses, library, theatre, museum, banks, baths, courts of justice, and other buildings cheerfully erected and gracefully arranged by its free and enlightened inhabitants—for their own use and pleasure, of course, but with a wise regard for mutual advantage and individual enjoyment, that insures the sympathy of every passing stranger; the more readily, too, as each discovers that he, even he, has been thought of, and that some study has been expended to give him pleasure? No, this is not the result to be looked for at present. Does the secret of beauty lie in the private buildings, the stores, the warehouses, the mansions, the villas, the hotels, the streets, or the cottages? There are probably as magnificent hotels and stores in the large cities of America as any where in the world. Architecture, within the last ten years, has managed to get a genuine foothold in this department of building; it has begun to *pay*, and that is an excellent sign, and one that offers food for reflection and solid encouragement; yet it is the few and not the many, even here, that speak of refinement, and a love of grace, which is as averse to meretricious display as it is to ungainly awkwardness. Among the private residences a great number are excellent; but still the mass are unsatisfactory in form, proportion, color, and light and shade. What is the reason of all this? Why is there comparatively so little beauty in American buildings? Some will say America is a dollar-loving country, without taste for the arts; others, that expense is the obstacle, and that the republican simplicity of America can not afford the luxury of good architecture. The latter of these solutions is clearly incorrect, for it is knowledge, and not money, that is the chief source of every pleasurable emotion that may be caused by a building. Indeed a simple, well-planned structure costs less to execute, for the accommodation obtained, than an ill-planned one; and the fact of its being agreeable and effective, or otherwise, does not depend on any ornament that may be superadded to the useful and necessary forms of which it is composed, but on the arrangement of those forms themselves, so that they may balance each other and suggest the pleasant ideas of harmonious proportion, fitness, and agreeable variety to the eye, and through the eye to the mind. All this is simply a matter of *study before* building, not of additional *cost in* building. The other solution of the problem, that Americans do not appreciate the beautiful, and do not care for it or value it, is a more specious but equally erroneous one. There are, doubtless, many obstructions that have hindered, and do hinder, the development of correct taste in the United States. The spring, however, is by no means dry, although these obstacles prevent its waters from flowing freely; and there is, in fact, no real difficulty that earnestness and ordinary patience may not overcome. One important evidence of a genuine longing for the beautiful may be at once pointed out. Almost every American has an equally unaffected, though not, of course, an equally appreciative, love for "the country." This love appears intuitive, and the possibility of ease and a country place or suburban cottage, large or small, is a vision that gives a zest to the labors of industrious thousands. This one simple fact is of marked importance; it shows that there is an innate homage to the natural in contradistinction to the artificial—a preference for the works of God to the works of man; and no matter what passing influences may prevent the perfect working of this tendency, there it exists; and with all its town-bred incongruities and frequently absurd shortcomings, it furnishes a valuable proof of inherent good, true, and healthy taste. Moreover, the greater includes the less. An actual love for nature, however crude it may be, speaks clearly of a possible love for art.

Till within a comparatively recent period the fine arts in America have been considered by the great bulk of the population as pomps and vanities so closely connected with superstition, popery, or aristocracy, that they must be eschewed accordingly, and the result is not *altogether* undesirable, though it has appeared to retard the advance of refinement and civilization. The awakening spirit of republicanism refused to acknowledge the value of art as it then existed, a tender hothouse plant ministering to the delights of a select few. The democratic element rebelled against this idea *in toto*, and tacitly, but none the less practically, demanded of art to thrive in the open air, in all weathers, for the benefit of all, if it was worth any thing, and if not, to perish as a troublesome and useless encumbrance. This was a severe course to take, and the effects are every where felt. But, after all, it had truth on its side; and candor must allow that no local, partial, class-recognizing advance in art, however individually valuable its examples might have been, could, in reality, have compensated for the disadvantage that would have attended it. Now, every step in advance, slow though it be, is a real step taken by the whole country. When we look at the ruins of old Rome, we say, What a great people! what temples! what mighty works! and undoubtedly Rome was really great *in individuals;* very great in a strong and clever minority, who spent with marked ability the labor of the weak and ignorant majority; but the *plebs*, the unlettered, unthought-of common people, were not great, nor were they taught to be so, and therefore Rome fell.

During the last hundred years there has been a continuous effort to give to the American millions the rudiments of self-reliant greatness, to abolish class legislation, and to sink the importance of individuals. "*Aut America aut nullus*"—"America or no *one*," has been, is, and will probably ever be the practical motto. It is not surprising, then, that the advancement in the arts has been somewhat less rapid than the progress in commercial prosperity and political importance. The conditions were new, and, it must be confessed, rather hard. Continuous ease and leisure readily welcome art, while constant action and industry require time to become acquainted with its merits. To the former, it may be a parasite and yet be supported; to the latter, it must be a friend or nothing. The great bulk of money that is laid out on building in the United States belongs to the active workers, and is spent by them and for them. The industrious classes, therefore, decide the national standard of architectural taste.

The question then occurs, How is this universal taste to be improved? There is the sound, healthy material, unprejudiced, open to conviction, with a real though not thoroughly understood desire for what is good and true—there is plenty of prosperity and opportunity, plenty of money and industry, plenty of every thing but education and the diffusion of knowledge. This language may seem inapplicable to America, to whom humanity is indebted for the successful introduction of the common school system, which lies at the root of every healthy idea of reform now at work in the world, but is, nevertheless, true. The genius of American art may, with justice, say of the genius of American education:

> If she be not so to me,
> What care I how fair she be!

Education must be liberal and comprehensive as well as universal and cheap, or the result will remain incomplete. To secure any thing permanently satisfactory in the matter of architecture, professors of ability, workmen of ability, and an appreciative, able public are necessary. It would seem that the architects practicing in America are not at present, in the majority of cases, born or bred in the United States. They have, therefore, to learn and unlearn much before the spirit instilled into their designs can be truly and genuinely American. There is no good reason now why this state of affairs should continue. Architecture is a profession likely to be in considerable request here for several hundred years at least, and the demand is steadily increasing. Why, then, should not parents speculate for their sons in this line? Why should not the article, as it is for home consumption, be raised at home? It is an honorable calling; not certainly offering such splendid fortunes as the merchant *may* realize, but it is a fair opening, and the only capital that it requires, beyond brains and industry, is the expense for books and an education. When a fair share of Young America enters upon this study heart and soul, as a means of earning an independent position, we may expect a rapid, natural development of the architectural resources of the country, and that the present meagre facilities for artistic education will be gradually increased; the schools and colleges, also, will probably be induced, after a time, to include in their course of study subjects calculated to discover and foster, in the rising generation, such natural gifts as have a bearing on these and similar matters.

To insure workmen of ability, a reasonable chance to improve is the chief thing wanted. So long as the general demand is for monotonous, commonplace, stereotyped work, the average of ability will necessarily be low; but with opportunity, good, cheap, illustrated works, and a spirited weekly paper devoted to the special discussion of the subjects interesting to architects, engineers, carpenters, masons, and all the other trades connected with building—a paper that would diffuse sound theoretical and practical information on the art in general and in detail throughout the whole country, the advance would be rapidly felt; for wherever there is an American, there at least, be he rich or poor, is a reader, a thinker, and an actor. Self-supporting schools of design for painters, decorators, modelers, carvers, paper-stainers, etc., must follow in due course, for the positiveness of the need would soon become evident, and the object would then be almost gained. With reference to the appreciative and able public, the press is the improving power that is to be mainly looked to. Cheap popular works on architecture in all its bearings, popular lectures, popular engravings—and hundreds of them, and yet all good—these are the simple, truthful, and effective means that are to influence the public, by supplying a medium through which it may see clearly, and thus be led to criticise freely, prefer wisely, and act judiciously. Every year offers proofs of an advancing interest in this subject, and shows an increasing desire to respond to it in newspapers, magazines, books, etc., while the public is certainly not slow to buy and read.

The truth is, not that America is a dollar-worshipping country, with a natural incapacity to enjoy the arts, but a dollar-making country, with restricted opportunities for popular, artistic education, *as yet;* but when this want is freely ministered to, in the spirit that it may be, and it is hoped will be, ere long, there is every reason to conjecture that correct architectural taste may be as generally diffused throughout the United States as we at present find the idea of a republican form of government. We shall *then* hope for genuine *originality* as well as intrinsic beauty in American buildings; and this interesting subject of originality is, perhaps, worthy of a separate analysis and consideration.

In the United States it would seem that diversities of style and strong contrasts of architectural design are a perfectly natural occurrence, when we take into account the early history of the nation and the circumstances under which it sprung into its present prominent position. Differences of manner should, therefore, be contemplated without any troublesome sense of inconsistency being awakened, for such a charge would hardly apply with justice to results so clearly inevitable. The art of building faithfully portrays the social history of the people to whose needs it ministers, but can not get beyond those boundaries. We must remember, therefore, that principles of action, perceptions, convictions, habits of thought, and customs are the directors of all architectural design, and that wherever and however it may exist, it is one of several national exponents, not an independent affair with a cut-and-dried theoretical existence. Good architecture of some kind must spring up in any society where there is a love of truth and nature, and a generally diffused spirit of politeness in the ordinary habits of thought. Wherever, on the other hand, there is a wide-spread carelessness as to the development of the refined and gentle perceptive faculties, there inevitably must be a monotonously deficient standard of existence, and very paltry architecture as a necessary consequence; for the senses being deadened by inaction or abuse, poor seeing, hearing, smelling, tasting, and feeling, naturally result, and are reflected in the art of building, which exists entirely by supplying the demands of the bodily organs, and always shows whether they are vulgar, uncontrolled masters, galled serfs, or gay, active workmen. It is, moreover, an art so constantly before us, in some form or other, that it can not help being a friend or enemy to the improvement of civilized beings all the days of their lives.

The individuality of the American people does not appear to depend extensively on derivation or tradition, but on the character of the institutions by which it is surrounded, and on the elasticity of action that ensues. It is a people composed of many differing elements, but these are all exposed to a fusing power so strong, and so incessantly at work, that a single generation is often sufficient to bring into marked prominence the latent sentiments and springs of action that constitute the individual part of the national character. The settler may, to the last, be somewhat divided in his opinions, but the settler's son is sure to be an American, as far as *politics* are concerned, although at this point the active influence on him of the new country may appear to cease, leaving *social* assimilation to come about much more slowly.

Each of the European nations that have contributed to the population of this country, has, in its religious and domestic character, distinctive peculiarities and preferences, harmless in themselves, as far as others are concerned, and of comparatively private interest. These take their chance of life in the new country unmolested. The press having, of course, a gradual influence over them, while the national habit of traveling, by offering opportunities for tacit observation and change of opinion, without loss of self-complacency, is constantly at work rubbing down the rough edges of egotism, and rounding off the hard angles of prejudice. This influence every day enlarges its sphere of action, and will, doubtless, help a good deal to clear away the obstructions that at present hamper the *social* progress of the spirit of republicanism. Here lies the root of the matter; for whenever this spirit is permitted to flow freely into its natural channels, without being dammed up into an exclusive political mill-stream, it must lead to considerable social unity, and we may then, *but not till then,* look for the exercise of a power of fusion in manners and arts equal in its grasp to the one now almost omnipotent in politics.

The religious convictions of every country have, necessarily, a highly important influence over its social advancement; and America, as far as art is concerned, has received, till lately, nothing but blows from this quarter. Meagre sectarianism and private intolerance, under the names of religious freedom and universal toleration, have been serious drawbacks. However, the respect hitherto paid to mere formalism is now on the wane, and something more life-like is demanded—loudly at intervals, silently always. Besides the generally prejudicial effect that has thus been produced, there exists, here and there, a more distinct opposition to artistic grace and elegance on the ground that they are useless luxuries; but this sentiment is so impious, and the punishment daily inflicted on it is so sad, that it ought to be thoroughly exploded. Every sect agrees that there can be but one Creator, therefore all our created organs, sensations, and capacities must emanate from this fountainhead, and be intended for use; for if they have another source, there must be two first causes; and if they are not intended for use, the power exercised in their construction must be absurdly employed. Of course, either of these assertions would be highly irreverent. The fact is, that the evil influence at work in the world can mar many things, but make nothing; it can invert opportunity, misapply means, overdo or leave undone, and thus produce unpleasant, because unnatural results, but it can originate absolutely nothing: all its lying is spoiled truth, all its ugliness spoiled beauty; it can not help being in every instance secondary and negative: therefore, the moment we arrive at any thing so distinctly positive as a sensation or perception, we may know at once that it is irrational on any pretended ground of morality to "hide the talent" or oppose its healthy exercise. Earnest vitality is the social and artistic need in America. Every good thing, originality included, may be anticipated from that, for wherever it exists it bears fruit a hundredfold; and the results of its influence on commerce show what may be expected when it pulsates as vigorously in the heart as in the pocket of this great republic. Cash will then assume its proper position, and money-spending will become the test of a man's ability instead of money-making.

In this country the wages of mechanics are good, and it is to be wished that they may ever remain so; but it is not equally desirable that the style of labor performed for those wages shall continue the same. On the other hand, it is to be hoped, and reasonably, when the subject becomes one of steady public interest, that the intelligence, skill, and taste of mechanics may be constantly heightened and improved, so that in time to come average ability may do easily and cheaply what is now considered superior out-of-the-way work. All would be the gainers and none the losers by this advancement; for without the increase of wages each man would be able, with the same amount of personal effort as formerly, to purchase from his neighbor more positively valuable results. It is palpably evident, indeed, that a high standard of life can be quite easily attained by the working-classes in America, that is to say, by all whose circumstances render it necessary that they should do something for a living. Still there is another section of the community to be provided for—the born rich. Individuals in this predicament, in some parts of the world, have a gratifying position at once accorded them on account of their property, but this is far from being the case in America. There is a great deal of toil and consequent wealth in the United States; still, it is money-making, not money made, that commands respect. The science of spending is imperfectly understood, and the unsatisfactory results are apparent enough; but the idea of a moneyed aristocracy is everywhere repelled at heart with a scorn so contemptuous that it can scarcely be called indignant. A dilemma springs up from this state of things. Idleness is abhorred by successful men; they insist, therefore, on their sons becoming lawyers, or doctors, or going into business. Then follows a failure, in the majority of cases; for the spur to exertion that makes such pursuits satisfy men, is, in these instances, entirely wanting, as pecuniary circumstances do not, in the least, require the effort. Rich Americans fear lest their offspring may be looked on as useless members of society, and the instinct that leads them to do so is well enough as far as it goes, but the natural independent comment on it all is, Why spend so much time in making and saving money if it is to be rather an incumbrance than otherwise to the next generation? The real difficulty, and it is a serious one, is the limited range allowed by custom to intellectual energy. It is neither fair to the individuals, nor to the society of which they are responsible units, that the sons of rich men should be tied down to one or two money-making pursuits; they ought to be in every department of literature, science, and art, not as dilettanti connoisseurs, but as earnest laborers, striving boldly for a higher national excellence than has yet been achieved. This is *their* proper post. Poor men can scarcely afford to occupy it. It is a glorious position, the only proper one for them to assume; and so long as they neglect it, so long will wealth be misunderstood and misapplied. The rich should study to be practical theorists, so that the less rich may be theoretical practitioners. Every young repulican of means in America should aim to be *aristocratic* in its literal sense; that is, to be "*aristos*"—the very best. He has advantages which his comrades have not. He can afford to give ample, unembarrassed study to any subject that suits his powers, and to work out its resources quietly and steadily. He should be one step in advance of the rest of creation, a leader in the foremost rank of the foremost band. The value of a class of men thus occupied would be unquestioned, and it would not be so unnatural then for a parent to labor for money, so that his son might enjoy the rightful opportunity to live an easy life of elevated action and noble exertion.

The nature of the pursuits men follow should be examined into and tested. As we are not good, we need preachers; as we are not straightforward, we must have lawyers; as we are not natural, we want doctors; and we are much indebted to all these gentlemen; but as we *are* virtuous, we ask for something besides, that shall be less negative and more actual. We demand poets, mechanics, philosophers, men of business, artists, authors, sailors, inventors. Possessing the capacities of all these in embryo, we ask, not that we may blindly admire the individual, but that we may fairly appropriate the spirit of his work, and be, when not laboring at our own specialty, at small cost, and in a quiet, general way, what each professor is in an individual, troublesome, and particular way. This seems to be the scope and intention of life with such a basis as American freedom; and exactly to the extent that it is recognized and acted on is the advance in art and science, and in all that makes the best part of life.

It is only in a state of society in which things are valued intrinsically, and not for what they will fetch, that any art can begin to progress or hope for a chance to become vital or original; and so long as the enjoyment of a purchase depends much on the opinion of others, and but little on its own merits, artistic invention is likely to remain at a stand-still. Taste must be real, unborrowed, and individual, to accomplish anything; and even a small allowance of earnest perceptive conviction is better than any amount of follow-my-leader opinion. If excellent architecture can give innocent pleasure, it is certainly worth having, and all Americans ought to have it with as little delay as possible; not for the sake of gratifying any petty spirit of rivalry, or indulging any national or local pride, but simply because it is *worth* having; on the same principle that every healthy man ought to enjoy dining daily, not on account of his being able to afford richer food than his neighbors, or because he happens to know a dozen people who live poorly (for if he can derive any appetite from such facts he is no true man), but solely because his good constitution requires regular sustenance.

In America perfect liberty, that absolute essential for healthy life, has been, in due course, talked for, fought for, legislated for, and, in these Free States, decidedly realized; and it seems, therefore, scarcely fair now to train all the best men to be lawyers and politicians, because the talent is more wanted somewhere else. The sensation of freedom is nothing more than the felt certainty of non-interference, and, however complete it may be, it can neither supply the will to do anything, nor suggest any deed to be done; it is like light, only perceptible when reflected from an object; it offers a solid rock on which to build, but not one idea for the superstructure adapted to it. In America this rock commands a boundless prospect, and no fitting or enduring edifice can be erected on it that does not include the most liberal manners, the most generous aspirations, the most noble institutions, and the most pure and beautiful arts that unfettered humanity is capable of conceiving. There has not, indeed, been, from the commencement of the world till this moment, an opportunity for the advance of the fine arts so replete with the material of true success as now exists in America; this advance is a question of choice, not time; of purpose, not ability; of direction, not force; there is *capacity* enough spread over all the country, and being wasted daily: it is *conviction* and *will* that are needed.

When the talent and energy that are fostered by American institutions are distributed with tolerable fairness, we shall, among other things, be justified in expecting to find in every architectural effort, not something so new that it is unintelligible, but some distinctive characteristics that show it to be a genuine American invention. These, however, can hardly be expected to depend much on the employment of really new forms. Webster and Clay were orators of originality, but their words were all old. Their stock in trade is common property in the form of a dictionary, and the boundary lines, over which neither ever ventured to pass, are fairly set forth in a good grammar. Any desire on their part to invent a brand-new language would have been, of course, absurd, and any wish to produce a brand-new style of building is, without doubt, an equally senseless chimera.

All previous experience in architecture is the inherited property of America, and should be taken every advantage of. Each beautiful thought, form and mode that is not unsuited to the climate and the people, ought to be studied, sifted, and tested, its principles elucidated, and itself improved on; but the past should always be looked on as a servant, not as a master.

Individual sentiment and education should be encouraged to act freely in every instance, and by degrees that important fact, a genuine public taste, will be fairly unfolded. The authority of precedents will then be unneeded, for actual ideas, such as "fitness," "unity," "variety," will give the critical standard to the general taste. Every individual of sound mind will then help to improve the national architecture, for each will resolutely refuse to admire any structure that does not seem agreeable to him or her individually, and all will freely insist on a right to call *good* whatever coincides with their untrammeled, but not uncultivated natural perceptions. Emerson says forcibly on this point, "Why need we copy the Doric or the Gothic model? Beauty, convenience, grandeur of thought, and quaint expression are as near to us as to any, and if the American artist will study with hope and love the precise thing to be done by him, considering the climate, the soil, the length of day, the wants of the people, the habit and form of government, he will create a home in which all these will find themselves fitted, and taste and sentiment will be satisfied also."

From: *Villas and Cottages*, by Calvert Vaux. New York: 1857, pages 13-24, 26-32. (Dover reprint, 1970).

Love of the Work

by

James Jackson Jarves

Our synopsis of the Art-Idea would be incomplete without referring to the condition of architecture in America. Strictly speaking, we have no architecture. If, as has happened to the Egyptians, Ninevites, Etruscans, Pelasgians, Aztecs, and Central American races, our buildings alone should be left, by some cataclysm of nations, to tell of our existence, what would they directly express of us? Absolutely nothing! Each civilized race, ancient or modern, has incarnated its own aesthetic life and character in definite forms of architecture, which show with great clearness their indigenous ideas and general conditions. A similar result will doubtless in time occur here. Meanwhile we must look at facts as they now exist. And the one intense, barren fact which stares us fixedly in the face is, that, were we annihilated tomorrow, nothing could be learned of us, as a distinctive race, from our architecture. It is simply substantial building, with ornamentation, orders, styles, or forms, borrowed or stolen from European races, an incongruous medley as a whole, developing no system or harmonious principle of adaptation, but chaotic, incomplete, and arbitrary, declaring plagiarism and superficiality, and proving beyond all question the absolute poverty of our imaginative faculties, and general absence of right feeling and correct taste. Whether we like it or not, this is the undeniable fact of 1864. And not merely this: an explorer of our ruins would often be at a loss to guess the uses or purposes of many of our public edifices. He could detect bastard Grecian temples in scores, but would never dream they were built for banks, colleges, or custom-houses. How could he account for ignoble and impoverished Gothic chapels, converted into libraries, of which there is so bad an example at Cambridge, Massachusetts, or indeed for any of the architectural anomalies which disfigure our soil and impeach our common sense, intensified as they frequently are by a total disregard of that fundamental law of art which demands the harmonious relation of things, condemning the use of stern granite or adamantine rock in styles where only beautiful marbles can be employed with aesthetic propriety, or of cold stones in lieu of brick, or the warmer and yet more plastic materials belonging of right to the variety and freedom of Gothic forms? If the mechanical features of our civilization were left to tell the story, our ocean-clippers, river-steamers, and industrial machines would show a different aspect. They bespeak an enterprise, invention, and development of the practical arts that proclaim the Americans to be a remarkable people. If, therefore, success attend them in whatever they give their hearts and hands to, it is but reasonable to infer that cultivation need but be stimulated in the direction of architecture to produce results commensurate with the advance in mechanical and industrial arts. If one doubt this, let him investigate the progress in shipbuilding from the point of view of beauty alone, and he will discover a success as complete in its way as was that of the builders of Gothic cathedrals and Grecian temples. And why? Simply, that American merchants took pride in naval architecture. Their hearts were in their work; their purses opened without stint; and they built the fastest and handsomest ships.

To excel in architecture we must warm up the blood to the work. The owner, officer, and sailor of a gallant ship love her with sympathy as of a human affinity. A ship is not *it*, but *she* and *her*, one of the family; the marvel of strength and beauty; a thing of life, to be tenderly and lovingly cared for and proudly spoken of. All the romance of the trader's heart—in the West, the steamboat holds a corresponding position in the taste and affections of the public—goes out bountifully towards the symmetrical, stately, graceful object of his adventurous skill and toil. Ocean-clippers and river-steamers are fast making way for locomotive and propeller, about which human affections scarce can cluster, and which art has yet to learn how to dignify and adorn. But the vital principle, *love of the work*, still lives, that gave to the sailing-vessel new grace and beauty, combining them with the highest qualities of utility and strength into a happy unity of form. As soon as an equal love is turned towards architecture, we may expect as rapid a development of beauty of material form on land as on the ocean.

Our forefathers built simply for protection and adaptation. Their style of dwelling-houses was suited to the climate, materials at hand, and social exigencies. Hence it was true and natural. They could not deal in artifice or plagiarism, because they had no tricks of beauty to display and nothing to copy. Over their simple truth of expression time has thrown the veil of rustic enchantment, so that the farm-houses still standing of the period of the Indian wars are a much more pleasurable feature of the landscape than their pretentious villa-successors of the nineteenth century.

The public buildings of our colonial period are interesting solely from association. Anything of architectural pretence, more destitute of beauty, it would be difficult to originate; and yet, as meagre a legacy as they are of the native styles of ancestral England and Holland at that date, they avoid the worst faults of ornamentation and plagiarism of later work. Any of them might have been sent over the seas to order, like a dress-coat, and placed wherever needed, without other thought than to get a substantial building for as little money as possible. Yet there is about them, as well as the aristocratic mansions of colonial times, a certain quiet dignity of constructural expression which bespeaks conscious rank and gentlemanly breeding. It is true, they have misplaced pilasters, pillars, and other incongruous thefts of classical architecture, in mathematical rank-and-file order upon wall-surfaces, with which they have nothing in common in feature or spirit, but, notwithstanding the pettinesses of the pettiest of the imitators of Wren or Jones, they are not overborne and crushed by them, but wear them with as self-possessed an air as their owners did foreign orders and titles, rejoicing in possessing conventional distinctions of rank not had by their neighbors.

Fergusson says, "There was not a building erected in the United States before A.D. 1814, worthy of being mentioned as an example of architectural art." This sweeping assertion may disturb the serenity of those who look upon the City Hall of New York, the State House at Boston, and buildings of their time and class as very wonderful. We agree entirely with the judgment of Fergusson from his standpoint of criticism. But there are details and features in many of the earlier buildings that are pleasurable and in good taste, while the edifices, as a whole, are not displeasing. The Boston State House is a symmetrical, well-proportioned building, simple and quiet in its application of classical details, with an overgrown lantern on a diminutive dome, but, as an entirety, effective and imposing. Its good taste is more in its negative than positive qualities, and happy adaptation of foreign styles to our wants, which at this early period almost savors of a germ of new thought. The New York City Hall is a meagre,

Renaissant building, with nothing new in expression or adaptation, and would find itself at home almost anywhere in Europe, without attracting notice of any kind.

Fergusson, who is an excellent guide in the forms of universal architecture, further states as a reason for our deficiency of original thought, that "an American has a great deal too much to do, and is always in too great a hurry to do it, ever to submit to the long, patient study and discipline requisite to master any style of architecture perfectly. Still less is he likely to submit to that amount of self-negation which is indispensable if a man would attempt to be original." This is too true for any one to gainsay it; neither would it lessen its force, to retort on the weak points of his countrymen. But perhaps he overstrains criticism in stating that "the perfection of art in an American's eyes would be the invention of a self-acting machine which should produce plans of cities, and designs for Gothic churches and classic monumental buildings, at so much per foot super, and so save all further thought or trouble." * Resentment at this caricature is checked when we remember that our countrymen have actually patented machines for producing sculpture, whether from life or copy; and that almost every new town *founded*—once they were allowed to grow—is on a rectangular, gridiron plan, utterly devoid of picturesque beauty or aesthetic design, as monotonous and unrefreshing as a table of logarithms. Such towns have no organic structure. They are all extremities, as if the human being was made up only of arms and legs, and his sole function to get about at right angles. The saving feature of Boston is that it has a heart, head, and lungs, as well as extremities. We refer to our towns in this connection, because the absence of taste and inventive thought in laying them out is at the root of corresponding weaknesses in architecture. "It is in vain to urge," says the same author, "the prosaic ugliness of such a system of laying out towns, or the vices of the way our architects *edit* buildings, after the free manner of using the scissors in making up a newspaper, when there is no feeling to perceive the deformity of the one, or knowledge to comprehend the absurdities of the other." It will be a healthful symptom of progress when we are willing to confess our deficiencies and seek remedies, instead of endeavoring to disguise them by lauding to the skies buildings styled architectural by those who erect them, but which do not possess the first principles of correct taste or beautiful design. Could the public criticise these edifices with the same

* Modern Architecture, Book IX, p. 436.

warm feeling and appreciative knowledge that is applied to naval architecture, we should soon see a different state of things, the sooner, because, having no examples of high art in architecture on our soil, we could more rapidly develop a style of our own.

. . . We have got a step beyond the notion, that, because a building or a portion of it is beautiful, it is desirable to repeat it without regarding the original intent, thus degrading architecture from a creative to an imitative process, and putting its forms upon a level with the copies of old masters which are imported by thousands as furniture decoration for our walls. The buildings we fix in our streets are like so many Old-World cousins come over on a visit, not having had time as yet to get other naturalization than Yankee sharpness and awkwardness of outline. We are glad to see them, though they bluntly tell us that we have many master-builders but no Giottos. It is encouraging, however, to begin to have a taste for what Giotto loved, though unable to create art in his spirit. In his day men *created* art. That is to say, they invented, designed, and composed with reference to home thoughts and needs. True architecture is not what so many fancy, simply ornamental building, but, as Fergusson emphatically observes, the accumulated creative and constructive powers of several minds harmoniously working out a great central idea. Everything is designed from a penetrative insight into its latent meaning, with reference to a certain position and use. The best men of each craft that enters into its constructive expression, painters, sculptors, carvers, moulders, stainers of glass, mosaicists, masons, carpenters, the very hodmen, all labor in unity of feeling for the one great object, which becomes to them the incarnated ambition of their lives, and into which enters a variety of language, fact, and feeling, having a word to all men, and commensurate with the harmonious variety of human capacity when stimulated to its fullest power. Not before we appreciate the possibilities of architecture in a grand combination of the intellectual and spiritual faculties, aroused to action by the deepest emotions, can we expect to create work to rival that of olden time.

From: *The Art-Idea,* by James Jackson Jarves. New York: 1864, pages 286–292, 299–300.

Towards the Organic

by

Louis Henri Sullivan

Growth and Decay

In seeking a clear, definite and full comprehension of the word, *organic*, we should at the beginning keep in mind the correlated words, organ, organize, organization, organism, and, what is still more important, what these words signify. All of these words imply the existence of a vital force and of a structure or mechanism whereby that force is made operative and manifest. I have already cautioned you against the fugacious nature of words, their peculiar tendency to transformation in meaning while they retain the same outward form. This is because the form of a word is not itself truly organic; it is arbitrary, and has very little inherent capacity to change in response to a change in significance—especially if the change be a subtle one. Beyond the mechanical changes that the grammarians call declensions, conjugations, compoundings, affixes, suffixes, etc., words can be modified or developed in significance only by association with other words—only when they are in rhythmical, organized motion. Statically words have little or no significance, as you may assure yourself by consulting any dictionary; but, when once they are treated dynamically and pictorially their power to convey thought increases enormously; still, let it always be understood that the powers are not in the words so much as in the mind and heart of him who uses them as his instrument. The thought, the feeling, the beauty is not so much in the words as in what the words suggest to the mind of the reader; and this power of suggestion is the power of the artist, the poet.

Some time ago you asked what connection there might be between words and architecture. There is this immediate and important connection—that architecture, for the past six centuries, has suffered from a growing accretion of words: It is now in fact overgrown and choked with meaningless words, silly words, vapid words—and meanwhile the reality has been lost in view and words and phrases have usurped the place of deeds, and, finally, phrase-making is accepted for architecture making: To such silly inanition have we come. If you doubt it, go to conventions, read the journals, listen to the papers and speeches. What are they?—words, words, words—mostly feeble words, mostly inconsequential, half-hearted, wholly sordid.

So, as we two together are seeking *things,* not words: As we are searching for *realities*—a word I love because I love the sense of life it stands for, the ten-fingered grasp of things it implies, the animalism and the spirituality of it—so, as we seek not words but realities, let us assume once for all that the architecture we seek is to be a reality not a word, or an evil aggregation of words as now.

The architecture that we see today has lost its organic quality. Like a man once strong but now old and ill, it no longer functions efficiently. It no longer speaks in tones of ringing eloquence as of yore. Its features have the pallid leer, the wistful, maudlin rictus of a countenance in decay. Its eye is lusterless, its ear is dulled, its vitals wasted. So moves it wearily toward a grave it cannot escape.

The architecture *we* seek shall be as a man active, alert, supple and strong, sound and sane. A man having five senses all awake; eyes that actually see, ears that truly hear; a man who *lives in the present,* who knows and feels the vibrant intensity of that ever-moving moment of existence that lies between the dead past and the unborn future, with heart to draw it in and mind to put it out—that portentous birth, that fertile moment which we call the hour, the very center and the soul of existence, that large abundant moment which we call *today.*

As a man who knows, who loves his day, who loves the sun, who loves life, who loves all animate things, who loves health and strength and kindliness, whose feet are upon the earth, whose ear is attuned to the ceaseless song of the spirit soaring ever as a lark in the bright sunny air: So shall our art be, and so shall our hearts be. Responsive to the throb of universal life, answering its urgent and inspiring call —so shall our lives be.

To live, really to live, is the consummation of existence. To half-live is to fail utterly, is to die standing.

All life is organic. It manifests itself through organs, through structures, through functions. That which is alive acts, organizes, grows, develops, unfolds, expands, differentiates, organ after organ, structure after structure, form after form, function after function. That which does not do these things is in *decay!* This is a *law,* not a word!

And decay proceeds as inevitably as growth: Functions decline, structures disintegrate, differentiations blur, the fabric dissolves, life disappears, death appears, time engulfs—the eternal night falls. Out of oblivion into oblivion, so goes the drama of created things—and of such is the history of an organism.

But it is the hey-day that is to interest us most deeply. For our art is an organism. To see it emerge from the matrix of humanity, to see it born of its conditions, to rock its cradle, to guard and ward it, to forecast its hope and promise—such shall be our friendly task. For the *New Architecture* is that child—come to stay, and grow, and bring the sunshine to our hearts.

For that which grows, grows by virtue of its life and strength, virtue of its nourishment, by reason of its energy. It grows through assimilation, upbuilding and organization; and, when it reaches maturity it propagates, it gives forth its kind, for this is the ultimate function of growth and maturity, and *this, too, is a law.*

Now shall a man prove inferior to a tree? Shall a tree give forth fruit true to itself, and shall a man give forth nothing in his art? . . .

It cannot be. For like begets its like, and this is a *law,* not a phrase. Nature throws with precision, and with most tenacious power develops its types and conserves them to their rhythmical endings.

But Man is capricious, wanton, headstrong—the most unnatural of the animals. Highly complex he degenerates with a corresponding ease, beginning, usually, like a tree, at the top or in the core. He is the only animal that voluntarily poisons himself physically and mentally. He is a paradox. He is a queer, foolish thing, and propagates folly—dies, and leaves others to wish he had never been born. Yet has he a saving grace: he knows in his heart that he is a fool, and yet, wishes in all sincerity that he were not.

And of such is contemporaneous American architecture: Pitiful in its folly—dying at the top and dead at the core, with here and there a gleam, a little gleam of regret. Functions without forms, forms without functions; details unrelated to masses, and masses unrelated to anything but folly, irresponsible, and grossly, callously ignorant; monuments to the feeble of mind and the shallow of heart; monuments to the mercenary hurly-burly of the hour; the distracted forms of a diseased and distracted function. Organic it is not. Inorganic it is becoming. Dissolution is its goal.

So you may learn, my son, what the word, organic, does *not* mean, by examining with the care of a pathologist this art in process of decay and putrefaction. In so doing you will get a broad side-light on the *true* meaning of the word, on the world of true activity of real life that it implies, and so, prepare your mind to grasp and absorb, little by little, its deep and rich meaning, and so to saturate yourself with the vital, impelling energy of its significance that, when your day comes you too may not be an imitation architect in your generation.

On the Historic Styles

A brief glance at the so-called "styles" of the past may now be opportune, and may assist us in clarifying our view of things contemporary. To begin with, my boy, disabuse your mind of this word "styles." It is a misnomer, or at the least reckoning, it is a term devoid of genuine significance as it is of honesty. Anyone who has, with a little industry, and a fair memory, read a "hand-book of architecture," can talk to you most glibly of the styles, remaining meanwhile grotesquely empty of head and heart concerning the art and the history of architecture as a form of expression, and, just as amusingly unable to weigh the objective or subjective values of any given building whatsoever, here, there or anywhere. What we so glibly call the styles are, and were, in their times and places, organizations or crystallizations of the thought and feeling of certain peoples; and they were done or they happened more or less consciously—but unerringly.

It is a not uncommon happening to hear the inquiry made: In what style is this building? And, if a categorical answer is given even though it be: This structure is in the Louis XIV style, with Gothic details, and Celtic ornaments, with adaptations to modern requirements, the questioner is satisfied; for the answer dove-tails into his preconception of architecture; namely, that it is a thing of styles.

Now suppose the answer to be not categorical, and to run something like this: The structure is a serious attempt, by a serious architect, to make a building grow naturally, out of all its conditions, logically and poetically, I doubt if the questioner would be satisfied; for the answer will not dove-tail with his preconception; and a man's preconception always governs unless he possess genuine culture.

Should he demur, and an argument follow, he is pretty sure to close it, to his satisfaction, in saying: Well, a good copy is the best that can be done: My friend, Mr. Blank, Architect, in whom I have great confidence, has told me so, repeatedly.

You will find it pretty difficult to convince such a man that there may now, as ever, exist a plastic and organic quality in the architectural art, ready at the hand of the Architect who has these qualities in his own mind. For his knowledge, such as it is, is ready-made, precisely as he believes architecture to be ready-made. It is needless to say that a genuine art cannot flourish within the range of such a man's influence. For such influence is ever a blight, not a nourishment. But all of this only in passing:

So, for our purposes, let us dismiss the word "styles" as meaningless, and seek a rational conception of our own. If it be true as I hold, and as I have told you, that a people can create only in its own *subjective* image, the Parthenon of the Greeks, for instance, was not done in the Greek style, but in the Greek subjectivity. The Parthenon was, in fact, the Greek nature, mind, heart, soul, beliefs, hopes, aspirations, known, felt and interpreted by a great Greek artist, and translated by him into an objective symbol of Greek civilization, called by us the Parthenon. In other words the Parthenon was Greek, not American; it arose out of the Greek life, was made by the Greeks, for the Greeks, it was a direct product sign and image of Greek civilization and expressed for them and for us the true essence of that civilization.

So, if, for the word style we substitute the word, civilization, we make at once a pronounced stride in advance toward an intelligent understanding of the *values* of the historical monuments of architecture.

Hereafter, when you look on one of your contemporary "good copies" of historical remains ask yourself the question: not in what *style*, but in what *civilization* is this building? and the absurdity, vulgarity, anachronism and solecism of the modern structure will be revealed to you in a most startling fashion. Of such and such a structure of the sort, for instance, manifestly we cannot say: this is a serious attempt, by a seriously minded architect, to make a building grow naturally, logically and poetically out of all its conditions, but no, this is an attempt, by a feeble-minded architect, living on the charity of modern American civilization, to reconstruct a part of the civilization of, say, Francis Ist, namely one of its buildings—a past and gone civilization, dead forever; and of which, he, this architect, can have no real knowledge, no true sense of its reality, not having lived as a part of it. Yet such is architecture, today, as endorsed by people of "culture" or no culture, who believe, or affect to believe that "a good copy is the best that can be done." For shame! How can culture, so-called, show itself more utterly shallow, than in this aspect of it?

Walk for a few blocks through the streets of New York, where "good copies" abound, and you will find, if I mistake not, a different "civilization" on every corner, and sub-civilizations, a plenty, in between—and yet nobody laughs! What has become of the sense of humor, the keen appreciation of the ridiculous, for which we Americans are noted? Yet nobody laughs! Isn't it queer?—when everybody would immoderately laugh if your coat and trousers were not of proper modern cut and fit. Yet here is an architectural cut and fit far more grotesque than the astronomers of Laputa, with all their scholarly ingenuity in doing things wrong end to, ever could have rivalled! But *we* look on gravely, nod our heads, and avow once more, that "a good copy is the best that can be done!"

Bear also in mind, my lad, while the continued and customary use of the word "styles" tends to confirm a popular notion that there were in the past *many* architectures, and that each one is now nicely packed up for our use under the label of a given style, that this popular and cultured notion is as unscientific as it is unnatural, unhistoric and inaccurate. It may pass, as a popular vagary expressive of the popular desire to "put on style," and as voicing the vulgar belief that putting on style is accomplished in "selecting a style."

It seems we "select" styles now-a-days.

I have even noted of late that it appears some "styles" are "correct"—others not.

But of us, who seek broad and convincing aspects of truth, there is now, as ever there has been and as ever there will be, but *one architecture,* of which the so-called styles were and are variants expressive of differences and changes in civilizations. For architecture, now, as ever, is *the need and the power to build!* How this need and this power have varied from time to time and place to place, climatically, ethnologically, following the shifting racial and personal moods of mind, body and soul, the history of building will show to you. . . .

It is primarily of importance to a just understanding of historical architecture, that you never lose sight of this unitary conception of the art—and that you hold it in your mind, together with all the variations of historic architectural expression, in a state of solution, or suspension, if I may use the term.

Nothing can more surely be fatal to a clear and just conception of the One Great Architectural Art, in all its fundamental simplicity and all its delightful and beautiful complexity, than the ready-made and cock-sure notions born of reading a few books or travel abroad.

It is Carlyle, I believe, who says in substance: The eye sees that which it brings the power to see. A wise saying, profound and true. Bear it, also, ever in mind. And, when your eye falls upon the great architecture of the past let it bring with it that higher power to see which is born of love, of reverence, of a noble sympathetic mind and a generous and kindly heart. And, likewise, when it falls upon the bastard periods, the periods of decay and death, let it bring with it the broad secure consciousness and the knowledge that spiritual decay is the cause at work behind them.

Then, the more deeply, the more intelligently you shall have used this power of seeing and shall have pursued its studies, the more fully and lastingly will you recognize and realize that *these works, good, bad and indifferent, are of the past, while you are of the present.* That the past is dead, and has been buried by a past that is dead: that the history of the past is a history of one vast procession of burials, and that nothing is at once so mutable and so steadfast as is Man—for Man is of the spirit.

I cannot, of course, in the span of our brief talks, undertake to go with you into a close view of the remains of a mighty architectural past—however fascinating such a view might be. For I have sought only to give you a sketch, not a finished study of our art. I must leave the details of historic study and exegesis to your own diligence and opportunity. All that I seek, is, to illuminate your path. But this I must say: That I do not see and cannot comprehend how anyone who truly reveres the great works of the past, can for a moment, dream of imitating them. The mere wish shows, to my view, a profound mental vacuity; and reveals this critical truth, namely, that the alleged reverence is a pretence, a fad, a humbug, and not a reality.

On the other hand: That these great works should inspire you with a Profound admiration, that they should cause to arise in your heart a powerful desire, not to imitate but to *emulate* them, I can readily understand; for such a feeling is born of sincerity and understanding and is worthy of a man and an architect.

It is the fashion to say that we are embarrassed by the richness of our heritage from the past; that it constitutes an obstruction to our progress, etc., etc. This sounds rather plausible and rather philosophical until we stop to consider that the statements really signify this:

That we are so puny of mind, heart and soul, that the great outpourings of the minds, hearts and souls of our predecessors cease to be an inspiration for us—that *they* arose to simplicity of mind; while *we* have fallen into simpleness of mind.

This may be true; but do not take it as your standard; for we are great or little as we choose to make ourselves.

Rather so simplify and enlarge and enrich your own mind that you come into a companionship with theirs, and then will grow within your own mind a power similar to theirs and you will no longer dread an embarrassment of riches, for spiritual riches can never embarrass him who is large in spirit—for the pride, the joy, the power of emulation surely will be his.

Conversely the *imitative vice,* being a cowardly, weak and ignoble one, leads us to appropriate, or, in plain English, *to steal the works of great minds rather than to emulate the greatness of the minds themselves!* And thus do we sink, deeper and deeper, into the mire of self-abasement, and moral decay and the artist accordingly ceases to be a man. . . .

I tell you, again, the need of the hour is for Men! Be a man!

And, in the manliness of your own soul, impart virility to your art!

When you shall carefully have studied the forms and the spirit of these historic structures, you will realize the more and the more impressively as you grow older, that the civilizations which produced them are definitely of the past—and that the ways thereof are not your ways.

The more deeply this truth sinks into your consciousness, the stronger will grow your conviction that never can you use these forms as they, who made them, used them. For the peculiar, characteristic subjectivity which animated these men, and which they infused into their works, has vanished with the physical presence of these men, their day and their generation.

From: *Kindergarten Chats,* by Louis Henri Sullivan. First published in the "Interstate Architect and Builder," 16 February 1901 to 8 February 1902. Revised by Sullivan in 1918, and edited by Claude Bragdon, these papers were first published as a book by the Scarab Fraternity Press, Lawrence, Kansas: 1934, pages 46–49, 170–176.

II

Roots in the Region

Early Foundations

by

Henry David Thoreau

As for a Shelter, I do not deny that this is now a necessary of life, though there are instances of men having done without it for long periods in colder countries than this. Samuel Laing says that "The Laplander in his skin dress, and in a skin bag which he puts over his head and shoulders, will sleep night after night on the snow—in a degree of cold which would extinguish the life of one exposed to it in any woollen clothing." He had seen them asleep thus. Yet he adds, "They are not hardier than other people." But, probably, man did not live long on earth without discovering the convenience which there is in a house, the domestic comforts, which phrase may have originally signified the satisfactions of the house more than of the family; though these must be extremely partial and occasional in those climates where the house is associated in our thoughts with winter or the rainy season chiefly, and two-thirds of the year, except for a parasol, is unnecessary. In our climate, in the summer, it was formerly almost solely a covering at night. In the Indian gazettes a wigwam was the symbol of a day's march, and a row of them cut or painted on the bark of a tree signified that so many times they had camped. Man was not made so large-limbed and robust but that he must seek to narrow his world, and wall in a space such as fitted him. He was at first bare and out of doors; but though this was pleasant enough in serene and warm weather, by daylight, the rainy season and the winter, to say nothing of the torrid sun, would perhaps have nipped his race in the bud if he had not made haste to clothe himself with the shelter of a house. Adam and Eve, according to the fable, wore the bower before other clothes. Man wanted a home, a place of warmth, or comfort, first of physical warmth, then the warmth of the affections.

We may imagine a time when, in the infancy of the human race, some enterprising mortal crept into a hollow in a rock for shelter. Every child begins the world again, to some extent, and loves to stay outdoors, even in wet and cold. It plays house as well as horse, having an instinct for it. Who does not remember the interest with which when young he looked at shelving rocks, or any approach to a cave? It was the natural yearning of that portion of our most primitive ancestor which still survived in us. From the cave we have advanced to roofs of palm leaves, of bark and boughs, of linen woven and stretched, of grass and straw, of boards and shingles, of stones and tiles. At last, we know not what it is to live in the open air, and our lives are domestic in more senses than we think. From the hearth to the field is a great distance. It would be well, perhaps, if we were to spend more of our days and nights without any obstruction between us and the celestial bodies, if the poet did not speak so much from under a roof, or the saint dwell there so long. Birds do not sing in caves, nor do doves cherish their innocence in dovecots.

However, if one designs to construct a dwelling-house, it behoves him to exercise a little Yankee shrewdness, lest after all he find himself in a work-house, a labyrinth without a clue, a museum, an almshouse, a prison, or a splendid mausoleum instead. Consider first how slight a shelter is absolutely necessary. I have seen Penobscot Indians, in this town, living in tents of thin cotton cloth, while the snow was nearly a foot deep around them, and I thought that they would be glad to have it deeper to keep out the wind. Formerly, when how to get my living honestly, with freedom left for my proper pursuits, was a question which vexed me even more than it does now, for unfortunately I am become somewhat callous, I used to see a large box by the railroad, six feet long by three wide, in which the labourers locked up their tools at night, and it suggested to me that every man who was hard pushed might get such a one for a dollar, and, having bored a few auger holes in it, to admit the air at least, get into it when it rained and at night, and hook down the lid, and so have freedom in his love, and in his soul be free. This did not appear the worst, nor by any means a despicable alternative. You could sit up as late as you pleased, and, whenever you got up, go abroad without any landlord or house-lord dogging you for rent. Many a man is harassed to death to pay the rent of a larger and more luxurious box who would not have frozen to death in such a box as this. I am far from jesting. Economy is a subject which admits of being treated with levity, but it cannot so be disposed of. A comfortable house, for a rude and hardy race, that lived mostly out of doors, was once made here almost entirely of such materials as nature furnished ready to their hands. Gookin, who was superintendent of the Indians subject to the Massachusetts Colony, writing in 1674, says "The best of their houses are covered very neatly, tight and warm, with barks of trees, slipped from their bodies at those seasons when the sap is up, and made into great flakes, with pressure of weighty timber, when they are green. . . . The meaner sort are covered with mats which they make of a kind of bulrush, and are also indifferently tight and warm, but not so good as the former. . . . Some I have seen, sixty or a hundred feet long and thirty feet broad. . . . I have often lodged in their wigwams, and found them as warm as the best English houses." He adds, that they were commonly carpeted and lined within with well-wrought embroidered mats, and were furnished with various utensils. The Indians had advanced so far as to regulate the effect of the wind by a mat suspended over the hole in the roof and moved by a string. Such a lodge was in the first instance constructed in a day or two at most, and taken down and put up in a few hours; and every family owned one, or its apartment in one.

In the savage state every family owns a shelter as good as the best, and sufficient for its coarser and simpler wants; but I think that I speak within bounds when I say that, though the birds of the air have their nests, and the foxes their holes, and the savages their wigwams, in modern civilised society not more than one half the families own a shelter. In the large towns and cities, where civilisation especially prevails, the number of those who own a shelter is a very small fraction of the whole. The rest pay an annual tax for this outside garment of all, become indispensable summer and winter, which would buy a village of Indian wigwams, but now helps to keep them poor as long as they live. I do not mean to insist here on the disadvantage of hiring compared with owning, but it is evident that the savage owns his shelter because it costs so little, while the civilised man hires his commonly because he cannot afford to own it; nor can he, in the long run, any better afford to hire. But, answers one, by merely paying this tax the poor civilised man secures an abode which is a palace compared with the savage's. An annual rent of from twenty-five to a hundred dollars—these are the country rates—entitles him to the benefit of the improvements of centuries, spacious apartments, clean paint and paper, Rumford fire-place, back plastering, Venetian blinds, copper pump, spring lock, a commodious cellar, and many other things. But how happens it that he who is said to enjoy these things is so commonly a *poor* civilised man, while the savage, who has them now, is rich as a savage? If it is asserted that civilisation is a real advance in the condition of man—and I think that it is, though only the wise improve their advantages—it must be shown that it has produced better dwellings without making them more costly; and the cost of a thing is the amount of what I will call life which is required to be exchanged for it, immediately or in the long run. An average house in this neighbourhood costs perhaps eight hundred dollars, and to lay up this sum will take from ten to fifteen years of the labourer's life, even if he is not encumbered with a family—estimating the pecuniary value of every man's labour at one dollar a day, for if some receive more, others receive less—so that he must have spent more than half his life commonly before *his* wigwam will be earned. If we suppose him to pay a rent instead, this is but a doubtful choice of evils. Would the savage have been wise to exchange his wigwam for a palace on these terms?

It may be guessed that I reduce almost the whole advantage of holding this superfluous property as a fund in store against the future, so far as the individual is concerned, mainly to the defraying of funeral expenses. But perhaps a man is not required to bury himself. Nevertheless this points to an important distinction between the civilised man and the savage; and, no doubt, they have designs on us for our benefit, in making the life of a civilised people an *institution*, in which the life of the individual is to a great extent absorbed, in order to preserve and perfect that of the race. But I wish to show at what a sacrifice this advantage is at present obtained, and to suggest that we may possibly so live as to secure all the advantage without suffering any of the disadvantage. What mean ye by saying that the poor ye have always with you, or that the fathers have eaten sour grapes, and the children's teeth are set on edge?

"As I live, saith the Lord God, ye shall not have occasion any more to use this proverb in Israel."

"Behold, all souls are mine; as the soul of the father, so also the soul of the son is mine: the soul that sinneth it shall die."

When I consider my neighbours, the farmers of Concord, who are at least as well off as the other classes, I find that for the most part they have been toiling twenty, thirty, or forty years, that they may become the real owners of their farms, which commonly they have inherited with encumbrances, or else bought with hired money—and we may regard one-third of that toil as the cost of their houses—but commonly they have not paid for them yet. It is true, the encumbrances sometimes outweigh the value of the farm, so that the farm itself becomes one great encumbrance, and still a man is found to inherit it, being well acquainted with it, as he says. On applying to the assessors, I am surprised to learn that they cannot at once name a dozen in the town who own their farms free and clear. If you would know the history of these homesteads, inquire at the bank where they are mortgaged. The man who has actually paid for his farm with labour on it is so rare that every neighbour can point to him. I doubt if there are three such men in Concord. What has been said of the merchants, that a very large majority, even ninety-seven in a hundred, are sure to fail, is equally true of the farmers. With regard to the merchants, however, one of them says pertinently that a great part of their failures are not genuine pecuniary failures, but merely failures to fulfil their engagements, because it is inconvenient—that is, it is the moral character that breaks down. But this puts an infinitely worse face on the matter, and suggests, beside that probably not even the other three succeed in saving their souls, but are perchance bankrupt in a worse sense than they who fail honestly. Bankruptcy and repudiation are the springboards from which much of our civilisation vaults and turns its somersets, but the savage stands on the unelastic plank of famine. Yet the Middlesex Cattle Show goes off here with *éclat* annually, as if all the joints of the agricultural machine were suet.

The farmer is endeavouring to solve the problem of a livelihood by a formula more complicated than the problem itself. To get his shoe strings he speculates in herds of cattle. With consummate skill he has set his trap with a hair-spring to catch comfort and independence, and then, as he turned away, got his own leg into it. This is the reason he is poor; and for a similar reason we are all poor in respect to a thousand savage comforts, though surrounded by luxuries. As Chapman sings—

> The false society of men—
> —for earthly greatness
> All heavenly comforts rarefies to air.

And when the farmer has got his house, he may not be the richer but the poorer for it, and it be the house that has got him. As I understand it, that was a valid objection urged by Momus against the house which Minerva made, that she "had not made it movable, by which means a bad neighbourhood might be avoided"; and it may still be urged, for our houses are such unwieldy property, that we are often imprisoned rather than housed in them; and the bad neighbourhood to be avoided is our own scurvy selves. I know one or two families, at least, in this town, who, for nearly a generation, have been wishing to sell their houses in the outskirts and move into the village, but have not been able to accomplish it, and only death will set them free.

Granted that the *majority* are able at last either to own or hire the modern house with all its improvements. While civilisation has been improving our houses, it has not equally improved the men who are to inhabit them. It has created palaces, but it was not so easy to create noblemen and kings. And *if the civilised man's pursuits are no worthier than the savage's, if he is employed the greater part of his life in obtaining gross necessaries and comforts merely, why should he have a better dwelling than the former?*

But how do the poor *minority* fare? Perhaps it will be found, that just in proportion as some have been placed in outward circumstances above the savage, others have been degraded below him. The luxury of one class is counterbalanced by the indigence of another. On the one side is the palace, on the other are the almshouse and "silent poor." The myriads who built the pyramids to be the tombs of the Pharaohs were fed on garlic, and it may be were not decently buried themselves. The mason who finishes the cornice of the palace returns at night perchance to a hut not so good as a wigwam. It is a mistake to suppose that, in a country where the usual evidences of civilisation exist, the condition of a very large body of the inhabitants may not be as degraded as that of savages. I refer to the degraded poor, not now to the degraded rich. To know this I should not need to look farther than to the shanties which everywhere border our railroads, that last improvement in civilisation; where I see in my daily walks human beings living in sties, and all winter with an open door, for the sake of light, without any visible, often imaginable, wood pile, and the forms of both old and young are permanently contracted by the long habit of shrinking from cold and misery, and the development of all their limbs and faculties is checked. It certainly is fair to look at that class by whose labour the works which distinguish this generation are accomplished. Such, too, to a greater or less extent, is the condition of the operatives of every denomination in England, which is the great workhouse of the world. Or I could refer you to Ireland, which is marked as one of the white or enlightened spots on the map. Contrast the physical condition of the Irish with that of the North American Indian, or the South Sea Islander, or any other savage race before it was degraded by contact with the civilised man. Yet I have no doubt that people's rulers are as wise as the average of civilised rulers. Their condition only proves what squalidness may consist with civilisation. I hardly need refer now to the labourers in our Southern States who produce the staple exports of this country, and are themselves a staple production of the South. But to confine myself to those who are said to be in *moderate* circumstances.

Most men appear never to have considered what a house is, and are actually though needlessly poor all their lives because they think that they must have such a one as their neighbours have. As if one were to wear any sort of coat which the tailor might cut out for him, or, gradually leaving off palm-leaf hat or cap of woodchuck skin complain of hard times because he could not afford to buy him a crown! It is possible to invent a house still more convenient and luxurious than we have, which yet all would admit that man could not afford to pay for. Shall we always study to obtain more of these things, and not sometimes to be content with less? Shall the respectable citizen thus gravely teach, by precept and example, the necessity of the young man's providing a certain number of superfluous glow-shoes, and umbrellas, and empty guest chambers for empty guests, before he dies? Why should not our furniture be as simple as the Arab's or the Indian's? When I think of the benefactors of the race, whom we have apotheosised as messengers from heaven, bearers of divine gifts to man, I do not see in my mind any retinue at their heels, any carload of fashionable furniture. Or what if I were to allow—would it not be a singular allowance?—that our furniture should be more complex than the Arab's in proportion as we are morally and intellectually his superiors! At present our houses are cluttered with it, and a good housewife would soon sweep out the greater part into the dust-hole, and not leave her morning's work undone. Morning work! By the blushes of Aurora and the Music of Memnon, what should be man's *morning work* in this world? I had three pieces of limestone on my desk, but I was terrified to find that they required to be dusted daily, when the furniture of my mind was all undusted still, and I threw them out the window in disgust. How, then, could I have a furnished house? I would rather sit in the open air, for no dust gathers on the grass, unless where man has broken ground.

It is the luxurious and dissipated who set the fashions which the herd so diligently follow. The traveller who stops at the best houses, so called, soon discovers this, for the publicans presume him to be a Sardanapalus, and if he resigned himself to their tender mercies he would soon be completely emasculated. I think that in the railroad car we are inclined to spend more on luxury than on safety and convenience, and it threatens without attaining these to become no better than a modern drawing-room, with its divans, and ottomans, and sunshades, and a hundred other oriental things, which we are taking west with us, invented for the ladies of the harem and the effeminate natives of the Celestial Empire, which Jonathan should be ashamed to know the names of. I would rather sit on a pumpkin and have it all to myself, than to be crowded on a velvet cushion. I would rather ride on earth in an ox-cart with a free circulation than go to heaven in the fancy car of an excursion train and breathe a *malaria* all the way.

The very simplicity and nakedness of man's life in the primitive ages imply this advantage at least, that they left him still but a sojourner in nature. When he was refreshed with food and sleep he contemplated his journey again. He dwelt, as it were, in a tent in this world, and was either threading the valleys, or crossing the plains, or climbing the mountain tops. But lo! men have become the tools of their tools. The man who independently plucked the fruits when he was hungry is become a farmer; and he who stood under a tree for shelter, a housekeeper. We now no longer camp as for a night, but have settled down on earth and forgotten heaven. We have adopted Christianity merely as an improved method of *agri*-culture. We have built for this world a family mansion, and for the next a family tomb. The best works of art are the expression of man's struggle to free himself from this condition, but the effect of our art is merely to make this low state comfortable and that higher state to be forgotten. There is actually no place in this village for a work of *fine* art, if any had come down to us, to stand, for our lives, our houses and streets, furnish no proper pedestal for it. There is not a nail to hang a picture on, nor a shaft to receive the bust of a hero or a saint. When I consider how our houses are built and paid for, or not paid for, and their internal economy managed and sustained, I wonder that the floor does not give way under the visitor while he is admiring the gewgaws upon the mantel-piece, and let him through into the cellar, to some solid and honest, though earthly foundation. I cannot but perceive that this so-called rich and refined life is a thing jumped at, and I do not get on in the enjoyment of the *fine* arts which adorn it, my attention being wholly occupied with the jump; for I remember that the greatest genuine leap due to human muscles alone, on record, is that of certain wandering Arabs, who are said to have cleared twenty-five feet on level ground. Without factitious support, man is sure to come to earth again beyond that distance. The first question which I am tempted to put to the proprietor of such great impropriety is, Who bolsters you? Are you one of the ninety-seven who fail, or the three who succeed? Answer me these questions, and then perhaps I may look at your baubles and find them ornamental. The cart before the horse is neither beautiful nor useful. Before we can adorn our houses with beautiful objects the walls must be stripped, and our lives must be stripped, and beautiful housekeeping and beautiful living be laid for a foundation: now, a taste for the beautiful is most cultivated out of doors, where there is no house and no housekeeper.

From: *Walden*, by Henry David Thoreau. Boston: 1854. From the World's Classics Edition, pages 22–33.

Rural Adaptation

by

Andrew Jackson Downing

Architecture, either practically considered, or viewed as an art of taste, is a subject so important and comprehensive in itself, that volumes would be requisite to do it justice. Buildings of every description, from the humble cottage to the lofty temple, are objects of such constant recurrence in every habitable part of the globe, and are so strikingly indicative of the intelligence, character, and taste of the inhabitants, that they possess in themselves a great and peculiar interest for the mind. To have a "local habitation,"—a permanent dwelling, that we can give the impress of our own mind, and identify with our own existence,—appears to be the ardent wish, sooner or later felt, of every man: excepting only those wandering sons of Ishmael, who pitch their tents with the same indifference, and as little desire to remain fixed, in the flowery plains of Persia, as in the sandy deserts of Sahara, or Arabia.

In a city or town, or its immediate vicinity, where space is limited, where buildings stand crowded together, and depend for their attractions entirely upon the style and manner of their construction, mere architectural effect, after convenience and fitness are consulted, is of course the only point to be kept in view. There the façade which meets the eye of the spectator from the public street, is enriched and made attractive by the display of architectural style and decoration; commensurate to the magnitude or importance of the edifice, and the whole, so far as the effect of the building is concerned, comes directly within the province of the architect alone.

With respect to this class of dwellings, we have little complaint to make, for many of our town residences are highly elegant and beautiful. But how shall we designate that singular perversity of taste, or rather that total want of it, which prompts the man, who, under the name of a villa residence, piles up in the free open country, amid the green fields, and beside the wanton gracefulness of luxuriant nature, a stiff modern "three story brick," which, like a well bred cockney with a true horror of the country, doggedly seems to refuse to enter into harmonious combination with any other object in the scene, but only serves to call up the exclamation,

> Avaunt, stiff pile! why didst thou stray
> From blocks congenial in Broadway!

Yet almost daily we see built up in the country huge combinations of boards and shingles, without the least attempts at adaptation to situation; and square masses of brick start up here and there, in the verdant slopes of our village suburbs appearing as if they had been transplanted, by some unlucky incantation, from the close-packed neighbourhood of city residence, and left accidentally in the country, or, as Sir Walter Scott has remarked, "had strayed out to the country for an airing."

What then are the proper characteristics of a rural residence? The answer to this, in a few words, is, such a dwelling, as from its various accommodations, not only gives ample space for all the comforts and conveniences of a country life, but by its varied and picturesque form and outline, its porches, verandas, etc., also appears to have some reasonable connection, or be in perfect keeping, with surrounding nature. *Architectural beauty* must be considered conjointly with the *beauty of the landscape* or situation. Buildings of almost every description, and particularly those for the habitation of man, will be considered by the mind of taste, not only as architectural objects of greater or less merit, but as component parts of the general scene; united with the surrounding lawn, embosomed in tufts of trees and shrubs, if properly designed and constructed, they will even serve to impress a character upon the surrounding landscape. Their effect will frequently be good or bad, not merely as they are excellent or indifferent examples of a certain style of building, but as they are happily or unhappily combined with the adjacent scenery. The intelligent observer will readily appreciate the truth of this, and acknowledge the value, as well as necessity, of something besides architectural knowledge. And he will perceive how much more likely to be successful, are the efforts of him, who in composing and constructing a rural residence, calls in to the aid of architecture, the genius of the landscape; —whose mind is imbued with a taste for beautiful scenery, and who so elegantly and ingeniously engrafts art upon nature, as to heighten her beauties; while by the harmonious union he throws a borrowed charm around his own creation.

The English, above all other people, are celebrated for their skill in what we consider *rural adaptation.* Their residences seem to be a part of the scenes where they are situated; for their exquisite taste and nice perception of the beauties of Landscape Gardening and rural scenery, lead them to erect those picturesque edifices, which by their varied outlines, seem in exquisite keeping with nature; while by the numberless climbing plants, shrubs, and fine ornamental trees with which they surround them, they form beautiful pictures of rural beauty. Even the various offices connected with the dwelling, partially concealed by groups of foliage, and contributing to the expression of domestic comfort, while they extend out, and give importance to the main edifice, also serve to connect it, in a less abrupt manner, with the grounds.

So different indeed is the general character of the cottage and villa architecture of England, that many an American, on looking over the illustrated works of their writers on domestic architecture, while he acknowledges their high scenic beauty, generally regards them in much the same light as he does Moore's description of the vale of Cashmere, in Lalla Rookh—beautiful imaginative creations of the artist, but which can never be realized in every-day life, and a comfortable dwelling. The fact however is, it is well known, quite the contrary; for many of the English country residences are really far more beautiful than the pictorial representations; and no people gather around themselves more of those little comforts and elegancies, which make up the sum total of *home,* than the inhabitants of that highly cultivated and gardenesque country.

The leading principles which should be our guide in Landscape or Rural Architecture, have been condensed by an able writer in the following heads. "1st, as a useful art, in *fitness for the end in view:* 2d, as an art of design, in *expression of purpose:* 3d, as an art of taste, in *expression of some particular architectural style.*"

The most enduring and permanent source of beauty is, undoubtedly, utility. In a country residence, therefore, of whatever character, the comfort and convenience of the various members of the family being the first and most important consideration, the quality of *fitness* is universally appreciated and placed in the first rank. In many of those articles of furniture or apparel which luxury or fashion has brought into use, fitness or convenience often gives way to beauty of form or texture: but in a habitation, intended to shelter us from the heat and cold, as well as to give us an opportunity to dispense the elegant hospitalities of refined life—the neglect of the various indispensable conveniences and comforts which an advanced state of civilization require, would be but poorly compensated for, by a fanciful exterior or a highly ornate style of building. Farther than this, *fitness* will extend to the choice of situation; selecting a sheltered site, neither too high, as upon the exposed summit of bleak hills, nor too low, as in the lowest bottoms of damp valleys; but preferring those middle grounds which, while they afford a free circulation of air, and a fine prospect, are not detrimental to the health or enjoyment of the occupants. A proper exposure is another subject, worthy of the attention of either the architect or proprietor, as there are stormy, and pleasant aspects or exposures in all climates.

However much the principle of *fitness* may be appreciated and acted upon in the United States, we have certainly great need of apology for the flagrant and almost constant violation of the second principle, viz: *the expression of purpose.* By the expression of purpose in buildings, is meant that architectural character, or *ensemble*, which distinctly points out the particular use or destination for which the edifice is intended. In a dwelling-house, the expression of purpose is conveyed by the chimney-tops, the porch or veranda, and those various appendages indicative of domestic enjoyment, which are needless, and therefore misplaced, in a public building. In a church, the spire or the dome, when present, at once stamps the building with the expression of purpose; and the few openings and plain exterior, with the absence of chimneys, are the suitable and easily recognized characteristics of the barn. Were any one to commit so violent an outrage upon the principle of the expression of purpose as to surmount his barns with the tall church spire, our feelings would at once cry out against the want of propriety. Yet how often do we meet in the northern states, with stables built after the models of Greek temples, and barns with elegant Venetian shutters—to say nothing of mansions with none but concealed chimney-tops, and without porches or appendages of any kind, to give the least hint to the mind of the doubting spectator, whether the edifice is a chapel, a bank, a hospital, or the private dwelling of a man of wealth and opulence!

"The expression of the purpose for which every building is erected," says the writer before quoted, "is the first and most essential beauty, and should be obvious from its architecture, although independent of any particular style; in the same manner as the reasons for things are altogether independent of the language in which they are conveyed. As in literary composition, no beauty of language can ever compensate for poverty of sense, so in architectural composition, no beauty of style can ever compensate for want of expression of purpose." Applying this excellent principle to our own country houses and their offices or out-buildings, we think every reasonable person will, at the first glance, see how lamentably deficient are many of the productions of our architects and builders, in one of the leading principles of the art. The most common form for an American country villa is the psuedo-Greek Temple; that is, a rectangular oblong building, with the chimney-tops concealed, if possible, and instead of a pretty and comfortable porch, veranda, or piazza, four, six, or eight lofty wooden columns are seen supporting a portico, so high as neither to afford an agreeable promenade, nor a sufficient shelter from the sun and rain.

There are two features, which it is now generally admitted, contribute strongly to the expression of purpose in a dwelling-house, and especially in a country residence. These are the chimney-tops and the entrance porch. Chimney-tops, with us, are generally square masses of brick, rising above the roof, and presenting certainly no very elegant appearance—which may perhaps serve as the apology of those who studiously conceal them. But in a climate where fires are requisite during a large portion of the year, chimney-tops are expressive of a certain comfort resulting from the use of them, which characterizes a building intended for a dwelling in that climate. Chimney-tops being never, or rarely, placed on those buildings intended for the inferior animals, are also undoubtedly strongly indicative of human habitations. Instead, therefore, of hiding or concealing them, they should be in all dwellings not only boldly avowed, but rendered ornamental; for whatever is a characteristic and necessary feature, should undoubtedly, if possible, be rendered elegant, or at least prevented from being ugly.

Much of the picturesque effect of the old English and Italian houses, undoubtedly arises from the handsome and curious stacks of chimneys, which spring out of their roofs. These, while they break and diversify the sky-outline of the building, enrich and give variety to its most bare and unornamented part. Examples are not wanting, in all the different styles of architecture, of handsome and characteristic chimneys, which may be adopted in any of our dwellings of a similar style. The Gothic, or old English chimney, with octagonal or cylindrical flues or shafts united in clusters, is made in a great variety of forms, either of bricks, or artificial stone. The former materials, moulded in the required shape, are highly taxed in England, while they may be very cheaply made here.

A Porch strengthens or conveys expression of purpose, because, instead of leaving the entrance door bare, as in manufactories and buildings of an inferior description, it serves both as a note of preparation, and an effectual shelter and protection to the entrance. Besides this, it gives a dignity and importance to that entrance, pointing it out to the stranger as the place of approach. A fine country house, without a porch or covered shelter to the doorway of some description, is therefore, as incomplete, to the correct eye, as a well-printed book without a title page, leaving the stranger to plunge at once in *media res,* without the friendly preparation of a single word of introduction. Porches are susceptible of every variety of form and decoration, from the embattled and buttressed portal of the Gothic castle, to the latticed arbor-porch of the cottage, around which the festoons of luxuriant climbing plants cluster, giving an effect not less beautiful than the richly carved capitals of the classic portico.

In this country, no architectural feature is more plainly expressive of purpose in our dwelling-houses than the *veranda,* or piazza. The unclouded splendor and fierce heat of our summer sun, render this very general appendage a source of real comfort and enjoyment; and the long veranda round many of our country residences stand in stead of the paved terraces of the English mansions as the place for promenade; while during the warmer portions of the season, half of the days or evenings are there passed in the enjoyment of the cool breezes, secure under low roofs supported by the open colonnade, from the solar rays, or the dews of night. The obvious utility of the veranda in this climate, (especially in the middle and southern states), will, therefore, excuse its adoption into any style of architecture that may be selected for our domestic uses, although abroad, buildings in the style in question, as the Gothic, for example, are not usually accompanied by such an appendage. An artist of the least taste or invention, will easily compose an addition, of this kind, that will be in good keeping with the rest of the edifice.

These various features, or parts of the building, with many others which convey *expression of purpose* in domestic architecture, because they recall to the mind the different uses to which they are applied, and the several enjoyments connected with them, also contribute greatly to the interest of the building itself, and heighten its good effect as part of a harmonious whole, in the landscape. The various projections and irregularities, caused by verandas, porticoes, etc., serve to connect the otherwise square masses of building, by gradual transition, with the ground about it.

The reader, who thus recognizes features as expressive of purpose in a dwelling intended for the habitation of man, we think, can be at no great loss to understand what would be characteristic in out-buildings or offices, farm-houses, lodges, stables, and the like, which are necessary structures on a villa or mansion residence of much size or importance. A proper regard to the expression of use or purpose, without interfering with beauty of style, will confer at all times another, viz. the beauty of truth, without which no building can be completely satisfactory. . . .

We have now to consider rural architecture under the guidance of the third leading principle, as *an art of taste*. The expression of architectural *style* in buildings is undoubtedly a matter of the first importance, and proper care being taken not to violate fitness, and expression of purpose, it may be considered as appealing most powerfully, at once, to the mind of almost every person. Indeed, with many, it is the only species of beauty which they perceive in buildings, and to it both convenience, and the expression of purpose, are often ignorantly sacrificed.

A marked style of architecture, appears to us to have claims for our admiration or preference for rural residences, for several reasons. As it is intrinsically beautiful in itself; as it interests us by means of the associations connected with it; as it is fitted to the wants and comforts of country life; and, as it is adapted to, or harmonizes with, the locality or scenery where it is located.

The harmonious union of buildings and scenery is a point of taste that appears to be but little understood in any country; and, mainly, we believe, because the architect and the landscape painter are seldom combined in the same person, or are seldom consulted together. It is for this reason that we so rarely see a country residence, or cottage and its grounds, making such a composition as a landscape painter would choose for his pencil. But it does not seem difficult, with a slight recurrence to the leading principle of unity of expression, to suggest a mode of immediately deciding which style of building is best adapted to harmonize with a certain kind of scenery.

From: *Landscape Architecture,* by Andrew Jackson Downing. New York: 1844, pages 339–349.

Frederick Law Olmsted's Contribution

by

Lewis Mumford

The influence of the land is sometimes looked upon as significant only in primitive conditions of life. With the coming of "civilization," that is to say, trade and manufacture and organized cities, the land is supposed to diminish in importance. As a matter of fact, the importance of the land increases with civilization: "Nature" as a system of interests and activities is one of the chief creations of the civilized man.

In a state of complete savagery, man's presence on the land is scarcely visible: if he lives off the land, he nevertheless makes little impression upon it. An open clearing or a midden of bones and broken crockery is all that marks his presence. As man learns to control his environment, his relationship with the land becomes more complicated: the plough and the axe and the hammer and the spade leave their mark on every feature of the landscape, from mountain top to valley bottom: the river bank is straightened, the harbor is dredged, the hill is terraced, the torrent is bridged, the natural vegetation is improved or altered by new importations: the whole aspect of the earth is changed. City life does not diminish these relations: it rather adds new ones.

The bridge, the garden, the ploughed field, the city, are the visible signs of men's relation with the land; they are all means of ordering the earth and making it fit for all the varieties and modes of human habitation. If man's exploitation of the land becomes reckless, then the interdependence of soils and civilizations is demonstrated by the gradual sapping of the civilization itself: if it is intelligent and thrifty, as in the agriculture of China and the hydraulic engineering of the Netherlands, then the civilization has some prospect of endurance. To understand the land, to appreciate the landscape, to turn to it for recreation, to cultivate it for food and energy, to reduce it to an orderly pattern for use—these functions belong more to an advanced state of society than they do to a primitive one. The continued culture of the land, and the culture of the mind through the land, is the mark of a high civilization.

Now, there are three main ways of modifying and humanizing the visible landscape. One of them is by agriculture and horticulture; it involves the orderly arrangement of the ploughed field and the woodlot, the meadow and the pasture, the road and the enclosure. When these functions are undertaken consciously and intelligently, as they were by the country gentlemen of England in the eighteenth century, for example, they lead to landscape design. The second method is by city development and architecture; and the third is by works of engineering—bridges, viaducts, canals, highroads, docks, harbours, dams. These three modes intermingle, and it is impossible to neglect one without spoiling the effect of the others. What is a beautiful city with bad drains, or a fine highway in a barren landscape?

Before the Civil War, the works of engineering in America, though modest in scale, were among the most genial that had been produced: around New York alone the High Bridge, a viaduct which carried the Croton water across the Harlem River, and the Croton system itself, with its lane of verdure carried against the side of the hills, with occasional breaks, from Croton to below Yonkers, was as fine in design as anything that had been produced within the city. In other parts of the country, the canals with their quiet towpaths, their little toll houses and bridges and locks, were happy improvements of the landscape; so that the reckless filling up of some of these canals in our own time, with their conversion into traffic highways, a wanton abandonment of all their recreative possibilities for summer and winter, is a black disgrace to the regions in which such misuse has occurred. At all events, the engineering of the wood-and-water stage of industrial economy, the stage marked by the water wheel and the local mill, the dirt highway and river and canal transportation and numerous agricultural villages, was aesthetically effective in its results. At its worst, it still left the landscape clear; and at its best, it gave the land comeliness.

With the coming of coal and iron and railroad transportation in the fifties, the whole picture altered. Railroad cuts were made with no thought of their effect on the landscape; the use of soft coal as a fuel cast a pall over the whole landscape and covered the cities into which the railroads nosed with grime; the slatternly habits of the pithead, the mine, the smeltery, and the blast furnace made their way into remote regions: indeed, wherever the railroad penetrated, it brought with it the characteristic paleotechnic disorder. Compare the actual physical landscape that surrounded the canal and the railroad: one is an elysium and the other is an inferno. The bargeman was notoriously a rough fellow, even poor Tom O'Leary who lost his dearie on the Erie Canal: but his vices did not extend much beyond the hailing distance of his oaths. Compare the coal-town of the post-Civil War Era, Altoona or Scranton, with the agricultural town of the canal and river era, Lancaster or Newburgh: the differences are no less striking than they are in a single community, like Bethlehem.

Rivers filled with refuse, inimical to fish and vegetation, flowed past cities covered with soot, which added to the industrial pollution of the streams by thus wasting, instead of utilizing for fertilizer, their human excrement. Mountain sides, first denuded of trees, lost their soil to the local torrents of spring that captured the run-off of the winter snows, now no longer retained and slowly seeping into the soil. Blight and waste came in with the boasted prosperities of the early industrial period: and at first the advantages and the defilements were so closely associated that people even prided themselves on the smoke of the thriving town—boasted, that is, of low efficiency in heating, wastage of carbon, and inability to make use of various useful gases and by-products! But this assault on the landscape was not confined to the industrial city: a parallel ruin went on in the countryside.

Millions of acres of arable land were thrown open at the two poles of Europe: America and Siberia. On to this land scrambled a horde of hungry people. Like men who had been starved too long of food, their impulse was to pluck ravenously at the first morsels that offered themselves, and not to concern themselves with either the manner in which it was cooked or its likelihood of eventually sitting well on the stomach. The result was a shiftless agriculture and an unstable rural life: two conditions that work against the slow permanent improvements that must be made in a cultivated landscape. Single-crop farming was characteristic of the new lands that were opened up in the West and the South: a method unsound economically and monotonous in its aesthetic results. Nathaniel Shaler tells in his autobiography how as late as the middle of the nineteenth century in Kentucky there was no systematic rotation or manuring, while as a result of timbermining one half of the arable soil of Northern Kentucky became unremunerative to plough tillage. The same story was written everywhere: the destruction of the forest, the depletion of the soil, the extirpation of wild life, the upsetting of the natural balance of organisms. It was in vain that the American proclaimed to the heavens that he loved his rocks and rills, his woods and templed hills: his actions were a derisive commentary on those pious words.

Land-hunger is one thing, and love of the soil is another. It is scarcely an exaggeration to say that it was only in the Brown Decades that the second attitude began to replace the first. This was not a process of romantic idealization: romanticism of the most touching sort was not, apparently, incompatible with bad farming and the general desecration of the wilderness: who could be more romantic today than the taxpayer who votes to build a concrete highway to a lonely mountain-top—making accessible that which is valuable only through its inaccessibility? On the contrary, the new sense of the land was scientific and realistic; it was chiefly the work of a handful of naturalists, geographers, and landscape planners. In Uncle Vanya, Chekhov presents a dissolute doctor whose one real passion is the restoration of the landscape to its fullest uses: undoubtedly, there were minds of this order, suddenly alive to the holocaust and disaster that had attended the vast land colonization of the nineteenth century, throughout Western Civilization.

The United States had its share of these men: Henry Thoreau, John Burroughs, George Perkins Marsh, Major Powell, Frederick Law Olmsted, John Muir, Charles Eliot, Jr., Nathaniel Southgate Shaler. The leaders of this movement here, the poet Thoreau and the scientific observer Marsh, by birth belonged to the Golden Day; but their influence did not begin to be effective until after the Civil War. The concern for the soil of America, as distinct from its republican institutions, was one of the genuine marks of the period. In the compendious survey of the country which closed the period, the book Shaler edited on the United States, the land was for the first time given its due place.

As the foundation of this whole movement, one cannot overestimate the part played by Thoreau: for unlike the artificers and decorators, he liked nature plain, and he showed the rewards that awaited a fresh attentive study of our local qualities and capacities. As a national influence, he belongs more properly to the period after the Civil War than to the days in which he lived: up to the time he died, only two of his books, *Walden*, and *A Week on the Concord and Merrimack Rivers,* had been published. Thoreau was not a naturalist like Audubon nor a scientist like Agassiz and Gray: his mission was not to find out the habits of wild creatures but to acclimate the mind of highly sensitive and civilized men to the natural possibilities of the environment: to make them see, smell, breathe, feel, touch the objects around them, and to find out how much nature could give that culture and civilization had left out of account.

This was different from the practical exploration of the wilderness that the pioneer was making: in fact, it was the diametric opposite. Any one who has looked for mushrooms knows how the pleasure and excitement of the hunt leads to a complete exclusion of every other trait of the landscape except the property of bearing mushrooms: the eye never raises from the ground, and it sees nothing except white umbrellas. The settlement of America was a large-scale mushroom hunt: in the pursuit of a single object, urban sites, coal mines, gold, or oil, every other attribute of the landscape was neglected. Thoreau concentrated on the totality of the natural environment—which, one may say almost without paradox, was the part that his contemporaries had forgotten. He observed the fields around Concord and knew when the wild flowers would bloom in them; he dallied with the fish in the river and boated slowly up the quiet waters; he took trips through the Maine woods; he explored the seashore and waded through the sands of Cape Cod; in short, he *tasted* the land.

This exploration did not lead to anything; it was not a preliminary step but an enjoyment in itself. Thoreau was not of course alone in testing these pleasures: but he was perhaps the first person in the country to devote himself to it systematically, and to touch every part of the natural environment with equal fervour and gusto. He not merely knew the land: he had also a political sense as to what should be done about it, and pointed out the necessity of following the noble example of the kings of England, in publicly preserving the wild places of the continent for our own enjoyment, lest, in the ruthless quest of possessions, men should lose a greater part of what was worth possessing. In Thoreau, the landscape was at last entering into the American's consciousness, no longer as "territory" dedicated to a republican form of government, nor yet as potential quarter sections, but as an inner treasure—one thing for the mountain man and another for the river man and a third for the beach man. The Currier and Ives prints of the forties and fifties show, in their naïve way, a similar interest: a definite school of landscape painters, the Catskill School, had at least a sense of locality, if only a feeble power of personal absorption and transmutation; and in the paintings of George Innes this feeling was more deeply expressed. Thoreau's influence was felt by the country boys around him. One of them, Myron Benton, in Dutchess County, New York, took a trip down the Webutuck in imitation of Thoreau and wrote rural verses: another, John Burroughs, devoted a good part of his life to writing upon nature and country life—proving himself Thoreau's disciple (despite the superior personal magnetism of Whitman), even when he criticized his master for inaccuracies of observation.

Thoreau died during the Civil War; but the ripples of influence spreading from his positive and selfcontained personality are still expanding. In our own day one of the most able advocates of regional planning is Mr. Benton MacKaye, an avowed disciple of Thoreau. In *The New Exploration*, Mr. MacKaye attempts to show the implication in terms of modern techniques and objectives of the sort of life and polity for which Thoreau had built the ideal framework. In his essay on Civil Disobedience, Thoreau outlined the policy of non-coöperation, that powerful weapon which Mahatma Gandhi has used to effect the paralysis of mere physical force. Thoreau's moral force, his political acumen, cannot be separated from his studies of nature: the man was a whole, and his thought cannot without undue violence be dismembered. To fancy that Thoreau has been made irrelevant by the Machine Age is to lose sight not merely of the point of his criticism, but of his actual historical position.

The naturalistic and biological influences which Thoreau expressed were, one must remember, later in getting started than the world of mechanism in which we now move: Descartes antedated Goethe, the first modern philosopher with a well-grounded intuition of the web of life, by almost two hundred years. Instead of looking upon Goethe and Thoreau as survivors from the past, to be finally obliterated by the relentless spread of a venal and mechanical civilization, it is perhaps more accurate to think of them as the forerunners of a fresh line of effort and action. It was, in fact, the reckless waste of life, the unbalancing of natural conditions, and the destruction of natural resources which followed the introduction of the machine and the migration of peoples that made imperative a new philosophy of nature: so long as nature was unspoiled we needed no philosophy.

Thoreau, more than any one else in America, acknowledged this need and gave expression to a positive philosophy. His *Walden*, his *Life on the Concord*, his *Cape Cod*, to say nothing of his journals, were both directly and indirectly the starting point of a whole movement. At a time when the cockney and the pioneer were dominant, both with a strong impulse against any fine use of the natural environment, Thoreau helped to set the tide moving in a contrary direction. He did not work alone; but his words must be put alongside the practical works and the concrete political programmes which followed during the Brown Decades: it is doubtful if these latter would have found themselves so quickly but for the help and popular understanding which his writings gave.

"Who would not rise to meet the expectation of the land?" That was a new challenge in the United States, where, at the opening of the Civil War, the expectations of political democracy, the expectations of bourgeois freedom, the expectation of equal opportunity and success under a system of private monopoly, had already grown sour and hopeless.

If the countryside ran down, as the result of the misappropriation and misuses of the land, the city was no less debauched. This was not for lack of good precedent. The original New England village had been planned as a definite communal unit: the pattern of common, school, church, town hall, inn, and houses had been worked out in relation to the need to exercise the direct political and economic functions of the community, and the result was as fine, on its limited scale, as anything the Old World could show. But the precedent was ignored. The greed to own land and profit by its increased increment outweighed the desire to build permanent and useful habitations.

While every city from the beginning of the nineteenth century looked forward to continued growth at an accelerating pace, the place of the city in the social economy was neglected, and its aesthetic aspect was forgotten. The American method of building cities during the nineteenth century was well pictured by Horace Cleveland, who, with Olmsted, was a pioneer landscape architect. His criticism could not be improved upon today.

"Before the introduction of the railroads," Cleveland pointed out, "the settlement of the West was by a process of accretion, a vanguard of hardy pioneers keeping ever in advance, enduring hardships and privations which could only be borne by men unaccustomed to the ordinary comforts of civilization. The better classes who followed were necessarily governed to a greater or less extent on whatever further improvements they attempted by the works of their predecessors, and nothing approaching to scientific or artistic designs or arrangements of extended areas, based upon wise forethought of future necessities, was attempted. The government survey of public lands formed the only basis of division, the only guide in laying out country roads or the streets of proposed towns; and if the towns grew into cities, it was simply by the indefinite extension of straight streets, running north, south, east or west, without regard to topographical features, or facilities of grading or drainage, and still less of any considerations of taste or convenience, which would have suggested a different environment. Every western traveller is familiar with the monotonous character of the towns resulting from the endless repetition of the dreary uniformity of rectangles which they present; yet the custom is so universal and offers such advantages in simplifying and facilitating descriptions and transfers of real estate that any attempt at the introduction of a different system encounters at once a strong feeling of popular prejudice."

The man who challenged this prejudice most successfully, and who almost single-handed laid the foundations for a better order in city building, was Frederick Law Olmsted. When Charles Eliot Norton said of him, towards the close of his career, that of all American artists he stood "first in the production of great works which answer the needs and give expression to the life of our immense and miscellaneous democracy" he did not exaggerate Olmsted's influence. From Central Park in New York to the Golden Gate Park in San Francisco, Olmsted dotted the country with parks: in the last twenty years of his career four town sites and twelve suburban districts were laid out by him. If, as Olmsted pointed out, the movement towards urban parks was almost an instinctive one throughout Western Civilization, after the middle of the nineteenth century, in reaction against the depression and misery of the industrial city, Olmsted gave it a rationale.

This remarkable man was the son of a Hartford merchant; and he was born in that city in 1822. In his youth, he boarded around with various ministers, to obtain his formal education: but a weakness in the eyes kept him from books, and he formed the habit of rambling about the countryside by himself. In 1842 he attended lectures at Yale; but the most important part of his early education was the three pilgrimages each a thousand miles or more that he made with his father, by horse, stage-coach, and canal-boat. The landscape itself was the first great influence on his mind: then came the popular writers of his day, Emerson, Lowell, Ruskin—that Ruskin whose paeans to Nature, the voluptuous worship of a starved young man, made the better part of *Modern Painters* more useful as a guide to scenery than to painting. As a boy he picked up in the public library two eighteenth century books that influenced him profoundly: Sir Uvedale Price on *The Picturesque* and Gilpin on *Forest Scenery*. He always treasured them.

Before settling down, he sailed in the forecastle to Canton (1843): the physical misery and brutality sated only temporarily his lust for travel, but he spent the ten years from 1847–1857 as an experimental farmer—not before he had served an apprenticeship with one of the best scientific farmers in New York State. In 1850 Olmsted made a tour of Europe, part of which he described in a book published in 1852, *The Walks and Talks of an American Farmer in England*. After this he made three journeys in the South: two through the slave States and one in Mexico and California. Olmsted had none of the prepossessions of the Abolitionist, and his report on the state of the South before the war is one of the most valuable first-hand Northern documents we possess: his very temperate picture of the beating of a young negress, calmly, coolly, by a matter-of-fact overseer was far more damning than the violent melodramatics of Mrs. Harriet Beecher Stowe. Olmsted's account of the ante-bellum South has well been compared with Young's picture of France before the Revolution.

This combination of wide travelling, shrewd observation, intelligent reading, and practical farming formed Olmsted's eduation: it was plainly a far more substantial discipline than the courses he had taken intermittently at Yale, never long enough to receive a degree. This was the American education at its best—when dispersed and fitful, lacking an inner core, it created the shiftless and all too adaptable pioneer: but, when integrated, as it was in literature by Whitman and Melville, in economics by Henry George, and in landscape design by Olmsted, it must be compared to the very best culture of the Renaissance for an equivalent. The proof of its efficacy lies in both the men and their works.

Meanwhile, Olmsted had gone into the publishing business with G. W. Curtis, and in 1855 and 1856 had edited the ill-fated Putnam's Magazine. What would he do next? Within two years he had found his centre. In 1857 he accepted the position of superintendent of Central Park; and the following year, having obtained the permission of his superior, the author of the first plan of Central Park, he joined with Calvert Vaux in submitting anonymously a new design for the Park—a design which won the prize. From that time on his work, as the saying is, was cut out for him.

The development of the farmer into the landscape architect took place in the healthiest manner possible. On his farm in South Side, Staten Island, Olmsted had entered fully into the rural life, serving on school committees, helping improve the highways, raising prize crops of wheat, turnips, fruit, importing an English machine, and establishing the first cylindrical drainage tile works in the country. He had found in travelling through the remoter parts of the country that carelessness or ingenuity in placing barns, stables, outbuildings, laundry yards, or in providing for conveniences to bring in supplies and carry out wastes, could help or hinder a farmer's life: even matters like the placing of a kitchen garden, or the determination of outlook or inlook, had a direct effect. Olmsted acquired a reputation among his neighbours for good judgment in these matters. He would be called in to give advice. Gradually his fame spread. Downing's partner at Newburgh, the young Englishman Calvert Vaux, had the intelligence to see Olmsted's possibilities. To say that Olmsted was not unprepared to plan and build Central Park hardly does justice to his qualifications: perhaps no one could have been better prepared.

The planning and planting of Central Park was the beginning of a stormy but fruitful public life. Born of the cosmopolitan knowledge and rural tastes of William Cullen Bryant, who viewed with alarm the encroachment of buildings on his country walks, Central Park was in 1851, when it was conceived, a monstrosity, a challenge, an affront.

Up to this time, with the exception of the New England commons, and a few parades like the Battery in New York and the Battery in Charleston, S. C., there was nothing that could be called a park in America. The park was an aristocratic symbol of the Old World: it cost money and it withdrew building lots from speculation: some opponents even believed that the pleasure ground would be used only by ruffians and gangsters, who would rob decent citizens or drive them out by their bawdy antics: others thought that the park would never be reached or visited by the common people. Even those who favoured the reservation of the land distrusted any efforts to improve it. Landscape architecture was an effeminancy: what was the country coming to?

One by one these objections were silenced, these anxieties allayed, these prejudices removed: but the process was a tedious one, and it was aggravated by the fact that the park was a convenient ball to kick around in party politics. The great part of the construction and planting was done in the four years between 1857 and 1861: eight hundred acres, chiefly rocks, swamps, barren pasture, were eventually transformed into lakes and meadows, wooded heights and grottoes, a fine mall and promenade, and a highroad and pedestrian walk system which, until the metropolis reached its present pitch of congestion, was ample to all the requirements of its use. But Olmsted had done something more than design a park, battle with politicians—he resigned at least five times—struggle with insolent and rascally city appointees, and protect his plantations against vandals: he had introduced an idea—the idea of using the landscape creatively. By making nature urbane he naturalized the city.

The American, a romantic by inheritance, had been stunned by large and awful phenomena of Nature: the Mammoth Caves of Kentucky, the sinuous length of the Mississippi, the high peaks of the Rockies. Olmsted taught him he could be pleased with a meadow and a few sheep—or a bare outcrop of schist with a summer house facing a small grove of pines. The landscape park had a right to exist by itself without museums, rinks, theatres, sideshows, or any of the other paraphernalia of "civilized life": its whole justification lay in the fact that it promoted the simple elementary pleasures of breathing deeply, stretching one's legs, basking in the sun. Such a notion was as deep an affront to the prevailing ideology of business as Herbert Spencer's defence of billiards: it seemed as crazy as the new landscapes of Monet, which spring out of the same natural and healthy impulses. Olmsted fought for this idea: he gave it a setting: he provided it with a rational justification. The landscape could be enjoyed, and the enjoyment could sometimes be heightened by the deliberate efforts of the designer. This notion seems ridiculously self-evident today; at the time Olmsted began his career neither the art nor its object were acknowledged. But the idea took on. Forest Park, St. Louis, Fairmount Park, Philadelphia, Prospect Park, Brooklyn, and Franklin Park, Boston, soon followed.

But Olmsted did something more than introduce the cultivated landscape as a means of urban recreation: those who have sought to protect this aspect of his work, particularly in Central Park, have too often forgotten that in 1870 he laid down the lines of a complete park programme on excellent social and hygienic grounds. By means of shade trees to line the street, wider malls and promenades and open squares, and a system of small recreation parks meant chiefly for the active forms of sport, he sought to make particular functions, not available in the landscape park because of either its character or its remoteness, play a part in the everyday life of the city. Moreover, he saw that the park could not be treated as an afterthought or a mere embellishment of a utilitarian plan otherwise complete.

"A park fairly well managed near a large town," he pointed out, "will surely become a new centre of that town. With the determination of location, size, and boundaries should therefore be associated the duty of arranging new trunk routes of communication between it and the distant parts of the town existing and forecasted. These may be either narrow informal elongations of the park, varying from two to five hundred feet in width and radiating irregularly from it, or, if, unfortunately, the town is already laid out in the unhappy way that New York and Brooklyn, San Francisco and Chicago, are . . . then we must probably adopt formal parkways. They should be so planned and constructed as never to be noisy and seldom crowded, and so also that the straightforward movement of pleasure-carriages need never to be obstructed, unless at absolutely necessary crossings, by slow-going vehicles used for commercial purposes. If possible, also, they should be branched or reticulated with other ways of a similar class. . . . It is a common error to regard a park as something to be produced complete in itself, as a picture to be painted on a canvas. It should rather be planned as one to be done in fresco, with constant consideration of exterior objects."

In short, by 1870, less than twenty years after the notion of a public landscape park had been introduced in this country, Olmsted had imaginatively grasped and defined all the related elements in a full park programme and a comprehensive city development. Between 1872 and 1895 he had a man-sized share in making this programme effective; but, despite the great improvements that have gone on in Washington, Chicago, Kansas City, Boston, there is not a large city in the country that has caught up with him.

Two final features in Olmsted's actual planning remain to be commented on. One was his respect for the natural topography. This was unusual enough in current American thought to make it the chief base of a suit for payment brought by his erstwhile superior, General Egbert Viele, who was also a Central Park competitor. Olmsted carried this respect from the park proper into the design of country estates and suburbs: he implanted it in pupils and collaborators like Horace Cleveland and Charles Eliot, Jr., to say nothing of those who succeeded to his practice. This utilization of the natural features of the landscape accounts, along with generous tree planting, for the surviving charm of the old-fashioned suburban development: such charm as was achieved, notably, in Roland Park, Baltimore, in the nineties.

A second characteristic of Central Park's design is perhaps even more important: the separation of the footways from the roadways and bridlepaths. It is only at inescapable intervals that these two different kinds of traffic artery even parallel each other: wherever there is the slightest possibility, Olmsted separates them by means of the overpass and underpass. Three considerations must have been in his mind: the safety of the pedestrian, the convenience of the driver, and the desirability of avoiding bustle and noise in parts of the city designed for relaxation and repose. In our own day, this essential principle has been carried a step further: into the residential neighbourhood. The best European and American town planners make the same differentiation between wheel and foot traffic as Olmsted did: indeed, in Radburn, N. J., Mr. Henry Wright has laid out a town in this fashion, with an internal park system completely out of the range of traffic. This modern design only adds to one's appreciation of Olmsted's power as an inventor. He had, without doubt, one of the best minds that the Brown Decades produced.*

To what good purpose that mind worked, at its best, one sees in the report that Olmsted made in 1886 to Leland Stanford on the plans and layout of his proposed University; and in the further execution of that design, as it later left his hands. No one has better analyzed the relation between soil, climate, landscape, and function than Olmsted did in this brief report.

"As I have been reflecting on what passed in our conferences at Palo Alto, I have been led more and more to feel that a permanently suitable plan for a great University in California must be studied with constant watchfulness against certain mental tendencies from which neither you, nor General Walker, nor I, nor anyone likely to have influence in the matter, can reasonably be supposed to be free. The subtle persistency of the class of tendencies to which I allude is shown in the fact that the English in India, after an experience there

* The following section has been added (1952).

of nearly two centuries, still order their lives in various particulars with absurd disregard of requirements of comfort and health, imposed by the climate, because they cannot dismiss from their minds standards of style, propriety, and taste, which are the result of their fathers' training under different climatic conditions.

"Because of less marked but not less positive differences of climate, with buildings and grounds arranged on the principles that have had control at Oxford and Cambridge, Harvard and Yale, Amherst and Williams, nothing like that which impresses a visitor as appropriate and pleasant in the general arrangement and environment of these colleges can be had in California. The same may be said with regard to other collections of buildings with semi-rural surroundings to which throngs of people are likely to resort. It would be impossible, for instance, in California to maintain simply such degree of neatness as is seen in the Eastern or in English institutions of that description, at ten times their outlay for the purpose. Yet if to secure some tolerable degree of neatness all who have to do with them should be required to pass from one building to another only upon certain prepared passages, as we pass on ordered lines between the beds of the old-fashioned flower garden, the result in neatness would not pay for the trouble it would cost.

"Neither turf nor any known substitute for covering unpaved surfaces between the buildings of a college can be used in California as turf is used in the East. Trees rooted in ground that is trampled as the ground is trampled about the college buildings of the East would be sickly, deformed, and short-lived. Arrangements upon which, in the climate of the Atlantic States, the beauty and comfort, not only of broad areas but even of streets and roads and yards depends, when reproduced as nearly as possible under the climate of California, will soon become unsuitable, dreary, and forlorn. An example of what is to be apprehended in this respect already appears at Berkeley.

"It has often been observed that the character of the buildings and grounds, the scenery and atmosphere, of Oxford has greatly aided English veneration for learning and is to all Oxford students a highly important element of a liberal education. It is surely a sad misfortune that a young man seeking a liberal education should be led, at the most impressible period of his life, to pass four years or more in an establishment the outward aspect of which is expressive of an illiterate and undisciplined mind, contemptuous of authority and that is essentially uncouth, ill-dressed, and ill-mannered.

"One of the largest of the college buildings at Amherst of masonry construction, not old nor in bad repair, but graceless and gracelessly placed, has been lately taken down because, as an offense to good taste, it had come through the advancing refinement of the times, to be no longer endurable. The same experience will, probably, by and by occur at Berkeley on a larger scale. I may predict this with more propriety because before the Amherst Trustees had thought of getting rid of the building to which I refer and fifteen years before they screwed their courage up to doing so, I had advised them that it would be only a question of time when that conclusion would be reached. What I have in mind at Berkeley is not alone that the buildings are in a "cheap and nasty" style, but that the disposition of them and of all the grounds and offices about them betrays heedlessness of the requirements of convenience and comfort under the conditions of the situation and climate.

"What I say, then, is that in the plan for a great University in California ideals must be given up that have been planted by all that we have found agreeable and have been led to regard as appropriate in the outward aspect of Eastern and English colleges. If we are to look for types of buildings and arrangements suitable to the climate of California it will rather be in those founded by the wiser men of Syria, Greece, Italy, and Spain. You will remember in what a different way from the English methods, the spirit of which we have inherited, the open spaces about nearly all buildings that you have seen in the south of Europe to which throngs of people resort, have been treated. In the great "front yard" of St. Peter's, for example, not a tree, nor a bush, nor a particle of turf has been made use of. This is not because Michael Angelo and his successors have been blind to the beauty of foliage and verdure in suitable places.

"For reasons that I have thus, I fear not successfully, tried to indicate, as well as because opportunity must be left open for enlarging particular buildings in the manner advised by General Walker and for continuously extending special departments of buildings as suggested in the beginning of this letter, it appears to me that all spaces not thus specifically reserved for well-defined purposes of usefulness, should, as much as possible, be avoided and a degree of compactness of arrangement anticipated in public ways and places, especially near the center of operations, that, having regard to Eastern and English standards should be regarded as illiberal and tasteless."

Olmsted's understanding of the problem of regional adaptation did not extend merely to the general layout and landscaping of the site: it likewise included an analysis of the type of structure that was suitable in this new setting. "Of several reasons for limiting these structures to one story," he pointed out, "the principal is that in a building of two or more stories the necessity for providing on the lower for any cross partitions or for the support of any considerable weight in the superstructures, has everywhere in older institutions been found to stand in the way of desirable revision of interior plans. It is considered that in anything thus likely to hinder the ready adoption in the future of new methods and conveniences for liberal education should be avoided." This admirable advice was only partly followed in the original architectural development of Stanford University; and it was flagrantly violated for the next half century in the character and layout and siting of most of the new buildings. For these mistakes the university paid grievously, not only in the earthquake of 1906, but in daily routine.

A generation passed before the one story school building, with completely flexible inner space, was first carried through, with adroitness, in the California schools designed by Neutra and by Kump; and this should now be recognized as an ideal type of universal application, not merely to elementary schools but to all educational buildings. And just as in Central Park Olmsted anticipated by almost a century the new order of town planning, so in the design of Stanford, he incorporated a permanent green belt a mile wide to separate the campus from Palo Alto. Thanks to Olmsted's grasp of the whole situation (aided by the unified ownership of the land) his plans for the campus and residential area of Stanford worked out into a miniature garden city that itself anticipated Howard's theoretical outline of this new type of community. But it is Olmsted's understanding of the regional basis of design that made his work preëminent in his own generation, and makes it significant to ours, which still has not fully caught up with him.

From: *The Brown Decades* by Lewis Mumford. New York: 1931, Dover reprint, 1955, pages 59-72, 80-93; Dover reprint, 1971, pages 26-32, 36-42.

The Regionalism of Richardson

by

Lewis Mumford

Henry Hobson Richardson was born on the Priestley plantation, in the Parish of St. James, Louisiana, in 1838; and his mother was Catherine Caroline Priestley, a granddaughter of the famous Dr. Priestley, the experimental philosopher who discovered oxygen, the radical whose views about the French Revolution provoked the ignorant to riot and drove him from his home in England to America. Before Richardson left Louisiana, his bent of mind was already established: he showed an interest in drawing, which was fostered by the best teachers available in New Orleans, and he had already evidenced a love for mathematics—always a useful trait in a young architect.

Like so many of the promising youth of the South, at this period, Richardson was destined for the army, and through Mr. Judah P. Benjamin, who was a friend of his father's, he got the chance of a cadetship at West Point. But Richardson had an impediment of speech, from which he suffered throughout his life; and this made him unfit for military service: hence he matriculated at Harvard; and in 1859, having been graduated, he went abroad to France, to become the second American student to study at the Ecole des Beaux-arts in Paris. He took up his work there in 1860.

With his French background in New Orleans, it is not surprising that Richardson should have sought to pursue his architectural studies in Paris, which was then pre-eminent in both the teaching and the practice of architecture: but this is perhaps the only point where his kinship with Jefferson becomes a positive one. Paris was Jefferson's finishing school as an architect; and it was in the South of France that his imagination was kindled. But the difference in their temperaments was so profound that each looked at a different aspect of France, each cherished a different fragment of its ancient civilization, each carried away a different image of the order to come. Richardson was too poor to go to the South of France while he was a student; for his family fortune, which had kept him going, vanished in the catastrophic conditions of wartime New Orleans. But if he had gone South, he would have been conscious, not of the Greek temples, but of the Romanesque churches. Richardson's Paris was the Paris of Victor Hugo and Viollet-le-Duc, the great medievalists; and though Richardson took part in a riot of protest over the appointment of Viollet-le-Duc to the head of the Beaux-arts, he did so as a loyal student, upholding the autonomy of his school against bureaucratic dictation, not as one who was insensible to the lessons that Viollet-le-Duc was then preaching, with such zeal and such scholarship. Only primitive sources, Viollet-le-Duc said, supply the basis for a long career; and once Richardson got past the finger lessons in planning, construction, and design, it was to the primitive sources of medieval architecture, in Syria and in Southern France, that he naturally turned for a starting point.

Before going into Richardson's achievements, it will be profitable, perhaps, to describe his character and background in a little more detail, in contrast to Jefferson's; for the two men were in every way the exact opposites; and each sums up not merely a different period but a different type of personality: indeed it is partly the preponderance of one or another of the types of personality represented by Richardson and Jefferson that gives to a cultural epoch its distinctive cast and flavor. Jefferson was the incarnation of the Age of Reason. He had the rationalist's love of clarity and measure; his mind was at home in law, politics, invention, in matters where it was thought well to keep the emotions out of the picture, as far as possible, lest they distort practical judgment. Order and measure had for him a definite esthetic appeal: these qualities, which seem so distasteful to the romantic mind, because they are based on abstract rules and formal relationships, undoubtedly made him feel a warm appreciative glow. The spare upright figure of Jefferson, with his unobtrusive urbanity and courtesy, his inner reserve, is a close match for his buildings. Colorful freehand sketches for his buildings are not what one would look for from Jefferson; and the fact is there are no such surviving memoranda; but on the contrary, there are pages of neat plans, ruled drawings, many of them done on squared paper covered, in a careful hand, with calculations of materials needed and costs.

Richardson's temperament was of an entirely different cast—just as his rapid freehand sketches, in which the building is felt as a whole before it is reorganized and re-modeled by more exact analysis, are profoundly different from Jefferson's neat drawings. If Jefferson was the man of reason, Richardson was the man of feeling and emotion: a man whose eyes reveled in color, whose fingertips delighted in textures, whose architectural forms were in a way the extension of his own bodily structure. Richardson was a man of Gargantuan frame, with great physical capacities and great appetites, built like a bison: a man of generous vitality who ate much and drank much, in an age that had ceased to regard gluttony as one of the deadly sins. When he passed through the streets of a foreign city, with two equally huge companions, the little street urchins thought that a circus parade had started and wanted to know when the dwarfs were coming. If William Blake was right in saying that Energy is eternal delight, Richardson was, through the sheer exuberance and overflow of his energies, a veritable mountain of delight; and as with maturity his energies waxed, in both the physical and the spiritual spheres, his architectural forms expanded accordingly. Apart from works of contemporary engineering, like the Eads Bridge and the Brooklyn Bridge, it is in Richardson's architecture that one first receives a dramatic expression of the fact that man, thanks to his mastery of coal and steam and iron and electricity, was now for the first time in control of colossal energies—far greater than those the builders of the Egyptian pyramids had wielded by marshaling together vast armies of slaves. His smaller buildings give one this sense no less than his great swaggering structures, like the Pittsburgh jail, where the stones that compose the arches are eight feet long, and all the other elements are in proportion.

No human being is ever free from emotion: so that what is important in the arts is the degree to which human emotion is exhibited, modulated, or repressed. Jefferson's reserves were deep. It was second nature for him to conceal his emotions. One day, when he returned from visiting a greater disaster that had happened to his estate—the bursting of a costly and irreplaceable dam—Jefferson treated the event in such a casual way that his house-guest did not have the faintest sense of the extent of the calamity until the left Monticello and heard the event discussed gravely by the people in Charlottesville. That was characteristic of the man. When Richardson, on the other hand, was chosen by the committee of the Springfield Church to execute his first important commission, he burst into tears on being informed of his success: unashamedly full of emotion because he at last had a chance to demonstrate his powers. By innate temperament Richardson was a full-blown example of the Romantic; and he was at home, therefore, in those periods of culture where vitality had counted for more than formal order or restrained ceremonial in daily life.

Fortunately for his success as an architect, fortunately, too, for his relations with his own industrial age, Richardson finished off his architectural training as a draughtsman in the office of Henri Labrouste, perhaps the foremost exponent of French rationalism in the middle of the nineteenth century. Labrouste's Bibliothéque Nationale, in Paris, built between 1858 and 1868, had used iron and glass far more extensively than they had ever been used on a comparable building; and thanks, perhaps, to Labrouste's influence, Richardson never shared the fashionable romantic contempt for contemporary problems and contemporary materials. Nevertheless, if he was called upon to make a choice between beauty and convenience, where not enough resources were available to make due provision for both, he resolutely held out for the fullest measure of beauty, because the feelings and emotions attached to the contemplation of beauty were in some sense sacred for him. Yet for the better part of ten years, Richardson's temperament was restrained by the current conventions in architecture. It took him all that time to formulate a more personal idiom.

In my last lecture I tried to indicate the underlying unity between classic architecture and the new type forms and mechanical methods that were transforming industrial production in the Western World. The romantic movement, which furnished the background for Richardson's early work was in essence a cry of protest against both the classic and the mechanical impulses: it recognized an enemy to life and feeling in both these philosophies. In reacting against rational, ordered forms, the romantics sometimes almost discarded form completely: in landscape gardening, for example, not merely did the leading theorists attempt to simulate wild nature, but they preferred irregular shapes to regular ones, even when they appeared in trees: dead branches, twisted stems, tangled foliage, were emblems of protest, not only against artificiality, but against art itself. This protest came chiefly from the middle classes: it was associated with a feeling that the old sanctities and pieties of religion were being threatened alike by the pagan culture of the Renaissance and by the mechanical inhumanity of the machine.

But there was something paradoxical about the protest. By serving as a counterweight to a brutal industrialism, it helped that industrialism to prosper: when life got too hot in the factory or the counting house, romanticism offered an exotic retreat for the private soul in artful Gothic cottages with nooks and towers, and in neo-Gothic churches. By making out of the architecture of the Middle Ages a fixed ideal, a standard for all later works of piety, as Pugin did in England and Upjohn in America, the romantics repeated the great mistake that the lovers of the classic had made during the Renaissance. Recognizing that the forms they loved were produced by a certain type of life, they mistakenly hoped that the reverse process was also possible, so that by recovering these forms they could make real once more the life that had first created them.

Unfortunately, dead forms do not produce living organisms. People who attempt to restore the outward form of tradition really deny both the validity of tradition and the integrity of the society in which they live. Worse than this: when the romanticists did this, they were in fact using the past as a master-mold from which to obtain mechanical reproductions for the present; so that in the very act of trying to escape the machine, when they were protesting most strenuously against it, they were nevertheless succumbing to its influences. If the freedom and vitality and rich emotions of romanticism were to count for anything, that freedom must mean emancipation from the Middle Ages, no less than from the classic or the Renaissance world: in other words, to be real, it must mean freedom to continue to experiment, to explore, to live the life demanded by their own times; since there is no logical reason why old castles and grist mills should be romantic objects, and suburban houses and factories should be altogether lacking in spirit, in taste, in imagination. So, too, the romantic must enjoy vitality wherever he finds it—not just in traditional forms and in earlier ages.

Most romantic architects never came to grips with this situation. They arrived at a compromise worthy of Dickens's famous architect, Mr. Pecksniff; whereby they applied their medieval formulas only to institutions that had some traditional connections with the past, like churches and colleges and upper class homes; and they held aloof from buildings that were crying aloud for more imaginative treatment—the steel bridges and the office buildings and the railroads and the factories that characterized the new age. There were exceptions to this rule; but they only established, more clearly than ever, that Gothic forms could not be conceived in cast-iron nor adapted to the culture of the iron age without both defacing the past and laming the future. The romantic theorists, for the greater part, were convicted in practice by their own doctrines; for they were right in holding that there is an organic connection between the forms of an age and the rest of its culture—its religion, its economic organization, its political institutions, its moral disciplines, its sense of the human personality; and therefore any formula that denies this contemporary connection is condemned to feebleness and sterility. Architectural forms, to be valid, must not merely be beautiful but timely. When the architect himself fails to understand and to command the forces with which he must work he only adds to the sum total of visible disorder.

By the time Richardson started work in America, in the late sixties, architectural anarchy had reached a point at which disorder had resulted almost in physical brutality, and ugliness conducted a constant assault and battery wherever one turned one's eye. When one beholds some of the famous buildings of the period, one must charitably assume that they were built by the blind for a generation that dwelt in darkness. Yet this period had established, by violent reaction against the past, a coarse vigor and a self-confidence in its own lights, which are necessary for any kind of architectural creativeness. By 1870, the words "novel" and "unique" were a recommendation in architecture; and so ignorant were people generally of the most elementary standards of esthetic cultivation, that they were open to originality, to a degree that better-educated people usually are not; and they were prepared, precisely because their taste was so lawless and undiscriminating, to welcome good architecture just as heartily as they appreciated the bad, simply because they did not know the difference.

Marshall Field and Company Wholesale House, Chicago, Illinois. Henry Hobson Richardson, architect. *Courtesy, Chicago Historical Society*.

Sever Hall, Harvard University; Cambridge, Massachusetts. Henry Hobson Richardson, architect.

Austin Hall, Harvard University; Cambridge, Massachusetts. Henry Hobson Richardson, architect. *Courtesy, The Museum of Modern Art, New York.*

Stoughton House, Cambridge, Massachusetts. Henry Hobson Richardson, architect.

For the first decade of his active life as an architect, Richardson's work was little above the level of contemporary taste: he, too, used the fashionable mansard roof; he, too, built churches with spires like a salamander's tail; his eye, too, still failed with elementary proportions, so that his narrow tower on the Worcester High School was almost painful, and even the main building of the Buffalo General Hospital, though it shows the beginnings of a new strength, was awkward in its proportions, and its high towers lack the base he finally achieved only in his famous Trinity Church in Boston. But this Richardson grew by leaps and bounds. One can scarcely believe that the Worcester High School and the Brattle Street Church in Boston were built by the same man, though only a few short years separate them. Yet it was not till the end of the seventies, with the building of Sever Hall in Harvard Yard in 1878 that Richardson, partly through experience, partly through intuitive understanding, began to understand that the old romantic formulae were fit only for the scrap heap and that a new task lay ahead of the architect. There was no use in the architect's wringing his hands over the imaginative beauties of the past: he must face the future and embody the life of his own people. His task, as Emerson said in one of his aphoristic verses, was to "give to pots and trays and pans grace and glimmer of romance." Warmth, color, imagination, in other words, do not depend upon the architect's working in a special style or with a special type of building: they are qualities that the good architect, who has command of both his materials and his human resources, can bring into every kind of work. Emotion cannot be imported into an architectural form by imitation of historic ornament or style: it must be felt and lived by the architect; it must govern his choice of materials, influence the rhythm of his composition, and be worked out in fresh terms, which belong to the age and place and pattern of culture in which the architect works. In other words, the emotional response and the rational response cannot be separated. "The beautiful rests on the foundation of the necessary." One must earn the right to have sensitive tastes and feelings by facing the practical tasks of one's own day.

Richardson's first biographer, Mrs. Schuyler Van Rensselaer, did well to remind her readers that Richardson "was born a creator, not a student, an innovator, not an antiquary. Feeling for the vital serviceableness of his art was very strong within him, and therefore he cared more to work on new than on traditional lines. What he loved best was the freshest problem. What he most rejoiced in was to give true yet beautiful expression to those needs which were wholly modern in their genesis, and had hitherto been overlooked by art. No architect so endowed as to be very strongly attracted by ecclesiastical work would have been likely to say what I once heard Richardson say: 'The things I want most to design are grain elevators and the interior of a great river steam boat.' " It was in the design, indeed, of new types of building that Richardson discovered his own sources of original design. It was in an entirely new kind of structure, the small town library and the suburban railroad station that his art first came to its perfection. Working through such forms, Richardson step by step threw off the old tags and the old ornaments, analyzed boldly the new functions to be performed by these buildings, and translated them into stone, brick and wooden forms that had both an inner logic and an outward shape of their own. In the five years between 1878 and 1883 Richardson emerged as one of the first architects of the modern age, one of the first who had found, in the commonplace occupations of the day, a source and an incentive for architectural creation. Richardson died in 1886—too early to have experimented with steel frame construction. But he did more than any other creative architect to prepare the imagination for that event.

Though Richardson's architecture was countrywide in its influence, though some of his best buildings are in Chicago and Pittsburgh—the Glessner House in Chicago and the Pittsburgh Court House and Jail—his work was deeply affected by the particular part of the country, New England, in which the first full opportunities for work were given to him. He interpreted that New England to itself and gave it a better sense of its own identity: he modified its Puritanic austerities: he gave to its buildings a color that they lacked: a color derived from its native granites and sandstones, from weathered shingles and from the autumnal tints of sumach and red oak that linger longer in the countryside of the North than any other colors. Richardson knew this part of the country too well, and loved it too heartily, to be deceived by the superficial whites and grays in which its older wooden houses. and even its brick buildings, like the State House in Boston, had been decked.

Richardson's somber autumnal colors went well with the period in which Richardson worked: they prevail so universally in the painting and the architecture of the period that I have called the period between 1865 and 1895, in imitation of the late Thomas Beer, the Brown Decades. One hears the sad notes of the aftermath of the War between the States in the novels of William Dean Howells as well as in the poetry of Lanier. It was a period of triumphant industrialism and rampant commercial enterprise, loud, spectacular, and vulgar: thousands of young men and women poured into the new industrial cities, to make their fortunes and to fritter away their lives. Whatever solidity and stability there had been in the country in the period before the war, now seemed to have vanished, or almost vanished, precisely in those sections of society that seemed most busy and successful. But the stern provincial culture of New England kept its grip for a generation: indeed the encouragement and opportunity given to Richardson was a proof of its integrity. And Richardson, in turn, gave back to his adopted region a reassuring sense of stability and strength in the series of buildings he designed.

Because Richardson delighted to use big stones with rough surfaces, or even, where glacial debris was at hand, to use enormous knobby boulders—as in the lodge on the Ames estate—one may misinterpret his love for these forms as a mere effort to re-instate a more primitive architectural past. The contrast between Richardson's big stone building and the light delicate constructions possible in modern architecture even serves to obscure, to some students, the essential continuity in spirit between Richardson's forms and those of later architects. Even a sympathetic and able critic, Montgomery Schuyler, once wittily said that Richardson's dwelling houses were not defensible except in a military sense. But the fact is, I believe, that Richardson was not merely purposefully dramatizing the energies of the new age: he was also trying to supply to the cultural life of his period some of the rugged masculine strength that he missed: he was as tired of an effeminate and puling architecture, as Walt Whitman was of effeminate and puling poets. And instead of succumbing to the patent instability of commercial enterprise during the Gilded Age, Richardson pitted his own solid powers against it: even his office buildings, like the great Marshall Field building in Chicago, look as if they were built for eternity. In these structures Richardson seems to say definitely to his contemporaries: Tear this building down ten years from now—if you can!

This dramatization of power and stability awakened an answering note in the breasts of his countrymen; for commissions poured into Richardson's office, from 1880 onward: his appeal, in his own generation, was a universal one. People of taste admired his work because he brought into the somewhat arid, conscientious rationalism of New

England a color and warmth that had hitherto been lacking. Here was an architect who called together the best contemporary sculptors and painters he could lay hands on, William Morris Hunt, who had studied with Millet, John La Farge, who had the Orient and the Occident at his fingertips; and Augustus Saint-Gaudens, the best of the younger sculptors; and under Richardson's tutelage a whole generation of craftsmen learned to build and carve in a fashion that had begun to die out, even in Europe, after the middle of the nineteenth century. At the same time, Richardson's work appealed, with no less trenchancy, to the lowbrows of his period: it met with equal success among the heavy-fisted gentlemen who were staking out the new American empire and binding it together in a web of steel rails and copper telegraph wires and white ticker-tape. There was a reason for this double success; for though the conscious aim of these Robber Barons, as Mr. Matthew Josephson has called them, was money, they were still close enough to the realities of the farm, the mill, and the factory to have a taste for buildings that talked to them in direct, simple terms they could understand. It was not the least of Richardson's architectural triumphs, that he made these creatures of carboniferous capitalism, these gigantic lizards and armored reptiles of the Industrial Age, feel at home in his buildings: they liked him and even fed out of his hands. They admired the indubitable masculinity of Richardson's architecture: it had a kinship with their own vitality, with their own kind of swagger. In the long role of Richardson's buildings there are little more than a handful of churches: homes, railroad stations, libraries, offices and public buildings, chiefly claimed his interest. This alone would be enough to separate Richardson from an earlier romantic architect, like Richard Upjohn.

Viewing Richardson's work as a whole, indeed, it is plain that his romanticism was a matter of ingrained temperament, based on a rich and copious emotional nature: his was not an architecture of escape. Quite the contrary: no one better confronted his age than Richardson did; no one exhibited more vigorously the strength to meet that age halfway and yet not be downed by its sordid vices, its contempt for beauty, its indifference to humanity. In Richardson's buildings the historic quarrel between the Utilitarian and the Romantic was for the first time resolved; for if Richardson was the first romantic architect to embrace, by creating fresh forms, the railroad station and the office building and all the other rising phenomena of the Industrial Age, he was also one of the first of those who served the machine to see that industrialism must be transformed by human purpose and by human feeling if it is adequately to serve modern man. Beauty, Richardson demonstrated, was not something that could be added to a purely practical structure, as a cook might use an icing to decorate a cake, or even to conceal the defects of a burnt cake: but it was rather something that must be worked into the whole architectural form from its very inception, and it must therefore rest on a warm, intimate knowledge of the function of the building. Handsome is as handsome does is the motto of this kind of design.

I have referred to Thomas Jefferson as an exponent of a universal order in architecture, as one of the chief exemplars of the international style of the eighteenth and early nineteenth centuries; and in contrast, I have characterized Richardson as a user of regional resources and as an interpreter of regional characteristics. And there is a patent sense in which this contrast is a true one. Both in his choice of materials and in his development of certain parts of the native New England tradition Richardson was our first true regional architect. It was Richardson who first made full use of the local quarries of New England—Milford granite, brown sandstone, Longmeadow stone, employing both the color and the texture of local stones in a way that gave them a new architectural value. It was Richardson, again, who took the traditional white cottage or farmhouse of New England, with its clapboard or shingled sides and its shingled roof, and who transformed this early type of house into the wide-windowed cottage, with its ample porch and open rambling rooms that embodied a new feeling for both the landscape in which it was placed and the requirements of domesticity. Richardson was not entirely alone in furthering this development; there were contemporaries like W. R. Emerson who were working along the same general lines; but under Richardson's hands the new type of shingled house reached a pitch of esthetic excellence which makes it one of the outstanding achievements in our whole architecture: even the colors he introduced, weathered browns, autumnal reds, and sage greens, brought it into harmony with the New England landscape. Here Richardson takes up the theme of the sumach and the red oak, the sweet fern and the lichened rock, the pine tree and the butternut; and by using their colors in subtle combinations he created country houses that belong as much to the autumnal or spring landscape, as the traditional white farmhouse does to the snowmantled winter one. One of the most successful of Richardson's cottages cost only $2500 to build. That is a test of the architect's imagination: his ability to accomplish much with modest means.

The thing to note about Richardson's cottages is that they were both a continuation of the established wood tradition, and a fresh creation within that form. But whereas our traditional farmhouses had their counterparts in England and Holland, Richardson's cottages belong wholly to their native soil. Now the land and the building were in complete harmony. One could never mistake these buildings for anything but what they are: New England homes. They belong to their setting in the same fashion that Robert Frost's poems belong to it. This indeed is the essence of a regional architecture; it is composed in such a fashion that it cannot be divorced from its landscape without losing something of its practical or its esthetic value—or both together. These cottages of Richardson's are, in addition, a proof of another important fact: that Richardson's success was not based upon ponderous forms of construction nor upon his mastery of a single material. Just as in Sever Hall in Harvard Richardson showed, more brilliantly than anyone had ever done in America, the inherent resources of brick, so in these vernacular cottages he showed the resources of a light framed construction with a shingle covering, entirely without ornament. More than any other architect he took advantage of the freedom of wooden construction, not alone in the planning of the rooms but in the wide range of sizes and shapes he used for his window openings.

In short, the handful of unpretentious country houses that Richardson designed not merely deserve to rank with the very best of his work: they were the best examples of an entirely native architecture that America could show before 1900. It is a vast pity that Richardson could not have made a similar essay to interpret the needs and possibilities of a regional architecture for the South; yet I hope I am not guilty of any base flattery if I say that, though this is regrettable, some measure of his success in New England surely derived from his original sense of family and place that came with his Southern heritage.

But in another sense, Richardson was much more than a regional architect. No less than Jefferson himself, Richardson was searching for a universal form; he was attempting to create a consistent and logical way of treating any architectural problem that came his way. One of his first visible efforts to align his more romantic inheritance with the needs of his own day came through his gradual discarding of ornament: particularly on the exteriors of his building. This was a departure of radical significance: the more radical in the eighteen-eighties when the word bare—as bare as a barn, as bare as a factory —was a synonym for ugliness. When Richardson built a railroad bridge, the masonry supports were as clean of ornament as the wholly utilitarian iron railings at the top; and when he built still another bridge in the Fenway in Boston, a superb example of his fresh feeling for masonry forms, that structure, though entirely of stone, depended only on his simple treatment of mass, contour, and texture for its esthetic success. The flaring curve of its piers is one of the high points of architectural form in bridge construction: it makes one regret that Richardson never had the opportunity to show his art in a great structure like the Brooklyn Bridge.

Instinctively, Richardson realized that his architecture must harmonize with the ever-spreading forms of the machine: therefore a certain economy, a certain spareness, a certain rigor were needed even in his most traditional structures. This new sense of modern form comes out fully in the Glessner House in Chicago. This is an E-shaped structure, formed about an inner courtyard. There is an almost complete lack of windows on the main street façade: only narrow openings to light the halls. And why? Because the street was noisy, dusty, and intrusive; and because, by turning his openings away from the street, Richardson threw all the rooms onto the quiet courtyard and garden, with a maximum of privacy, solitude, and beauty. He felt no need for any kind of decorative flourish to mark this building as a human dwelling: one had only to put one's feet inside to discover how thoroughly the plan and disposition of the rooms furthered the purposes for which they were intended. Today's descriptive word for this guiding principle is functionalism. It is one of the universal attributes of modern architecture.

As Richardson's architecture matured, he approached steadily to rational and universal forms: even in his most regional architecture, he established principles of design that were of far wider application. Much as he loved the simple solidity of a stone wall, he realized in his bones that the age of steel frame construction and continuous windows was approaching; and in one of the last of his buildings, the Pray building in Boston, he deliberately subordinated the solids, brought the windows out to the walls to form an almost continuous surface of glass between the narrow brick piers, up and down the façade. This design was already, in form if not in construction, an anticipation of the logical treatment of the skyscraper: in this building, Richardson was actually ahead of the architects in New York and

Chicago who were professedly building skyscrapers, without their having the faintest notion of how to express the structure. In fine, Richardson transcended by his actual development as an architect all the descriptive tags the architectural historian would apply to him. He began as a romantic architect, but he was far more than that; he became a regional architect; but he was more than that; and in the end, he was an able utilitarian and rational architect; but *precisely because he had never lost his romanticism and his regionalism,* he was also far more than *that.* It was indeed by his robust combination of all these elements that Richardson achieved a unity and completeness that few architects in the nineteenth century possessed. No other architect so well embodied his age; no other so well transcended it, as Richardson did in the best buildings of the last eight years of his life. Richardson's work was in a true sense an integration of all the dominant forces in his period; not merely the practical forces, but the spiritual and cultural forces.

So it was not the Romanesque style of architecture, but Richardson himself, who turned out to be the primitive source of modern architecture, at least in the United States. Was it any wonder that his architecture, demanding as it did a great personal capacity for embracing the most diverse and even contradictory forces of his age, was so often caricatured by his smaller contemporaries, who imitated the bare forms and had no insight into the mind that had created them? Richardson had not a few talented disciples in his office; some, like Stanford White, had left him even before he died: but none was strong enough to carry on his work, once the master himself could no longer give the lead and guide the outcome. But by the same token, it is not strange that Richardson's spirit, becoming manifest during the eighties in the few great buildings he built in Chicago, had a powerful influence upon the brilliant young architects of the Middle West; and in particular, that it should have affected the most original and able of them—Leroy Buffington, Louis Sullivan, and John Wellborn Root. Eventually, through the early work of Howard and Maybeck, it was to have a direct influence upon the present generation of San Francisco architects.

Richardson's work, with his bearings upon the architecture that followed, with his remoter meaning for us in the future, is hard to part with without recording a regret, as profound as it is vain, that he did not live for another decade, to carry his work to a final stage of fruition. He was forced to lay down his tools in mid-career; for he died at the age of forty-eight; and in the reaction toward the classic and the colonial that characterized American architecture during the nineties, it was Jefferson rather than Richardson that profited. It would have been a happier fate for American form if the emergence of one great Southern architecture from undeserved neglect had not been canceled out by the submergence of the other, into a neglect equally undeserved. For each of these men was great in his particular way, and each succeeded in embodying a particular moment of American life and culture—Jefferson, that of the humanistic and classical inheritance which came to life pre-eminently on the Southern plantation; Richardson, those newer romantic and utilitarian currents, now impersonal and mechanical, now sentimental and burgeoning with insuppressible vitality, which characterized the nineteenth century. There are important lessons to be learned directly from both careers: there were further lessons that could be discovered only through trial and experiment, in the work of later architects, and through reflection upon the changing social needs of a later generation.

From: *The South in Architecture,* by Lewis Mumford. New York: 1941, pages 81–110.

Nature as Architect

by

Frank Lloyd Wright

The Bad Lands

Speaking of our trip to the Big Bad Lands, Black Hills, and Spearfish Canyon: I've been about the world a lot and pretty much over our own country; but I was totally unprepared for that revolution called the Dakota Bad Lands. From Mitchell, Paul Bellamy was driving a fair seventy over the brown Dakota prairie to reach the Bad Lands before sunset. About four, afternoon, something came into view that made me sit up straight and look at Bellamy to see if he saw what I saw. "Oh," said he, "you've seen nothing yet." But I had. What I saw gave me an indescribable sense of mysterious otherwhere—a distant architecture, ethereal, touched, only touched with a sense of Egyptian, Mayan drift and silhouette. As we came closer a templed realm definitely stood ambient in air before my astonished "scene," loving but scene-jaded gaze. The streamline working on a vast plateau of solid cream white clay, something like "calichi," had sculptured this familiar world into one unfamiliar but entrancing.

Endless trabeations surmounted by or rising into pyramid (obelisk) and temple, ethereal in color and exquisitely chiseled in endless detail, they began to reach to infinity spreading into the sky on every side; an endless supernatural world more spiritual than earth but created out of it. As we rode, or seemed to be floating upon a splendid winding road that seemed to understand it all and just where to go, we rose and fell between its delicate parallels of rose and cream and sublime shapes, chalk white, fretted against a blue sky with high floating clouds; the sky itself seemed only there to cleanse and light the vast harmonious building scheme.

Of course I am an architect and that ride through the land of pure line and evanescent color affected me strangely. Here was the element, architecture, cut of the body of the ground itself, beggaring human imagination, prostrating the simplicities of man before the great cosmic simplicity. Reverence, yes, awe. Deep satisfaction, harmoniouslike great music drifted over the senses until a new sacred realm was born of light, delicate color and ever changing but immaculate form wherein not even the senses could touch bottom, top, nor sides of its vast respose.

Here, for once, came complete release from materiality. Communion with what man often calls "God" is inevitable in this place. It is everywhere around him and when the man emerges to the brown plateau and looks back, as I did, the sun now setting, a pale moon rising in darkening rose and blue sky as rays of last light drifted over, linking drifting water lines of dark rose in pallid creamy walls, gently playing with the sky line, with mingled obelisks, terraces, and temples more beautiful than thought, eternal, who knows, a strange sense of inner experience will come to him of a crisis in his perception of what he has termed beauty. He will leave that place a more humble, seeking soul than when he went in to this pure appeal to his spirit. He will know baptism in its higher than sectarian sense.

Let sculptors come to the Bad Lands. Let painters come. But first of all the true architect should come. He who could interpret this vast gift of nature in terms of human habitation so that Americans on their own continent might glimpse a new and higher civilization certainly, and touch it and feel it as they lived in it and deserved to call it their own. Yes, I say the aspects of the Dakota Bad Lands have more spiritual quality to impart to the mind of America than anything else in it made by man's God.

I turned to Bellamy and finally said, "But how is it that I've heard so little of this miracle and we, toward the Atlantic, have heard so much of the Grand Canyon when this is even more miraculous?"

"Oh," said he slyly, "we are not on the through line to the coast."

"Never mind," I said, "all the better eventually." And we drove on to the famous Black Hills which the fame of Borglum's work had already brought to my attention.

Next day, Bellamy again at the wheel, from fine little Rapid City, well set in low hills (what could not that town do for itself if it knew how to live accordingly), several of us drove up another finely laid-out road that seemed to know what the region was all about, through scenery I had often heard of as beautiful. But a more flesh and blood kind of beauty. The beauty that appeals surely to a human being because he is human and brother to the tree and respects individualistic rock formations. Here they are great but not too great. All has the charm of human scale which many great Western scenes lack, and invites the wanderer to enter into the spirit of it all and rest. No home for man the Rocky Mountains; no, nor perhaps the Bad Lands, yet; but an ideal home; these Black Hills. Do not think from this that the Hills are unexciting. They are exciting but they stir a different region of the soul; we call it the heart probably. There are stone needles, stone spires, stone piles and stone blades, artificial lakes, tall beautiful pines, wooded gorges, more free standing and sculptured rock masses in nature's own style than one has ever seen before grouped in one area. So it seems fitting that some hand of man should brush aside the realistic veil of a stained weathered rock and let the mind of man himself envision his own greatness and his fate alongside the titanic handiwork of nature. Human nature, let us hope eventually nature's higher nature, found its hand for this in Gutzon Borglum's masterhand and the face of the great leader of his country. The noble countenance emerges from Rushmore as though the spirit of the mountain had heard a human prayer and itself became a human countenance. The countenance haunts you as you ride rises; winds and falls with you as freight through depths of pine woods; huge rocks standing about you, themselves statues of a more elemental thought than Gutzon Borglum's: the cosmic urge.

We passed by a quiet land-locked lake (Stockade Lake) that seems to be there with a man-made white sand shore to invite you to get out and stay and rest and drink in the breath of the pines as the breezes print themselves on the surface of the placid water. This Black Hills country has charm, inviting you to get out and go about or stay about. It is a lingering kind of human satisfaction for the soul, hungry of a tired body, the recreation of any jaded mind compelled to live by the abacus, money.

You may think all this the feeling of the moment, a mood, and because I was in good company. But no! I am an old soldier of the spirit, a veteran in time, place, and man. I could not be mistaken. Go and see.

We wound on upward to Sylvan Lake, a gem spot in the Hills where South Dakota plans to entertain her guests. It may be that South Dakota sees a body of water so seldom that her citizens overvalue it for the lake is artificial and small, but what a setting! Here a sweeping mountain resort, with the lake as a vignette seen below, could be a masterful thing of the kind, woven in with the great rich rock and tree foreground, framing the vistas of this spot; another and a higher kind of nature understanding well and loving the earth from which it springs, loving it too much to imitate it.

Harney Peak loomed to one side. Turning from the little rock-defended, rock-bound lake your gaze travels away along blue ridges ornamented by great rock piles to distant blue mountain tops, as far away as the human eye can go beneath the clouds. Round about you, rugged strength, forest depths, primeval earth at best; well, an architect is speaking.

There was a hotel there once but nature disposed of it in her inscrutable way, for cause. It was ugly.

Notwithstanding the expenditure of riches, so far, there were wonders left for tomorrow. And "Spitz," as I felt like calling him by now, came with Ted Lusk's car to drive me to Spearfish Canyon. I felt a little dull toward Spearfish. I had seen two marvels unique in the scenery of the world. I felt headed in for an anticlimax and said so. The boys said, no. These South Dakota boys by now had me where I believed that they knew their stuff. They couldn't have built those superb roads in the Bad Lands and Black Hills if they didn't know. So I patiently waited and visited with "Spitz" as we rode away. We stopped at Homestake, of which everyone has heard, and saw how a primitive gold mining operation has been turned over to the power of the machine and remains primitive just the same. The resources of machinery couldn't change the original steps or even the original way of mining except to cut down the manpower involved. By afternoon we got in by Spearfish, a mountain torrent beginning a canyon 26 miles long. Not very interesting at first, I had seen so many; the Western States are full of them as everyone knows. The road here is haphazard as hazard was and is none too good. "Spitz" drove well, fortunately. And the stream itself was something but after a half-hour things began to happen. We would be headed straight for gigantic white walls trabeated in ledges from which pines sprouted and grew in precisely the manner of the pictorial dreams of the great Chinese painters, the greatest painters who ever lived. We were in the land of the Sung and Ming masters. Whoever knows their idealizations of nature in the Chinese landscape painting of those great periods, and they were mostly landscapes, can see the character of the Spearfish ensemble.

Great horizontal rock walls abruptly rising above torrential streams, their stratified surfaces decorated (it is the word) with red pine stems carving stratified branches in horizontal textures over the cream white walls, multiplied red pine trunks and the black green masses of the pine rhythmically repeating pattern, climbing, climbing until the sky disappeared or was a narrow rift of blue as the clear water poured over pebbles or pooled under the heavy masses of green at the foot of the grand rock walls. Well, here was something again different. As different as could be from Bad Lands or Black Hills or anything I had actually seen, a stately exposition of what decorated walls on enormous scale can do and be. The Chinese predicted and depicted it. This continued for miles and miles without palling or growing in the least stale. We drove out, finally, and turned away from Spearfish town to get back, two architects drunk with primal scene painting, to Gutzon Borglum's little dinner. A third type of earthly marvel was now added to the two. All unique and unparalleled elsewhere in our country.

But now came an unexpected experience. That drive from the Canyon "Spearfish" to Rapid City. Does anyone who knows California and Arizona know that in the softly modeled brown surfaces of South Dakota binding these three wonders together is a terrain greater in charm than any to be found in either? A sweep of modeling and a tender color (it is early September) and a variety of aspect matchless anywhere?

No, I shall be burned for a heretic when I make the statement. But I should be thanked as a prophet and hailed as a discoverer by that jaded public who have "seen everything" and stick to the "through lines." The greatest scenic wonders of the world I know now are touched on grand safe highways but not on railroads. My hat is off to South Dakota's treasures and the men who made them.

Go to South Dakota, but drive there. It is so near to us all and yet I never knew, nor had ever heard much about its southwestern treasure house until Gutzon Borglum went out there to work and Senator Norbeck invited me to see it.

I hope the noble inheritance, for that is what it is, won't be exploited too much and spoiled as lesser beauty spots in our country have been spoiled and will not continue to be marred by the nature imitator with his "rustic" effects, piled boulders, peeled logs, and imitation of camp style primitive gabled buildings. Nature needs from man not imitation but interpretation. It is quite another story, as you may learn.

The Soil of the Southwest

I, too, have discovered this America that is Arizona. It will seem strange to the small group of fortunate people who intelligently live here that anyone in their Nation should have to "discover" Arizona after seeing the Grand Canyon. But the remarkable beauty peculiar to this southern Arizona region is quite undiscovered by the grand-average American, or for that matter, by the upper American. This I believe is about to change, and the inevitable boom accompanying such discoveries of the picturesque and climate in the United States will probably come, a rubbish heap, to set Arizona backward a decade or two. That doesn't matter so much, if Arizona clings faithfully to its desert beauty and takes care of it. The desert with its rim of arid mountains spotted like the leopard's skin or tattooed with amazing patterns of creation, is a grand garden the like of which in sheer beauty of space and pattern does not exist, I think, in the world. This great desert garden is Arizona's chief asset. Of course, water poured on certain portions of it will make oases of citrus trees, grapefruit, oranges, lettuce, and melons and they will be rolling east to market just as they do in other arid States. But the American people need not come rolling in here for things like that. They will come because this desert has extraordinary beauty all its own and come to breathe the incomparably pure air here on account of the desert. They will come to get away from weather, come to play, and some of them to stay in the invigorating sunshine. All of Arizona is not a large enough playground for the United States so it may well remain caviar to the general, and prosper mightily.

Compared to the clean, intoxicating air, sweeping vistas and astonishing plant life especially created in the crannies and on the ranges of this desert garden, all else in Arizona is insignificant—even if considered by way of the realtor as "property." Los Angeles has oversold by billions a winter climate wholly inferior to this one of the Salt River Valley which lay quietly undiscovered behind the mountain ranges that cut it off from the too well-known California coast until, now, Californians are coming here to winter.

Here in the Salt River Valley is winter climate in unexampled perfection, due almost wholly to the vast surrounding desert. I dread to see this incomparable natural garden marred, to be eventually spoiled by the candy makers and cactus hunters and careless fire builders and period house builders as well as Indian or Mexican "hut" builders, who will soon destroy the beautiful natural plant growths of the more accessible parts unless the people manage somehow to stop them.

To take the life of one desert plant that is naturally otherwise is to betray this greatest gift nature has yet given in trust to any people. Those who come here to live must eat. They must go out and dig irrigation ditches to earn more money, to make them strong to go out and dig more ditches. And date palms and fig trees, grapefruit, and orange groves are all desirable and beautiful things in themselves where they belong but not to be compared in money-getting value to the noble sahuaro, the wicked cholla, the desert spring called the bianana, the golden paloverde, mesquite, and greasebush, the ocatillo and the ironwood's violet profusion under the canopy of Arizona blue.

For the architect what a marvel of construction that sahuaro! Or the latticed stalk of the cholla! Nature, driven to economize in materials by hard conditions, develops, in the sahuaro, a system of economy of materials in a reinforcement of vertical rods, a plaiting of tendons that holds the structure bolt upright for six centuries or more.

Study the stalk of the cholla for a pattern of latticed steel structure or the structure of the stem of the ocatillo that waves its red flags from the tops of a spray of slender plaited whips 15 feet long.

What a building that would be with a sense of those streamlined spaces in its plan, walled like the sahuaro, textured like it, too, by the nature of its construction. For the desert is no place for plain, hard walls; all is sculptured wind and water. All is patterned and textured in the desert, the rocks and reptiles no less than cacti. A desert building should be nobly simple in outline as the region is sculptured, and have learned from the cactus secrets of straight-line patterns for its forms playing with the light and softening the building into its proper place among the organic desert creations, each heightening the beauty of the other. We do not yet understand pattern for one thing because it is an attribute of a very high and older civilization. We now try to think ornament useless or we continue to go wrong with it by trying to emphasize with it when nature intended it to soften, conceal, and harmonize. Nature herself always does just that very thing with it as you will see if you will go to school to the desert.

But nature never "sticks ornament or sheer pattern on." She gets it all out of the inside by way of the way it grows. It is always *of* the thing. Plain house walls that defy the sun and jump out to your eyes from the desert forty miles or more away are not true desert buildings in any cultivated sense. The Indian Hopi house is no desert house in this sense. Even were it no base imitation for us, it is too loud. The projecting poles soften it with shadows a very little; the Indians got that far with it. But the Indian learned from the desert when he made pots or mats or beadwork or clothed himself. He got something of the spirit of the desert into all those things as we may see. The rattlesnake, the Gila monster and the cacti taught him. Architecture, the great art, except on primitive terms, was beyond him as music and literature were. The fine arts are in themselves a finer civilization, or ought to be as they once were. The broken or dotted line is the line for the desert; not the hard line nor the continuous knife edge. And in that comes a new type of structure for the spaces. You will see that the desert abhors sun defiance as nature abhors a vacuum. Sun acceptance as a condition of survival is everywhere evident. That means organic pattern integral ornament in everything. Sun acceptance in building means the dotted line and wall surfaces that eagerly take the light and play with it, break it up, or drink it in until the sunlight blends the building into place with the creation around it. Man's imagination is none too lively but the task is not too great to harmonize his building masses with topography and typify his building walls with the nature creation they consort with, by taking the abstract designs inherent in all desert growth and weaving them quietly in good order into the abstract fabric of his own work whenever he makes anything. That is to say, make the essential spirit of the thing, however or whatever it is, come through as object.

The human threat to the beauty of the desert garden might be avoided if the builder as architect would only go to school to the desert in this sense and learn the harmonious contrasts or sympathetic treatments for his walls that would, thus, "belong."

Is this organic expression too difficult for us at this stage of our development? Well, then, plant trees and vines, water them and cover your walls with them. Trees and vines native to the conditions here. Be quiet at any cost. Blot out your intrusion as you best can.

I believe that the Arizona "drains" and "washes" and the grand square miles of desert floor out here are worth more eventually even in terms of the gold standard than the irrigation ditches, although not so quick to the department stores, I admit. And I must admit also that the irrigated oases to a certain extent are necessary to the life that is coming into the desert to remain. But I hope Arizona won't, as California did, get the cart before the horse. I hope ranching and the vigorous enterprise in drinking and eating won't go far enough to in any degree spoil the desert garden that will soon bring wealth to the various Arizona pioneers just as it already brings beautiful life to millions of faded, jaded dwellers, refugees from our American cities. The cities are all slums by comparison. This conservation of desert creation should be even more important to government than the conservation of the forests, important as any conservation of water in the mountain streams.

Should the legislature of the State neglect to protect its true reserves in this respect, eventually, yes, even its greatest financial resource, the Federal Government should take them over and protect them or future Arizona may yet curse its short-sighted, short-lived legislators.

Arizona, too, already needs less salesmanship and more statesmanship as less building and more architecture.

From: *Frank Lloyd Wright on Architecture*, edited by Frederick L. Gutheim. New York: 1941, pages 191–199.

Environment as a Natural Resource

by

Benton MacKaye

Environment is outward influence. It is defined as "the sum of the influences which affect an organism from without." It appears to be extrinsic rather than intrinsic. It belongs to what we call the "outer world," which appears to be different from the "inner mind." But what else is the outer world but an extension of the inner mind? It is certainly a form of life in which every inner life takes share. Environment is the influence upon *each* inner mind of the thing shared by *every* inner mind: it is the common layer of air which we all breathe—the filament which binds our separate lives. "Look out and not in," we are told, for when we look *out* we thereby look *in*—to our fellow souls on earth. Environment, therefore, provides a sort of *common mind*—the total life which every life must share: it is the least common denominator of our inner selves.

"All the world's a stage and all the men and women merely players."

Stage and players, setting and activity—these, as we have noted, are the two halves of environment. But what is a "player"? A player is one who *lives:* one who practices neither toil nor decreation but the inspired "activity" where work and play are one. "I work an hour a day," said Steinmetz, "and spend fourteen hours at engineering." Let us take the liberty of translating this remark: "I toil or do chores for an hour a day and spend fourteen hours at play, which in my case in engineering." Steinmetz was a "player." So was Darwin—Whistler—and Wordsworth—and Beethoven. These were big players: most of us are little players; or rather we can learn to be as soon as we learn machines. This kind of playing—the Steinmetz, Whistler, Wordsworth, Beethoven variety—constitutes that sort of activity which we call *living.* Stage or setting plus such activity constitute the kind of environment sought in our new exploration: it is the environment to Mother Earth and God's Nature; it is *environment, the natural resource.*

And this is nothing less than the *indigenous environment.* Indigenous is defined as "innate, inherent, intrinsic." Isaac Taylor said that "joy and hope are emotions indigeous to the human mind." The three elemental environments which we have cited (the primeval, the communal, and the urban) appear to be, like "joy and hope" themselves, "indigenous to the human mind." So it is the indigenous environment, and no other, which constitutes the *natural resource.*

The indigenous environment, is, as we have stated, a psychologic resource. It is one of the energy resources. Energy is converted from a potential to an actual condition in three ways: mechanical conversion, biologic conversion, psychologic conversion. Let us consider them.

Mechanical conversion is illustrated by the water wheel or turbine; it can be illustrated also by the process of burning coal under a steam boiler. Coal consists of wood formed in the luxuriant forests of the carboniferous age. Wood is "bottled sunshine" or bottled solar energy, which, through burning, is converted first into heat, next into steam pressure, and finally into actual motion. Thus the energy which in the coal heap of the locomotive-tender lies dormant and inevident is rendered sensible and evident in the moving train of freight cars. The energy as shown in the moving freight cars is easily perceived by the human senses—of sight, of sound, of contact—and so we call it "actual." The same energy when reposing in the coal heap is not outwardly perceived by any of the senses, but we can figure it out as a possibility, and so we call the energy "potential."

Biologic conversion is illustrated by the process of absorption which takes place in the leaves of trees. We have said that wood is "bottled sunshine." The "sunshine" or solar energy is bottled in the tree trunk through this process of absorption. The leaves, under the action of the sun's direct rays during the summer growing season, take from the surrounding air a certain gas (carbon dioxide) and cause it to "flow" down through the twigs and branches and stem so as to form an enveloping layer of wood, or "annual ring," which surrounds the stem and each of the branches. By this enveloping and "fattening" process the tree trunk grows from year to year, the only growing part of the tree being this outer ring or layer (the *cambium layer* as it is called). As the invisible energy in a heap of coal is converted under the locomotive-boiler into the visible motion of the freight cars, so the energy in an unseen gas and the sun's direct rays is converted in the leaves into the visible substance of wood. Thus one form of latent energy (that in the sun's rays) is converted into another form of latent energy (that in the wood of the tree's trunk). Thus also is invisible matter (carbon dioxide gas) converted into visible matter (the wood substance of the tree's trunk).

Psychologic conversion of energy may be illustrated by certain processes and reactions of the human brain and mind upon the thing which we have called environment. As in the leaves and cambium layer of the tree an unseen gas is converted into visible and solid wood, just so in the cells of the human brain another sort of unseen (or obscure) reality is transformed into substantial evidence. The diffused beauty of a landscape which to the ordinary eye is obscure and perhaps inevident, is, through the brain-action and skill of the artist, captured and placed on sturdy canvas for all to see and comprehend. The elusive thrill of an early spring morning is caught by a Wordsworth or a Whitman and placed before us upon the printed page. The deeply moving rhythm which with us ordinary folks passes by unnoticed is detected by a Chopin, translated by a Paderewski, and placed within our souls to make them richer. In each case a thing of beauty is lifted from the common cerebellum of creation and made a joy forever; an unseen reality is focused to our duller senses to give them appetite for vision; the potential happiness resident in "natural setting" is rendered actual.

In all three of these ways of converting energy (the mechanical, the biologic, and the psychologic), that which is inevident and potential is turned into something which is evident and actual. In each instance also there is a *base* and a *reaction.* Coal is a base, the burning of it is reaction; carbon dioxide is a base, the absorption of it is reaction: the landscape is a base, the painting of it is reaction.

Environment, like every other natural resource, is developed by means of a reaction directed toward a base. Another name for base is "stage" or "setting"; another name for reaction is "activity." We have noted the reaction or activity of the landscape painter; of the poet and of the musician. All of these activities are forms of art; all are carried on by "players." As the material resources and those of mechanical energy are developed by means of the various activities classed as *industry,* so the resource of environment is developed by means of the various activities of the fine arts, or *culture.* Each one of these activities develops a portion of the resource—it picks out (rightly) its own little fragment to be emphasized: but the complete development—the development of *environment as such*—requires a *synthesis* of arts. It requires more than each art working by itself; it requires all arts, working all together. . . .

The most fundamental portion of the indigenous environment consists of the primeval. For the other portions (the communal and the urban) are found ultimately to be but compounds of the primeval. The primeval is "The All" of visible creation: it is the known quantity from which we came, as God is the unknown. The primeval is bequeathed to us by God alone; all other environments are bequeathed by God with man's assistance; and with man comes in the element of fallacy. Man's needs, of course, require sturdy changes in any environment which comes unmodified from "the hands of its Maker." And yet the less an environment is affected by human hands, the greater the range of human minds it unites. The unmodified environment, apparently, approaches closest to the common mind of all humanity: it is the one thing which is agreeable to all our inner minds. Some one has said that discord has no basis in eternity. It seems to have no basis in the primeval environment as it comes to us unmodified by the animal world. The primeval, on the contrary, seems to possess an innate harmony, and this must be why it appeals to us as an innate environment.

The most appealing harmony, perhaps, of the primeval is its ever-recurring youth—the opening of the springtime and the dawning of the day. The sense of eternity thus generated has been captured by Thoreau and put in simple words. He says: "I have been as sincere a worshipper of Aurora as the Greeks. . . . Morning brings back the heroic ages. . . . There is something cosmical about it. . . . Little is to be expected of that day to which we are not awakened by our own newly-acquired aspirations from within, to a higher life than we fell asleep from." And again: "Morning is when I am awake and there is a dawn in me. . . . We must learn to reawaken and keep ourselves awake, not by mechanical aids, but by an infinite expectation of the dawn."

This sentiment is concretely illustrated in the growth of a tree's stem or trunk. This grows, as we have noted, by the accumulation of concentric enveloping layers, or annual rings. The annual ring is the result of the growth of the "cambium layer" above mentioned. The cambium during the dormant months of autumn and winter consists of a thin film of potential growth awaiting the "dawn" of the spring's sunshine and loosened energy. During the months of spring and summer the fluid cambium layer, deriving its substance through the leaves from the ethereal carbon dioxide of the air, forms itself into the solid wood of the annual ring and thereby of the tree's trunk. Again, in the autumn, the cambium becomes a film of potentiality awaiting once more the "dawn." And so from year to year ad infinitum. For the cambium, left unmolested, is a thing of eternal life. It may be killed, but it will never of itself die. The cambium of an oak tree five hundred years of age is just as "young" as that of the oak sapling three years of age. The tree itself becomes in time too large to hold the cambium together, or else it is attacked by some disease, and thus the cambium is "killed." Else it would go on forever as a perennial potentiality—a force and spirit that has learned to reawaken, and *keep* itself awake, by "an infinite expectation of the dawn."

There seems to be within the primeval that measured cadence between expectation and fulfillment which goes to the bottom of all harmony. Harmony is happiness. It consists not of superlatives; neither is it made of promises: it is produced by the journey in between. It is pianissimo leading to crescendo: the potential pristine green of early April leading to the crashing red and yellow of October; the first snow flakes before Thanksgiving leading to the jovial blizzards of February; the feeling of 4 A.M. leading up to that of 4 P.M.—and then, with taps and sunset, the promise of *another* day and of a higher life than the one we fall asleep from. "To him whose elastic and vigorous thought keeps pace with the sun, the day is a perpetual morning." "Morning" consists of one dawn plus the expectation of another; "morning" is a continuing symphony—the onward march of primeval nature.

The opposite of symphony is cacophony. Symphony seems to be an inherent quality of all creation; cacophony comes as an intruder on creation. Both things occur within the primeval world: symphony is indigenous to the primeval world, but cacophony is intrusive or exogenous. In this the animal kingdom is chief offender: the sentient beings of creation have been the breakers of the peace. The struggle for existence is a story of cacophony, and the higher we go in the animal scale, the greater seems to be the discord. The struggle throughout concerns the raw fact of sustenance; with the higher animals it concerns, in addition, the other raw fact of reproduction. The robin apparently selects his mate without collision or other discord and sings his merry springtime song as part of nature's symphony. But bull moose have the habit of fighting to a finish for possession of the female, and the remains of their locked horns give evidence of the fierce futility of their cacophony. The simian is probably the very worst of all the animals in his sins against creation, and man is the worst of all the simians. The story of Adam and Eve, though false in fact, is profound in truth. Man's cacophony has developed around both classes of raw facts—sustenance and reproduction: it relates to two main problems: (1) that of *sustenance* and *industry;* (2) that of *reproduction and the home.* The first problem is a portion of the struggle for existence; the second is this plus an attempt toward the attainment of real living. Let us take a look at each.

The cacophony attending man's struggle for existence and his development of industry has been so blatant and notorious as to give the impression that it is desired for its own sake. War is the only part of business which has been set to music. This is because the cacophony of battle is so precise a replica of hell that symphony must be resorted to as a syrenic means to lure men into it. Truly stirring rhythm is thus developed along with imbecilic war-cries; art as pure emotion is advanced along the right of way, while reason and perspective are sidetracked for a quieter day. But aside from war, the cacophony of business and industry is seldom camouflaged so far as outward aspects go. The hideousness of business and industry, both in the producing and the sales departments, is left exposed in all its nakedness, from the grimy, smoke-belching factory of the industrial suburb to the notorious billboard along the motor road. This apparently sought-for cacophonous environment applies not only to the industrial plants themselves, but to the stabling and housing of their workers. A vivid picture of this "lust to make the world intolerable" is presented by Mr. H. L. Mencken in a recent essay on "Hideous Steel Towns of Pennsylvania." Here are some significant passages:

"The other day, coming out of Pittsburgh by train, I rolled eastward for an hour through the coal and steel towns of Westmoreland county. . . . Here was the very heart of industrial America, the richest and grandest nation ever seen on earth—and here was a scene so dreadfully hideous, so intolerably bleak and forlorn, that it reduced the whole aspiration of man to a sort of joke.

The country itself is not uncomely. . . . But [it contains] the most loathsome towns and villages ever seen by mortal eye . . . as if some titanic and aberrant genius, uncompromisingly inimical to men, had devoted all the ingenuity of hell to the making of them. . . . It seems incredible that mere ignorance should have achieved such masterpieces of horror. There is a voluptuous quality in them. They look deliberate.*

Mr. Mencken pictures other striking instances—here in the mighty world-empire of Appalachian America—of reducing man's apiration to a joke. This situation he calls "deliberate." Well, perhaps it is. The workers dwelling in these steel towns are, as is well known, in profound rebellion against their condition in life. They and American workers generally are fighting deliberately and definitely for higher pay and for longer hours of leisure. They are fighting, incidentally and vaguely, for "better living-conditions." The demand for *time* in which to play and "live" is deliberate and articulate, but the demand for *space* is incidental and inarticulate. The average worker (and the average man or woman) oftentimes seems, to some of us, to be actually desirous of a cacophonous environment. But this probably is not really true. He merely is not ravenous for a symphonious environment; and the feeble demand for the one looks like a "deliberate" demand for the other.

The demand for a symphonious environment appears to play no serious part in the problem of *sustenance and industry:* it does, however, play the leading rôle in the problem of *reproduction and the home.* Cacophony in the home, though plentiful, is recognized as a fundamental evil, and as the one indeed which strikes at the integrity of the institution itself. The home is conceived as in symphony. In

* "Hideous Steel Towns of Pennsylvania," by H. L. Mencken. *Boston Herald*, Sunday, January 23, 1927.

nothing else do lovers meet. That is their whole game—to create a symphonious environment—an harmonious "common mind." But in each individual mind there are usually certain portions not common to the other fellow's: these portions (pertaining to "the one" and not to "the two") sometimes trespass on the common denominator: then comes the cacophony. These trespasses vary greatly—from the little ripplings known as "lovers' quarrels" to the invading state of mind called "incompatibility." As with lovers, or the husband and wife, so with the family and home: the basic desire and ambition—the sole point of the institution—is an atmosphere and environment of mutual harmonious living; when discord comes, as it so often does, it comes as an invader and as something foreign to the basic stuff. As with the home, so with the community and with human society generally: symphony is indigenous, cacophony is exogenous.

The purely indigenous environment is essentially a symphonious environment; and it is nothing else. It is the source and support of all true living. The indigenous environment is the basic natural resource of civilization as a "spiritual form"; all the other natural resources (the soils, the ores, the waters, the forests) are basic of civilization as a "material fact." Man *lives* not by bread alone—nor by clothing, nor by shelter. One more big category needs to be provided: it is an extension of the category which we call "shelter." Each one of us, each family of us, needs a roof, and warmth, and light, and water supply, and some degree of sanitation. But it takes more than these to make a home. Each group of us who live in the same town need houses and stores and streets and churches and school buildings: but it takes more than these to make a real community. The nation as a whole needs towns and roads and industries and a great deal of other material plant: but it takes more than these to make a pleasant land to live in. Mere "shelter," therefore, will not suffice. We need a further category. This is environment: it is a particular kind of environment—*indigenous, innate, symphonious environment.*

The environment described by Mr. Mencken (in the Pittsburgh region) is the very opposite of this. He describes the exogenous environment—none other indeed than our old acquaintance, the metropolitan environment. He describes it correctly—as an intrusion into the indigenous environment. The latter, "the country itself," he says, is "not uncomely," but it is invaded by "the most loathsome towns and villages ever seen by mortal eye." Mr. Mencken is describing nothing more or less than the metropolitan invasion. He describes this as something "uncompromisingly inimical" to man, as something "so intolerably bleak and forlorn" as to reduce the whole aspiration of man to "a sort of joke." We have here "the country itself" of the Allegheny Mountains—the indigenous, innate, symphonious environment—invaded by the metropolitan flood—and *exogenous, unnatural, cacophonous environment.*

As rational men and women, plainly, we would develop the one and control the other.

From: *The New Exploration,* by Benton MacKaye. New York: 1928, pages 134–145.

III

The Role of the Machine

The Development of Modern Style

by

Joseph Warren Yost

The human race finds itself endowed with two distinct classes of desire—one to perpetuate, the other to enjoy its existence. What necessity requires seldom performs its office without administering to the desire for pleasure. Utility makes her demands to perpetuate life, art to provide enjoyment. While the capacity of the race to provide was exhausted in supplying its necessities, art was impossible. It was only when he had so far conquered the forces of nature as to leave some time and some energy unexpended, after his needs were supplied, that man could or did, turn his mind to the contemplation, and his hand to the realization, of that which was ornamental. It is only out of the surplus strength of hand and brain that works of art proceed. . . .

Architecture being an art of precedence, forms and motives when once accepted, tend to perpetuate themselves in use, even for long periods after their original meaning is forgotten—possibly in materials for which they were not intended, and in which they never would have been produced. It was many a century from the early timber buildings of Egypt to the mastabas of the fifth dynasty, yet we have the crystallization of wood construction in these later productions in granite and limestone. It was two thousand years from the wooden sun-shelter of Chaldea to the palaces of Esarhaddon, but some of the details familiar to the eye of the early ages, when both civilization and Architecture were in a formative condition, were retained in the best materials the later Mesopotamian empires could furnish. Some of the details in palaces of Assyria, which were built two hundred years before the time of Pericles, not only were transported twelve hundred miles to the new civilization on the Mediterranean, but were carried from their origin in sun-dried brick to the marble of classic times. The guilloche from the palace of Ashurbanipal, and which was older than Hellenic civilization, is still retained among us as one of our most effective ornaments.

But not greater was the conservatism which resisted any change in form and decoration, in the empires of antiquity, than is the conservatism of more modern times—even in our own country, in the nineteenth century. While we claim to be free to adopt any detail we please, we are, nevertheless, copying the detail of past ages—not only using it in the material where it reached its perfection, but in any other material that we have at hand, and without reference to whether the material is suitable for the detail or not, and without much thinking of the place and manner in which it was formerly employed.

The cause of this tenacity of historic forms rests, probably, in the fact that the most fertile mind—much less the average designer—is not able to produce, from the use of the material and the purposes in the structure, an entirely original supply of forms—especially within the limit of time allowed for the purpose. This demand for more than can be wrought out for the occasion, causes continuance in the habit of copying direct-copying even more thoughtlessly—from existing buildings and familiar designs. Again, through the sense of sight, forms fix themselves in the mind, and when the designer is called upon to use *some* form, he naturally turns first to those which "hang on memory's wall."

But while this tenacity of old forms must be recognized in the consideration of our subject, it is equally true that no material has ever become the chief, in a class of buildings, without lending the influence of its qualities to the design of the structures where it was used. Very soon a new requirement has arisen that could not be met by the old materials, and for which the new would answer—and the new was forced into prominence—lending a new quality, in proportion or detail, to the design.

But what is new must begin with the old as a basis, so that the style of our times will be influenced not only by new materials brought into use, but also by those which have been in use, and which have already lent their impression to the work of the past; because Architecture is a record of past, as well as a statement of present conditions.

Our subject is undoubtedly intended to include not only past, but future influence as well, upon the development of style. The past will be historic, the future prophetic. There is not as much to disagree about in that which has passed, as in that which is to come, and yet no two persons will make quite the same selection of facts from which to form an opinion, even of what now exists—hence opinions must differ. But when it comes to what is to occur in the future, the field for difference of opinion widens. It may be that opinions printed now will be read with much mirth—if they are read at all—after what is to happen has happened. But with all the past as a foundation—as a base upon which to support predictions of the future—it may be that some little part of the future can be estimated.

The materials of which buildings are erected always affect the design to a greater or less extent. All historic styles of Architecture possess certain peculiarities of form and detail induced by the character of the material, in the use of which the style was developed. Any style will have a definable relation to the materials available when it is undergoing formation. History presents some interesting proofs of the influence of material on style. The great buildings of the Nile Valley, which have lived to carry the story of Egyptian civilization across a silence of so many centuries, bear unmistakable evidence of the abundance of stone at the beginning of Egyptian greatness, which the ancient Mesopotamian cities could rise from their earth-bound sleep of 2,000 years, and exhibit their buildings to prove the scarcity of stone in that country, when Ourkam bid his nation of thinkers erect temples for the worship of Ishtar. Even the Greek, who crystallized the toys of his youth in the monuments of his manhood, never forgot the timber which built the shelter for his ancestry. . . .

The wonderful difference between the proportions of modern buildings since steel construction has come into use, and those which were the prevailing custom prior to that date, is noticeable upon all hands—particularly in this country. The most remarkable of these changes is the extraordinary height to which buildings are now carried in some American cities. Another noticeable change is the great unbroken window surface closed in by plate glass, which prior to the present age was impossible. Not only the exterior but the interior of the buildings has been greatly changed by reason of steel construction. Vast floor spaces are now opened up, with but few small supports for what is above, and the same is repeated story after story. To whatever extent plate glass has made it easier to furnish light, its use has resulted in great benefit to humanity, whether it has overturned former Architectural notions or not. To whatever extent steel construction has made it possible to have lighter, better and safer buildings, more ample and better arranged floor space, more comfortable and safer offices, it has been a benefit to mankind, even though it may have entirely over-reached our ability to govern it, as an Architectural element. No more need be said of the possibility of extending floor space without being broken by roof supports, than to call attention to the main hall of the Liberal Arts building at the Columbian Exposition at Chicago—a room two hundred feet high, without a post or pier anywhere to break the well night "boundless continuity" of floor space. In this direction it may be said that steel construction opens up a possibility of greatness hitherto unknown. This is one decided influence already realized. If you say this is more of a feat of engineering than of Architecture, I say in reply, that this is only because architecture has not been able, as yet, to measure up to its privilege under the reign of glass and steel. While these possibilities have had an extensive influence upon the height of buildings, the extension of rooms and the question of light, . . . it is perhaps not the direction in which we are supposed to discuss this question.

Let us turn to the influence that steel and plate glass have exerted upon the exterior of these buildings. Here their influence is written in legible lines by the numerous *attempts* which have been made to vary the proportions of historic styles of Architecture to fit the requirements which have come with the use of these two hitherto unknown materials. These *attempts* are mostly failures, as viewed from an artistic or Architectural standpoint—no, they are not failures, they are only unsuccessful efforts. They are not failures, for they prove to us what *not* to do, and that we must know. Their influence is negative, but it is wholesome. They prove to us that our ideas must be reformed and expressed in a different Architectural language. Up to date we have witnessed the building of walls—or what seemed to be walls—two hundred feet high, supported only on small piers, scarcely able, if they *were* piers, to sustain their own weight. We have tried hard to admire the result, but have failed. The untruthfulness of the expression was too evident. Then, we have built walls very plain and simple, and that seemed to have a negative kind of merit, but we were not satisfied with it. Next, we have tried to decorate the façades—supposed to be walls—with forms from one style of Architecture or another, and, like the man with the road in Arkansas, whichever style we have tried, we wish we had tried some other one. Then we have lost our patience and decided that steel, as a building material, was a destroyer of our peace, and we have tried to get city councils to pass ordinances, saying that steel construction should not be allowed. We have tried to drive it out of town, by limiting the height to which buildings might go. Then, when we find these efforts a failure, we go back and try some other style of Architecture, and perhaps we plaster the details of a Greek temple or Venetian palace all over a sixteen-story front, and try to comfort ourselves with the fact that we have done as well as anybody else. We place columns one, two and three stories high, upon the top of each other, or by interspersing them with a few tiers of impossible arches, resulting in a sort of Architectural grille, which looks as if it ought to be built lying down, as it apparently has no ability to stand up. And we feel real mad at some newspaper critic for saying that "it looks as though the builder had got hold of the elevation with the wrong end up." After this we meet with our brethren of the profession, . . . and we solemnly resolve that tall buildings are an Architectural monstrosity.

This seems to be the history of the past. It is largely a record of our failure to accommodate our Architectural notions, and the details of historic styles, to the new conditions induced by the use of steel and plate glass. But what of the future?

It so occurs that plate glass and steel construction are directly opposite in character, and yet both work toward the same end. The steel may be said to be the positive quantity, and the glass the negative quantity. The steel is the solid—the glass the void. The glass can fill the space which the more positive material does not care to occupy. The great strength of steel posts tends to reduce the width of piers, and glass stands ready to fill the increased space between. The great strength of steel girders tends to widen the space between posts, and the glass is ready at hand for the greater duty of closing the larger opening. It may be said, therefore, that if steel construction is the master, plate glass is a faithful servant. The great strength of steel has a tendency to reduce the solids and increase the voids, to reduce the thickness of walls, and decrease the depths of shadows. The character of posts and lintels is such as to induce the use of straight lines, and the same influence is exerted by the difficulty in using curves in the windows filled with plate glass. The influence of these characteristics would be in the direction of angularity of style.

Being a material quickly affected by fire and weather, steel must be enclosed by some shield for protection. Instead of its brick or terra cotta covering attempting to preserve the appearance of a wall, when it has lost the substance of a wall, it will, by and by, fall into its true position as a covering for the steel, and begin to take the form of, and exhibit, probably in conventionalized form, the detail natural to the steel construction itself. Already it is seen that to attempt to make a building, the frame of which is steel, look like a stone building or a brick building, is a caricature on all decent building art. It is not less an Architectural fraud—an artistic monstrosity—to imitate a brick building by the forms used, when steel constitutes the chief building material, and when the brick, if left alone as it appears, would not stand for a moment. But as the steel will give certain suggestions to the form of the covering, which are natural to the steel construction and not to the covering material, the material used for the covering, on the other hand, will tend to give to the design certain of its own peculiarities. Hitherto the covering has practically given all, and the steel nothing, to the detail. The constructive forms of the past have been continued in use, as well as the decorative motives, whether they are suited to the material in which they are wrought or not.

Sixteen-story buildings have sought to avoid the appearance of height by adopting some manner of design by which their real altitude could be partially concealed. Breadth and comparative lowness have become such desirable qualities, in our minds, that we have been willing to make that seem low which was not low, and solidity and repose have been so desirable, that we have sought to supply the appearance of these qualities to buildings where the whole purpose was in the opposite direction. But it has become evident to the intelligent designer that we must stop trying to make a twelve-story building look like a distorted Greek temple, and must stop trying to use forms which must be distorted in their proportions in order to fit requirements at variance with any which such forms can properly answer. The fact is that the problem of a design in steel and plate glass for a tall building, is a new one, and it cannot be solved by the old rules. There is no use trying to convince ourselves, or anybody else, that the little piers laid up with brick, are real piers. We see at a glance they are not. They would be crushed instantly if they were. There is no use trying to lead anybody into the idea that a brick or stone wall can be laid across a twenty-foot void, with nothing to support it. There is no use trying to conceal the fact that what we see is only a covering of the real building material, on whose efficiency the structure depends. There is no use trying to hold longer to the antiquated notion that only comparatively low buildings are Architecturally creditable. There is no use either, of our entertaining the idea that because steel cannot be successfully used in proportions suitable to stone, that, therefore, steel is not a good material for Architectural purposes.

The fact is that the wall and pier and buttress, hitherto the strength and support of the building, have no reason for an existence under the new conditions. It is therefore possible to conventionalize them as the Greeks did the wooden cornice when they built in marble, or it is possible to omit them altogether as features of the design, as the builders of the middle ages did with the entablature, when they had no further use for it.

There seem to be four parts to be disposed of in the design for a modern steel building. First, the continuous posts, second, the lintels between stories, third, the panels of brick or other material which fill the space between posts and lintels, and fourth, the windows. It seems to me, that while the steel must be concealed from the elements, it should not be concealed in the design, and that the surface of the building should take the form of a covering of continuous posts, and a covering of horizontal members between posts, and the filling in of the panels which intervene. It would seem also, that none of these three should be so designed as to make believe that it is the support for the structure, but the covering of posts and lintels should show that it is a covering, and a covering only, of that which is the support of all. It would seem furthermore, that this screen and covering should take on its true character, and appear to be what it really is, and not pretend to be a wall.

The reflex influence of this change from old ideas, in the design of buildings where steel is really used, will be a tendency to harmonize the design of other buildings, to express an Architectural relationship with them.

Thus we have the influence of steel construction and plate glass; first, the tendency to greatness, especially in the direction of greater altitude and greater dimensions for interiors; second, a tendency toward angularity of style; third, a tendency to better illumination; fourth, a tendency to decrease ponderosity of structure; fifth, a tendency to entire reformation in the use of forms and motives of ornament. . . .

From: *The Influence of Steel Construction and of Plate Glass upon the Development of Modern Style*, by Joseph Watten Yost. "The Proceedings of the Thirtieth Annual Convention of American Institute of Architects," 1896, pages 52–58.

The Brooklyn Bridge as a Monument

by

Montgomery Schuyler

The total length of the bridge is 5989 feet, of which the central span between the towers is 1595 feet 6 inches, the "land spans" from the towers to the anchorages each 930 feet, the approach on the New York side 1562 feet 6 inches, and on the steeper Brooklyn side 971 feet. These dimensions do not make this the longest bridge in the world. But when it was built there was no single span which approached the central span over the East River; and though it has since been exceeded by two spans of the Forth Bridge, in Scotland (1710 feet each, sustained by cantilevers), it remains by far the largest example of a chain-bridge. It is half as long again as Roebling's Cincinnati Bridge (1057 feet between towers), and nearly twice as long as the same engineer's Niagara Bridge (821 feet). The span of the ill-fated bridge over the Ohio at Wheeling, which was built in 1848, and blown down in 1854, was 1010 feet. Noteworthy suspension-bridges in Europe are Telford's, over the Menai Straits (589 feet), finished in 1825; Chaley's bridge, at Fribourg (870 feet), finished in 1834; and Tierney Clark's bridge over the Danube at Pesth (670 feet), finished in 1849. The longest spans bridged otherwise than by a roadway hung from cables are the central spans of Stephenson's Britania (box girder) Bridge (459 feet), of Ead's St. Louis Bridge, of steel arches (520 feet), and of the beautiful Washington Bridge, of steel arches, at New York (510 feet). The largest span of an arch of masonry known to have been built in a bridge (251 feet) was in that built in the fourteenth century, and destroyed by Carmagnola in the fifteenth, which crossed the Adda at Trezzo. The largest now standing (220 feet) is an American work, the arch designed and built by General Meigs to carry the Washington Aqueduct over Cabin John Creek. The second is that of the Grosvenor Bridge at Chester (200 feet), and the third the central arch of London Bridge (152 feet).

The Brooklyn Bridge is thus one of the mechanical wonders of the world, one of the greatest and most characteristic of the monuments of the nineteenth century. Its towers, at least, bid fair to outlast every structure of which they command a view. Everybody recalls Macaulay's prophecy of the time "when some traveller from New Zealand shall, in the midst of a vast solitude, take his stand upon a broken arch of London Bridge, to sketch the ruins of St. Paul's." But when our New-Zealander takes his stand above the saddles that are now ridden by the cables of the bridge, to look over the side of a forsaken city, there will be no ruins of churches—at least, of churches now in being—for him to sketch or see. The web of woven steel that now hangs between the stark masses of the towers may have disappeared, its slender filaments rusted into nothingness under the slow corrosion of the centuries. Its builders and the generation for which they wrought may have been as long forgotten as are now the builders of the Pyramids, whereof the traveller, "as he paceth amazedly those deserts," asks the Historic Muse "who builded them; and she mumbleth something, but what it is he heareth not." It is not unimaginable that our future archeologist, looking from one of these towers upon the solitude of a mastless river and a dispeopled land, may have no other means of reconstructing our civilization than that which is furnished him by the tower on which he stands. What will his judgment of us be?

This, or something like this, ought to be a question with every man who builds a structure which is meant to outlast him, whether it be a temple of religion or a work of bare utility like this. It so happens that the work which is likely to be our most durable monument, and to convey some knowledge of us to the most remote posterity, is a work of bare utility; not a shrine, not a fortress, not a palace, but a bridge. This is in itself characteristic of our time. It is true of no other people since the Romans, and of none before. Like the Roman remains, the duration of this work of ours will show that we knew how to build. "A Roman work," we often hear it said of the bridge, and it is in many ways true. It is far beyond any Roman monument in refinement of mechanical skill. It is Roman in its massiveness and durability. It is Roman, too, in its disregard of art, in resting satisfied with the practical solution of the great problem of its builders, without a sign of that skill which would have explained and emphasized the process of construction at every step, and everywhere, in whole and in part, made the structure tell of the work it was doing. There have been periods in history when this aesthetic purpose would have seemed to the builder of such a monument as much a matter of course, as necessary a part of his work, as the practical purpose which animated the designer of the Brooklyn Bridge. It would have seemed so to the engineer of a bridge in Athens in the second century before our era, or to the engineer of a bridge in Western Europe in the thirteenth century of our era. The utilitarian treatment of our monument is as striking and as characteristic a mark of the period as its utilitarian purpose. It is a noble work of engineering; it is not a work of architecture.

The most strictly scientific of constructors would scarcely take the ground that he did not care how his work looked, when his work was so conspicuous and so durable as the Brooklyn Bridge, and he must be aware that a training in scientific construction alone will not secure an architectural result. It is more probable that he looks upon the current architectural devices as frivolous and irrelevant to the work upon which he is engaged, and consoles himself for his ignorance of them by contempt. Architecture is to him the unintelligent use of building material. Assuredly this view is borne out by a majority of the "architecturesque" buildings that he sees, and he does not lack express authority for it. Whereas the engineer's definition of good masonry is "the least material to perform a certain duty," Mr. Fergusson declares that "an architect ought always to allow himself such a margin of strength that he may disregard or play with his construction;" and Mr. Ruskin defines architecture to be the addition to a building of unnecessary features. An engineer has, therefore, some warrant for considering that he is sacrificing to the graces and doing all that can reasonably be expected of him to produce an architectural monument, if in designing the piers of a chain-bridge he employs an unnecessary amount of material and adds unnecessary features. But if we go back to the time when engineers were artists, and study what a modern scientific writer has described as "that paragon of constructive skill, a Pointed cathedral," we shall find that the architecture and the construction cannot be disjoined. The work of the mediaeval builder in his capacity of artist was to expound, emphasize, and refine upon the work he did in his capacity of constructor, and to develop and heighten its inherent effect. And it is of this kind of skill that the work of the modern engineer, in so far as he is only an engineer, shows no trace.

Reduced to its simplest expression, and as it has actually been used for unknown periods in Asia and in South America, a suspension-bridge consists of two parallel ropes swung from side to side of a ravine, and carrying the platform over which the passenger walks. As the span increases, so that the dip makes the ropes impracticable, the land ends of the ropes are hoisted some distance above the roadway which they carry. If nothing can be found there strong enough to hold them, they are simply passed over, say, forked trees, and the ends made fast to other trees or held down with stones. This is the essential construction of the Brooklyn Bridge. The ropes become four cables sixteen inches thick, of 5541 steel wires; the forked tree becomes a tower 276 feet high, and 8260 square feet in area at the base; the bowlder to hold down the end of the rope becomes a mass of masonry of 60,000 tons' weight; the shaky platform becomes a great street, 85 feet wide, of five firm roadways. But the man who first carried his rope over the forked tree was the inventor of the arrangement which, developed through all the refinements of modern mechanics, forms the groundwork of the Brooklyn Bridge.

This statement of the germinal idea of a chain-bridge will, perhaps, give a clearer notion of the functions of the several parts of the Brooklyn Bridge than a consideration of the complicated structure in its ultimate evolution, in which these functions are partly lost sight of. But if the structure had been architecturally designed, these things would have been emphasized at every point and in every way. The function of the great "towers," so called, being merely to hold up the cables, it is plain that three isolated piers would have performed that function, and the stability of these piers, loaded as they are by the cables, would have very possibly been assured, even if they had been completely detached from each other. But in order at once to stiffen and to load them, so as to make the area of resistance to the force of the wind equal to the whole area of the towers, the openings through which the roadways run are closed above by steep pointed arches, and the spandrels of these filled with a wall which rises to the summit of the piers, where a flat coping covers the whole. There is a woeful lack of expression in this arrangement. The piers should assert themselves starkly and unmistakably as the bones of the structure, and the wall above the arches be subordinated to a mere filling. It should be distinctly withdrawn from the face of the piers instead of being, as in fact it is, only distinguished from them by their shallow and ineffectual projections. It should be distinctly dropped below their summits instead of rising to the same height, and being included under a common cornice. To see what a difference in effect this very obvious differentiation of parts would have been made, glance at the sketch of a suspension-bridge at Minneapolis. This is not, upon the whole, a laudable design, and it contains several survivals of conventional architectural forms meaningless in their present place. But the mere subduing of the archway to a strut between the piers explains—not forcibly, perhaps, nor elegantly, but unmistakably—the main purpose of the structure, and the functional relation of its parts. A drawing of one of the towers of the Brooklyn Bridge without its cables would tell the spectator nothing; the structure itself will tell our New-Zealander nothing of its uses. With its flat top and its level coping, indicating that the whole was meant to be evenly loaded, it would seem to be the base of a missing superstructure rather than what it is.

The flatness of the top alone conceals instead of expressing the structure. It is of the first practical necessity that the great cables should move freely in their saddles, so as always to keep the pressure upon the piers directly vertical, and very ingenious appliances have been employed to attain this end, and to avoid chafing the cables. But the design of the piers themselves tells us absolutely nothing of all this. The cable simply disappears on one side and reappears on the other, as if it were two separate cables, one on each side, instead of one continuous chain. Look at this section at the top of the tower, and see how an exquisite refinement of mechanical arrangement may coexist with absolute insensibility to the desirableness even of an architectural expression of this arrangement. The architecture of this crowning member of the tower has nothing whatever to do with the purpose for which the structure exists. Is it not perfectly evident that an architectural expression of this mechanical arrangement would require that the line of the summit, instead of this meaningless flat coping, should, to begin with, be a crest of roof, its double slope following the line of the cable which it shelters? Here the very channel through which the cable runs is not designed, but is a mere hole occurring casually, and not by premeditation, in the midst of the mouldings which form the cornice of the tower. This is architectural barbarism.

Other opportunities offered for architectural expression in the towers themselves were in the treatment of the buttresses, in the treatment of the balconies which girdle the tower at the height of the roadway, and in the modelling of the arches. The girth of each of the towers at the water-line is 398 feet. The reduction is effected by means of five or six offsets, which withdraw each face of the tower four feet between the bottom and the top, and each end six feet. The counterforts, eight in all, on the sides of the outer piers and on the faces of all the piers, are mere applied strips, very shallow in proportion to their width, and terminating in the capital-like projections which are casually pierced to receive the cables. It may make, perhaps, no serious difference in the mechanical efficiency of these counter-forts whether their area be narrow and deep or broad and shallow. But an increase of depth in proportion to width would of itself, with its higher lights and sharper shadows, have made forcible masses of what are now ineffectual features. This inherent effect would be very greatly enhanced if the offsets themselves were accentuated by sharp and decisive modelling. As it is, emphasis seems to have been studiously avoided. The offsets are merely long batterings of the wall, which do nothing to separate the piers into related parts with definite transitions, and so to refine the crudity of the masses. To see the difference between a mechanical and a monumental conception of a great structure, compare these towers with the front of Amiens, or of Strasburg, or of Notre Dame of Paris. Of course the designer of a modern bridge must not attempt to reproduce in his work "those misty masses of multitudinous pinnacle and diademed tower." That would be a more fatal fault than the rudeness and crudeness with which we have to charge the design of the towers of the Brooklyn Bridge. The ornament of the cathedrals, so far as it is separable from their structure, has nothing for the designer of the bridge even of suggestion. But to see how masses may be modelled so as to be made to speak, look at the modelled masses of the tower of Amiens, the stark lines of essential structure framing the screen of wall between them, in contrast with the uniform deadness here of buttress and curtain wall; the crisp emphasis of lines of light and hollows of black shade which mark the transitions between parts of structure in the west front of Rheims, in contrast with the lack of emphasis in the offsets of the bridge tower; the spirit of the gargoyled balconies that belt the towers of Notre Dame, and the spiritlessness of the parapeted balconies that encircle the tower of the bridge. And note, too (we are not now speaking of the decoration of the cathedrals), that all this transcendent superiority arises merely from a development and emphasis of the inherent expression of the masses themselves, which in the bridge are left so crude, and in the cathedral towers are refined so far. It need not, and indeed should not, have been carried so far in this architecture of reason and utility as in the architecture of a poetical religion. The mere rudiments of those works would have furnished all the expression that is necessary or desirable here. But these rudiments are wanting. What can we say but that the designer of the cathedral began where the designer of the bridge left off? If our New-Zealander should extend his travels, and come upon these monuments also, what would be his surprise at finding documentary proof that the bridge was built six hundred years after the cathedrals, and that the generation which built the bridge looked backward and downward upon the generation which built the cathedrals as rude and barbarous and unreasoning in comparison with themselves!

What we have said of the towers is true also of the anchorages. The bowlder which the Peruvian rolls upon the end of his rope to hold it down is here a mass of 60,000 tons. Scientifically it is adjusted to its purpose, no doubt, with the most exact nicety. Artistically it is still but a bowlder rolled upon a rope. It would probably be impracticable to exhibit the anchor plate which takes the ultimate strain of this mile and more of cable, though we may be sure that our Greek or our Gothic bridge-builder would not have admitted its impracticability without as exhaustive an investigation as the modern bridge-builder has given to the mechanical aspects of his problem. But it was certainly practicable to indicate the function of the anchorage itself, to build it up in masses which should seem to hold the cable to the earth, or a double arch like—or rather unlike—the double arch of the main tower, turned between piers which should visibly answer the same purpose. Instead of either of these, or of any technical device for the same purpose, the weight above is a crude mass, so far from being adapted to its function in its form, that one has to look with some care to find it from the street below, and to distinguish it from the approaches.

What we have called the balconies at the level of the roadway are not "practical" balconies, since they open from the driveways, and not from the walk, and are not accessible as points of view. The purpose of a projection at this point is to secure as great a breadth as possible for the system of wind-braces under the floor of the bridge. This purpose is attained by the projection, but is only masked by the imitations of balconies, instead of being architecturally expressed, as it might have been unmistakably expressed, by the bold projection of a granite spur from the angle of the pier.

There are, probably, few arches in the world—certainly there can be none outside of works of modern engineering—of anything like the span, height, thickness, and conspicuousness of those in the bridge towers which are so little effective. Like the brute mass of wall above them, they are impressive only by magnitude. The great depth of the archway is only seen as a matter of mensuration, not felt as a poetical impression, as it would have been if the labors of the constructor had been supplemented by the labors of an artist; if the shallow strips of pier had become real buttresses, and the jamb and arch had been narrowed by emphatic successions of withdrawal, instead of being merely tunnelled through the mass; if the intrados of the arch itself had been accentuated by modelling, instead of being weakened by the actual recession of its voussoirs behind the plane of the wall.

The approaches themselves are greatly impressive, as indeed the towers are also, by magnitude and massiveness. The street bridges are uniformly imposing by size and span, and especially attractive also by reason of the fact that through them we get what is to be got nowhere else in our rectangular city, glimpses and "bits" of buildings. The most successful of them all, and the most successful feature architecturally of all the masonry of the bridge, is the simple, massive, and low bridge of two arches which spans North William Street, in New York. The arcades between the streets are imposing by number and repetition as well as by massiveness, and by the Roman durability which marks all the work. They suffer, however, from two causes. The coping, the arches, and the piers, which are the emphatic parts of structure, are lighter in color than the unemphasized and rock-faced fields of the wall, and this is always a misfortune when it is not an error. The arches are of the form called "Florentine"—that is to say, round within and pointed without. The deepest voussoirs are thus those at the crown of the arch. This is the reverse of the disposition which would be dictated by mechanical considerations alone. Architecturally it has the drawback of interrupting at every arch the successive and diminishing wheelings which make a long arcade of great openings so impressive in a perspective view. The form seems to have been chosen on account of the facility it afforded, by lengthening the upper voussoirs, to conform the ridge line of the arches to the slope of the roadway, while keeping the springing line horizontal.

This gradual diminution of the arches shoreward enhances the apparent length of the approach looking in that direction, but correspondingly shortens it looking towards the bridge; and it seems, upon the whole, that it would have been better to carry the arches through level, without attempting to dissemble the difference between their line and that of the roadway. There are some shabby and flimsy details or iron work, which mar the monumental effect of the great roadway itself, while the design of the iron stations at either end is grossly illiterate, and discreditable to the great work. Imitations in cast-iron of stone capitals surmount and emphatically contradict posts profusely studded with bolt-heads; and other solecisms, alike against constructional reason and architectural tradition, are rife in these unfortunate edifices, which do what they can to vulgarize the great structure to which they give access.

Vulgarity certainly cannot be charged against any integral portion of the great work itself. There is nothing frivolous and nothing ostentatious even in the details we have noted, and in which we have not been so much criticising the crowning work of a great engineer's career as noting the spirit of our age. It is scarcely fair to say, even, as was said by an architectural journal when the completion of the bridge was doubtful, that if it were left incomplete its towers would stand "in unnecessary ugliness." Its defects in design are not misdeeds, but shortcomings. They are the defects of being rudimentary, of not being completely developed. The anatomy of the towers and of the anchorages is not brought out in their modelling. Their fingers, so to speak, are all thumbs. Their impressiveness is inherent in their mass, and is what it could not help being. The ugliest of great bridges is undoubtedly Stephenson's Britannia Bridge; and this is ugly, not because it is square and straight, but because it tells nothing of itself. It is a mere flat surface, and almost absolutely inexpressive, compared, for example, with such a piece of ironwork as the truss which carries the roadway of the bridge over Franklin Square, in which the function of every joint and member is apparent. But a far nobler thing than this is the central span of the great bridge itself, its roadway slowly sweeping upward to meet the swift swoop of its cables. We have complained of the lack of expression in the towers of their anatomy, but this is anatomy only, a skeletonized structure in which, as in a scientific diagram, we see—even the layman sees—the interplay of forces represented by an abstraction of lines. What monument of any architecture can speak its story more clearly and more forcibly that this gossamer architecture, through which its purpose, like "the spider's touch"—

So exquisitely fine,
Feels at each thread, and lives along the line?

This aerial bow, as it hangs between the busy cities, "curving on a sky imbrued with color," is perfect as an organism of nature. It is an organism of nature. There was no question in the mind of its designer of "good taste" or of appearance. He learned the law that struck its curves, the law that fixed the strength and the relation of its parts, and he applied the law. His work is beautiful, as the work of a ship-builder is unfailingly beautiful in the forms and outlines in which he is only studying "what the water likes," without a thought of beauty, and as it is almost unfailingly ugly when he does what he likes for the sake of beauty. The designer of the Brooklyn Bridge has made a beautiful structure out of an exquisite refinement of utility, in a work in which the lines of forces constitute the structure. Where a more massive material forbade him to skeletonize the structure, and the lines of effort and resistance needed to be brought out by modelling, he has failed to bring them out, and his structure is only as impressive as it needs must be. It has not helped his work, as we have seen, to trust his own sense of beauty, and to contradict or to conceal what he was doing in accordance with its dictates. As little would it have helped him to invoke the aid of a commonplace architect to plaster his structure with triglyphs or to indent it with trefoils. But an architect who pursued his calling in the spirit and with the skill of the mediaeval builders of whom we have been speaking, who knew in his province the lesson the engineer has re-enforced in his, that "Nature can only be commanded by obeying her," and that the function of an organism, in art as in nature, must determine its form—such an architect might have helped the designer of the Brooklyn Bridge to make it one of the noblest monuments of architecture in the world, as it is one of the greatest and most honorable works of engineering.

From: *American Architecture*, by Montgomery Schuyler. New York: 1891, pages 68–85.

The Art and Craft of the Machine

by

Frank Lloyd Wright

No one, I hope, has come here tonight for a sociological prescription for the cure of evils peculiar to this Machine Age. For I come to you as an Architect to say my word for the right use upon such new materials as we have, of our great substitute for tools—Machines. There is no thrift in any craft until the tools are mastered; nor will there be a worthy social order in America until the elements by which America does its work are mastered by American Society. Nor can there be an Art worth the man or the name until these elements are grasped and truthfully idealized in whatever we as a people try to make. Although these elemental truths should be commonplace enough by now, as a people we do not understand them nor do we see the way to apply them. We are probably richer in raw materials for our use as workmen, citizens or artists than any other nation,—but outside mechanical genius for mere contrivance we are not good workmen, nor, beyond adventitious or propitious respect for property, are we as good citizens as we should be, nor are we artists at all. We are one and all, consciously or unconsciously, mastered by our fascinating automatic "implements," using them as substitutes for tools. To make this assertion clear I offer you evidence I have found in the field of Architecture. It is still a field in which the pulse of the age throbs beneath much shabby finery and one broad enough (God knows) to represent the errors and possibilities common to our time-serving Time.

Architects in the past have embodied the spirit common to their own life and to the life of the society in which they lived in the most noble of all noble records—Buildings. They wrought these valuable records with the primitive tools at their command and whatever these records have to say to us today would be utterly insignificant if not wholly illegible were tools suited to another and different conditions stupidly forced to work upon them; blindly compelled to do work to which they were not fitted, work which they could only spoil.

In this age of steel and steam the tools with which civilization's true record will be written are scientific thoughts made operative in iron and bronze and steel and in the plastic processes which characterize this age, all of which we call Machines. The Electric Lamp is in this sense a Machine. New materials in the man-Machines have made the physical body of this age what it is as distinguished from former ages. They have made our era the Machine Age—wherein locomotive engines, engines of industry, engines of light or engines of war or steamships take the place works of Art took in previous history. Today we have a Scientist or an Inventor in place of a Shakespeare or a Dante. Captains of Industry are modern substitutes, not only for Kings and Potentates, but, I am afraid, for great Artists as well. And yet—man-made environment is the truest, most characteristic of all human records. Let a man build and you have him. You may not have all he is, but certainly he is what you have. Usually you will have his outline. Though the elements may be in him to enable him to grow out of his present self-made characterization, few men are ever belied by self-made environment. Certainly no historical period was ever so misrepresented. Chicago in its ugliness today becomes as true an expression of the *life* lived here as is any center on earth where men come together closely to live it out or fight it out. Man is a selecting principle, gathering his like to him wherever he goes. The intensifying of his existence by close contact, too, flashes out the human record vividly in his background and his surroundings. But somewhere—somehow—in our age, although signs of the times are not wanting, beauty in this expression is forfeited—the record is illegible when not ignoble. We must walk blindfolded through the streets of this, or any great modern American city, to fail to see that all this magnificent resource of machine-power and superior material has brought to us, so far, is degradation. All of the Art forms sacred to The Art of Old are, by us, prostitute.

On every side we see evidence of inglorious quarrel between things as they were and things as they must be and are. This shame a certain merciful ignorance on our part mistakes for glorious achievement. We believe in our greatness when we have tossed up a Pantheon to the god of money in a night or two, like the Illinois Trust Building or the Chicago National Bank. And it is our glory to get together a mammoth aggregation of Roman monuments, sarcophagi and temples for a Post Office in a year or two. On Michigan Avenue Montgomery Ward presents us with a nondescript Florentine Palace with a grand campanile for a "Farmer Grocery" and it is as common with us as it is elsewhere to find the giant stone Palladian "orders" overhanging plate glass shop fronts. Show windows beneath Gothic office buildings, the office-middle topped by Parthenons, or models of any old sacrificial temple, are a common sight. Every commercial interest in any American town, in fact, is scurrying for respectability by seeking some advertising connection, at least, with the "Classic." A commercial Renaissance is here; the Renaissance of "the ass in the lion's skin." This much, at least, we owe to the late Columbian Fair—that triumph of modern civilization in 1893 will go down in American Architectural history, when it is properly recorded, as a mortgage upon posterity that posterity must repudiate not only as usurious but as forged.

In our so-called "Sky-Scrapers" (latest and most famous business-building triumph), good granite or Bedford stone is cut into the fashion of the Italian followers of Phidias and his Greek slaves. Blocks so cut are cunningly arranged about a structure of steel beams and shafts (which structure secretly robs them of any real meaning), in order to make the finished building resemble the architecture bepictured by Palladio and Vitruvius—in the schoolbooks. It is quite as feasible to begin putting on this Italian trimming at the cornice, and come on down to the base as it is to work, as the less fortunate Italians were forced to do, from the base upward. Yes, "from the top down" is often the actual method employed. The keystone of a Roman or Gothic arch may now be "set"—that is to say "hung"—and the voussoirs stuck alongside or "hung" on downward to the haunches. Finally this mask, completed, takes on the feature of the pure "Classic," or any variety of "Renaissance" or whatever catches the fancy or fixes the "convictions" of the designer. Most likely, an education in Art has "fixed" both. Our Chicago University, "a seat of learning," is just as far removed from truth. If environment is significant and indicative, what does this highly reactionary, extensive and expensive scene-painting by means of hybrid Collegiate Gothic signify? Because of Oxford it seems to be generally accepted as "appropriate for scholastic purposes." Yet, why should an American University in a land of Democratic ideals in a Machine Age be characterized by second-hand adaptation of Gothic forms, themselves adapted previously to our own adoption by a feudalistic age with tools to use and conditions to face totally different from anything we can call our own? The Public Library is again Asinine Renaissance, bones sticking through the flesh because the interior was planned by a shrewd Library Board—while an "Art-Architect" (the term is Chicago's, not mine) was "hired" to "put the architecture on it." The "classical" aspect of the sham-front must be preserved at any cost to sense. Nine out of ten public buildings in almost any American city are the same.

On Michigan Avenue, too, we pass another pretentious structure, this time fashioned as inculcated by the Ecole des Beaux Arts after the ideals and methods of a Graeco-Roman, inartistic, grandly brutal civilization, a civilization that borrowed everything but its jurisprudence. Its essential tool was the slave. Here at the top of our Culture is the Chicago Art Institute, and very like other Art Institutes. Between lions—realistic—Kemyss would have them so because Barye did—we come beneath some stone millinery into the grandly useless lobby. Here French's noble statue of the Republic confronts us—she too, Imperial. The grand introduction over, we go further on to find amid plaster casts of antiquity, earnest students patiently gleaning a half-acre or more of archaeological dry-bones, arming here for industrial conquest, in other words to go out and try to make a living by making some valuable impression upon the Machine Age in which they live. Their fundamental tool in this business about which they will know just this much less than nothing, is—the Machine. In this acre or more not one relic has any vital relation to things as they are for these students, except for the blessed circumstance that they are more or less beautiful things in themselves—bodying forth the beauty of "once upon a time." These students at best are to concoct from a study of the aspect of these blind reverences an extract of antiquity suited to modern needs, meanwhile knowing nothing of modern needs, permitted to care nothing for them, and knowing just as little of the needs of the ancients which made the objects they now study. The tyros are taught in the name of John Ruskin and William Morris to shun and despise the essential tool of their Age as a matter commercial and antagonistic to Art. So in time they go forth, each armed with his little Academic extract, applying it as a sticking-plaster from without, wherever it can be made to stick, many helplessly knowing in their hearts that it should be a development from within—but how? And this is an education in Art in these United States, A. D. 1901. Climb now the grand monumental stairway to see the results of this cultural effort—we call it "education"—hanging over the walls of the Exhibition Galleries. You will find there the same empty reverences to the past at cost to the present and of doubtful value to the future, unless a curse is valuable. Here you may see fruits of the lust and pride of the patron-collector but how shamefully little to show by way of encouraging patronage by the Artist of his own day and generation. This is a Temple of the Fine Arts. A sacred place! It should be the heart-center, the emotional inspiration of a great national industrial activity, but here we find Tradition not as an *inspiring* spirit animating progress. No. Now more in the *past* than ever! No more, now, than an ancient mummy, a dead letter. A "precedent" is a "hang over" to copy, the copy to be copied for Machine reproduction, to be shamelessly reproduced until demoralized utterly or unrecognizable.

More unfortunate, however, than all this fiasco, is the Fiasco al Fresco. The suburban house-parade is more servile still. Any popular avenue or suburb will show the polyglot encampment displaying, on the neatly kept little plots, a theatrical desire on the part of fairly respectable people to live in Chateaux, Manor Houses, Venetian Palaces, Feudal Castles, and Queen Anne Cottages. Many with sufficient hardihood abide in abortions of the Carpenter-Architect, our very own General Grant Gothic perhaps, intended to beat all the "lovely periods" at their own game and succeeding. Look within all this typical monotony-in variety and see there the machine-made copies of handicraft originals; in fact, unless you, the householder, are fortunate indeed, possessed of extraordinary taste and opportunity, all you possess is in some degree a machine-made example of vitiated handicraft, imitation antique furniture made antique by the Machine, itself of all abominations the most abominable. Everything must be curved and carved and carved and turned. The whole mass a tortured sprawl supposed artistic. And the floor-coverings? Probably machine-weavings of Oriental Rug patterns—pattern and texture mechanically perfect; or worse, your walls are papered with paper-imitations of old tapestry, imitation patterns and imitation textures, stamped or printed by the Machine; imitations under foot, imitations overhead and imitations all round about you. You are sunk in "Imitation." Your much-moulded woodwork is stained "antique." Inevitably you have a white-and-gold "reception-room" with a few gilded chairs, an overwrought piano, and withal, about you a general cheap machine-made "profusion" of—copies of copies of original imitations. To you, proud proprietors—do these things thus degraded mean anything aside from vogue and price? Aside from your sense of quantitative ownership, do you perceive in them some fine fitness in form, line and color to the purposes which they serve? Are the chairs to sit in, the tables to use, the couch comfortable, and are all harmoniously related to each other and to your own life? Do many of the furnishings or any of the window-millinery serve any purpose at all of which you can think? Do you enjoy in "things" the least appreciation of truth in beautiful guise? If not, you are a victim of habit, a habit evidence enough of the stagnation of an outgrown Art. Here we have the curse of stupidity—a cheap substitute for ancient Art and Craft which has no vital meaning in your own life or our time. You line the box you live in as a magpie lines its nest. You need not be ashamed to confess your ignorance of the meaning of all this, because not only you, but every one else, is hopelessly ignorant concerning it; it is "impossible." Imitations of imitations, copies of copies, cheap expedients, lack of integrity, some few blind gropings for simplicity to give hope to the picture. That is all.

Why wonder what has become of the grand spirit of Art that made, in times past, man's reflection in his environment a godlike thing. *This* is what has become of it! Of all conditions, this one at home is most deplorable, for to the homes of this country we must look for any beginning of the awakening of an artistic conscience which will change this parasitic condition to independent growth. The homes of the people will change before public buildings can possibly change.

Glance now for a moment behind this adventitious scene-painting passing, at home, for Art in the Nineteenth Century. Try to sense the true conditions underlying all, and which you betray and belie in the name of Culture. Study with me for a moment the engine which produces this wreckage and builds you, thus cheapened and ridiculous, into an ignoble record.

Here is this thing we call the Machine, contrary to the principle of organic growth, but imitating it, working irresistibly the will of Man through the medium of men. All of us are drawn helplessly into its mesh as we tread our daily round. And its offices—call them "services"—have become the commonplace background of modern existence; yes, and sad to say, in too many lives the foreground, middle distance and future. At best we ourselves are already become or are becoming some cooperative part in a vast machinery. It is, with us, as though we were controlled by some great crystallizing principle going on in Nature all around us and going on, in spite of ourselves, even in our very own *natures*. If you would see how interwoven it is, this thing we call the Machine, with the warp and the woof of civilization, if indeed it is not now the very basis of civilization itself, go at nightfall when all is simplified and made suggestive, to the top of our newest Skyscraper, the Masonic Temple. There you may see how in the image of material man, at once his glory and his menace, is this thing we call a City. Beneath you is the monster stretching out into the far distance. High overhead hangs a stagnant pall, its fetid breath reddened with light from myriad eyes endlessly, everywhere blinking. Thousands of acres of cellular tissue outspread, enmeshed by an intricate network of veins and arteries radiating into the gloom. Circulating there with muffled ominous roar is the ceaseless activity to whose necessities it all conforms. This wondrous tissue is knit and knit again and inter-knit with a nervous system, marvellously effective and complete, with delicate filaments for hearing and knowing the pulse of its own organism, acting intelligently upon the ligaments and tendons of motive impulse, and in it all is flowing the impelling electric fluid of man's own life. And the labored breathing, murmur, clangor, and the roar—how the voice of this monstrous force rises to proclaim the marvel of its structure! Near at hand, the ghastly warning boom from the deep throats of vessels heavily seeking inlet to the waterway below, answered by the echoing clangor of the bridge bells. A distant shriek grows nearer, more ominous, as the bells warn the living current from the swinging bridge and a vessel cuts for a moment the flow of the nearer artery. Closing then upon the great vessel's stately passage the double bridge is just in time to receive in a rush of steam the avalanche of blood and metal hurled across it;—a streak of light gone roaring into the night on glittering bands of steel; an avalanche encircled in its flight by slender magic lines, clicking faithfully from station to station—its nervous herald, its warning and its protection.

Nearer, in the building ablaze with midnight activity, a spotless paper band is streaming into the marvel of the multiple-press, receiving indelibly the impression of human hopes and fears, throbbing in the pulse of this great activity, as infallibly as the gray-matter of the human brain receives the impression of the senses. The impressions come forth as millions of neatly folded, perfected news-sheets, teeming with vivid appeals to good and evil passions;—weaving a web of intercommunication so far-reaching that distance becomes as nothing, the thought of one man in one corner of the earth on one day visible on the next to all men. The doings of all the world are reflected here as in a glass—so marvellously sensitive this simple band streaming endlessly from day to day becomes in the grasp of the multiple-press.

If the pulse of this great activity—automatons working night and day in every line of industry, to the power of which the tremor of the mammoth steel skeleton beneath your feet is but an awe-inspiring response—is thrilling, what of the prolific, silent obedience to man's will underlying it all? If this power must be uprooted that civilization may live, then civilization is already doomed. Remain to contemplate this wonder until the twinkling lights perish in groups, or follow one by one, leaving others to live through the gloom; fires are banked, tumult slowly dies to an echo here and there. Then the darkened pall is gradually lifted and moonlight outlines the shadowy, sullen masses of structure, structure deeply cut here and there by half-luminous channels. Huge patches of shadow in shade and darkness commingle mysteriously in the block-like plan with box-like skylines—contrasting strangely with the broad surface of the lake beside, placid and resplendent with a silver gleam. Remain, I say, to reflect that the texture of the city, this great Machine, is the warp upon which will be woven the woof and pattern of the Democracy we pray for. Realize that it has been deposited here, particle by particle, in blind obedience to law—Law no less organic so far as we are concerned than the laws of the great solar universe. That universe, too, in a sense, is but an obedient machine.

Magnificent power! And it confronts the young Architect and his Artist comrades now, with no other beauty—a lusty material giant without trace of ideality, absurdly disguised by garments long torn to tatters or contemptuously tossed aside, outgrown. Within our own recollection we have all been horrified at the bitter cost of this ruthless development—appalled to see this great power driven by Greed over the innocent and defenseless—we have seen bread snatched from the mouths of sober and industrious men, honorable occupations going to the wall with a riot, a feeble strike, or a stifled moan, outclassed, outdone, outlived by the Machine. The workman himself has come to regard this relentless force as his Nemesis and combines against machinery in the trades with a wild despair that dashes itself to pieces, while the Artist blissfully dreaming in the halls we have just visited or walking blindly abroad in the paths of the past, berates his own people for lack-luster senses, rails against industrial conditions that neither afford him his opportunity, nor, he says, can appreciate him as he, panderer to ill-gotten luxury, folding his hands, starves to death. "Innocuous martyr upon the cross of Art!" One by one, tens by tens, soon thousands by thousands, handicraftsmen and parasitic artists succumb to the inevitable as one man at a Machine does the work of from five to fifty men in the same time, with all the Art there is meanwhile prostituting to old methods and misunderstood ideals the far greater new possibilities due to this same Machine, and doing this disgracefully in the name of the Beautiful!

American Society has the essential tool of its own age by the blade, as lacerated hands everywhere testify!

See the magnificent prowess of this unqualified power—strewing our surroundings with the mangled corpses of a happier time. We live amid ghostly relics whose pattern once stood for cultivated luxury and now stands for an ignorant matter of taste. With no regard for first principles of common sense the letter of Tradition is recklessly fed into rapacious maws of machines until the reproduction, reproduced *ad nauseam,* may be had for five, ten or ninety-nine cents although the worthy original cost ages of toil and patient culture. This might seem like progress, were it not for the fact that these butchered forms, the life entirely gone out of them, are now harmful parasites, belittling and falsifying any true perception of normal beauty the Creator may have seen fit to implant in us on our own account. Any idea whatever of fitness to purpose or of harmony between form and use is gone from us. It is lacking in these things one and all, because it is so sadly lacking in us. And as for making the best of our own conditions or repudiating the terms on which this vulgar insult to Tradition is produced, thereby insuring and rectifying the industrial fabric thus wasted or enslaved by base imitation—the mere idea is abnormal, as I have found myself to my sorrow.

And among the Few, the favored chosen Few who love Art by nature and would devote their energies to it so that it may live and let them live—any training they can seek would still be a protest against the Machine as the Creator of all this iniquity, when (God knows) it is no more than the Creature.

But, I say, usurped by Greed and deserted by its natural interpreter, the Artist, the Machine is only the creature, not the Creator of this iniquity! I say the Machine has noble possibilities unwillingly forced to this degradation, degraded by the Arts themselves. Insofar as the true capacity of the Machine is concerned it is itself the crazed victim of Artist-impotence. Why will the American Artist not see that human thought in our age is stripping off its old form and donning another; why is the Artist unable to see that this is his glorious opportunity to create and reap anew?

But let us be practical—let us go now afield for evident instances of Machine abuse or abuse by the Machine. I will show you typical abuses that should serve to suggest to any mind, capable of thought, that the Machine is, to begin with, a marvellous simplifier in no merely negative sense. Come now, with me, and see examples which show that these craft-engines may be the modern emancipator of the creative mind. We may find them to be the regenerator of the creative conscience in our America, as well, so soon as a stultified "Culture" will allow them to be so used.

First—as perhaps wood is most available of home-building materials, naturally then the most abused—let us now glance at wood. Elaborate machinery has been invented for no other purpose than to imitate the wood-carving of early handicraft patterns. Result? No good joinery. None salable without some horrible glued-on botchwork meaning nothing, unless it means that "Art and Craft" (by salesmanship) has fixed in the minds of the masses the elaborate old hand-carved chair as ultimate ideal. The miserable tribute to this perversion yielded by Grand Rapids alone would mar the face of Art beyond repair, to say nothing of the weird or fussy joinery of spindles and jig-sawing, beamed, braced and elaborated to outdo in sentimentality the sentiment of some erstwhile overwrought "antique." The beauty of wood lies in its qualities as wood, strange as this may seem. Why does it take so much imagination—just to see that? Treatments that fail to bring out those qualities, foremost, are not *plastic,* therefore no longer appropriate. The inappropriate cannot be beautiful.

The Machine at work on wood will itself teach us—and we seem so far to have left it to the Machine to do so—that certain simple forms and handling serve to bring out the beauty of wood, and to retain its character, and that certain other forms and handling do not bring out its beauty, but spoil it. All wood-carving is apt to be a forcing of this material likely to destroy the finer possibilities of wood as we may know those possibilities now. In itself wood has beauty of marking, exquisite texture, and delicate nuances of color that carving is likely to destroy. The Machines used in woodwork will show that by unlimited power in cutting, shaping, smoothing, and by the tireless repeat, they have emancipated beauties of wood-nature, making possible, without waste, beautiful surface treatments and clean strong forms that veneers of Sheraton or Chippendale only hinted at with dire extravagance. Beauty unknown even to the Middle Ages. These machines have undoubtedly placed within reach of the designer a technique enabling him to realize the true nature of wood in his designs harmoniously with man's sense of beauty, satisfying his material needs with such economy as to put this beauty of wood in use within the reach of every one. But the advantages of the Machines are wasted and we suffer from a riot of aesthetic murder and everywhere live with debased handicraft.

Then, at random, let us take, say, the worker in marbles—his gang-saws, planers, pneumatic chisels and rubbing-beds have made it possible to reduce blocks ten feet long, six feet deep, and two feet thick to sheets or thin slabs an inch in thickness within a few hours, so it is now possible to use a precious material as ordinary wall covering. The slab may be turned and matched at the edges to develop exquisite pattern, emancipating hundreds of superficial feet of characteristic drawing in pure marble colors that formerly wasted in the heart of a great expensive block in the thickness of the wall. Here again a distinctly new architectural use may bring out a beauty of marbles consistent with Nature and impossible to handicraft. But what happens? The "Artist" persists in taking dishonest advantage of this practice, building up imitations of solid piers with moulded caps and bases, cunningly uniting the slabs at the edge until detection is difficult except to the trained eye. His method does not change to develop the beauty of a new technical possibility; no, the "Artist" is simply enabled to "fake" more architecture, make more piers and column shafts because he can now make them hollow! His architecture becomes no more worthy in itself than the cheap faker that he himself is, for his classical forms not only falsify the method which used to be and belie the method that is, but they cheat progress of its due. For convincing evidence see any Public Library or Art Institute, the Congressional Library at Washington, or the Boston Library.

In the stone-cutting trade the stone-planer has made it possible to cut upon stone any given moulded surface, or to ingrain upon that surface any lovely texture the cunning brain may devise, and do it as it never was possible to do it by hand. What is it doing? Giving us as near an imitation of hand tooth-chiselling as possible, imitating mouldings specially adapted to wood, making possible the lavish use of miles of meaningless moulded string courses, cornices, base courses —the giant power meanwhile sneered at by the "Artist" because it fails to render the wavering delicacy of "touch" resulting from the imperfections of hand-work.

No architect, this man! No—or he would excel that "antique" quality by the design of the contour of his sections, making a telling point of the very perfection he dreads, and so sensibly designing, for the prolific dexterity of the machine, work which it can do so well that hand-work would seem insufferably crude by comparison. The deadly facility this one machine has given "book architecture" is rivalled only by the facility given to it by galvanized iron itself. And if, incontinently, you will still have tracery in stone, you may arrive at acres of it now consistently with the economy of other features of this still fundamental "trade." You may try to imitate the hand-carving of the ancients in this matter, baffled by the craft and tenderness of the originals, or you may give the pneumatic chisel and power-plane suitable work to do which would mean a changed style, a shift in the spiritual center of the ideal now controlling the use of stone in constructing modern stone-buildings.

You will find in studying the group of ancient materials, wood and stone foremost among them, that they have all been rendered fit for *plastic* use by the Machine! The Machine itself steadily making available for economic use the very quality in these things now needed to satisfy its own art equation. Burned clay—we call it Terra Cotta—is another conspicuous instance of the advantage of the "process." Modern machines (and a process is a machine) have rendered this material as sensitive to the creative brain as a dry plate is to the lens of the camera. A marvellous simplifier, this material, rightly used. The artist is enabled to clothe the steel structure, now becoming characteristic of this era, with modestly beautiful, plastic robes instead of five or more different kinds of material now aggregated in confused features and parts, "composed" and supposedly picturesque, but really a species of cheap millinery to be mocked and warped by the sun, eventually beaten by wind and rain into a variegated heap of trash. But when these great possibilities of simplicity, the gift of the Machine, get to us by way of the Architect, we have only a base imitation of the hand-tooled blocks—pilaster-cap and base, voussoirs and carved spandrels of the laborious man-handled stonecrop of an ancient people's architecture!

The modern processes of casting in metal are modern machines too, approaching perfection, capable of perpetuating the imagery of the most vividly poetic mind without hindrance—putting permanence and grace within reach of every one, heretofore forced to sit supine with the Italians at their Belshazzar-feast of "Renaissance." Yes, without exaggeration, multitudes of processes, many new, more coming, await sympathetic interpretation, such as the galvano-plastic and its electrical brethren—a prolific horde, now cheap fakers imitating "real" bronzes and all manner of metallic antiques, secretly damning all of them in their vitals, if not openly giving them away. And there is electro-glazing, shunned because its straight lines in glasswork are too severely clean and delicate. Straight lines it seems are not so susceptible to the traditional designer's lack of touch. Stream lines and straight lines are to him severely unbeautiful. "Curved is the line of beauty"—says he! As though Nature would not know what to do with its own rectilinear!

The familiar lithograph, too, is the prince of an entire province of new reproductive but unproductive processes. Each and every one have their individualities and therefore have possibilities of their own. See what Whistler made and the Germans are making of the lithograph:—one note sounded in the gamut of its possibilities. But that note rings true to process as the sheen of the butterfly's wing to that wing. Yet, having fallen into disrepute, the most this particular "machine" did for us, until Whistler picked it up, was to give us the cheap imitative effects of painting, mostly for advertising purposes. This is the use made of machinery in the abuse of materials by men. And still more important than all we have yet discussed here is the new element entering industry in this material we call steel. The structural necessity which once shaped Parthenons, Pantheons, Cathedrals, is fast being reduced by the Machine to a skeleton of steel or its equivalent, complete in itself without the Artist-Craftsman's touch. They are now building Gothic Cathedrals in California upon a steel skeleton. Is it not easy to see that the myriad ways of satisfying ancient structural necessities known to us through the books as the art of building, vanish, become History? The mainspring of their physical existence now removed, their spiritual center has shifted and nothing remains but the impassive features of a dead face. Such is our "Classic" architecture.

For centuries this insensate or insane abuse of great opportunity in the name of Culture has made cleanly, strenthy and true simplicity impossible in Art or Architecture, whereas now we might reach the heights of creative Art. Rightly used the very curse Machinery puts upon handicraft should emancipate the artist from temptation to petty structural deceit and end this wearisome struggle to make things seem what they are not and can never be. Then the Machine itself, eventually, will satisfy the simple terms of its modern art equation as the ball of clay in the sculptor's hand yields to his desire—ending forever this nostalgic masquerade led by a stultified Culture in the name of Art.

Yes, although he does not know it, the Artist is now free to work his rational will with freedom unknown to structural tradition. Units of construction have enlarged, rhythms have been simplified and etherealized, space is more spacious and the sense of it may enter into every building, great or small. The architect is no longer hampered by the stone arch of the Romans or by the stone beam of the Greeks. Why then does he cling to the grammatical phrases of those ancient methods of construction when such phrases are in his modern work empty lies, and himself an inevitable liar as well.

Already, as we stand today, the Machine has weakened the artist to the point of destruction and antiquated the craftsman altogether. Earlier forms of Art are by abuse all but destroyed. The whole matter has been reduced to mere pose. Instead of joyful creation we have all around about us poisonous tastes—foolish attitudes. With some little of the flame of the old love, and creditable but pitiful enthusiasm, the young artist still keeps on working, making miserable mischief with lofty motives; perhaps, because his heart has not kept in touch or in sympathy with his scientific brother's head, being out of step with the forward marching of his own time.

Now, let us remember in forming this new Arts and Crafts Society at Hull House that every people has done its work, therefore evolved its art as an expression of its own life, using the best tools; and that means the most economic and effective tools or contrivances it knew: the tools most successful in saving valuable human effort. The chattel slave was the essential tool of Greek civilization, therefore of its Art. We have discarded this tool and would refuse the return of the Art of the Greeks were slavery the terms of its restoration, and slavery, in some form, would be the terms.

But in Grecian Art two flowers did find spiritual expression—the Acanthus and the Honeysuckle. In the Art of Egypt—similarly we see the Papyrus, the Lotus. In Japan the Chrysanthemum and many other flowers. The Art of the Occident has made no such sympathetic interpretation since that time, with due credit given to the English Rose and the French Fleur-de-Lys, and as things are now the West may never make one. But to get from some native plant an expression of its native character in terms of imperishable stone to be fitted perfectly to its place in structure, and without loss of vital significance, is one great phase of great Art. It means that Greek or Egyptian found a revelation of the inmost life and character of the Lotus and Acanthus in terms of Lotus or Acanthus Life. That was what happened when the Art of these people had done with the plants they most loved. This imaginative process is known only to the creative Artist. Conventionalization, it is called. Really it is the dramatizing of an object—truest "drama." To enlarge upon this simple figure, as an Artist, it seems to me that this complex matter of civilization is itself at bottom some such conventionalizing process, or must be so to be successful and endure.

Just as any Artist-Craftsman, wishing to use a beloved flower for the stone capital of a column-shaft in his building must conventionalize the flower, that is, find the pattern of its life-principle in terms of stone as a material before he can rightly use it as a beautiful factor in his building, so education must take the natural man, to "civilize" him. And this great new power of the dangerous Machine we must learn to understand and then learn to use as this valuable "*conventionalizing*" agent. But in the construction of a society as in the construction of a great building, the elemental conventionalizing process is dangerous, for without the inspiration or inner light of the true Artist—the quality of the flower—its very life—is lost, leaving a withered husk in the place of living expression.

Therefore, Society, in this conventionalizing process or Culture, has a task even more dangerous than has the Architect in creating his building forms, because instead of having a plant-leaf and a fixed material as ancient architecture had, we have a sentient man with a fluid soul. So without the inner light of a sound philosophy of Art (the Educator too, must now be Artist), the life of the man will be sacrificed and Society gain an automaton or a machine-made moron instead of a noble creative Citizen!

If education is doomed to fail in this process, utterly—then the man slips back to rudimentary animalism or goes on into decay. Society degenerates or has a mere realistic creature instead of the idealistic creator needed. The world will have to record more "great dead cities."

To keep the Artist-figure of the flower *dramatized for human purposes*—the Socialist would bow his neck in altruistic submission to the "Harmonious" whole; his conventionalization or dramatization of the human being would be like a poor stone-craftsman's attempt to conventionalize the beloved plant with the living character of leaf and flower left out. The Anarchist would pluck the flower as it grows and use it as it is for what it is—with essential reality left out.

The Hereditary Aristocrat has always justified his existence by his ability, owing to fortunate propinquity, to appropriate the flower to his own uses after the craftsman has given it life and character, and has kept the craftsman too by promising him his flower back if he behaves himself well. The Plutocrat does virtually the same thing by means of "interests." But the true Democrat will take the human plant as it grows and—in the spirit of using the means at hand to put life into his conventionalization—preserve the individuality of the plant to protect the flower, which is its very life, getting from both a living expression of essential man-character fitted perfectly to a place in Society with no loss of vital significance. Fine Art is this flower of the Man. When Education has become creative and Art again prophetic of the natural means by which we are to grow—we call it "progress"—we will, by means of the Creative Artist, possess this monstrous tool of our civilization as it now possesses us.

Grasp and use the power of scientific automatons in this *creative sense*, and their terrible forces are not antagonistic to any fine individualistic quality in man. He will find their collective mechanistic forces capable of bringing to the individual a more adequate life, and the outward expression of the inner man as seen in his environment will be genuine revelation of his inner life and higher purpose. Not until then will America be free!

This new American Liberty is of the sort that declares man free only when he has found his work and effective means to achieve a life of his own. The means once found, he will find his due place. The man of our country will thus make his own way, and *grow* to the natural place thus due him, promised—yes, promised by our charter, the Declaration of Independence. But this place of his is not to be made over to fit him by reform, nor shall it be brought down to him by concession, but will become his by his own use of the means at hand. He must *himself* build a new world. The day of the individual is not over—instead, it is just about to begin. The Machine does not write the doom of Liberty, but is waiting at man's hand as a peerless tool, for him to use to put foundations beneath a genuine Democracy. Then the Machine may conquer human drudgery to some purpose, taking it upon itself to broaden, lengthen, strengthen and deepen the life of the simplest man. What limits do we dare imagine to an Art that is organic fruit of an adequate life for the individual! Although this power is now murderous, chained to botchwork and bunglers' ambitions, the creative Artist will take it surely into his hand and, in the name of Liberty, swiftly undo the deadly mischief it has created.

From: *Modern Architecture* (Kahn Lectures for 1930) by Frank Lloyd Wright. Princeton: 1931, pages 7–23. (This is Wright's famous lecture originally delivered at Hull House, Chicago, in 1901.)

Craftsmen: Machines: Speed

by

Frederick Lee Ackerman

Plans were on the boards for a vast amount of construction—the tallest office building, the largest hotel, the largest apartment house, the largest factory, and in Greater New York, a flood of tax exemption dwellings. Subways were in prospect, greater in length than the systems already bursting with traffic. The largest tunnel was under construction; more were in prospect. Across the Hudson was to be thrown a colossal bridge requiring twice as much steel as went into the making of the five great spans across the East River. So ran the year end (1922) summaries of events and forecasts of events to come in the world of building.

But shot through these summaries of events and forecasts were qualifying references to probable "labor troubles." Without exception writers referred to a seemingly new factor in the case; a "shortage" of skilled handicraft workmen hung like a cloud obscuring all but the bare forecasts of events to come. So some space was devoted to the prospect of developing the "open shop" and to what was being said and done toward the training of apprentices sufficiently skilled to carry on this work. The training of apprentices was a hopeful sign. But it would take time; and the number that could be so trained appeared pitifully small when set in relation to the number required to do the work in prospect. Altogether the shortage of handicraft workmen, upon whose knowledge and skill hung the erection of all these great projects, loomed as large among the events to come as did the projects themselves.

But what, precisely, had the writers in mind when they used the current term "shortage"? Has there been a falling away in the number of building trades handicraft workmen in relation to the population? Have potential handicraft building trades workmen, by reason of the long period of training required and the seasonal nature of employment in the building trades, gone into factories; have they become clerks, salesmen and chauffeurs? Has Europe ceased to pour in upon us a fresh supply of craftsmen already trained, as has been the case during the last half century? If such was the meaning which the writers attached to the term "shortage," it would have but partially covered the case.

For "shortage" has come to cover more than an actual falling away of numbers in the handicraft trades—more than a relative falling away of numbers in relation to population. Building operations, for example, which but a short time ago would have been viewed as creditable industrial performances within a span of eighteen months are now as a matter of course scheduled for completion within twelve, ten, eight or even six months' time. That is to say, the increasing demand for an ever more rapid turnover of funds involved in building, as expressed in the diminishing length of time assigned to the work of erection, is alone sufficient to turn a "normal" supply of building trades workmen into a "shortage."

The erection of buildings in the field goes on by the handicraft process, the pace of which is set by the workman and his tools. Some gains in productivity have taken effect here and there in the processes of erection since the introduction of the machine and mechanical power. But the methods and processes involved in the erection of small structures, which as yet, constitute the bulk of building, have hardly been touched by science, modern mechanical invention, the use of mechanical power or the process of quantity production. The work of the mason, the carpenter, the lather, the plasterer, the roofer, the tile setter, the painter and much of the work performed by "common labor" is carried on in the same (industrial) manner as was the case before the introduction of the machine. It is not to be denied that many of the materials used in building arrive at the job in a more nearly finished state than formerly. But in the case of such materials and forms much of the work of assembling is done by handicraft workmen at the plant. Many new devices—largely the product of machine industry—are now deemed necessary in the finished building. But the use of these devices adds to the handicraft work involved in erection. So that, after due allowance has been made for the use of machines, mechanical power and the process of quantity production now involved in building erection, it remains approximately true that the erection of buildings is carried on at the pace of handicraft industry. The erection of buildings in the field is, after all, hand work.

But production as a whole is now carried on by the machine process, the pace of which is given by the machine driven by mechanical power. The machine process is inordinately productive and its productivity is an ever expanding function of scientific research, mechanical invention and the matter of fact engineering point of view with respect to the use of material resources and knowledge. So that the quota of handicraft workmen capable of keeping pace with the machine and the process of quantity production, or the number capable of using the products of the mechanical industries producing the materials which handicraft workmen turn into buildings should be a varying and an ever expanding number.[1]

Contrast, for example, the fabrication of cotton goods with the erection of buildings. Mechanical industry has increased the rate of producing materials and forms preparatory to the erection of buildings. But it has not materially increased the per-man speed of erection, whereas the introduction of the machine revolutionized the fabrication of cotton and increased the speed of production many fold. Again, contrast agricultural production as it is carried on throughout the West. At no point has the erection of buildings been touched by such a revolutionary change as took place when the machine process, through the production of harvesting machinery, sent to the discard the hoe, the scythe, the cradle and the flail. In contrast with the fabrication of cotton and the production of the basic agricultural products the erection of buildings belongs to an older—a slower order of industry.

The same factors which have operated to reduce the space of time consumed in the erection of buildings—that is to say, increase the speed of erection—have operated also to increase the speed of their obsolescence. A very large percentage of the structures erected within our rapidly expanding cities serve in the first instance as a medium for the turnover of funds. This turnover of funds takes place through sale of the property following close upon the erection of the structure

[1] No doubt objection will be offered to this broad statement; it will be pointed out that there is now a shortage of machine-made building materials and supplies. But there is slight ground for assuming that the shortage of materials is due to any lack of industrial capacity. It would seem to be a function of pecuniary management and control.

or it takes place after the building has served its purpose for some time as an investment, or for paying taxes upon the land, while the land appreciates in value sufficiently to warrant the destruction of the building. In the typical case several structures of ascending value in turn occupy a plot of land before the cost of the structure reaches a point where it no longer appears likely that further appreciation of the land will exceed the cost of the last structure to be erected upon it.[2]

[2] In less than five years following completion, the hot water supply lines in the office building where I do my work had been renewed. In the apartment house where I live the work of replacing hot and cold water lines began eight years following completion. I am told by plumbing contractors that the latter case is fairly typical of structures in New York built within the last quarter century.

Now, it takes a larger number of plumbers to reinstall than it does to do the work in the first instance. Some say twice as much labor is involved. So that it follows that we shall require in New York, for some time to come, a multiple of that number which would now be required had a policy of durable building been in force when all of these up-to-date, modern structures were erected.

It is stated that the home owners of the country spend well over half a billion dollars annually in the repair and renewal of rusted metal work, and that the greater volume of this work could be avoided through the use in the first instance of more durable material. After making due allowance for the volume of repairs and renewals which would attend the use of the most durable materials and for the cost of the materials used in such work, there still remains a large percentage of this half billion which represents nothing but waste—waste of money, materials and waste of handicraft labor.

Some idea of the magnitude and velocity already reached in the process of demolition and replacement in Manhattan may be gained from a tabulation by S. W. Straus & Co., appearing in the New York *Times* of May 17, from which the following is quoted: "Every year the equivalent of a city of 500 buildings is demolished on Manhattan Island, and every year a similar city of most imposing types of construction rises to replace the city that has disappeared."

An extract from the tabulation discloses the following figures:

	Buildings Completed				Buildings Demolished			
Year	Total	Dwellings	Tenements	Hotels, etc.	Total	Dwellings	Tenements	Hotels, etc.
1913	581	26	160	8	750	341	194	4
1914	432	35	119	13	657	304	255	40
1915	348	26	133	9	584	325	98	132
1916	316	17	145	8	654	307	90	1
1917	345	8	85	7	261	39	37	0
1918	195	7	20	3	373	110	44	4
1919	166	4	5	6	687	154	81	5
1920	253	4	26	8	679	284	111	4
1921	433	63	31	7	457	129	128	2
1922	540	45	102	9	634	249	220	3
Total ten years	3,609	235	926	78	5,736	2,242	1,258	165

So that as it works out in the typical case, a premium is placed upon the erection of low cost structures, which is the same as saying under the current interpretation, non-durable structures. From the production of non-durable structures it follows as an unavoidable consequence that repairing, renewing and demolishing, and the replacement of old structures by new must be carried on at such an increased rate as to volume and speed as durability diminishes, or as the speed of obsolescence increases from the above or from other well known causes which need not be discussed here.

This bears directly upon the point in question in that repairing, renewing, demolition and the erection of replacements is done by handicraftsmen; and increased speed in the field of handicraft production is to be had only through the use of additional handicraft workmen.

If for good and sufficient business reasons we elect to use non-durable elements in our buildings in place of elements whose life span is a century or more, then it follows that the quota of handicraft workmen involved in the use of such materials must be increased by a multiple which corresponds to the relatively shorter life of the non-durable element. The significance of this may be readily seen when we note that the relative life of two materials which may be used for a given purpose in building may be expressed by the ratio of one to ten. Or if for what may be gained from a rapid appreciation of land values we elect to diminish the life of the structures we build, it again follows that the quota of handicraft workmen must be augmented in the proportion that we shorten the life of our structures generally. So that, strange as it may seem, out of the increasing speed of decay, the speed of obsolescence, and the extent to which demolition is carried on for purposes of profit, there arises in this era of credit economy and machine production the need for a quota of handicraft workmen not merely actually larger, but relatively larger than was needed during the days of slow moving, handicraft industry when men built with their hands and a few tools all that was built.

A "shortage" of handicraft workmen in the building trades, it would therefore seem, is not to be passed over lightly as a mal-adjustment which may be readily overcome by open shop methods of employment or by more adequate provision for their training. For it is not likely that the potential productivity of the machine process will remain stationary. Viewed from the standpoint of technology the productivity of the machine process is due to increase many fold. And one may safely predict not only a demand for single building operations of ever increasing magnitude, but a demand for even greater speed of erection. Evidently we have now reached a phase, in the development of our industrial system, where we must take account of the fact that it is composed of a great number of closely related and interdependent industrial units and that these units group themselves in two widely differing categories with respect to method and productivity. The modern industrial system is part handicraft and part mechanical.

This observation is highly significant when viewed solely as an industrial fact. But it takes on added significance when account is taken of the condition that modern industry is carried on by the rule of credit economy—investment for a profit. Industrial activity is now organized around the prospect of remunerative turnover of funds. Hence the rate of productivity—the speed—of the mechanical industries sets the pace at which it appears desirable—nay, necessary to carry on the erection of buildings.

But the erection of buildings does not as yet lend itself to the machine process nor to the methods of quantity production as that term has come to be understood. For the most part, it is a handicraft process. From which it follows that, in so far as the handicraft industries of building are essential to the operation of the industrial system as a whole, to that extent the productivity of handicraft industry limits the pace.

Certainly, far reaching consequences should be due to follow in train upon the development of such a condition—an industrial system, two great and vital parts of which run at two widely differing rates of productivity.[3] One would expect, for example, to find a differential accorded that element which of a necessity produces at the lower rate of speed in order to induce a greater number to enter that field. Thus might one interpret the many forms of housing subsidies which were resorted to so generally throughout the Western World in the decade or so before the war; or even our more recent tax exemption of dwellings in the State of New York. Not that such an interpretation is to be taken as a complete genetic account of the rise of the housing problem: it recognizes, rather, a causal factor of first magnitude in the action of so generally subsidizing the building industry as against other industries which produce necessities. It was a way of

[3] The productivity of the various industries is here conceived in relation to the productivity of the untrained human unit involved, which is used as the base of reference.

speeding up—of increasing the rate of productivity of that element of the industrial system which had fallen behind.

Under such an industrial system the employers of handicraft workmen should go to the greatest pains to develop and maintain a condition of impotence among those whom they employ. For only under a thoroughly coercive system of employment would it seem possible to maintain control over workmen who had fallen heir to a condition wherein their numbers automatically constituted a "shortage" whenever the industrial system began to pick up speed or to produce at the rate demanded by the use of credit and as set by the potential productivity of the basic mechanical industries. In the same way the industries which stand over as handicraft should constitute the weakest point in the line that offers resistance against the demands which workmen now and again see fit to make in their own behalf. By and large, the center of labor disturbances and the maximum gains secured by labor lie within the frontiers of handicraft industry.

It is true, the common stock of knowledge and the skill upon which turn the productivity of the modern industrial system is no longer borne by the handicraft workmen as was approximately the case during the early stages of the era of handicraft. But this is also true with respect to all the other groups that likewise constitute the productive units of the modern industrial system.

The position, but not the importance, of the handicraft workman has undergone a change. He no longer serves as the central figure in the industrial system as a whole. But he retains his position as the central figure in many great sectors of the system where his knowledge and his skill are quite as indispensable as is the technological knowledge of the scientist and the engineer.

The length of time required of the handicraft workman in order that he may learn to do his work competently differs but slightly from that required of the scientist and the engineer. This is not to say that the periods of training in the case of the handicraft workman, the scientist and the engineer, all come to a close within the same space of time. It is to remark that in so far as touches the run of handicraft workmen and the run of engineers and scientists, a period of from four to six years is . . . deemed necessary to fit them to function. . . .

This similarity with respect to the length of time required in preparation and with respect to the importance of training has evidently been overlooked in the case of the handicraft workman. For ever greater stress has been laid upon the training of the engineer and the scientist, while the training of the handicraft workman has been left to chance where real obstacles have not been set in the way. These two contrasting attitudes toward the training of those who make up the productive factors serve but to increase the already widening discrepancy as between the productivity of handicraft and machine industry in that the abilities of the scientist and the engineer are very largely drawn upon to increase the speed or the productivity of the latter.

The handicraft workman in essential industries—particularly in the building industry—now occupies a peculiar position in that any technological advance in machine design or any attempt to launch building operations of still greater magnitude, or any attempt to bring such operations to completion within a still shorter space of time or the more general use of non-durable materials or the more rapid obsolescence of buildings brought about by whatever cause, automatically pushes the handicraft workmen over into a position where their numbers appear insufficient to do the work.

What is apparently in store, barring more effective retardation of the productive processes of industry through the operation of the price system, is the granting of price differentials to the handicraft industries or to such mechanical industries as depend largely upon handicraft work to complete the process. Such price differentials, in the case of labor, must be sufficient to overcome the handicap of the years of training required of the handicraft workman as against the days, weeks or at most months required of those who perform the run of operations in mechanical industry. They also must cover the handicap of seasonal work and work subject to weather, as against continuous employment in an industrial plant. There is the further handicap of the relatively lower status; handicraft work is rated as more or less degrading.

Beyond these factors are those which touch the handicraft industries as a whole and point to the granting of further differentials. Any increase in productivity of mechanical industry, due to the application of scientific knowledge, which would indicate the possibility of a more rapid turnover of funds in the processes of production or in the use of the product—any greater gains to be had from investment—any more general use of non-durable materials, any increase in the speed at which the process of obsolescence takes place in buildings by reason of the materials out of which they are built or by reason of appreciation of land values due to congestion—any of these make for the need of more handicraft workmen which again points to the necessity of granting a further price differential.

It is to run counter to a well established opinion to suggest that the handicraft workman of the machine era still holds a position similar in point of strategic value, to that which he held during the era when production was a matter of handicraft only. But to the extent that business ends are served, to the extent that the modern community needs what he produces out of his knowledge and skill, to that extent the modern handicraft workman stands secure in that position which he gained during the era of handicraft.

It has been assumed that the handicraft workman, carrying an indispensable body of knowledge and skill without which buildings could not be erected and many of the processes of machine industry carried on, might be dealt with according to the latest businesslike formula of "handling labor"—that his labor might be classified as a commodity. But by treating labor as a commodity it becomes subject to the rules of purchase and sale as formulated by business traffic. In a business situation, such as constitutes our own time, such a classification, under the circumstances referred to, has its distinct advantages from the standpoint of the handicraft workman. For it follows under such a classification of his abilities that he is thrown into a position of possessing something which may be readily advanced in price under conditions of shortage; and the economic factors involved make directly for such a condition in the ordinary run of events.

To deal with such constantly recurring conditions of shortage of skilled handicraft workmen as are due to arise out of the businesslike management of production, plans will be laid to prevent an undue increase in wages. Recourse will be had to whatever gives promise of weakening the force of organization. Facilities will be developed for training apprentices and some attempts will be made to smooth out the employment curse. The use of loan credit with respect to building will be curtailed whenever a check upon building promises a reduction in wages. And a general curtailment of building all 'round will no doubt be suggested. The cost to the community at large of these various measures will not be rated as too high a price to pay for the power which such measures will give the business community over organized labor. A general curtailment of building operations will then be organized and the partial curtailment of building activities will be hailed as a "solution."

But it will be a "solution" only in the sense that it will reduce the item of wages in the cost of building. It will be the reverse of a solution in that it will operate to increase the discrepancy as between the supply of buildings and the number of buildings needed. But even in the face of so obvious a fact, such a move will appeal to "enlightened common sense" as the only satisfactory way of dealing with the problem. Which all goes to show how far the price system has run in shaping our point of view and in controlling our action. Tangible performance need no longer appear among the items of evidence which go to make up the account of work well done.

From: *Craftsmen—Machines—Credit—Speed*, by Frederick Lee Ackerman. "The Journal of the American Institute of Architects," June 1923, pages 249–252.

Machinery and the Modern Style

by

Lewis Mumford

It has taken our architects and interior decorators a long time to realize that there is a modern style in building, as well as a classic and mediaeval style. By far the greater number of edifices that have been put up within the last hundred years have been patterned in a mold with which neither the current materials nor the methods of workmanship have had very much to do. There have been, it is true, such grand monstrosities as the Crystal Palace, whose architectural significance has not, I believe, been fully appreciated: but the Crystal Palace is the frozen bud of a plant that has hardly had the opportunity to flower. The modern building has not dared to be itself. Our early skyscrapers, for example, were not designed on the assumption that skeletons of steel could reach higher into the air than buildings had ever before reached: they were constructed on the theory that a tall building was a solid column, and that it must therefore have a base, a shaft, and a capital. As a result of this stuffy misconception years passed before the extravagant aspirations that steel had made possible were even faintly realized in the Woolworth and Bush Towers.

The outcome of the failure to develop a modern style is that the contemporary city has the air of a ransacked museum, with all its various rooms and periods placed on exhibition. Up to the present all that we can call a modern style consists of misappropriated fragments

Old Grand Central Depot, New York. *Courtesy, The J. Clarence Davies Collection, The Museum of the City of New York.*

The Brooklyn Bridge by John A. Roebling and Washington A. Roebling.

Pavillon de l'Esprit Nouveau, Internation Exposition of Decorative Art; Paris, France. Le Corbusier and P. Jeanneret, architects. ***Courtesy, The Museum of Modern Art, New York.***

Home Insurance Building, Chicago, Illinois. William Le Baron Jenney, architect. ***Courtesy, Chicago Historical Society.***

of antiquity. What our contemporary buildings represent of modern life is its encyclopaedic acquaintance with the past: what they fail bravely to exhibit are the characteristic achievements of technology by which our daily activities have been molded into a hundred new patterns. Quite frequently the incongruity between our architectural "styles" and our secular habits is so flagrant as to constitute an aesthetic misdemeanor. Perhaps the best examples of ineptitude are the water fountains in the New York Public Library: from the mouth of the conventional marble lion there spouts, not water, alas! but a patented, sanitary drinking device with a hard nickeled surface. That is the sort of hole in which a classically trained architect finds himself when he begins to fill up his Greek and Roman frame with apparatus designed to meet strictly modern requirements. Without any hope of persuading the community to live a Roman life, he attempts to make the community live in a Roman building.

Yet, although our more ostentatious architecture has not developed a modern style, a fresh tradition has been stealing in upon us, like the proverbial thief in the night. In the fulfillment of some peculiarly contemporary purpose the modern style has here and there been introduced; and since the difficulty of creating a new structure is not so great when the functions it performs are themselves new, there is nothing strange in the fact that the two main sources of the modern style at present are the subways and the cheap popular lunchrooms. Because our subways and lunchrooms have been constructed with as strict an eye to ways and means and ends as a mediaeval guild hall or a Roman amphitheatre, these modern structures have come increasingly to possess that intelligibility of purpose and that integrity of execution which mark what can properly be called a "style."

There is, indeed, perhaps finer promise of a living art behind one of those white-rimmed glass fronts, where white-winged chefs pour white batter upon an immaculate griddle, than there is, for example, in the Cathedral of St. John the Divine, which it has taken so much labor and reconsideration to build. This will very likely seem a malicious paradox to those who fancy that "style" is nothing more than a pleasing superfluity that can be added to or withdrawn from a work of utilitarian art at will—like a sheet of veneer. Those who appreciate the sociological insight of Ruskin and Morris, however, believe that a "style" is fundamentally the outcome of a way of living, that it ramifiies through all the activities of a community, and that it is the reasoned expression, in some particular work, of the complex of social and technological experience that grows out of a community's life. From this latter point of view a Child's restaurant is nearer to the source of a contemporary style than a building by Stanford White or Ralph Cram.

Let me disarm criticism by confessing that we are only at the beginning of a modern style, and that the beginning is crude. Lured into the void of a modern lunchroom by the vision of thick disks of golden batter basking on the griddle, one is struck immediately upon entrance by a cacophonous chorus of china and metal. From the polished tiles of the white interior comes a frigid glare, and it is difficult not to associate this surgical immaculacy with that of a ward in the better sort of hospital. The cleanliness is, in fact, blatant: the restaurant is like a soap which not merely removes the dirt efficiently but adds a gratuitous odor of antiseptics by which, as it were, to call attention to its performance. These defects of overstatement have discredited the modern style; they have drawn attention away from the fact that there *is* a style. Yet here is an equipment, harmonious in almost every detail, which could not possibly have exhibited itself in the world before 1880. If one looks carefully at the floors, the cutlery, the tables, the chairs, and the rest of the fixtures one discovers that there is not an object in the place which is not a machine product. What does that mean? Cheapness, standardization, monotony, ugliness one is perhaps tempted at first to answer; but this is by no means all.

Of its kind every article in the modern lunchroom is excellent, and its excellence is due to the fact that it has been made by a machine, and that it exhibits the accuracy, the fine finish, and the unerring fidelity to design which makes machine work delightful to everyone who knows how to take pleasure in geometrical perfection. If there are no surprises in a modern scheme of decoration and equipment there are likewise no disappointments. The whole structure is as neat, as chaste, and as inevitable as a demonstration in Euclid. There is no messiness, no "more-or-less" in the economy of the machine: once it has achieved a certain level of workmanship it can remain there, if the materials hold out, forever. Other ages have recorded great achievements in manufacture; but it has remained for the modern age to attain a hair's breadth perfection. We do not readily complain of monotony when an object is genuinely perfect. It is only an imperfect form that makes us long for a change, or, as we pregnantly say, an alteration. One can wander for hours through a forest of beeches, each tree a lean pole reaching up into a green vault, without the slightest sense of monotony; whereas one cannot walk for five minutes through the by-streets of a Philadelphia or a London suburb without wishing to destroy the mechanical sameness of the ugly little hutches the jerry-builder has erected. It is not the monotony of a machine product that hurts, but some manifest inadequacy to human uses.

Now the test of a living style is its ability to beget new forms and fresh variations. The imitative "period" decorations that are made by machine in a Grand Rapids furniture factory fall within limits that are defined by the patterns which have survived from other ages: they are as incapable of yielding fresh designs as a mummy is of begetting a family. One of the things that should cause us to be hopeful about the naïve modern style is that it is already undergoing improvements: the Bronx subway extension in New York is as great an advance over the old-fashioned system, aesthetically, as the first American subways were over the Picadilly tube. In the restaurants a similar development has been going on. Recently a couple of lunchrooms were opened on Fifth Avenue whose scheme of decoration has retained the fine congruity with the machinery of cooking and service that marks a genuine style, and at the same time has a mellowness and a refinement which brings a grateful relief from the jangling whiteness of the earlier regime. These new restaurants are as good, on their scale, as the trainhall of the Pennsylvania Station in New York, and they are good in the same way—they perform a necessary purpose with urbanity, distinction and grace. In them the modern style has reached a maturer development through which the logic of the machine is reconciled with the decent aesthetic requirements of humanity.

How is it that the modern style has been so slow to realize itself—is still so timid, so partial, so inadequate? Is its crudity not due to the fact that our architects have thought that true art lay elsewhere, in Greek temples and Roman baths and Adam residences and what not, and so they have not given the lunchroom and the subway station the degree of passionate attention which would make them perfect in design as well as in execution? This "division in the records of the mind" accounts, I believe, for the peculiar barrenness and frigidity of the early machine style: its vices were due not to the presence of machine work but to the absence of a vivifying human imagination.

Up to the present the machine style has fallen short of its possibilities largely for two reasons. In the early part of the industrial period the designer attempted to qualify the mechanical rigidity of his materials by introducing forms which were antipathetic to the functions which they performed. The iron cornucopias and flowers that Ruskin railed at, for example, typify this weak attempt to mollify the machine; and the flowery decorations that one can still see on some old model of the typewriter arose out of the same fallacy. The second reason for its frustration was that when the designer paid due attention to mechanical efficiency, he neglected to carry out those final developments of form and material which—so far from being vague excrescences, like ferrous foliage—were essential to their human enjoyment beyond the mean requirements of use.

To create designs that will respect the logic of the machine and at the same time have regard for the vagaries of human psychology is the problem whose solution will give us a satisfactory, genuine modern style. We have yet to see what humane fulfillments the machine may bring about when we finally come to grips with it, and neither allow ourselves to be overridden by a crude and boisterous utilitarianism nor turn a repugnant, ineffectual face completely away from the instrument which promises—at least promises!—to liberate the community.

From: *The New Republic,* by Lewis Mumford. New York: August 3, 1921, pages 263–265.

The Balloon Frame and Industrialization

by

Sigfried Giedion

The balloon frame is closely connected with the level of industrialization which had been reached in America. Its invention practically converted building in wood from a complicated craft, practiced by skilled labor, into an industry.

The principle of the balloon frame involves the substitution of thin plates and studs—running the entire height of the building and held together only by nails—for the ancient and expensive method of construction with mortised and tenoned joints. To put together a house like a box, using only nails—this must have seemed utterly revolutionary to carpenters. Naturally enough, the balloon frame met with attack at the start: "The Balloon Frame has passed through and survived the theory, ridicule, and abuse of all who have seen fit to attack it. . . . Its name was given in contempt by those old fogy mechanics who had been brought up to rob a stick of timber of all its strength and durability, by cutting it full of mortices, tenons and auger holes, and then supposing it to be stronger than a far lighter stick differently applied, and with all its capabilities unimpaired. . . . The name of 'Basket Frame' would convey a better impression, but the name 'Balloon' has long ago outlived the derision which suggested it."

The balloon frame marks the point at which industrialization began to penetrate housing. Just as the trades of the watchmaker, the butcher, the baker, the tailor were transformed into industries, so too the balloon frame led to the replacement of the skilled carpenter by the unskilled laborer.

"A man and a boy can now (1865) attain the same results, with ease, that twenty men could on an old-fashioned frame. . . . "The principle of Balloon Framing is the true one for strength, as well as for economy. If a mechanic is employed, the Balloon Frame can be put up *for forty per cent less money* than the mortice and tenon frame."

"Without machine-made nails the balloon frame would be economic nonsense. It was only when machinery had made nails cheaper, and "cut nails of steel and iron and nails made of wire could be furnished of excellent quality and at a cost much less than old-fashioned wrought-iron nails (that) the comparatively expensive system of house framing with mortise and tenon began to be supplanted by a more economic system dependent entirely upon the efficacy of nailing."

The invention of the balloon frame really coincides with the improvement of sawmill machinery as well as with the mass production of nails.

Several machines for cutting and heading nails were developed in both England and the United States toward the end of the eighteenth century. Thomas Clifford patented such a device in 1790, and about the same time a similar machine was invented by Jacob Perkins of Newburyport. A machine which cut, shaped, and headed tacks in a single operation at the rate of sixty thousand a day was patented by Jesse Reed in 1807.

"When the manufacture of cut nails was first undertaken, wrought nails cost 25 cents a pound. . . . This made their use for houses and fences difficult." All this changed with the introduction of machinery. The price of nails was suddenly reduced. "In 1828 the production was so brisk that the price was reduced to 8 cents a pound. . . . In 1833 the rapidity of production had brought prices down to 5 cents . . . in 1842, 3 cents. . . ."

The balloon frame has an established connection with the conquest of the West from Chicago to the Pacific Coast.

Contemporaries knew quite well that houses would never have sprung up with such incredible rapidity—either on the prairies or within the big cities—had it not been for this construction.

"With the application of machinery, the labor of house building has been greatly lessened, and the western prairies are dotted over with houses which have been *shipped there all made*, and the various pieces numbered." Another observer goes further: "If it had not been for the knowledge of the balloon-frame, Chicago and San Francisco could never have arisen, as they did, from little villages to great cities in a single year."

At the period when the West was being built up, contemporaries called "the method of construction known as 'balloon framing' the most important contribution to our domestic architecture."

To me it seems very characteristic of the negligence with which contemporary history is treated that no dictionary of architecture or construction gives a precise answer to the question of who invented the balloon frame and when it was invented. . . .

Even as far back as the fifties and sixties there seems to have been no certainty with regard to the invention of the balloon frame. One early witness, writing in 1872, relates that "when it was first used is not known with any definiteness, but it has within the last fifty years replaced the old method of construction."

Woodward, in 1869, confesses that "the early history of the Balloon Frame, is somewhat obscure, there being no well authenticated statements of its origin. It may, however, be traced back to the early settlement of our prairie countries, where it was impossible to obtain heavy timber and skillful mechanics. . . . The Balloon Frame belongs to no one person; nobody claims it as an invention, and yet in the art of construction it is one of the most sensible improvements that has ever been made."

Nevertheless, the balloon frame does seem to have had an inventor and to have emanated from one particular town. . . .

The inventor of the balloon frame was George W. Snow. He was born at Keene, New Hampshire, September 16, 1797, of an old American family which traced back to the *Mayflower*.

He must have been a rather reckless spirit, since he first left the family homestead for New York and afterwards went to Detroit with his wife. Under rather primitive conditions he crossed the state of Michigan, and finally, in a canoe paddled by an Indian guide, he reached the mouth of the Chicago River, July 12, 1832. The small community he found there—there were only two hundred and fifty inhabitants—pleased his pioneer temperament. He took an active part in its affairs for many years: in 1833, when Chicago became a city, Snow was appointed its first assessor and surveyor; he was elected alderman in 1849, and made drainage commissioner the same year; he was at one time chief of the pioneer hook and ladder company.

As one of his descendants remarks in a letter, like many of the first settlers Snow was something of a jack-of-all-trades. He was one of the earliest of the Chicago lumber dealers, purchasing "Carver's Lumber-yard" in 1835. He owned considerable land and conducted a real estate business. He was a building contractor, as well as a general contractor and financier.

Snow was not merely a surveyor; he had been educated as a civil engineer in his youth. This technical training may have led him to the invention of the balloon frame. How this came about and what his struggles were we do not know. The tag, "balloon frame," was a mere nickname, a jocular reference to the lightness of this new type of construction.

There are several confirmations of the tradition in Snow's family that he invented the balloon frame. Its invention is credited to him by Andreas in his *History of Chicago*, and in *Industrial Chicago,* the most important book on the development of Chicago, we read that "the balloon frame is the joint idea of George W. Snow and necessity." Andreas' statement is based on the words of one of Snow's fellow townsmen, the architect, J. M. Van Osdel, who arrived in Chicago in 1837. In an article, "The History of Chicago Architecture," published in a Chicago monthly of the early eighties, Van Osdel remarks that "Mr. Snow was the inventor of the 'balloon frame' method of constructing wooden buildings, which in this city completely superseded the old style of framing with posts, girts, beams and braces."

George Snow's name is nearly unknown. There is no portrait of him in any of the local histories, but one was obtained from a family album which reveals a face at once full of puritan energy and of human sensitivity.

The first building in balloon frame was St. Mary's Church in Chicago, the earliest of the Catholic churches of the city. "In July 1833 a number of men are found erecting a church on Lake Street near State Street." Old builders prophesied its collapse. In the short term of its existence this church was razed and re-erected three times.

Until the seventies the balloon frame was called simply "Chicago construction," as we learn from a report of United States Commissioner H. Bowen, published in Washington in 1869. Bowen speaks of the western farmhouse which was forwarded in sections to the Paris Universal Exposition of 1867 as being of "Chicago construction."

The balloon frame, then, is associated with Chicago, like the skyscraper construction which, half a century later, was also called simply "Chicago construction."

The balloon-frame building with its skeleton of thin machine-cut studs and its covering of clapboards grew out of the seventeenth-century farmhouses of the early settlers. Snow was familiar with such houses in his home state of New Hampshire and his wife's home, Connecticut, where they were especially common. In these houses comparatively thin and narrow studs were used as intermediary framing, with the whole construction tied together by the clapboard covering.

George Snow started with these traditional methods, changing and adapting them to meet the new possibilities of production in a way which was as simple as it was ingenious.

The balloon frame has kept its vitality for a whole century and is still used extensively. This simple and efficient construction is thoroughly adapted to the requirements of contemporary architects. Many of Richard J. Neutra's houses in Texas and southern California reveal the elegance and lightness which are innate qualities of the balloon-frame skeleton.

From: *Space, Time and Architecture*,
by Sigfried Giedion. Cambridge, Mass.:
1949, pages 281–288.

Carson Pirie Scott & Company, Chicago, Illinois. Louis Henri Sullivan, architect. Right: Detail of cast iron over entrance.

IV

Integration in Chicago

The Chicago Renascence

by

Montgomery Schuyler

To begin with a paradox, the feature of Chicago is its featurelessness. There is scarcely any capital, ancient or modern, to which the site supplies so little of a visible reason of being. The prairie and the lake meet at a level, a liquid plain and a plain of mud that cannot properly be called solid, with nothing but the change of material to break the expanse. Indeed, when there is a breeze, the surface of Lake Michigan would be distinctly more diversified than that of the adjoining land, but for the handiwork of man. In point of fact, Chicago is of course explained by the confluence here of the two branches of the Chicago River. These have determined the site, the plan, and the building of the town, but one can scarcely describe as natural features the two sinuous ditches that drain the prairie into the lake, apparently in defiance of the law that water runs, and even oozes, down hill. Streams, however narrow and sluggish they may be, so they be themselves available for traffic, operate an obstruction to traffic by land; and it is the fact that for some distance from the junction the south fork of the river flows parallel with the shore of the lake, and within a half-mile of it, which establishes in this enclosure the commercial centre of Chicago. Even the slight obstacle interposed to traffic by the confluent streams, bridged and tunnelled as they are, has sufficed greatly to raise the cost of land within this area, in comparison with that outside, and to compel here the erection of the towering structures that are the most characteristic and the most impressive monuments of the town.

In character and impressiveness these by no means disappoint the stranger's expectations, but in number and extent they do, rather. For what one expects of Chicago, before anything else, is modernness. In most things one's expectations are fully realized. It is the most contemporaneous of capitals, and in the appearance of its people and their talk in the streets and in the clubs and in the newspapers it fairly palpitates with "actuality." Nevertheless, the general aspect of the business quarter is distinctly old-fashioned, and this even to the effete Oriental from New York or Boston. The elevator is nearly a quarter of a century old, and the first specimens of "elevator architecture," the Western Union and the "Tribune" buildings in New York, are very nearly coeval with the great fire in Chicago. One would have supposed that the rebuilders of Chicago would have seized upon this hint with avidity, and that its compressed commercial quarter would have made up in altitude what it lacked in area. In fact, not only are the great modern office buildings still exceptional in the most costly and most crowded district, but it is astonishing to hear that the oldest of them is scarcely more than seven years of age. "Men's deeds are after as they have been accustomed"—and the first impulse of the burnt-out merchants of Chicago was not to seize the opportunity the clean sweep of the fire had given them to improve their warehouses and office buildings, but to provide themselves straightway with places in which they could find shelter and do business. The consequence was that the new buildings of the burnt district were planned and designed, as well as built, with the utmost possible speed, and the rebuilding was for the most part done by the same architects who had built the old Chicago, and who took even less thought the second time than they had taken the first, by reason of the greater pressure upon them. The American commercial Renaissance, commonly expressed in cast-iron, was in its full efflorescence just before the fire. The material was discredited by that calamity, but unhappily not the forms it had taken, and in Chicago we may see, what is scarcely to be seen anywhere else in the world, fronts in cast-iron, themselves imitated from lithic architecture, again imitated in masonry, with the modifications reproduced that had been made necessary by the use of the less trustworthy material. This ignoble process is facilitated by the material at hand, a limestone of which slabs can be had in sizes that simulate exactly the castings from which the treatment of them is derived. After the exposure of a few months to the bituminous fumes it is really impossible to tell one of these reproductions from the original, which very likely adjoins it. Masonry and metal alike appear to have come from a foundry, rather than from a quarry, and to have been moulded according to the stock patterns of some architectural iron-works. The lifelessness and thoughtlessness of the iron-founders' work predominate in the streets devoted to the retail trade, and the picturesque tourist in Chicago is thus compelled to traverse many miles of street fronts quite as dismal and as monotonous as the commercial architecture of any other modern town.

There is a compensation for this in what at first sight seems to be one of its aggravations. The buildings which wear these stereotyped street fronts are much lower and less capacious than the increasing exigencies of business require, and than the introduction of the elevator makes possible, and they could not be other than cheap and flimsy in construction. Naturally the rebuilders of Chicago talked a great deal about "absolutely fire-proof" construction, but as naturally they did very little of it. The necessity for immediate accommodation, at a minimum of cost, was overwhelming, and cheap and hasty construction cannot be fire-proof construction. Accordingly, the majority of the commercial buildings now standing in Chicago are as really provisional and temporary as the tents and shanties, pitched almost on the embers of the fire, which they succeeded. The time being now ripe for replacing them by structures more capacious and durable, it is a matter for congratulation that there is nothing in the existing buildings of such practical or architectural value as to make anybody regret or obstruct the substitution.

Even if the old-fashioned architects who rebuilt Chicago had been anxious to reconstruct it according to the best and newest lights, it would have been quite out of their power to do so unaided. The erection of a twelve-story building anywhere involves an amount of mechanical consideration and a degree of engineering skill that are quite beyond the practitioners of the American metallic Renaissance. In Chicago the problem is more complicated than elsewhere, because these towering and massive structures ultimately rest upon a quagmire that is not less but more untrustworthy the deeper one digs. The distribution of the weight by carrying the foundations down to a trustworthy bottom, and increasing the area of the supporting piers as they descend, is not practicable here, nor, for the same reason, can it be done by piling. It is managed, in the heaviest buildings, by floating them upon a raft of concrete and railroad iron, spread a few feet below the surface, so that there are no cellars in the business quarter, and the subterranean activities that are so striking in the elevator buildings of New York are quite unknown. If the architects of the old Chicago, to whom their former clients naturally applied to rear the phoenix of the new, had been seized with the ambition of building Babels, they would doubtless have made as wild work practically as they certainly would have made artistically in the confusion of architectural tongues that would have fallen upon them. It is in every point of view fortunate that the modernization of the town was reserved for the better-trained designers of a younger generation.

It might be expected that the architecture of Chicago would be severely utilitarian in purpose if not in design, and this is the case. The city may be said to consist of places of business and places of residence. There are no churches, for example, that fairly represent the skill of the architects. The best of them are scarcely worthy of extensive discussion here, while the worst of them might suitably illustrate the work projected by a ribald wit on "The Comic Aspects of Christianity." Among other things, it follows from this deficiency that Chicago lacks almost altogether, in any general view that can be had of it, the variety and animation that are imparted to the sky line of a town seen from the water, or from an eminence, by a "tiara of proud towers," even when these are not specially attractive in outline or in detail, nor especially fortunate in their grouping. There is nothing, for example, in the aspect of Chicago from the lake, or from any attainable point of view, that is comparable to the sky line of the Back Bay of Boston, as seen from the Cambridge bridge, or of lower New York from either river. The towering buildings are almost wholly flat-roofed, and their stark, rectangular outlines cannot take on picturesqueness, even under the friendly drapery of the smoke that overhangs the commercial quarter during six days of the week. The architect of the Dearborn Station was very happily inspired when he relieved the prevailing monotony with the quaint and striking clock-tower that adjoins that structure.

The secular public buildings of Chicago are much more noteworthy than the churches, but upon the whole they bear scarcely so large a relation to the mass of private building as one would expect from the wealth and the public spirit of the town, and with one or two very noteworthy exceptions, recent as many of them are, they were built too early. The most discussed of them is the city and county building, and this has been discussed for reasons quite alien to its architecture, the halves of what was originally a single design having been assigned to different architects. The original design has been followed in the main, and the result is an edifice that certainly makes a distinctive impression. A building, completely detached, 340 feet by 280 in area, and considerably over 100 feet high, can scarcely fail to make an impression by dint of mere magnitude, but there is rather more than that in the city and county building. The parts are few and large, but five stories appearing, the masonry is massive, and the projecting and pedimented porticoes are on an ample scale. These things give the building a certain effect of sumptuosity and swagger that ally it rather to the Parisian than to the Peorian Renaissance. The effect is marred by certain drawbacks of detail, and by one that is scarcely of detail, the extreme meanness and baldness of the attic, in which, for the only time in the building, the openings seem to be arranged with some reference to their uses, and in which accordingly they have a painfully pinched and huddled appearance. In the decorative detail there is apparent a divergency of views between the two architects appointed to carry out the divided halves of the united design. The municipal designer—or possibly it is the county gentleman—has been content to stand upon the ancient ways, and to introduce no detail for which he has not found Ludovican precedent, while his rival is of a more aspiring mind, and has endeavored to carry out the precepts of the late Thomas Jefferson, by classicizing things modern. His excursions are not very daring, and consist mainly in such substitutions as that of an Indian's head for the antique mask, in a frieze of conventionalized American foliage. He has attained what must be in such an attempt the gratifying success of converting his modern material to a result as dull and lifeless and uninteresting as his prototype. It does not, however, impair the grandiosity of the general effect. This is impaired, not merely by the poverty of design already noted in the attic, but also by the niggardliness shown in dividing the polished granite column of the porticoes into several drums, though monoliths are plainly indicated by their dimensions, and by the general scale of the masonry. The small economy is the more injurious, because a noble regardlessness of expense is of the essence of the architecture, and an integral part of its effectiveness. The most monumental feature of the projected building has never been supplied—a huge arch in the centre of each of the shorter fronts, giving access to the central court, and marking the division between the property of the city and of the county. It is possible that the failure to finish this arch has proceeded from the political conflict that has left its scars upon the building elsewhere. There is an obvious practical difficulty in intrusting the two halves of an arch to rival architects and rival contractors. However that may be, the arch is unbuilt, and the entrance to the central court is a mere rift in the wall. The practical townspeople have seized the opportunity thus presented by the unoccupied space of free quarters for the all-pervading buggy. With a contempt for the constituted authorities have gone far to justify, they tether their horses in the shadow of their chief civic monument, like so many Arabs under the pillars of Palmyra or Persepolis, and heighten the impression of being the relic of an extinct race that is given to the pile not only by its unfinished state and by the stains of smoke, undistinguishable from those of time, but by its entirely exotic architecture. As the newly-landed Irishman, making his way up Broadway from Castle Garden, is said to have exclaimed, when he came in sight of the City Hall, that "that never was built in this country," so the stranger in Chicago is tempted to declare of its municipal building that it could not have been reared by the same race of whose building activities the other evidences surround him. This single example Ludovican architecture recalls, as most examples of it do, Thackeray's caricature of its Maecenas. Despoiled of its periwigs and its high heels, that is to say, of its architecture, which is easily separable from it, the building would merely lose all its character, without losing anything that belongs to it as a building.

Nevertheless this municipal building has its character, and in comparison with the next most famous public building of Chicago, it vindicates the wisdom of its architect in subjecting himself to the safeguard of a style of which, moreover, his work shows a real study. The style may be absolutely irrelevant both to our needs and to our ideas, as irrelevant as the political system of Louis XIV which it recalls. Its formulas may seem quite empty, but they gather dignity, if not meaning, when contrasted with the work of an avid "swallower of formulas," like the architect of the Board of Trade. His work is of no style, a proposition that is not invalidated by the probability that he himself would call it "American eclectic Gothic." We all know what the untutored and aboriginal architect stretches that term to cover. There is no doubt about its being characteristically modern and American; one might say characteristically Western, if he did not recall equally free and untrammelled exuberances in the Atlantic States. But it is impossible to ascribe to it any architectural merit, unless a complete disregard for precedent is to be imputed for righteousness, whether it proceed from ignorance or from contempt. And, indeed, there are not many other structures in the United States, of equal cost and pretension, which equally with this combine the dignity of a commercial traveller with the bland repose of St. Vitus. It is difficult to contemplate its bustling and uneasy façade without feeling a certain sympathy with the mob of anarchists that "demonstrated" under its windows on the night of its opening. If they really were anarchists, it was very ungrateful of them, for one would go far to find a more perfect expression of anarchy in architecture, and it is conceivable that they were instigated by an outraged architectural critic in disguise. If that ring-leader had been caught and arraigned, he could have maintained, with much better reason, the plea that Gustave Courbet made for his share in the destruction of the column of the Place Vendome, that his opposition to the monument was not political, but aesthetic.

Fortunately there is no other among the public or quasi-public buildings of Chicago of which the architecture is so hopeless and so irresponsible—no other that would so baffle the palaeontological Paley who should seek in it evidences of design, and that does not exhibit, at least, an architectural purpose, carried out with more or less of consistency and success. At the very centre of the commercial water front there was wisely reserved from traffic in the rebuilding of the town the "Lake Park," a mile in extent, and some hundreds of feet in depth, which not only serves the purpose of affording a view of the lake from the business quarter, but also secures an effective foreground for the buildings that line its landward edge. One of the oldest of these, young as all of them are, is the "Art Institute," designed by Messrs. Burnham & Root. This is of a moderate altitude, and suffers somewhat from being dwarfed by the elevator buildings erected since, being but of three stories and a roof; but no neighbor could make it other than a vigorous and effective work, as dignified as the Board of Trade is uneasy, and as quiet as that is noisy. It is extremely simple in composition, as will be seen, and it bears very little ornament, this being for the most part concentrated upon the ample and deeply moulded archway of the entrance. It owes its effectiveness to the clearness of its division into the three main parts of base and superstructure and roof, to the harmonious relation between them, and to the differences in the treatment of them that enhance this harmony. The Aristotelian precept that a work of art must have a beginning, a middle, and an end, is nowhere more conspicuously valid than in architecture, and nowhere does the neglect of it entail more unfortunate consequences. The severity of the basement, with its plain rectangular openings, is an effective introduction to the somewhat lighter and more open fenestration of the second and third stories, which are grouped to form the second term in the proportion, and this in turn to the range of openings in the gable of the shorter front, and to the row of peaked dormers in the longer that animate the sky-line and complete the composition. The impressiveness of the fronts is very greatly deepened by the vigorous framing of massive angle piers in which they are enclosed, the vigor of which is enhanced by the solid pinnacled turrets, corbelled out above the second story, that help to weight them, and that visibly abut the outward thrust of the arcades. It may be significant, with reference to the tendency of Western architecture, that this admirable building, admirable in the sobriety and moderation that are facilitated by its moderate size, is precisely what one would not expect to find in Chicago, so little is there evident in it of an intention to "collar the eye," or to challenge the attention it so very well repays.

In part, as we have just intimated, this modesty may be ascribed to the modest dimensions of the building. At any rate, it was out of the question in another important quasi-public building, which is the latest, and, at this writing, the loudest of the lions of Chicago—the Auditorium. Whatever else a ten-story building, nearly 300 feet by more than 350 in area and 140 in height, with a tower rising 80 feet farther, may happen to be, it must be conspicuous, and it is no wise possible that its designer should make it appear bashful or unobtrusive. Of however retiring a disposition he may be, in such a situation he must brazen it out. It is in his power to adopt a very simple or a very elaborate treatment, and to imperil the success of his work by making it dull on the one hand or unquiet on the other. Messrs. Adler & Sullivan, the architects of the Auditorium, have chosen the better part in treating their huge fronts with great severity, insomuch that the building can scarcely be said to exhibit any "features," except the triple entrance on the lake front, with its overhanging balcony, and the square tower that rises over the southern front to a height of 225 feet. While they did wisely in showing that monotony had fewer terrors for them than restlessness, the monotony that undoubtedly amounts to a defect in the aspect of the completed work is by no means wholly or mainly attributable to them. A place of popular entertainment, constructed upon a scale and with a massiveness to which we can scarcely find a parallel since Roman days, would present one of the worthiest and most interesting problems a modern architect could have if he were left to solve it unhampered. It is quite difficult enough to tax the power of any designer without any complications. The problem of design in the Chicago Auditorium is much complicated with requirements entirely irrelevant to its main purpose. The lobbies, the auditorium, and the stage of a great theatre, which are its essential parts, are all susceptible of an exterior expression more truthful and more striking than has yet been attained, in spite of many earnest and interesting essays. In the interior of the Auditorium, where the architects were left free, they have devoted themselves to solving their real problem with a high degree of success, and have attained an impressive simplicity and largeness. We are not dealing with interiors, however, and they were required to envelop the outside of their theatre in a shell of many-storied commercial architecture, which forbade them even to try for a monumental expression of their great hall. In the main, their exterior appears and must be judged only as a "business block." They have their exits and their entrances, and it is really only in these features that the exterior betrays the primary purpose of the building. The tower, even, is evidently not so much monumental as utilitarian. It is prepared for in the substructure only by a slight and inadequate projection of the piers, while it is itself obviously destined for profitable occupancy, being a small three-story business block, superimposed upon a huge ten-story business block. Such a structure cannot be converted into a monumental feature by making it more massive at the top that it is at the bottom, even though the massiveness be as artistically accentuated as it is in the tower of the Auditorium by the powerful open colonnade and the strong machicolated cornice in which it culminates. Waiving, as the designers have been compelled to do, the main purpose of the structure, and considering it as a commercial building, the Auditorium does not leave very much to be desired. The basement, especially, which consists of three stories of granite darker than the limestone of the superstructure, and appropriately rough-faced, is a vigorous and dignified performance, in which the expression of rugged strength is enhanced by the small and deep openings, and in which the necessarily large openings of the ground-floor are prevented from enfeebling the design by the massiveness of the lintels and flat arches that enclose them, and of the piers and pillars by which these are supported. The superstructure is scarcely worthy of this basement. The triple vertical division of the wall is effectively proportioned, but a much stronger demarcation is needed between the second and third members than is furnished by the discontinuous sill-course of the eighth story, while a greater projection, a greater depth, and a more vigorous modelling of the main cornice, and an enrichment of the attic beneath, would go far to relieve the baldness and monotony that are the defects of the design, and that are scarcely to be condoned because there are architectural faults much worse and much more frequent, which the designers have avoided. It is only, as has been said, in the entrances that they have been permitted to exhibit the object of the building. Really, it is only in the entrance on the Lake front, for the triplet of stilted arches at the base of the tower is not a very felicitous or a very congruous feature. The three low arches of the Lake front are of a Roman largeness—true vomitoria—and their effectiveness is increased by the simplicity of their treatment, by the ample lateral abutment provided for them, and by the long and shallow balcony that overhangs them. With the arches themselves this makes a very impressive feature, albeit the balcony is a very questionable feature. Even to the layman there must be a latent contradiction in the intercalation of the pillar to relieve the bearing of a lintel, when the pillar is referred to an unsupported shelf, obviously lighter and weaker than the lintel itself. This contradiction is not explained away by the vigor and massiveness of the shallow corbels that really account for the alternate columns, and it suggests that the construction so exhibited is not the true construction at all, and leaves this latter to be inferred without any help from the architecture. Even if one waives his objection to architectural forms that do not agree with the structural facts, it is surely not pedantic to require that the construction asserted by the forms shall be plausible to the extent of agreeing with itself. It is a pity that there should be such a drawback from a feature so effective; but the drawback does not prevent the feature from being effective, nor do the shortcomings we have been considering in the design of the Auditorium, nor even the much more serious obstacle that was inherent in the problem and imposed upon the architects, prevent it from being a very impressive structure, and justifying the pride with which it is regarded by all patriotic Chicagoans.

But, as has been intimated, it is not in monumental edifices that the characteristic building of Chicago is to be looked for. The "business block," entirely utilitarian in purpose, and monumental only in magnitude and in solidity of construction, is the true and typical embodiment in building of the Chicago idea. This might be said, of course, of any American city. Undoubtedly the most remarkable achievements of our architects and the most creditable have been in commercial architecture. But in this respect Chicago is more American than any of the Eastern cities, where there are signs, even in the commercial quarters, of division of interest and infirmity of purpose. In none of them does the building bespeak such a singleness of devotion, or indicate that life means so exclusively a living. Even the exceptions prove the rule by such tokens as the modest dimensions of the Art Institute and the concealment of the Auditorium in the heart of a business block. It does not by any means follow that the business blocks are uninteresting. There are singularly few exceptions to the rule of dismalness in the buildings that were hurriedly run up after the fire. One of these exceptions, the American Express Company, has an extrinsic interest as being the work of Mr. Richardson, and as being, so far as it need be classified, an example of Victorian Gothic, although its openings are all lintelled, instead of the Provençal Romanesque to which its author afterwards addicted himself with such success. So successful an example is it that an eminent but possibly bilious English architect, who visited Chicago at an early stage of the rebuilding, declared it to be the only thing in the town worth looking at—a judgment that does not seem so harsh to the tourist of to-day who compares it with its thus disesteemed contemporaries. It is a sober and straightforward performance in a safe monochrome of olive sandstone, and it thus lacks the note of that variety of Victorian Gothic that Mr. Ruskin's eloquence stimulated untrained American designers to produce, in which the restlessness of unstudied forms is still further tormented by the spotty application of color. From this variety of Victorian Gothic, Chicago is happily free. A gabled building in brick and sandstone opposite the Palmer House is almost a unique, and not at all an unfavorable, example. The business streets that are now merely dismal would have been much more aggressively painful if the incapable architects who built them had deviated from the comparative safety of their cast-iron Renaissance into a style that put them upon their individual want of resources. Moreover, throughout the commercial quarter any attempt at a structural use of color is sure shortly to be frustrated by coal-smoke. Upon the whole, it is a matter for congratulation that the earlier rebuilders of Chicago, being what they were, should have been so ignorant or careless of what was going on elsewhere, which, had they been aware of it, they would have been quite certain to misapply. Not only did they thus escape the frantic result that came of Victorian Gothic in untutored hands, but they escaped the pettiness and puerility that resulted of "Queen Anne," even when it was done by designers who ought to have known better. These pages contain a disparagement of that curious mode of building in a paper written when it was dressed in its little brief authority and playing its most fantastic tricks. Now it is so well recognized that Queen Anne is dead, that it seems strange educated architects ever could have fancied they detected the promise and potency of architectural life in her cold remains. This most evanescent of fashions seems never to have prevailed in Chicago at all.

One of the earliest of the more modern and characteristic of the commercial structures of Chicago, the Field Building, is by Mr. Richardson also, a huge warehouse covering a whole square, and seven stories high. With such an opportunity, Mr. Richardson could be trusted implicitly at least to make the most of his dimensions, and large as the building is in fact, it looks interminably big. Its bigness is made apparent by the simplicity of its treatment and the absence of any lateral division whatever. Simplicity, indeed, could scarcely go further. The vast expanses of the fronts are unrelieved by any ornament except a leaf in the cornice, and a rudimentary capital in the piers and mullions of the colonnaded attic. The effect of the mass is due wholly to its magnitude, to the disposition of its openings and to the emphatic exhibition of the masonic structure. The openings, except in the attic, and except for an ample pier reserved at each corner, are equally spaced throughout. The vertical division is limited to a sharp separation from the intermediate wall veil of the basement on one hand, and of the attic on the other. It must be owned that there is even a distinct infelicity in the arrangement of the five stories of this intermediate wall, the two superposed arcades, the upper of which, by reason of its multiplied supports, is the more solid of aspect, and between which there is no harmonious relation, but contrariwise a competition. Nevertheless, the main division is so clear, and the handling throughout so vigorous, as to carry off even a more serious defect. Nothing of its kind could be more impressive than the rugged expanse of masonry, of which the bonding is expressed throughout, and which in the granite basement becomes Cyclopean in scale, and in the doorway especially Cyclopean in rude strength. The great pile is one of the most interesting as it is one of the most individual examples of American commercial building. In it the vulgarity of the "commercial palace" is gratefully conspicuous by its absence, and it is as monumental in its massiveness and durability as it is grimly utilitarian in expression.

It is in this observance of the proprieties of commercial architecture, and in this self-denying rejection of an ornateness improper to it, that the best of the commercial architecture of Chicago is a welcome surprise to the tourist from the East. When the rebuilding of the business quarter of Boston was in progress, and while that city was for the most part congratulating itself upon the display of the skill of its architects for which the fire had opened a field, Mr. Richardson observed to the author of these remarks that there was more character in the plain and solid warehouses that had been destroyed than in the florid edifices by which they had been replaced. The saying was just, for the burned Boston was as unmistakably commercial as much of the rebuilt Boston is irrelevantly palatial. In the warehouse just noticed, Mr. Richardson himself resisted this besetting temptation of the architect, and his work certainly loses nothing of the simplicity which, with the uninstructed builders of old Boston, was in large part mere ignorance and unskilfulness, but emphasizes it by the superior power of distributing his masses that belonged to him as a trained and sensitive designer; for the resources of an artist are required to give an artistic and poignant expression even of rudeness. The rebuilt commercial quarter of Boston is by no means an extreme example of misplaced ornateness. Within the past three or four years Wall Street has been converted from the hum-drum respectability of an old-fashioned business thoroughfare to a street of commercial palaces, the aspect of which must contain an element of grievousness to the judicious, who see that the builders have lavished their repertory of ornament and variety on buildings to which nobody resorts for pleasure, but everybody for business alone, and that they have left themselves nothing further to do in the way of enrichment when they come to do temples and palaces, properly so called. Mr. Ruskin has fallen into deep, and largely into deserved discredit as an architectural critic, by promulgating rhapsodies as dogmas. His intellectual frivolity is even more evident and irritating by reason of the moral earnestness that attends it, recalling that perfervid pulpiteer of whom a like-minded eulogist affirmed that "he wielded his prurient imagination like a battle-axe in the service of the Lord of Hosts." All the same, lovers of architecture owe him gratitude for his eloquent inculcation of some of the truths that he arrived at by feeling, however inconclusive is the reasoning by which he endeavors to support them, and one of these is the text, so much preached from in the "Seven Lamps," that "where rest is forbidden, so is ornament." Wall Street and the business quarter of Boston, and every commercial palace in every city, violate, in differing degrees, this plain dictate of good sense and good taste, even in the very rare instances in which the misplacement of the ornateness is the worst thing that can be alleged against it. In the best of the commercial buildings of Chicago there is nothing visible of the conflict of which we hear so much from architects, mostly in the way of complaint, between the claims of "art" and the claims of utility, nor any evidence of a desire to get the better of a practical client by smuggling architecture upon him, and deceiving him for his own good and the glory of his architect. It is a very good lesson to see how the strictly architectural success of the commercial buildings is apt to be directly in proportion to the renunciation by the designers of conventional "architecturesqueness," and to their loyal acceptance at all points of the utilitarian conditions under which they are working. . . .

We have been speaking, of course, of the better commercial edifices, and it is by no means to be inferred that Chicago does not contain "elevator buildings" as disunited and absurd and restless as those of any other American town. About these select few, also, there is nothing especially characteristic. They might be in New York, or Boston, or Philadelphia, for any local color that they exhibit. It is otherwise with the commercial buildings designed by Messrs. Burnham & Root. With the striking exception of Mr. Richardson's Field Building, the names of these designers connote what there is of characteristically Chicagoan in the architecture of the business streets, so that, after all, the individuality is not local, but personal. The untimely and deplorable death of John Wellborn Root makes it proper to say that the individuality was mainly his. It consists largely in a clearer perception than one finds elsewhere of the limitations and conditions of commercial architecture, or in a more austere and self-denying acting upon that perception. This is the quality that such towering structures as the Insurance Exchange, the Phoenix Building, and "The Rookery" have in common, and that clearly distinguishes them from the mass of commercial palaces in Chicago or elsewhere. There is no sacrifice to picturesqueness of the utilitarian purpose in their general form, as in the composition of the Owings Building, and no denial of it in detail, as in the irrelevant arcade of the Studebaker Building. Their flat roofs are not tormented into protuberances in order to animate their sky-lines, and those of them that are built around an interior court are frankly hypacthral. Nor is there in any of them any incongruous preciousness of material. They are of brick, brown or red, upon stone basements, and the ornament is such, and only such, as is needed to express and to emphasize the structural divisions and dispositions. These are negative merits, it is true, but as our commercial architecture goes, they are not less meritorious on that account, and one is inclined to wish that the architects of all the commercial palaces might attend to the preachments upon the fitness of things that these edifices deliver, for they have very positive merits also. They are all architectural compositions, and not mere walls promiscuously pierced with openings, or, what is much commoner, mere ranges of openings scantily framed in strips of wall. They are sharply and unmistakably divided into the parts that every building needs to be a work of architecture, the members that mark the division are carefully and successfully adjusted with reference to their place and their scale, and the treatment of the different parts is so varied as to avoid both monotony and miscellany. The angle piers, upon the visible sufficiency of which the effectiveness, especially of a lofty building, so largely depends, never fail in this sufficiency, and the superior solidity that the basement of any building needs as a building, when it cannot be attained in fact by reason of commercial exigencies, is suggested in a more rugged and more massive treatment not less than in the employment of a visibly stronger material. These dispositions are aided by the devices at the command of the architect. The angle piers are weighted to the eye by the solid corbelled pinnacles at the top, as in the Insurance Exchange and the Rookery, or stiffened by a slight withdrawal that gives an additional vertical line on each side of the arris, as in the Phoenix, while the same purpose is partly subserved in the Rookery by the projection from the angle of the tall metallic lantern standards that repeat and enforce this line. The lateral division of the principal fronts is similar in all three structures. A narrow central compartment is distinguished in treatment, by an actual projection or by the thickening of the pier, from the longer wings, while the coincidence of this central division with the main entrance relieves the arrangement from the unpleasant look of an arrangement obviously forced or arbitrary. In the Insurance Exchange the centre is signalized by a balconied projection over the entrance, extending through the architectural basement—the dado, so to speak, which is here the principal division; by a widening of the pier and a concentration of the central openings in the second division, and above by an interruption of the otherwise unbroken arcade that traverses the attic. In the Rookery it is marked by a slight projection, which above is still further projected into tall corbelled pinnacles, and the wall thus bounded is slightly bowed, and its openings diminished and multiplied. In the Phoenix Building this bowing is carried so much further as to result in a corbelled oriel, extending through four stories, and repeated on a smaller scale at each end of the principal front and in the centre of each shorter front. This feature may perhaps be excepted from the general praise the buildings deserve of a strict adherence to their utilitarian purpose. Not that even in Chicago a business man may not have occasion to look out of the window, nor that, if he does, he may not be pardoned for desiring to extend his view beyond the walls and windows of over the way. An oriel-window is not necessarily an incongruity in a "business block," but the treatment of these oriels is a little fantastic and a little ornate for their destination, and belongs rather to domestic than to commercial architecture, and it is not in any case fortunate. This is the sole exception, however, to be made on this score. The entrances, to be sure, are enriched with a decoration beyond the mere expression of the structure which has elsewhere been the rule, but they do not appear incongruous. The entrance to a building that houses the population of a considerable village must be wide, and if its height were regulated by that of the human figure it would resemble the burrow by which the Esquimau gains access to his snow-hut, and become a manifest absurdity as the portal of a ten-story building. It must be large and conspicuous, and it should be stately, and it were a "very cynical asperity" to deny to the designer the privilege of enhancing by ornament the necessary stateliness of the one feature of his building which must arrest, for a moment at least, the attention of the most preoccupied visitor. It cannot be said that such a feature as the entrance of the Phoenix Building is intensely characteristic of a modern business block, but it can be said that in its place it does not in the least disturb the impression the structure makes of a modern business block. If beauty be its own excuse for being, this entrance needs no other, for assuredly it is one of the most beautiful and artistic works that American architecture has to show, so admirably proportioned it is, and so admirably detailed, so clear and emphatic without exaggeration is the expression of the structure, and so rich and refined the ornament. Upon the whole these buildings, by far the most successful and impressive of the business buildings of Chicago, not merely attest the skill of their architects, but reward their self-denial in making the design for a commercial building out of its own elements, however unpromising these may seem; in permitting the building, in a word, to impose its design upon them and in following its indications, rather than in imposing upon the building a design derived from anything but a consideration of its own requirements. Hence it is that, without showing anywhere any strain after originality, these structures are more original than structures in which such a strain is evident. "The merit of originality is not novelty; it is sincerity." The designer did not permit himself to be diverted from the problem in hand by a consideration of the irrelevant beauties of Roman theatres, or Florentine palaces, or Flemish town-halls, and accordingly the work is not reminiscent of these nor of any previous architectural types, of which so many contemporary buildings have the air of being adaptations under extreme difficulties. It is to the same directness and sincerity in the attempt to solve a novel problem that these buildings owe what is not their least attraction, in the sense they convey of a reserved power. The architect of a commercial palace seems often to be discharging his architectural vocabulary and wreaking his entire faculty of expression upon that contradiction in terms. Some of the buildings of which we have been speaking exhibit this prodigality. There is something especially grateful and welcome in turning from one of them to a building like one of those now in question, which suggests by comparison that, after he had completed the design of it, the architect might still have had something left—in his portfolios and in his intellect.

Another characteristic of the domestic architecture of Chicago there is—less prevalent than this absence of pretentiousness and mere display, but still prevalent enough to be very noteworthy—and that is the evidence it affords of an admiration for the work of Mr. Richardson, which, if not inordinate, is at least undiscriminating and misapplied. What region of our land, indeed, is not full of his labors, done vicariously, and with a zeal not according to knowledge? In Chicago his misunderstood example has fructified much more in the quarters of residence than in the business quarters, insomuch that one can scarcely walk around a square, either in the north or in the south side, without seeing some familiar feature or detail, which has often been borrowed outright from one of his works, and is reproduced without reference to its context. Now the great and merited success of Richardson was as personal and incommunicable as any artistic success can be. It was due to his faculty of reducing a complicated problem to its simplest and most forcible expression. More specifically, it was due to his faculty for seizing some feature of his building, developing it into predominance, and skilfully subordinating the rest of his composition to it, until this feature became the building. It was his power of disposing masses, his insistence upon largeness and simplicity, his impatience of niggling, his straightforward and virile handling of his tasks, that made his successes brilliant, and even his failures interesting. Very much of all this is a matter of temperament, and Richardson's best buildings were the express images of that impetuous and exuberant personality that all who knew him remember. He used to tell of a tourist from Holland in whom admiration for his art had induced a desire to make his acquaintance, and who upon being introduced to him exclaimed: "Oh, Mr. Richardson, how you are like your work!" "Now, wasn't that a Dutch remark?" Richardson concluded the story. Indeed, the tact of the salutation must be admitted to have been somewhat Batavian, but it was not without critical value. One cannot conceive of Richardson's work as having been done by an anaemic architect, or by a self-distrustful architect, or by a professor of architecture, faithful as his own professional preparation had been. There is a distinction well recognized in the art to which architecture has more or less plausibly been likened that is no less valid as applied to architecture itself—the distinction between "school music" and "bravura music." If we adopt this distinction, Richardson must be classed among the bravura performers in architecture, who are eligible rather for admiration than for study. Assuredly designers will get nothing but good from his work if they learn from it to try for largeness and simplicity, to avoid niggling, and to consider first of all the disposition of their masses. But these are merits that cannot be transferred from a photograph. They are quite independent of a fondness for the Provençal Romanesque, and still more of an exaggeration of the depth of voussoirs and of the dwarfishness of pillars. These things are readily enough imitable, as nearly every block of dwellings in Chicago testifies, but they are scarcely worth imitating. In Richardson's best work there is apt to be some questionable detail, since the success or failure of his building is commonly decided before the consideration of detail arises, and it is this questionable detail that the imitators are apt to reproduce without asking it any questions. Moreover, it will probably be agreed by most students that Richardson's city houses are, upon the whole, and in spite of some noteworthy exceptions, the least successful of his works. As it happens, there are two of them in Chicago itself, one on the north side and one on the south, and if their author had done nothing else, it is likely that they would be accepted rather as warnings than as examples. The principal front of the former has the simple leading motive that one seldom fails to find in the work of its architect, in the central open loggia of each of its three stories, flanked on each side by an abutment of solid wall, and the apportionment of the front between voids and solids is just and felicitous. Three loggie seem an excessive allowance for the town-house of a single family; but if we waive this point as an affair between the architect and his client exclusively, it must be owned that the arrangement supplies a motive susceptible of very effective development. In this case it cannot be said to have been developed effectively; nay, it can hardly be said to have been developed in an architectural sense at all, and the result proves that though a skilful disposition of masses is much, it is not everything. We have just been saying that the success or failure of Richardson's work was in a great degree independent of the merit of the detail, but this dwelling scarcely exhibits any detail. This is the more a drawback because the loggia is a feature of which lightness and openness is the essential characteristic, and which seems, therefore, to demand a certain elegance of treatment, as was recognized alike by the architects of the Gothic and the Renaissance palaces in Italy, from which we derive the feature and the name. It is, indeed, in the contrast between the lightened and enriched fenestration of the centre and the massiveness of the flanking walls that the potential effectiveness of the arrangement resides. Here, however, there is no lightening and no enrichment. Rude vigor characterizes as much the enclosed arcades as the enclosing walls, and becomes as much the predominant expression of the front of a dwelling of moderate dimensions as of the huge façades of the Field warehouse. Such modelling as is introduced tends rather to enforce than to mitigate this expression, for the piers of the lower arcade are squared, and the intercalated shafts of the upper are doubled perpendicularly to the front, as are the shafts of the colonnade above, so as to lay an additional stress upon the thickness of a wall that is here manifestly a mere screen. The continuation of the abacus of the arcade through the wall and its reappearance as the transom of the flanking windows is an effective device that loses some of its effectiveness from its introduction into both arcades. It scarcely modifies the impression the front makes of lacking detail altogether. The double-dentilled string-course that marks off and corbels out the attic is virtually the only moulding the front shows. Yet the need of mouldings is not less now than it was in the remote antiquity when a forgotten Egyptian artist perceived the necessity of some expedient to subdivide a wall, to mark a level, to sharpen or to soften a transition. For three thousand years his successors have agreed with him, and for a modern architect to abjure the use of these devices is to deny himself the rhetoric of his art. The incompleteness that comes of this abjuration in the present instance must be apparent to the least-trained layman, who vaguely feels that "something is the matter" with the building thus deprived of a source of expression, for which the texture given to the whole front by the exhibition of the bonding of the masonry, skilful and successful as this is it itself, by no means compensates. The sensitive architect must yearn to set the stone-cutters at work anew to bring out the expression of those parts that are especially in need of rhetorical exposition, to accentuate the sills of the arcades, to define and refine their arches, to emphasize the continuous line of the abacus, and especially to mark the summit of the sloping basement, which now is merged into the plane of the main wall, without the suggestion of a plinth. It is conceivable that an architect might, by the skilful employment of color, so treat a front, without the least projection or recess from top to bottom or from end to end, as to make us forget to deplore the absence of mouldings. Some interesting attempts in that direction have, in fact, been made, and complete success in such an attempt would be entitled to the praise of a tour de force. But when in a monochromatic wall the designer omits the members that should express and emphasize and adorn his structural dispositions without offering any substitute for them, his building will appear, as this dwelling appears, a work merely "blocked out" and left unfinished; and if it be the work of a highly endowed and highly accomplished designer like Richardson, the deficiency must be set down merely as an unlucky caprice. We have been speaking exclusively of the longer front, since it is manifest that the shorter shares its incompleteness, without the partial compensation of a strong and striking composition, which would carry off much unsuccessful detail, though it is not strong enough to carry off the lack of detail, even with the powerful and simple roof that covers the whole—in itself an admirable and entirely satisfactory piece of work.

Capriciousness may with as much justice be charged upon the only other example of Richardson's domestic architecture in Chicago, which, even more than the house we have been considering, arrests attention and prevents apathy, but which also seems even more from the purpose of domestic architecture. Upon the longer though less conspicuous front it lacks any central and controlling motive; and on the shorter and more conspicuous, this motive, about which the architect so seldom leaves the beholder in any doubt, is obscured by the addition at one end of a series of openings irrelevant to it, having no counterpart upon the other, and serving to weaken at a critical point the wall, the emphasis of whose massiveness and lateral expanse may be said to be the whole purport of the design, to which everything else is quite ruthlessly sacrificed. For this the building is kept as low as possible, insomuch that the ridge of its rather steep roof only reaches the level of the third story of the adjoining house. For this the openings are diminished in size upon both sides, insomuch that the ridge of its rather steep roof only reaches the level of the third story of the adjoining house. For this the openings are diminished in size upon both sides, insomuch that they become mere orifices for the admission of light, and in number upon the long side, insomuch that the designer seems to regard them as annoying interruptions to his essay in the treatment of blank wall. A granite wall over a hundred and fifty feet long, as in the side of this dwelling, almost unbroken, and with its structure clearly exhibited, is sure enough to arrest and strike the beholder; and so is the shorter front, in which the same treatment prevails, with a little more of ungracious concession to practical needs in the more numerous openings; but the beholder can scarcely accept the result as an eligible residence. The treatment is, even more strictly than in the house on the north side, an exposition of masonry. There is here, to be sure, some decorative detail in the filling of the head of the doorway and in the sill above it, but this detail is so minute, in the case of the egg-and-dart that adorns the sill, so microscopic, that it does not count at all in the general effect. A moulding that does count in the general effect, and that vindicates itself at the expense of the structural features not thus developed, is the main cornice, an emphatic and appropriate profile. In this building there seems to be a real attempt to supply the place of mouldings by modifications of the masonry, which in the other forms an unvaried reticulation over the whole surface. In this not only are the horizontal joints accentuated, and the vertical joints slurred so as to assist very greatly in the emphasis of length, but the courses that are structurally of unusual importance, the sills and lintels of the openings, are doubled in width thus strongly belting the building at their several levels. Here again a device that needs only to be expressed in modelling to answer an artistic purpose fails to make up for the absence of modelling. The merits of the building as a building, however, are much effaced when it is considered as a dwelling, and the structure ceases to be defensible, except, indeed, in a military sense. The whole aspect of the exterior is so gloomy and forbidding and unhomelike that but for its neighborhood one would infer its purpose to be not domestic, but penal. Lovelace has assured us that "stone walls do not a prison make," but when a building consists as exclusively as possible of bare stone walls, it irresistibly suggests a place of involuntary seclusion, even though minds especially "innocent and quiet" might take it for a hermitage. Indeed, if one were to take it for a dwelling expressive of the character of its inmates, he must suppose it to be the abode of a recluse or a misanthrope, though when Timon secures a large plot upon a fashionable avenue, and erects a costly building to show his aversion to the society of his kind, he exposes the sincerity of his misanthropical sentiments to suspicion. Assuming that the owner does not profess such sentiments, but is much like his fellow-citizens, the character of his abode must be referred to a whim on the part of his architect—a Titanic, or rather a Gargantuan freak. For there is at least nothing petty or puerile about the design of these houses. They bear an unmistakably strong and individual stamp, and failures as, upon the whole, they must be called, they really increase the admiration aroused by their author's successes for the power of design that can make even wilful error so interesting.

From: *American Architecture*, by Montgomery Schuyler, New York: 1892, pages 24–161 (with omissions).

The Economics of Steel Frame Construction

by

Montgomery Schuyler

It is impossible fairly to estimate the work of the leading architects of Chicago without some preliminary reference to the conditions of their work. In part, perhaps in the main, these are the same conditions that preside over the evolution of American architecture in general, but some of them are really local, and those of them that are general are applied in Chicago with a peculiar strictness and intensity. It is from this stringency of application that the characteristics of Chicago building come, and that it comes that the individuality of that building is so much more local than it is general that from the first sight of a new Chicago building one can "place" it so much more readily than one can assign it to its particular author. Here, more than elsewhere, "the individual withers, and the world is more and more."

Of course, what I have in mind in saying this is "the heart of Chicago," the business quarter, for it is by that that Chicago is characterized, especially in its architecture. Its architectural expressions are twofold only, places of business and places of residence. It would be impossible to mention another great city of which this is so strictly true. It is indeed curious how the composite image of Chicago that remains in one's memory as the sum of innumerable individual impressions is made up exclusively of the sky-scraper of the city and the dwellings of the suburbs. Not a church enters into it, so as to count, as churches count for so much elsewhere. Scarcely a

Tacoma Building, Chicago, Illinois. William Holabird and Martin Roche, architects. *Courtesy, Chicago Historical Society.*

Great Northern Hotel, Chicago, Illinois. John Wellborn Root and Daniel Burnham, architects. *Courtesy, Chicago Historical Society.*

Reliance Building, Chicago, Illinois. John Wellborn Root and Daniel Burnham, architects. ***Courtesy, Chicago Historical Society.***

public building enters into it. There is the old Art Institute, indeed, excellent and impressive building. There is the new Art Institute, scholarly and academic, and the new library, of a more modern and exuberant as well as of a more vigorous aspect, and there is the city and county building which is exuberant exclusively. Still later, there is the Newberry Library at one end of the town and the Chicago University at the other. But this brief list, which must be very nearly exhaustive, is not a list of characteristic buildings. In spite of the respectable dimensions of several of these in longitude and latitude their inferiority in the third and most characteristic dimension of altitude denotes that they are incidental and episodical to the real task of the architects, which is to produce sky-scrapers and homes,—and factories, indeed, which architecturally are neither here nor there, but which occupy much of the attention and contribute much to the incomes of the busiest architects. The deficiency of churches, which in magnitude and costliness are commensurate with the populousness and wealth of the city, and in architectural interest are comparable with its utilitarian structures, is a fact that must strike every stranger. The men who project and "finance" the utilitarian buildings are the same men who are ready to incur expenditures for public purposes with a generosity and a public spirit that are elsewhere unparalleled, and that constitute one of the justest of the boasts of the place. But it seems that churches do not enter into their scheme of public benefaction, and any lavishness of expenditure on churches appears to strike them as a little frivolous and dilettante. There is a kernel of real meaning and applicability in the legend of the inhabitant of a "boom town" further to the West, who was bragging about the hotels and the saloons and the "opera house" of it to a stranger, who at last inquired about the churches. "Well, no," *Occidentalis Gloriosus* had to own; "there was some talk about one, but the boys thought it would look too dudish." Whether the Chicago man thinks that he can do without monumental churches, or is only postponing them till a more convenient season, the lack of them restricts the range of architectural practice to a simplicity unknown in older cities. Theatres would elsewhere constitute a variation and a relief, and Chicago is a very playgoing place, but it no more possesses a monumental theatre than a monumental church. It has no more a Nouvel Opera than it has a Notre Dame. Burke, speaking of the new London theatres of a century ago, described them as "large and lofty piles, which lift their broad shoulders in gigantic pride, almost emulous of the temples of God," and in more than one modern capital the emulation has been carried further. In Chicago the theatres are housed in "huge and lofty piles," but they are not altogether monumental for the reason that they are but incidents of the piles. The two theatres that are of the chief architectural interest interiorly, and one of them is of the greatest architectural interest, are inclosed and in great part concealed, the one in a hotel and the other in an office building. The fact is very characteristic. It is the characteristic fact, for in the dwellings there is little of strictly local color. They might be in Buffalo, or in St. Paul, or in a suburb of any American city. Hardly in New York, because the expanse of Chicago permits a spaciousness and a detachment that the projector of a town-house upon cramped Manhattan Island cannot afford, or thinks he cannot, which comes to the same thing. It is only "the heart of Chicago" that is straightened for room. It is accordingly only in the heart of Chicago that we find Chicago buildings. Even before the introduction of the "Chicago construction," which first appeared in the Home Insurance building some six years ago, the sky-scrapers were noticeable for two Chicagoan characteristics, their extreme altitude and their strictly utilitarian treatment. Now that the Chicago construction has come to prevail, they are still noteworthy in comparison with the sky-scraper of other towns for these same qualities. And this brings me to remark upon the very great share which the Chicago "business man" has had in the evolution of commercial architecture in Chicago, a share not less important than that of the architects, and not less important for being in the main negative. We all like to hear the intelligent foreigner upon the characteristic manifestations of our national spirit, if he be candid as well as intelligent, to see ourselves as others see us, and it gives me pleasure to quote a very intelligent and a very candid foreigner, M. Paul Bourget, in "Outre Mer," upon the commercial architecture of Chicago, what he says is so true and so well put:

> At one moment you have around you only "buildings." They scale the sky with their eighteen, with their twenty stories. The architect who has built, or rather who has plotted them, has renounced colonnades, mouldings, classical embellishments. He has frankly accepted the condition imposed by the speculator; multiplying as many times as possible the value of the bit of ground at the base in multiplying the supposed offices. It is a problem capable of interesting only an engineer, one would sup-

> pose. Nothing of the kind. The simple force of need is such a principle of beauty, and these buildings so conspicuously manifest that need that in contemplating them you experience a singular emotion. The sketch appears here of a new kind of art, an art of democracy, made by the crowd and for the crowd, an art of science in which the certainty of natural laws gives to audacities in appearance the most unbridled, the tranquillity of geometrical figures.

It is noteworthy that the observer had seen and described New York before he saw Chicago. The circumstance makes more striking his recognition that it is in Chicago that the type of office building has been most clearly detached and elucidated. One is arrested by the averment that this art, so evidently made "for the crowd," is also made "by the crowd," since a crowd cannot be an artist, one is inclined to say. But there is not only the general consideration that in architecture an artist cannot even produce without the cooperation of his public, and cannot go on producing without being popular. There is the particular consideration that in this strictly utilitarian building the requirements are imposed with a stringency elsewhere unknown in the same degree, and very greatly to the advantage of the architecture. Elsewhere the designer of a business building commonly attempts to persuade or to hoodwink his client into sacrificing something of utility to "art," and when he succeeds, it is commonly perceptible that the sacrifice has been in vain, and that the building would have been better for its artistic purpose if it had been better for its practical purpose. There used to be an absurd story current in New York of how that the owner of two examples of florid classic in cast-iron (the Gilsey Building in lower Broadway and the Gilsey House in upper Broadway they were), exclaimed, when the second was finished, that now he had done enough for art, and henceforth he meant to build as a matter of business. Commercial architecture in Chicago is long past that stage, and that it is so is due rather to the business man than to the architect. In this way and to this extent the architecture is made "by the crowd," is an architecture of the people and by the people as well as for the people. I asked one of the successful architects of Chicago what would happen if the designer of a commercial building sacrificed the practical availableness of one or more of its stories to the assumed exigencies of architecture, as has often been done in New York, and as has been done in several aggravated and conspicuous instances that will readily occur to the reader familiar with recent building there. His answer was suggestive: "Why, the word would be passed and he would never get another to do. No, we never try those tricks on our business men. They are too wide-awake." Another successful architect explained to me his procedure in designing a sky-scraper. "I get from my engineer a statement of the minimum thickness of the steel post and its enclosure of terra cotta. Then I establish the minimum depth of floor beam and the minimum height of the sill from the floor to accommodate what must go between them. These are the data of my design." It is not the question whether the piers would not look better for somewhat more of massiveness, whether the skeleton could not be more "padded round with flesh and fat" to its aesthetic advantage, without too serious an infringement upon its suitableness for its purpose, whether the designer could not make a workable compromise between what it might please him to call his artistic conscience and the duty he owes as the agent and adviser of the owner in directing an investment for the largest possible return. Modern commercial architecture in general, when it is done by artistic designers, is such a compromise. It bears the scars of a conflict, if not between the architect and the client, between the claims of utility and art, or I should prefer to say between the facts of the case and the notions of the architect. It is only the work of the "artchitect," the work that nobody looks at twice or thinks of once, or cares to talk about, that evinces a purpose, not indeed to fulfil perfectly the real requirements of the building, but to carry out the "artchitect's" confused notion of the owner's confused notion of the manner of satisfying those requirements. That is as different a matter as possible from putting the resources of a trained and artistic intelligence absolutely at the service of an employer, and the results are as different as possible. The architects of Chicago are not so radically different as all this from architects elsewhere. They are different on compulsion. They have "frankly accepted the conditions imposed by the speculator," (the word I translate "frankly" is *brutalement*, and I wish that M. Bourget had chosen to say "loyally" instead), because they are really imposed, and there is no getting away from them, if one would win and keep the reputation of a "practical" architect. And mark that the business men who impose these conditions are not the most private-spirited; they are the most public-spirited body of business men of any commercial city in the world. They are willing to make the most generous sacrifices for their city to provide it with ornaments and trophies which shall make it something more than a centre of pig-sticking and grain-handling. They are willing to play the part of Maecenas to the fine arts, only they insist that they will not play it "during business hours." They are too clear-headed to allow themselves or their architects to confuse their several and distinct capacities of money-makers and Maecenases. If they allow themselves to be confused upon this point, in the first place they would not have so much money to do their public benefactions withal, and in the second place their commercial architecture would not have the character that in fact it has, and that comes from their insistence upon a rigid adherence to the real requirements of their commercial undertakings. Into that architecture, then, their influence enters as a very potent factor, and, whatever the architect beginning his practice in Chicago with his head full of "classical embellishments" may have thought or said, it enters, as every discerning beholder must now perceive, as a very beneficent factor.

In one respect, and this a respect that more or less affects commercial architecture everywhere, the influence is not beneficial. The architect is too much pressed for time. His client is aware that parsimony is not economy, and is willing to give him all the money that he really needs. He is aware also that mere greediness defeats its own purpose, that to erect a very lofty building on a very restricted site is to increase the comparative cost both of building and of maintenance, and that to occupy with rentable apartments space that is needed for light and air is a very costly proceeding. In all such things he shows a spirit of large and intelligent liberality. But it is especially true of him, what our French critic has noted as a national characteristic, that he cannot spare time. From the hour that the ground for a new building is put at his disposal the work of construction must go on at the highest rate of speed. If the plans are not matured at that moment, they must be executed in their immaturity, or with such ripening only as can be allowed while the work is actually going forward. There is after that no time left for the leisurely correction and completion upon which artistic perfection depends. There is no atmosphere in the world that less resembles "the still air of delightful studies" than that of the heart of Chicago. And so the successful practitioner of architecture in Chicago is primarily an administrator. He absolutely must be that. If he be secondarily an artist, all the better; but in that case he is an artist working under pressure, a condition which is peculiarly abhorrent to the "artistic temperament." All the questions of arrangement of construction and of design which enter into the design of that very complicated organism, the modern office building, are presented at once, with a peremptory demand for an immediate answer. In the answer to them must concur the constructor, the designer and the "practical man." Whether these three are united in one person or distributed among three, the primary and co-ordinating qualification is that of an administrator. "The readiness is all." A busy practitioner must have his professional apparatus, including his professional library, at his fingers' ends. The irrefutable criticism in the Vicar of Wakefield that "the picture would have been better if the artist had taken more pains," is irrelevant. It is not a question whether the study of another month might not invigorate the masses and chasten the detail. The foundation-plans must be ready as soon as the ground is cleared, and the building must not at any stage wait a day for drawings. Here, it is true, the general uniformity of the problem is a great resource to the designer. An architect who lives by and upon office buildings has always, it is to be presumed, designs adumbrated in his mind—alternative designs, very possibly, for past buildings, rejected as less eligible for the past purpose than the design executed, but more eligible for the future purpose, or designs entirely ideal, drawn from a consideration of the abstract sky-scraper. Much of the preliminary and general work of design may thus be done before the commission arrives, much more than if the practice were more varied. But with whatever mitigations there may be of the conditions, the conditions are so especially stringent in Chicago as to make the successes all the more remarkable. And, indeed, it would be worse than idle to find fault with the conditions because, as we have seen, the successes have been won by an absolute loyalty to the conditions, and by the frank abandonment of every architectural convention that comes in conflict with them.

From: *A Critique of the Works of Adler and Sullivan,* by Montgomery Schuyler. Great American Architects Series. "The Architectural Record," December, 1895.

The First Skyscraper

by

Col. W. A. Starrett

Before some architect could attempt to carry masonry walls even higher, the skyscraper appeared. In the fall of 1883, W. L. B. Jenney was commissioned by the Home Insurance Company of New York to design a Chicago office building for them. Others had built cast-iron into their masonry walls and piers and used wrought-iron floor beams, but Jenney went a long and daring step farther. He actually carried out what no one ever had done in theory or practice before—took the dead load off his walls and placed it on a skeleton framework of iron concealed inside the masonry—cast-iron columns and wrought-iron *I* beams, bolting the beams to the columns with angle-iron brackets.

When the framework had reached the sixth floor, a letter came to Mr. Jenney from the Carnegie-Phipps Steel Company of Pittsburgh. It stated that they were now rolling Bessemer steel beams and asked permission to substitute these for wrought-iron beams on the remaining floors. Jenney agreed, and the resultant shipment was the first ever made of structural steel, in the modern sense. The columns continued to be cast-iron, however, since plates and angles of steel, of which the later steel columns were built up, had not yet been rolled.

This Home Insurance Building, the first of all skyscrapers, still stands at La Salle and Adams Streets; originally ten stories, two more floors were added later. It was started May 1, 1884, and finished in the fall of 1885.

It is true, however, that L. S. Buffington, a young architect of Minneapolis, had dreamed of skeleton steel structures as early as 1880. His inspiration was gained from the speculations of a French architect, LeDuc, who had, years before, in a discourse on architecture, written: "A practical architect might not unnaturally conceive the idea of erecting a vast edifice whose frame should be entirely of iron, enclosing that frame and preserving it by means of a casing of stone." Pursuant to the inspiration that this reading gave him, Mr. Buffington set about conceiving multi-storied structures. He dreamed of buildings twenty, thirty, fifty, and even a hundred stories high, and made fantastic sketches. These dream buildings he christened, "cloud-scrapers." * He even went so far as to make the engineering calculations as to how heavy the columns might have to be in these buildings of various heights. But for one reason or another, he delayed making any application for patents until about 1887 or 1888. We know, of course, that already the Home Insurance Building had been completed two or three years before. Moreover, it is questionable whether Mr. Buffington could have secured backing to erect any of his dream structures, and whether any of the designs he had made were capable of practical construction. The fact is, regardless of his claim to prior invention, it was Mr. Jenney who put the problem to practical test, and to him belongs the credit, in spite of the commendable excursion of Mr. Buffington into the field of fancy. It is of interest to record that, for several years after skyscrapers commenced to appear in Chicago, Mr. Buffington threatened suit against the owners for infringement of his patents, and it is my recollection that, in one or two cases, he actually started proceedings, but the prior application of the principle by Mr. Jenney largely defeated his case.

The next great step forward came a year later from the office of Burnham & Root. Their twelve-story Rookery Building copied the Jenney skeleton framework, but the foundations pioneered the present steel-grillage design. Instead of setting the Rookery on a series of bulky stone-and-cement pyramids, Burnham & Root designed footings of two courses of railroad steel laid at right angles to each other and embedded in concrete, with steel *I* beams crossing the upper courses. John M. Ewen was, at that time, chief engineer for Burnham & Root, and my eldest brother, Theodore, was then a draftsman in the office. It was he, I believe, who first suggested this use of railroad rails.

Laymen may find this explanation obscure; but if the reader does not understand how it was done, he will understand the effect. What was accomplished was a better burden-bearing foundation, occupying only a fraction of the space of the pyramidal footings and requiring an excavation of as little as three feet.

Though an advance on the isolated masonry pier, this still was a complacent acceptance of a floating foundation. When I was a young-

*** The word skyscraper probably came from the Port of New York. The highest sail on a clipper ship was so called. (L. M.)**

ster in Chicago, it was not uncommon for large buildings to be as much as three or four inches out of plumb, a condition frequently noticeable in the chatter of the elevators. It was a general practice then to allow for as much as a foot of settling, and sidewalks were canted upward from the curb line at as much of an angle as the builder dared, in the hope that, when the building did settle, the sidewalks would sink with it to their true plane. The extent of the settling, unfortunately, had to be guessed at.

The real answer to the problem, of course, was to carry the piers to hard-pan or bed-rock at seventy-five or one hundred feet and seal out the water to provide a basement; but engineers did not yet know how to combat water and caving soils, except awkwardly, at prohibitive expense. In recent years just such foundations have been carried through the muck and sand and the underlying blue clay to rock or hard-pan under some of those old buildings—even such a massive structure as the Masonic Temple—while business went on as usual above. The method is to take the columns one by one, catch them up on girders that span to cribbings placed adjacent, thus forming a temporary straddle between cribs, with the column base dangling over the hole of a now open caisson. These caissons finished to hard-pan are filled with concrete and the dangling base securely embedded. The cribbing is then removed, and the old column rests securely on a new foundation.

And as engineers learned in the early '90's how to tame the ground water, they went back and dug basements under some of these pioneer buildings. A sheath piling first was run down to hold back the sand and water, then the excavation was sealed with a lining of concrete, pitch and five plies of tar paper. A sump was left as an outlet for the ground water constantly thrusting upward and threatening to flood the basement. Pumps keep going year in and out to draw off this water. It is the refinement of this method which now is used in almost all deep basements where water and shifting soils are met.

Though we no longer would build a twelve-story structure on grillages floating on soggy earth and shifting sand, we continue to use this same grillage of steel and concrete as a footing for every pier hole, deep or shallow. What is the necessity in bed-rock, you may ask. Can any mortal-made weight crush the rocky shell of Mother Earth? To an extent, yes. A weight of 1,000 tons resting directly on rock will tend to powder the surface of that rock, however hard; and inasmuch as a variation of a fraction of an inch is to be avoided in foundations, we have to distribute that enormous burden on a spread of steel grillage laid on top of the rock. Moreover, as a practical matter, it is important to have a reasonable spread to a footing on which a column stands to facilitate steel erection, for the bases and grillage are carefully and accurately set level, and the column is bolted to the base before the derrick lets go of it; otherwise it would topple and fall.

The passer-by who stops from a fascination he cannot explain to watch a steam shovel snorting in a hole, imagines that the deeper the hole, the higher the building is to be. This does not follow. We can scrape away two or three feet of earth and run up a fifty-story building or more, if beneath that few feet of earth is bed-rock. If we quarry deeply into the solid rock with air drills and explosives, it is to provide basement and sub-basement space demanded by operating, not engineering, necessities. Contrarily, in swampy ground, we may have to dig one hundred feet to bed-rock to support a ten-story building, and this necessitates pneumatic caissons or some other complex form of foundation construction.

Now, in 1887, one year further along, Holabird & Roche, architects, in collaboration with Purdy & Henderson, bridge engineers, both of which firms are still active, combined and improved upon the achievements of Jenney and of Burnham & Root and designed the fourteen-story Tacoma Building. The outer walls on the two street frontages were purely curtains of brick and terra cotta, carried at each floor by steel spandrel beams attached to cast-iron columns; and here first was seen the startling spectacle of bricklayers beginning to lay walls midway between roof and ground. The Tacoma was the first structure ever built in which any outer wall carried no burden and served no purpose other than ornamentation and the keeping out of wind and weather, which became one of the fundamentals of skyscraper design. The two other walls were masonry and self-supporting. The foundations were the isolated footings with steel members devised by Burnham & Root.

George A. Fuller appears on the scene here as the builder of the Tacoma. He came to Chicago a few years earlier from Worcester, Massachusetts. He was a new type of contractor, pioneering an administrative revolution in construction. Contractors until now usually had been boss carpenters or masons, men of a little capital and foremanship, but generally of no technical education, who executed subcontracts under the supervision of the architects. This was feasible in small enterprises, but as buildings grew in magnitude architects were overwhelmed with a multiplicity of burdens for which many of them had little training and no aptitude. Fuller raised contracting from a limited trade to both an industry and a profession, visualizing the building problem in its entirety—promotion, finance, engineering, labor and materials; and the architect reverted to his original function of design.

Fuller first was a salesman who sought out property owners and promoted new buildings; secondly, an expert who understood the income possibilities and necessities of office buildings; then a financier who arranged the needful capital and credits; next an engineer competent to oversee every phase of modern building; and lastly, a business executive, buying and assembling materials to the best advantage and commanding a staff of assistants and an army of sub-contractors and laborers. That is the building business as it exists to-day.

Fuller was an engineer, but a builder need not of necessity be an engineer, and it is measurably true that great engineers are not likely to be good builders; the jobs are too unlike. A sound engineering knowledge is of great value to a builder if he first has the other needful qualities, more particularly because an engineer, in his education, learns to observe how things are put together. But the involved calculations necessary to great structures are worked out in advance for the builder by a professional structural engineer. If there were such a thing as a technically educated business manager, he would be the ideal builder, for we are administrators and executives, not specialist technicians. George A. Fuller died in his forty-ninth year, in 1900. He was the victim of his own tremendous driving power and the demands that the building business often imposes.

There were other pioneers, of course, some very great names in this skyscraper field, but I did not come into such close contact with them. John Griffiths of Chicago was another like Fuller, but he never extended his sphere of influence to other cities as Fuller did. In the East, Marc Eidlitz established a name for ability and integrity as a builder, to-day made even more illustrious by his sons, who carry on with increased vigor the original organization of their father. Norcross in New England laid the foundations for some of the finest traditions of the modern building industry. And in New York, Charles T. Wills and John I. Downey left their everlasting impress on the building profession by the fine structures they erected. In Philadelphia, John T. Windrim, a pioneer architect of the era of the Centennial and after, gave inspiration to the sudden skyscraper development of that city and left a heritage of some of the best structures in Philadelphia. It was he who designed and supervised the construction of the Pennsylvania Railroad office building, a splendid achievement in engineering and construction. His son carries on as one of the country's leading architects, and the skyscrapers to his credit in Philadelphia are many.

In 1889, the skyscraper evolved into a form the fundamentals of which have come down unchanged in high-building practice. In that year Burnham & Root designed and built the Rand-McNally Building, the first skeleton structure of rolled-steel beams and columns built up of standard bridge-steel shapes and riveted together. Jenney's Leiter Building, a few months later, was the first without a single self-supporting wall, as his Fair Building in 1891 was the first to employ Z bar columns. Then, in 1890, Burnham & Root designed the Masonic Temple, twenty-one stories of steel on floating, spread foundations, the highest building in the world, and one of the seven wonders thereof for the next few years.

Thus the skyscraper was a quick evolution of some six or seven years, achieved in Chicago and fathered by no one or two men. As Corydon T. Purdy, who himself had an important role in its genesis, wrote in 1895:

> This reversal of building methods, this change about in the function and use of masonry walls, and the introduction of such new conditions in large buildings, is a real revolution the extent of which hardly can be realized. The result is that the constructive side of the problem has reached its most perfect development in Chicago practice. The rapidity and history of its development can be readily traced in that city. A new idea is tried to a limited extent in one building; a bolder application is attempted in the next; another idea, originating in another office, is worked out the same way. Thus the evolution proceeds and honors are extremely hard to divide.

From: *Skyscrapers and the Men Who Build Them,* by W. A. Starrett. New York: 1928, pages 27–35.

Function and Environment

by

Dankmar Adler

The writer of an article recently published in *Lippincott's Magazine,* summarizes the law of architectural design in the sentence "form follows function," and endeavors to condense into three words what others have vainly tried to enunciate in numerous treatises and in bulky volumes on the Philosophy of Art. If it was necessary to state in a three-worded aphorism the entire law of architectural design and composition, nothing could have better suited the purpose than the words quoted above from the pen of that clear thinker and brilliant writer, Louis H. Sullivan.

Every architectural work has a "function," a purpose which has called it into being, and its success is measured by the degree of approximation to fulfilment of "functions" which characterizes its "form."

From this one might infer that it is only necessary to divide into a few classes the functions to be served by architectural structures and to determine the form best adapted to each, and thus develop an infallibly correct system of architectural design from which none may deviate without incurring the reproach of ignorance and lack of culture.

We would then have an architecture somewhat more scientific and vastly more practical, but as trite and as devoid of the interest imparted by the creative impulse, as is the architecture founded upon the principle, *Form follows historic precedent,* which stamps as barbaric every structure for which the architect has failed to provide an academically and historically correct mask and costume, and which treats as heresy an attempt to do, not as the Romans did in the year 1, but to do as one thinks the Romans might have done in the year 1896.

Returning to Mr. Sullivan's aphorism, we find that he bases it upon studies and observations of nature, which, carried a little further, show that although the common function of all organic creation is to maintain and propagate the various species, yet an ever changing environment has produced an infinite number of species and innumerable differences in individuals of each species.

Therefore, if "form follows function," it does not follow in a straight line, nor in accordance with a simple mathematical formula, but along the lines of curves whose elements are always changing and never alike; and if the lines of development and growth of vegetable and animal organisms are infinitely differentiated, the processes of untrammeled human thought and human emotions are even more subtle in the differences and shadings of their manifestations, while the natural variations in conditions of human environment are as great as those which influence the developments of form in the lower organisms; and human work is further modified by necessary artificial conditions and circumstances.

Therefore, before accepting Mr. Sullivan's statement of the underlying law upon which all good architectural design and all true architectural style is founded, it may be well to amend it, and say: "function and environment determine form," using the words environment and form in their broadest sense.

The functions served by the work of the architect have expanded but little, and have varied still less within the limits of the historic records of architecture, nor has there been much change until the last quarter of this century in those conditions of environments which comprise the structural and decorative materials at the disposal of the architect.

The great epochs in the development of architectural styles are respectively characterized by the introduction of the beam and lintel, the Roman arch and vault, and the pointed arch and its characteristic vaultings. It is our good fortune to have inherited all that was accomplished by the many generations who lived and thought and worked in those epochs. We are still more blessed in being allowed the privilege of participating in the creation and in witnessing the birth of another epoch of architectural design, the form or style of which will be founded upon the discovery of the steel pillar, the steel beam, the clear sheet of plate glass, electric light and mechanical ventilation, all devoted to the service of functions or wants created by the greater intensity of modern life and by improved means of communication between places and men.

Probably there were those in Greece who deplored the departure from correct and historic Assyrian and Egyptian architecture, which had to be made in order to originate and establish the most exquisitely finished and most fully and logically developed architectural style the world has known. And when the sturdy but gross-minded Roman used and modified Greek prototypes in accordance with his coarser and more aggressive mentality, and when finally he introduced the arch and the vault, and substituted for the refined and elegant treatment of the severe and regular forms inseparable from beam and lintel construction, a bold and comparatively unrefined treatment of the more irregular and picturesque forms made possible by the discovery of the arch, the new departure was certainly as displeasing and distressing to the purists and scholars of that day, as were in latter days the works of those alleged barbarians whose efforts to utilize to the utmost the means and knowledge at their command, created the styles known as Byzantine and Romanesque, and finally that culmination of protest against dry-as-dust tradition, the styles which scholars and men of culture derisively named after the barbarian Goths.

So also in our day many of those who have been taught to understand and love and honor forms and traditions transmitted from past ages, shrink from contact with the new materials and processes; and noting the inevitable modifications of time-honored theory and practice, lift their voices in protest against legitimising forms which are the offspring of newly arisen functions and of newly discovered conditions of environment.

And yet each historic style was called into being in obedience to new developments of function and environment, and each was in its day an iconoclastic innovation upon well established and firmly founded practice.

Therefore we are justified in assuming that the new conditions will exert a marked influence on architectural style in our day and in the future.

It is the duty of those, who by familiarity with the historical styles are best fitted for this task, to ascertain the creative principles and laws which underlie the architectural styles of bygone periods of greatest artistic achievement, and to apply these principles to the utilization of the means placed at the disposal of the architect of our day for satisfying the requirements of the day.

The American architect who travels in Europe and studies the architecture of the many ages which have preceded the last century, is impressed and charmed by the freedom and naïveté with which consciousness of the fact that each age is the heir of all preceding ages is proclaimed in the composition and in the detail of so many structures. Nothing can be more interesting than the observation of the existence of a living vigorous style, joyous in the consciousness of life, free to assimilate the old and to create the new. Nor is it unprofitable to follow a style from the exuberance of its youthful vigor to old age and decadence, to ossification and crystallization into an inert and lifeless set of fixed and unalterable rules, into a fetish to be worshiped by future generations; in other words, into an academic historic style.

But after one has taken it all in, there is one impression stronger than all others. It is the consciousness of the zeal and earnestness of the all-pervading endeavor to utilize all the means at command, that the form and expression of each structure might conform to its function, whether that were the worship of God, or the glorification of guild or municipality; whether intended to serve the lavish display of the wealth and dignity of the great noble, or to house the humble burgher, each kind of structure has its individuality, and of these again each gives expression to the character and personality of its occupant.

Our generation has in many ways shown itself worthy of its heirship of so many ages of material and scientific progress, and has given expression to its appreciation of its good fortune by transmitting to the future an inheritance still more valuable than that which has fallen to its lot.

What can the architect do, that he also may prove himself worthy of opportunities so much greater than those enjoyed by his predecessors?

Human nature has limitations which circumscribe and define the attainable in Literature and Art. There will be none greater than Homer, than Moses, than David, than Shakespeare, than Phidias, than Leonardo da Vinci, than Raphael, than Michael Angelo, no author, no sculptor, no painter, no architect can, as an artist, expect to excel those who have gone before. But the architect is not only an artist, but also an engineer, a man of science and a man of affairs. In these latter capacities the architect of today has at his command instrumentalities and opportunities unknown to his predecessors. Were he an artist only, the giant strides which science and by its aid industry, communication and traffic have made in the past fifty years would leave him by the wayside, content as are his fellow artists of the brush and chisel to admire the onward rush—to be with it but not of it, to be dazed by its splendor, and to thrive and wax fat under the patronage of those who imitate and control the movement of modern material progress.

But architecture is not permitted to remain placidly contemplative of the march of events. The architect is not allowed to wait until, seized by an irresistible impulse from within, he gives the world the fruit of his studies and musings. He is of the world as well as in it. The world of today has greater need of his aid than had any previous period, and he is pressed into its service and must work for it and with it, no matter whether or not urged by the spirit within him. The world must have buildings; it will have them adapted to its wants and functions; it will insist upon the utilization of the best of the materials and processes which scientific and industrial progress place at its disposal. The architect must, therefore, fit himself for the duties thrust upon him. The world calls upon him to do the work of today with the tools of today, not as a tyro, not as one who must first learn how, but as an architect, a master worker, as one of whom the world believes that familiarity which he has acquired with the processes by which the work of other periods has been accomplished makes him better fitted for the work of today, and that he will press into its service all the experience of many ages and epochs.

Michael Angelo was painter, sculptor; architect, diplomat, but above all, and in all, an artist. An important factor in his greatness as an architect was his familiarity with the techniques of the auxiliary and subsidiary arts, sciences and crafts, the command of which devolves upon the architect. The great Buonarotti did not disdain to learn the metal founder's, the quarry worker's, and other crafts in order to be the better able to carry out the plans which his great mind had conceived. Were he among us now, he would be in the front rank of the experts and specialists in all the modern arts and sciences which have arisen to perplex and worry the artist architect wedded to the traditions, processes and materials of the past. And being Master of specialties and details, he would as General, muster them all into martial array for overcoming the difficulties incident to the expanded and diversified demands which our time makes upon the architect.

Few, perhaps none of us, can be equal to Buonarotti, but all can emulate him and his zeal and capacity for hard work. We, too, can become impatient and contemptuous of the performance of auxiliaries and specialists, and dismissing them, can ourselves acquire a knowledge of the technique of their arts and sciences and crafts, and in the furnace heat of zeal and enthusiasm for the attainment of a great end, combine all that we honor in the lore and traditions of our profession with the discoveries and achievements of the science of today, pour all into the mold of contemporary requirements and bring forth our contribution to the architecture of the new world, the new age of steel, electricity and scientific progress.

For several years it has been the fashion among the professors of our art to decry the new materials and processes of construction and condemn their most noteworthy applications to the service of requirements born of modern conditions. The contributions which modern science has made to our power to command and utilize the materials and forces of nature, and the increased and expanded opportunities for the creation of useful and beautiful works which modern society has given us, have been looked upon askance. And it is greatly to be regretted that some of those whose works have proved them well qualified to determine under the new environments the forms best adapted to the old, as well as the new functions, have been most persistent in their condemnatory utterances against the new problems which they themselves were so successfully solving.

What I have written is intended to be a protest against the dogma that Art in Architecture ended with the Renaissance, a denial of the assumption that the use of materials and processes and wants and functions unknown to the Masters who flourished in that glorious period or to their predecessors in other eras of great artistic vigor in architecture is incompatible with the performance of truly artistic work.

I wish to maintain that the steel pillar and beam and other contemporary contributions to the materials and processes of building construction, that the modern business building, and many other so-called monstrosities, are as legitimate contributions to architectural art, as were in their day, when first introduced, the stone pier and lintel, the brick wall or pier, the arch, the vault, the roofed temple, the vaulted basilica, the spired and buttressed cathedral. All that is wanting is the will and the ability to make proper use of these newly discovered agencies.

The new materials and processes, the new requirements, should not, however, in their introduction into architecture and in their assimilation by our art, be treated as things apart and by themselves, but as related to and part of all that has gone before in the long history of human and artistic progress.

The author of today has at his disposal and does not disdain to use an enlarged vocabulary; the musician has a greater range of instruments, a richer and fuller orchestration; and the great composer deems it a privilege to be able to evolve combinations of tone that were unattainable to his predecessors. And even if the painter of today uses the same pigments, and depicts the same phases of animate and inanimate nature, and he uses the same marble, and both painter and sculptor play upon the same gamut of human emotions, as did their prototypes for many generations, that is no reason why the architect should look askance upon new instrumentalities and new opportunities for developing and enlarging the scope of his art.

Let us then welcome the prosaic output of furnace and mill, and even the unpromising and garish sheet of plate glass. If they are always used where they are wanted and as they are wanted and never where they are not wanted, nor as they are not wanted, we shall have taken the first step toward the transmutation of these utterances of scientific prose into the language of poetry and art. In the nature of things the block of rough stone, the lump of clay, the log of timber, all are apparently as uncompromisingly unpoetic and inartistic as these much dreaded and imprecated modern intruders into the programme of architectural composition. . . . What they have of poetic suggestion and significance they owe to the genius of man, and what man has done with them, man can do with other media. Let us not stand back and admit that we are unable to learn from our predecessors how difficulties are overcome, how victory is wrested from apparent defeat.

Yet another word. I have quoted the dictum "form follows function" and have modified it into the words "function and environment determine form."

Steel pillars and steel beams occupy so little space that in order to enclose structures of which they are the essential supporting parts, they must be furnished with a filling if a space enclosing structure is to be erected, and steel posts and beams to be adequately protected against possible attacks of fire must receive bulky fire protective coverings. In these fillings and coverings we obtain media for artistic treatment which may be handled solely with reference to the desire to adapt "form" to "function."

From this I deduce that the influence of the new materials and processes will tend to a more free and less trammelled treatment of architectural design, and that the striving for the creation of ideally perfect form will be less hampered by limitations incident to the use of refractory materials of construction.

From: *The Influence of Steel Construction and Plate Glass Upon Style,* by Dankmar Adler. "The Proceedings of the Thirtieth Annual Convention of American Institute of Architects," 1896, pages 58–64.

The Chicago Period in Retrospect

by

Louis Henri Sullivan

In Chicago, the progress of the building art from 1880 onward was phenomenal. The earlier days had been given over to four-inch ashlar fronts, cylinder glass, and galvanized iron cornices, with cast-iron columns and lintels below; with interior construction of wood joists, posts and girders; continuous and rule-of-thumb foundations of "dimension stone." Plate glass and mirrors came from Belgium and France; rolled iron beams—rare and precious—came from Belgium; Portland cement from England. The only available American cements were "Rosendale," "Louisville" and "Utica"—called natural or hydraulic cements. Brownstone could be had from Connecticut, marble from Vermont, granite from Maine. Interior equipments such as heating, plumbing, drainage, and elevators or lifts, were to a degree, primitive. Of timber and lumber—soft and hard woods—there was an abundance. This general statement applies mainly to the business district, although there were some solid structures to be seen. And it should be noted that before the great fire, a few attempts had been made to build "fireproof" on the assumption that bare iron would resist fire. As to the residential districts, there were increasing indications of pride and display, for rich men were already being thrust up by the mass. The vast acreage and square mileage, however, consisted of frame dwellings; for, as has been said, Chicago was the greatest lumber market "in the world." . . .

The Middle West at that time was dominantly agricultural; wheat, corn, other grains, hogs, while cattle and sheep roamed the unfenced ranges of the Far Western plains. Lumbering was a great industry with its attendant saw mills and planing mills, and there were immense lumber yards along the south branch of the Chicago River, which on occasion made gallant bonfires. And it so happened that, as Louis heard a banquet orator remark, in the spread eagle fashion of the day, Chicago is "the center of a vast contiguous territory."

Great grain elevators gave accent to the branches of the river. There was huge slaughter at the Stock Yards, as droves of steers, hogs and sheep moved bellowing, squealing, bleating or silently anxious as they crowded the runways to their reward. The agonized look in the eyes of a steer as his nose was pulled silently down tight to the floor ring, in useless protest, the blow on the crown of the skull; and endless procession of oncoming hogs hanging single file by the heel—a pandemonium of terror—one by one reaching the man in the blood-pit; the knife pushed into a soft throat then down, a crimson gush, a turn in the trolley, and object drops into the scalding trough, thence on its way to the coterie of skilled surgeons, who manipulate with amazing celerity. Then comes the next one and the next one and the next, as they have been coming ever since, and will come.

Surely the story of the hog is not without human interest. The beginning, a cute bit of activity, tugging in competition with brothers and sisters of the litter, pushing aside the titman, while she who brought these little ones to the light lies stretched full length on her side, twitching a corkscrew tail, flapping the one ear, grunting softly even musically as the little ones push and paw, heaving a sigh now and again, moving and replacing a foot, flies buzzing about thick as the barnyard odors; other hogs of the group moving waywardly in idle curiosity, grunting conversationally, commenting on things as they are; others asleep. The farmer comes at times, leans over the fence and speculates on hog cholera; for these are his precious ones; they are to transmute his corn. Mentally he estimates their weights; he regards the sucklings with earnest eyes; he will shave on Sunday next. To him this is routine, not that high comedy of rural tranquillity, in peace and contentment, seen by the poet's eye, as he hangs his harp upon the willow and works the handle of the pump, and converses in city speech with the farmer of fiction and of fact, in the good old days, as the kitchen door opens suddenly and the farm wife throws out slops and disappears as quickly. Such were the home surroundings of the pretty white suckling, such were to form the background of his culture; all one family, crops and farmer, weather fair or untoward, big barn, little house, barnyard and fields, horses, ploughs, harrows, and their kin; cows, chickens, turkeys, ducks, all one family, with the little pig's cousins that romped and played—one perhaps to dream and go to Congress, others to dream and, when the time should come that their country needed them, would answer their country's call, it may be to fill little holes in the ground where poppies grow and bloom.

Meanwhile the little white suckling grows to full pig stature, which signifies he has become a hog, with all a hog's background of culture. He, too, answers his country's call, though himself not directly bent on making the world safe for democracy. He is placed by his friends in a palace car with many of his kind, equally idealistic, equally educated. The laden train moves onward. At the sidings our hero is watered to save shrinkage, and through the open spaces between the slats—the train at rest—he gazes at a new sort of human being, men doing this and that; they, too, answering their country's call, at so much per call, and he wonders at a huge black creature passing by grunting most horribly. Again the train moves on, stops, and moves on. In due time what was once the pink and white suckling, meets the man with the knife. But he is not murdered, he is merely slaughtered. Yet his earthly career is not ended; for soon he goes forth again into the work—much subdivided it is true—to seek out the tables of rich and poor alike, there to be welcomed and rejoiced in as benefactor of mankind. Thus may a hog rise to the heights of altruism. It does not pay to assume lowly origins as finalities, for it is shown that good may come out of the sty, as out of the manger. Thus the life story of the hog gains in human interest and glory, as we view his transfiguration into a higher form of life, wherein he is not dead but sleepeth. And yet, upon reflection, what about other pink and whites at the breast today? Are they to grow up within a culture which shall demand of them their immolation? or shall they not?

Inasmuch as all distinguished strangers, upon arrival in the city, at once were taken to the Stock Yards, not to be slaughtered, it is true, but to view with salutary wonder the prodigious goings on, and to be crammed with statistics and oratory concerning how Chicago feeds the world; and inasmuch as the reporter's first query would be: "How do you like Chicago?" Next, invariably: "Have you seen the Stock Yards?" and the third, possibly: "Have you viewed our beautiful system of parks and boulevards?" it may be assumed that in the cultural system prevailing in those days of long ago, the butcher stood at the peak of social eminence, while slightly below him were ranged the overloads of grain, lumber, and merchandising. Of manufacturing, ordinarily so called, there was little, and the units were scattering and small.

Then, presto, as it were, came a magic change. The city had become the center of a great radiating system of railways, the lake traffic changed from sail to steam. The population had grown to five hundred thousand by 1880, and reached a million in 1890; and this, from a pitiful 4,000 in 1837, at which time, by charter, the village became a city. Thus Chicago grew and flourished by virtue of pressure from without—the pressure of forest, field and plain, the mines of copper, iron and coal, and the human pressure of those who crowded in upon it from all sides seeking fortune. Thus the year 1880 may be set as the zero hour of an amazing expansion, for by that time the city had recovered from the shock of the panic of 1873. Manufacturing expanded with incredible rapidity, and the building industry took on an organizing definition. With the advance in land values, and a growing sense of financial stability, investors awakened to opportunity, and speculators and promoters were at high feast. The tendency in commercial buildings was toward increasing stability, durability, and height, with ever bettering equipment. The telephone appeared, and electric lighting systems. Iron columns and girders were now encased in fireproofing materials, hydraulic elevators came into established use, superseding those operated by steam or gas. Sanitary appliances kept pace with the rest.

The essential scheme of construction, however, was that of solid masonry enclosing-and-supporting walls. The "Montauk" Block had reached the height of nine stories and was regarded with wonder. Then came the Auditorium Building with its immense mass of ten stories, its tower, weighing thirty million pounds, equivalent to twenty stories—a tower of solid masonry carried on a "floating" foundation; a great raft 67 by 100 feet. Meanwhile Burnham and Root had prepared plans for a 16-story solid masonry office building to be called the "Monadnock." As this was to be a big jump from nine stories, construction was postponed until it should be seen whether or not the Auditorium Tower would go to China of its own free will. The great tower, however, politely declined to go to China, or rudely rack the main building, because it had been trained by its architects concerning the etiquette of the situation, and, like a good and gentle tower, quietly responded to a manipulation of pig iron within its base. Then the "Monadnock" went ahead; an amazing cliff of brickwork, rising sheer and stark, with a subtlety of line and surface, a direct singleness of purpose, that gave one the thrill of romance. It was the first and last word of its kind; a great word in its day, but its day van-

Monadnock Building, Chicago, Illinois. John Wellborn Root and Daniel Burnham, architects.

Auditorium Building, Chicago, Illinois. Dankmar Adler and Louis Henri Sullivan, architects. *Courtesy, Chicago Historical Society.*

Interior of Auditorium Building. View from the balcony. *Courtesy, Chicago Historical Society.*

ished almost over night, leaving it to stand as a symbol, as a solitary monument, marking the high tide of masonry construction as applied to commercial structures.

The Bessemer process of making "mild" steel had for some time been in operation in the Pennsylvania mills, but the output had been limited to steel rails; structural shapes were still rolled out of iron. The Bessemer process itself was revolutionary, and the story of its early trials and tribulations, its ultimate success, form a special chapter in the bible of modern industry.

Now in the process of things we have called a flow, and which is frequently spoken of as evolution—a word fast losing its significance—the tall commercial building arose from the pressure of land values, the land values from pressure of population, the pressure of population from external pressure, as has been said. But an office building could not rise above stairway height without a means of vertical transportation. Thus pressure was brought on the brain of mechanical engineer whose creative imagination and industry brought forth the passenger elevator, which when fairly developed as to safety, speed and control, removed the limit from the number of stories. But it was inherent in the nature of masonry construction, in its turn to fix a new limit of height, as its ever thickening walls ate up ground and floor space of ever increasing value, as the pressure of population rapidly increased.

Meanwhile the use of concrete in heavy construction was spreading, and the application of railroad iron to distribute concentrated loads on the foundations, the character of which became thereby radically changed from pyramids to flat affairs, thus liberating basement space; but this added basement space was of comparatively little value owing to deficiency in headroom due to the shallowness of the street sewers. Then joined in the flow an invention of English origin, an automatic pneumatic ejector, which rendered basement depths independent of sewer levels. But to get full value from this appliance, foundations would have to be carried much deeper, in new buildings. With heavy walls and gravity retaining walls, the operation would be hazardous and of doubtful value. It became evident that the very tall masonry office building was in its nature economically unfit as ground values steadily rose. Not only did its thick walls entail loss of space and therefore revenue, but its unavoidably small window openings could not furnish the proper . . . ratio of glass area to rentable floor area.

Thus arose a crisis, a seeming *impasse*. What was to do? Architects made attempts at solutions by carrying the outer spans of floor loads on cast columns next to the masonry piers, but this method was of small avail, and of limited application as to height. The attempts, moreover, did not rest on any basic principle, therefore the squabblings as to priority are so much piffle. The problem of the tall office building had not been solved, because the solution had not been sought within the problem itself—within its inherent nature. And it may be here remarked after years of observation, that the truth most difficult to grasp, especially by the intellectuals, is this truth: That every problem of whatsoever name or nature, contains and suggests its own solution; and, the solution reached, it is invariably found to be simple in nature, basic, and clearly allied to common sense. This is what Monsieur Clopet really meant when he said to Louis in his Paris student days: "Our demonstrations will be such as to admit of no exception." Monsieur Clopet carried the principle no further than his mathematics, but Louis saw in a flash the immensity and minuteness of its application, and what a world of research lay before him; for with the passing of the flash he saw dimly as through a veil, and it needed long years for the vision to reclarify and find its formula.

As a rule, inventions—which are truly solutions—are not arrived at quickly. They may seem to appear suddenly, but the groundwork has usually been long in preparing. It is of the essence of this philosophy that man's needs are balanced by his powers. That as the needs increase the powers increase. . . .

So in this instance, the Chicago activity in erecting high buildings finally attracted the attention of the local sales managers of Eastern rolling mills; and their engineers were set at work. The mills for some time past had been rolling those structural shapes that had long been in use in bridge work. Their own ground work thus was prepared. It was a matter of vision in salesmanship based upon engineering imagination and technique. Thus the idea of a steel frame which should carry *all* the load was tentatively presented to Chicago architects.

The passion to *sell* is the impelling power in American life. Manufacturing is subsidiary and adventitious. But selling must be based on a semblance of service—the satisfaction of a need. The need was there, the capacity to satisfy was there, but contact was not there. Then came the flash of imagination which saw the single thing. The trick was turned; and there swiftly came into being something new under the sun. For the true steel-frame structure stands unique in the flowing of a man and his works; a brilliant material example of man's capacity to satisfy his needs through the exercise of his natural powers. The tall steel-frame structure may have its aspects of beneficence; but so long as a man may say: "I shall do as I please with my own," it presents opposite aspects of social menace and danger. For such is the complexity, the complication, the intricacy of modern feudal society; such is its neurasthenia, its hyperesthesia, its precarious instability, that not a move may be made in any one of its manifold activities, according to its code, without creating risk and danger in its wake; as will be, further on, elaborated.

The architects of Chicago welcomed the steel frame and did something with it. The architects of the East were appalled by it and could make no contribution to it. In fact, the tall office buildings fronting the narrow streets and lanes of lower New York were provincialisms, gross departures from the law of common sense. For the tall office building loses its validity when the surroundings are uncongenial to its nature; and when such buildings are crowded together upon narrow streets or lanes they become mutually destructive. The social significance of the tall building is in finality its most important phase. In and by itself, considered *solus* so to speak, the lofty steel frame makes a powerful appeal to the architectural imagination where there is any. Where imagination is absent and its place usurped by timid pedantry the case is hopeless. The appeal and the inspiration lie, of course, in the element of loftiness, in the suggestion of slenderness and aspiration, the soaring quality as of a thing rising from the earth as a unitary utterance, Dionysian in beauty. The failure to perceive this simple truth has resulted in a throng of monstrosities, snobbish and maudlin or brashly insolent and thick-lipped in speech; in either case a defamation and denial of man's finest powers.

In Chicago the tall office building would seem to have arisen spontaneously, in response to favoring physical conditions, and the economic pressure as then sanctified, combined with the daring of promoters.

The construction and mechanical equipment soon developed into engineering triumphs. Architects, with a considerable measure of success, undertook to give a commensurate external treatment. The art of design in Chicago had begun to take on a recognizable character of its own. The future looked bright. The flag was in the breeze. . . .

From: *The Autobiography of an Idea*, by Louis Henri Sullivan. New York: 1924, pages 304-314. (Dover reprint, 1956).

Taliesin, Spring Green, Wisconsin. Frank Lloyd Wright, architect.
Courtesy, Chicago Historical Society.

V

Client, Architect and House

Client and Architect

by

Mariana Griswold Van Rensselaer

Fancy a painter unable to make pictures except when some one says to him: Paint now, paint this or that, and paint it thus and so; or a poet or musician forced to wait for similar behests, and getting them, very often, in the shape of uncongenial themes and narrow limitations. Imagine this and you will realize the architect's actual position, and the contrast between his life and that of other artists. Of course, the difference is neither accidental nor designed, but inevitable. It is the natural result of the fact that architecture is not an art pure and simple. It has a practical side. Its products are not mere objects of beauty. They are useful objects made beautiful, and they cannot be spun out of the artist's brain, but must cost a great deal of money. When useful, costly things which take up a great deal of space are in question, demand must precede supply. The poet or the painter caters to the public's taste; the architect serves the public's express wishes.

These facts mean two things. They mean that the architect must be something more than an artist, and that the client has a part to play which is only less important—which from one point of view is even more important—than the architect's own. As neither perfectly fulfils his duty in America to-day, it may be worth while to define in brief what that duty is. Let us begin with the client.

The client—whether a unit or that multiple of units called a committee—should remember that architecture is not practical only, but that its aesthetic side is as inevitable and important as its utilitarian, should realize that he who meddles with artistic things owes a duty to others as well as to himself, and know that this is especially the case when the result is to stand conspicuously before the public eye. It is false to say that there are structures which need not be "architectural" at all; that men may build at times, yet put all thoughts of art aside. Everything that ever was built is a good work of architecture or a bad one. If it plainly shows that its builders did not even try to make it good, it is only the more inexcusably bad. We are not naïve savages. We know that if a man is hungry for good or for beauty our obligation is the same, and we must give him the best that opportunity allows. When we insist that our neighbors shall daily look upon barrenness or deformity, when we fill what before was placid, empty space with crying shapes of ugliness, we are bad citizens, brutal neighbors. Some one has said that to build a hideous house is to indulge in the worst form of selfishness, and I am not sure that he exaggerated much.

Thus the client, whatever he means to build, should look about him for an architect, in the sense of a man who values at its highest the artistic side of every problem, great or small, elaborate or simple, and has thoroughly prepared himself to treat it. This is the first and the greatest commandment: an artist is needed for an "unimportant" as well as for an "important" building. Indeed, these words should not be used as they commonly are; for architectural things are most important in their aggregate, and in making up this aggregate it is the smaller units which play the larger part. If every twenty-five-foot house in New York could be made truly excellent, inside and out, would we not gladly give in exchange our few large and sumptuous buildings?

The second commandment is that when we set an artist to work we should let him work as freely as possible. "Undoubtedly," you may say; "but who is to decide just what is meant by these words?" In a letter I received not long ago from an American architect I find the following answer; it may sound startling, but, believe me, none could be more true and wise:

> The public must first learn to trust us as it does lawyers or doctors, before architecture can develop into a great art. Only when a public has learned to put its interests in building into the hands of trustees who are architects, can the latter do their best work. Any examples otherwise produced are accidental and not healthful developments.

That is to say, the architect's client should reason with himself somewhat in this fashion: Here is a problem to be solved which is very difficult, as demanding both a practical and an artistic solution. Here is a man whose profession it is to deal with such problems. The respect I feel for professional skill in other directions, artistic or practical, as the case may be, I should now feel with double strength. Of course, I must tell him exactly what I want, as I must describe my state of body to my doctor or my business tangle to my man-of-law. But, this done, I should feel sure that he will know best how my wants can be supplied. Of course, he is working for me, but so is my doctor, so is my lawyer. I am not more interested in the outcome of his efforts than of theirs; it is not a sign of folly, a confession of disgraceful ignorance, to defer to professional skill when they are concerned: the folly would be, and the ignorance and disgrace, did I try to doctor myself or plead my own cause, or, after engaging some one more competent to do it for me, did I dictate to him, cavil at him, and hamper his hand at every turn. And by just so much as is more subtile and, so to say, more professional than anything else, by just so much ought I to be most modest, most scrupulous, most trusting, when her ministrants are at work for me.

But this, American Public, is exactly what you do not say to yourself, except of very recent years, and in the very rarest instances. You do not see that it is just as foolish to refuse professional help in building as in law or medicine, and a great deal more selfish; nor, when you ask an architect's help do you follow and help him with half enough docility and trust. You must have your own say about his work, and your own share of credit if it succeeds. Truly, you own the result. But it belongs also to the artist and to the world at large, and their interests are quite as important as your own. The architect, it cannot be said too often, works only when you give him the chance, and only as you permit. Just now our art is in a transition stage. This is a crucial time, when every effort is of such importance that you would be glad to escape from all responsibility, eager to shift it all upon the architect, if you were only a little less ignorant with regard to the depth of your own ignorance. What you ought to know is that in any profession, and especially in so complicated a one as this, the weakest professional is likely to do better than the cleverest amateur.

Whatever you want, then, go to an architect for it; not to a carpenter, or a mason, or your own still more profound incompetence. Tell him all your practical, material desires, and insist that they shall be respected. That is to say, if you are quite sure what they are, and quite certain that it is possible to respect them. This is by no means always the case. To be unsettled, vague, self-contradictory, unpractical, impossible, is one of your most common faults, and one for the inevitable results of which you are only too apt to blame your architect. Settle your practical desires and state them clearly; and, if you will, pour out your vague aesthetic wishes; try to explain those crude artistic preferences, those misty, formless visions which you are pleased to call "my own ideas." But then go home, and leave him who is a trained artist, an experienced planner and constructor, to work out your problem in his own way. If what you get is exactly what you want, be very thankful; say that you are; and give the credit where credit is due. And if what you get is not quite all you want, or exactly what you think it ought to be, why, be thankful still; for the chances are (nay, the certainty is) that, had you interfered, the result would have been more unsatisfactory still.

This, then, American Public, is, as I conceive it, your duty in matters architectural. Or—for I must now confess that I have been playing the part of special pleader—this would be your duty, everywhere and always, and without possibility of doubt, if the architectural profession also recognized its duty clearly and was unanimously bent on its fulfillment.

In turning now to you, The Profession, can it be said that you have no shortcomings? Are there not many things in your attitude towards your client and towards your art which must be reformed, if you, if he, and if that art are to profit and to prosper as they should? Of course, you will agree that the public should trust you as it trusts the legal or the medical profession. But are you sure that you deserve to be trusted to quite the same extent? We are pretty certain that any lawyer or physician "in good standing" will do his very best for us. He may be stupid, but he is not likely to be uneducated, careless, or unfaithful. They would teach us to have the same confidence in you; but does experience prove that we always can? When we ask you and pay you to do a certain definite thing, can we feel confident that you will know how best to do it, and will do it as exactly as you can? that you will not slight it in favor of more interesting work, and will not causelessly alter it into something more like your own idea of what we ought to want? Can we feel confident that, if the task is small and cheap, you will approach it as carefully as though it were large and costly, or that, when we name the sum we want to pay, you will scrupulously respect the limitation, and scrupulously give us the most and the best you can within it? Many men in other professions sin by making things cost more in the end than they said they would in the beginning; but do they sin as frequently, frankly, and light-heartedly, or with as many specious maxims in excuse, as you? Do not say that the conditions differ. Of course they do, and of course in your case they are singularly complex and difficult. But your responsibility is increased, not lessened, by the fact. If it is peculiarly hard for you to make your clients understand the difference between a desirable or necessary increase in cost and an increase which comes merely from wilfulness, carelessness, selfish ambition, or stupidity on your part, then it is peculiarly needful that you should never be careless or selfish or more stupid than poor mortality is sometimes allowed to be. If it is essential that your client should have more confidence in you than in his lawyer or physician, then you should be still more conscientious. You should work unusually hard to inspire that trust which to you, and to the general progress of your art, is so absolutely indispensable. And this I do not think that, as a profession viewed in the mass, you yet have done.

I know that as a whole—as an Architectural Profession really worthy of the name, as something different from a mere body of building creatures—you are very young in America. Every one who cares for our art must recognize this fact, must see in your youth lusty strength, right ambition, and healthful promise; must have followed your progress thus far with admiration, and must believe in your future. If you could hear all that is said about you by serious and critical observers, I am afraid you would grow conceited. You are by no means conceited now. Indeed, you hardly realize as yet what surprisingly good work you have done as compared, not with your fathers only, but with your rivals over sea. Yet with all the respect, gratitude, and admiration that they feel for you, I think such observers see that you have faults, and that they are faults of character rather than of artistic endowment. Now, faults of character do not greatly matter with artists who paint or carve or even write, but with you they matter in the most vital way. An architect cannot shut himself up in his closet. He must come in contact with the public both as artist and as man; the public must trust him, while it need only weigh the poet and the painter after the act; and their product it may take or leave, while it is obliged to keep whatever you bestow. Therefore it is that, as men and artists, you must set yourselves a lofty standard. You must respect yourselves, respect each other, respect your client, and respect your art (each for its own sake and always all together). . . .

Let me hasten to say that there are some among you who fulfil this ideal. There are American architects who come pretty near to being models of all an architect should be. That is,—for I want to explain myself quite clearly,—they have prepared themselves in a thorough, all-round way to deserve the professional title; they think in the first place of their art and what it demands of them, in the second place of their client and his inalienable rights, and only in the third place of themselves; and in thinking of themselves it is still for art they care more than for pecuniary profit. To do all this means much labor and constant self-abnegation. But they know that they are artists, and if they did not mean to do it all, ought they to pretend to the artist's name or standing or reward?

Does this look like a fancy picture in your eyes, American Public? It is a faithful portrait, drawn from more than one original. As a picture of the whole profession it would, indeed, be flattering; yet it ought to be such a picture; and until it is, or, at least, until some distinct approach is made to the qualities it exhibits, the profession as a whole will never win the position it should, the public as a whole will never take the attitude it ought, and our art as a whole will never have the best chance of development. I may quote again, as a summing-up, from the letter already cited. It was written hastily for private reading, not as a formal confession of faith. . . .

"I have never spoken to you on the subject of the responsibility of my profession in this new country, where we have to create its status, but I feel its importance most keenly. The public must first learn to trust us as it does doctors or lawyers, before architecture can develop into a great art. . . . Therefore, every architect, no matter what his genius, who shows any lack of conscience or devotion to the responsibility his client has laid upon him, does more to ruin the cause of true architectural advance than any design of his creation can counterbalance. . . . I am proud of the men in my office. Thus far they have been but average fellows, but all seem quickly to feel the responsibility and dignity of their profession, and learn to accept the self-restraint and sacrifice it entails. . . . Of myself I may say that I have never yet had a chance to do anything great, but I have been patiently fitting myself for that opportunity (should it ever come) by trying my best and uttermost on everything, no matter how unimportant it may be; and I do not really think that anything has ever passed through the hands of our firm that greater care could at the time have improved."

Is not this, in truth, the heart of the matter—loyal trust on the client's part, loyal service on the architect's? When we say that the architect should think first of his art, do we not mean that he should prove that some kind of art may result from the faithful solution of the given problem? If he reveres his art, and wishes to make the public revere it, he should never doubt of its capacity. And if he is sure that in the given problem his capacity cannot keep touch with the capacity of art, then, as an artist, he has no right to meddle with it—whatever he might decide to do as a mere money-making man.

Which, now, will be more in fault, public or profession, if there does not soon grow up that happy accord upon which the future of our art depends? If loyal trust is not the rule, and does not always meet with loyal service, where chiefly rests the responsibility of developing a better state of things? Chiefly, I think, upon the public; and for several reasons.

In the first place, it is the public which in each given case must take the initiative. The architect cannot choose his client; the client must choose his architect, and it is his own fault if to-day he does not choose a good one. Then, in the second place, the profession, with all its faults, has certainly gone further than the public on the road to ideal excellence. The great advance it has made in recent years towards loyal service—which means, be it remembered, both competent and conscientious service—has been due to its own right instincts. The public has never asked that its architects should fit themselves better for their work than they did in former years; nor when they have thus fitted themselves is it properly conscious of the fact or properly grateful for it. Do we clearly see the kind and degree of difference which marks off our good buildings from our bad ones? Do we so intelligently, so persistently, encourage trained ability that untrained incompetence need feel greatly discouraged?

Nor are we more careful to foster professional honor and frankness than to foster true art. That system of competitions which has been supposed the best aid to art and the best protection for the client is answerable for much that we deplore. Open, unpaid competitions are an abomination. It is folly, and something worse, to ask the members of a respectable profession to show us their ideas for nothing, and to expect to get their best ideas or the ideas of the best among them. Limited, paid competitions, where certain chosen artists are asked to submit schemes for comparison, and are promised a fair reward for their trouble, should stand on a different footing. But they are often managed with so total a lack of respect on the client's part, not only for art, but for mere labor, and so total a disregard for the precepts of business good-faith and common honesty, that they, too, have become a by-word and reproach. I cannot dwell upon this thorny subject here; those who care to pursue it may take a file of the *American Architect and Building News* and look up the references under the index heading "Competition." Let me only beg of my reader that, whether he be architect or client, he will never countenance in any way an unpaid competition; that, if as a client he shares in the management of a paid one, he will keep the Eighth and Ninth Commandments—will mean what he says and say what he means and stand honestly by his meanings and sayings, and will not try to get something for nothing, or more than he asked for the price he agreed to pay; and that, if as an architect he takes part in such an enterprise, he will try not to break the Tenth Commandment in deed, or word or thought.

But a competition is a make-shift at best. In the majority of cases an architect should be chosen in the same way as any other professional adviser. It is easy to discover his standing among members of his own profession, easy to estimate his past results, and easy to draw conclusions from the effect he produces upon you as a man. Or, if all this is not always easy, it is not as hard or as risky as to judge from those architectural drawings which are so misleading to the untrained eye. Of course, it is more difficult to make sure in advance of conscientiousness than of capacity. But, as a general rule (which is not, perhaps, without exceptions), capacity implies at least artistic conscientiousness, for it means thorough preparatory training; and such training means right ambitions, since no strong external pressure has enforced it.

The subject of architectural drawings is too important to be passed over with a word. Much of our trouble in the past has come because the public does not understand that it takes an architect's eye, or, at least, an experienced eye, to read an architectural drawing rightly. At its best it is a conventionalized thing; at its worst it is about as mendacious a thing as one could find. The effects a novice admires most on paper are often the very ones he will not notice or will not admire in the building. The points which on paper seem least important are often those which will tell most strongly in brick or stone. Even that picture which is called a perspective cannot easily be understood; and a plan, a section, an elevation, are not pictures at all, but signs and symbols, which the novice often misconceives most entirely just when he thinks he has unravelled every knot. It should be a maxim, therefore, that never in competitions of any kind should judgment be pronounced without the taking of expert testimony. The interests of the client and those of the architect both demand that some competent artist, not himself concerned in the matter, should be asked —and paid—to explain the submitted designs.

Even apart from competitions, the public's conduct is not what it should be to encourage loyal service. Often enough in all his dealings the client shows a disregard for truth, honesty, and business methods which he would find very shocking were the architect the sinner and he the sufferer. And when the work is complete, he constantly takes credit for good ideas which do not belong to him, blames his architect for defects that his own ignorant demands have brought about, and, above all, cries out against an excess in cost that has been necessitated by changes from the original scheme which he himself has suggested.

Finally, our building customs are not yet arranged on a genuine business basis, and this is chiefly the fault of the public. With the best will in the world, a client rarely knows what he has a right to expect from his architect in the way of executive service, and almost always expects too much. "Superintendence" is a bone of contention between them, and will so remain until the public realizes all that is meant by architectural work, as a combination of art and science, and is willing to pay a fairer price than at present for its proper execution.*

In short, the American architect has less reason to trust the American public implicitly than the public has to put confidence in him. Therefore upon the client even more than upon the architect—and yet upon him, too, in no inconsiderable measure—lies at this moment the responsibility of improving our condition in matters architectural. If we are to have that reciprocal loyalty in trust and service from which alone can grow a healthy, prolific, and truly national art, the public must learn to bear itself as intelligently and honorably as the profession does to-day, and thus encourage the profession to still greater conscientiousness.

* See *American Architect and Building News.* "Building Superintendence"; and *Century* magazine, January, 1889, "Are We Just to Our Architects?"

From: *The Client and Architect,* by Mariana Griswold Van Rensselaer. "The North American Review," September, 1890, pages 319–328.

Coonley Playhouse, Riverside, Illinois. Frank Lloyd Wright, architect. *Courtesy, The Museum of Modern Art, New York.*

Midway Gardens, Chicago, Illinois. Frank Lloyd Wright, architect. *Courtesy, The Museum of Modern Art, New York.*

Bradley House, Woods Hole, Massachusetts. George G. Elmslie and W. G. Purcell, architects. *Courtesy, Wayne Andrews.*

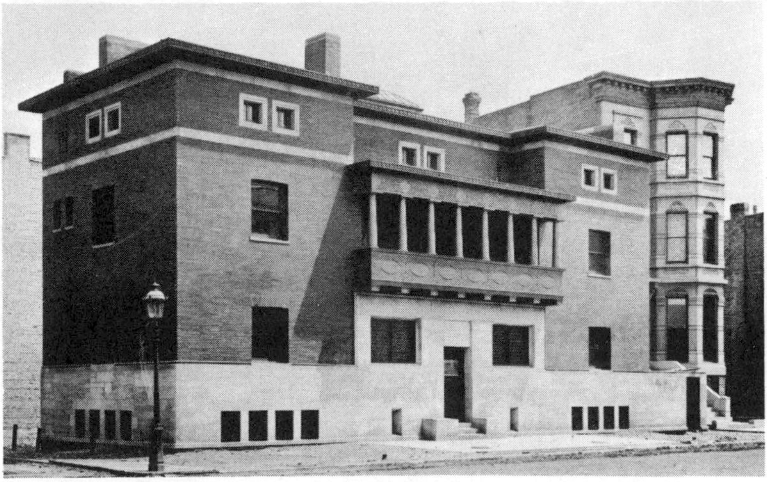

Charnley House, Chicago, Illinois. Dankmar Adler and Louis Henri Sullivan, architects; Frank Lloyd Wright, designer. *Courtesy, Chicago Historical Society.*

The Equipment of the Architect

by

John Wellborn Root

As a man of the century the typical client wants knowledge more than anything else, and what he needs when off the track is only information to put him right. To combat his whims with whims equally unreasoning, to fight his groundless notions of style with our groundless notions, to make him cease laying down law equally as questionable—all this is the height of folly. Ours is no more a position of unassailable virtue than his. With what thin disguise of recently acquired saintliness do we protest that a thing is bad to-day which yesterday we ceased doing and to-morrow will do again! Fashion becomes our only fortress. We fight our battles behind bulwarks made of stays and ruffs, laces and ribbons, baggy and tight trousers, snuff-boxes and smelling-salts, "Queen Anne" gables, and "Neo-jacobean" bays and "Romanesque" turrets; battlements behind which we risk our professional lives to-day, and which, to-morrow, we blow into oblivion with a sneer. For our own self-respect, for the dignity of our own position, for the sake of an architecture which shall have within it some vital germ, let us come out from our petticoat fortress and fight our battles in open field. In science and literature, in art, is heard, loudly calling, the voice of reason. For any branch of human knowledge or imagination or aspiration to shut itself from this cry is death.

In his relations with his clients the architect must take a position as reasonable as that which he occupies to his design and to himself. In the present catholic condition of art there seems to be no reason for violent prepossessions or any shirking of persistent "whys"; for any notions we may have of a possible solution for a problem as yet unstudied should have at least the merit of being suggested by the inherent elements of the problem; and this being true, a statement of the possible solution and its reasons will certainly carry weight. Much more will an equally frank statement carry weight when the problem has been in all its bearings carefully considered and the best solution arrived at. In architecture, as in all other arts, it is granted that while reason may be pushed very far, it must finally stop short of full attainment, leaving this for the higher faculties of taste and imagination. Reason should lead the way, however, and imagination take wings from a height to which reason has already climbed. This reasonable plane for the contact of architect and client removes from between them much of that false view which assumes that art is an arcanum too profound for uninitiated minds, a Court of the Priests upon which unwashed feet may not tread. There is no danger that great things or even good things in art will ever be born to the sterile mind, or that the creative gift of a true artist will be profaned by a perfect comprehension of the unwashed.

The art of architecture, moreover, is different from other arts in the largeness of this purely reasonable and (if the word be allowed) explainable side. Not to avail himself of this fact is for the architect a great mistake, for when the client has fully grasped the reasons for that part of a design which can be explained, he is inspired to completer trust for those parts which lie in the realm of the imagination and fancy. Often by such an interview floods of light will be shed upon questions otherwise vague and indeterminate, and methods of solving them will be indicated which will have a pertinence and beauty not otherwise attainable. It is not uncommon that an intelligent layman will have a breadth of view in architectural matters which will not be suspected if he be held rigidly to professional interviews. He lacks technical vocabulary; he fears perhaps to express an opinion which from a professional point of view will seem ridiculous; he hesitates to commit himself to what may be out of style. All this is wrong and should be discouraged. His opinions and tastes may be the result of careful study and close observation by a mind at once acute, discriminating and retentive; and, moreover, may have for the architect an especial value because they have been formed without professional prepossessions. The technical and professional point of view in art is not always the truest. Artists are often victims of artificially acquired judgment, when unaided vision in dry light should be the only communication with the mind. How great would be the value to an architect of being able at will to free himself from all the prejudices and theories which in his practice have grown about him, and for an occasional hour see as an intelligent layman may see! This is possible unfortunately at second-hand, but at second-hand it is possible. If, however, it is to be done, care must be taken that for the time being the mind is not swayed by the very professional habit that prevents its own clear sight. Statements will be made, opinions expressed which will be shocking enough to archaeologists and art critics; questions will be asked impossible to answer; the profound student and brilliant designer of the moment before may find himself dangerously near a most unpleasant unmasking. This is as it should be and should not be shirked.

The temptation is almost irresistible often to take refuge in the books, among the Greeks, among the French; to seek cover in the darkness of the middle ages, or concealment in the glitter of the seventeenth century; to quote precedents, and turn to buildings erected by great men. All this is nonsense. Be assured that no reason is good, no answer worth giving that does not spring from the present question and is not inherently connected with it. It is of course very easy to say what men of other times, did, but it is not easy to tell whether our conceptions of those men and their surroundings are true to the life, or are pictures painted by ourselves and without models. No building nor architect of this or any other time can be a conclusive precedent until we get a stenographic report of the interviews which were held between the architect and his client, and even this is incomplete without a photograph of both.

It will be seen that this tends directly against the literal use of historic styles. True. But so much the better for the styles as we understand them. A style has never been made by copying with the loving care of a dry-as-dust some preceding style. Styles grow by the careful study of all the conditions which lie about each architectural problem, and thus while each will have its distinct differentiation from all others, broad influences of climate, of national habits and institutions will in time create the type, and this is the only style worth considering. This position is reasonable and is susceptible of rational statement. It does not mean the monstrous method, sometimes advocated, which would gather fragments from all ages and build them into one hideous whole. It does not mean the reconciliation in one design of "the chaste beauty of the Greek with the rugged strength of the Egyptian," which is as if nature should essay a combination of the chaste beauty of the gazelle with the rugged strength of the rhinoceros. It means rather to use all that men have done, to use it all intelligently and consistently, with study and the nicest discrimination, and to make sure that the particular thing chosen for the given purpose shall be the best fitted for that purpose—shall in short grow out of it. This is as obvious as to say that a man's exterior form shall be the result of his interior structure, that his skin and hair shall be colored by the climate where he lives; and being thus obvious it becomes the true position to assume in relation to the client. Answers to his questions, corrections of his false, and approval of his right, tastes, estimating the value of his suggestions and the possibility of their realization—all these are possible upon this plane.

Having thus mastered the outer conditions of the problem—its theorem—we pass to its solution. We sit down with the conditions before us. What next? The mind wanders; the question seems barren of interest. How shall we quicken and concentrate the mind—how give interest to the problem? First, saturate ourselves with it; fully realize all of its essential conditions. This may take time, which seems wasted, for meanwhile the design does not seem to grow. But wait: What sort of a town is the house to be in? How wide are the streets it faces? Where do the prevalent winds blow from? How much hot and cold weather has the town? How much rain? Which way is south? How far from the street is the house to stand? Has the town smoky or clear air? What are the native building materials? What is the character of the workmen likely to be employed? Is the occupant of the house a student? a family man? a public man with many friends? one who has many guests? who gives many entertainments? Is he a man fond of display, or one who shirks it and rather prefers the simplicity of "solid comfort"? These and many other questions will suggest themselves, and being answered will, when added to suggestions obtained directly from the client, point out very plainly the general solution of the problem. This assumes that the architect will frankly accept the consequences involved in each answer, and also that he is not burdened by prepossessions so strong as to prevent his acting dispassionately.

Before proceeding with our design, one other point must be carefully weighed, as it will exercise upon the character of the building a very strong influence:—What sort of houses is the new house to have for its neighbors? Probably in no country in the world are architects so indifferent to this as in America. Here, if any attention is given to the matter, it is for the purpose of avoiding deference to the neighbors, of making the house as emphatic a contrast as possible. The existing houses are old and quiet? Then the new house must be as spick-and-span and as noisy and offensive as we can make it. The old houses are broad and low? The new house must stand tip-toe to the clouds. The old houses are of stone? The new house must be of brick, and as red as possible. Thus we succeed in compelling every passer-by to stop and gaze upon our new house, but this gaze is too often that of baleful fascination, as one finds his eyes riveted by the antics of a drunken man. Any new design should be carefully adjusted to its neighbors. If out of key with them, it becomes invariably impertinent and offensive, be the design as clever as you please.

Assuming now that the architect has been brought into entire sympathy with his client, that he has fully mastered the environments and conditions of his problem, he is prepared for its actual solution. The stage of mental preparation, based as it is upon the previous exchange of ideas between client and adviser, has undoubtedly brought about a tolerably trustworthy scheme of general procedure. We have now to determine more accurately what form our design shall take. It is not probable that any first study will be best, and for this reason it seems a waste of time even to consider the first study until several other sketches of plans and designs shall have been made, differing from each other as widely or as slightly as may be. Then an intelligent comparison becomes possible. To make this first comparison as little prejudiced as possible, it is wise to make each rough study independently, if possible with scarcely the memory of the others, and also (so far as the design is concerned) to make it as rapidly as possible. Thus the impression left upon the mind at the moment of production is less lasting, and the sketches come back to us from their temporary seclusion as if they were the work of another man. They can be criticised therefore without bias, and from among them can be determined more accurately the true path. From this test-sketching come new light and more accurate direction, and the design is ready to take on a growth more nearly like its full development.

Further study will probably bring us to our libraries. Books are dangerous things and need most careful handling. Reference to them will often tend to confuse ideas which before were well defined, and inject others totally irrelevant to the case in hand. In this hour with books, reject as unworthy of consideration everything, however fascinating, which conflicts with the predetermined plan of procedure, and beware of a single detail which suggests itself as perfectly appropriate for our purpose. Nothing found in a book will add a feather's weight to a really good design if it be bodily transferred, or indeed transferred with anything of literal translation. For this reason the study of the hour should be close and sympathetic, continued until the mind is fully refreshed and inspired by a process precisely similar to that by which it became saturated with preliminary conditions. Then shut the book and do not go back to your design; do something else. After a day or two, find what impressions remain with you and work them out of yourself without reference to the originals. Any impression which remains so vague that reference must be made to the original source before it can be made to assume coherent and approximately satisfactory shape should be thrown aside as worthless. It is undigested food from which no muscle or vitality can be expected, and in the varied constitutions of men some mental foods as often disagree with individuals as physical foods. This fact is so palpable that it often becomes a question, not of accident but of constitution. Some architects can no more digest a bit of thirteenth-century detail than they can digest a nail. The only difference is that they readily learn whether the nail has been digested, while they may not know if the detail has been.

During this time the critical study of the house plans will have been going on; each minutest point will have been discussed, and this not only in relation to the convenience and beauty of the interior, but also in its capabilities of artistic external treatment. The development of the design and of the plan should in all cases go on together; one should never get away from the other. No feature should ever be allowed to form into a plan, about the external treatment of which the architect has not a well defined idea.

By study and sketching we are now prepared to make a somewhat carefully rendered design of the building as we intend it to be. At this stage of the design we are open to dangers which arise from several causes, different in architecture from other arts, but still dangerous. Several of these are loss of scale; over-application or wrong application of detail, and hence a loss of simplicity; loss of homogeneity. To avoid the loss of scale, it is of course necessary to realize through every means in our power the exact meaning of each part sketched in terms of the executed work; . . . and therefore not a single drawing should be made to a scale which has not been mastered.

Over-application of detail will be avoided by similar means as loss of scale; but, beyond what may be taught by observation, is the simple law that beautiful detail is a precious commodity, not to be prodigally flung away, but to be used with wise discrimination. A broad wall surface should fairly cry out for an ornament before it gets one, and also a moulding or a column. In a drawing every plain surface or moulding seems of much less interest than when built or cut. Nature steps in here, and nature's decorations of sunshine and shadow, her warm glow of ever beautiful colors, varied and enriched by rain and wind, are always lovely, while our decorations often fall short of loveliness. . . . If, however, the mind is surcharged with brilliant inspirations, consistent, truthful, poetic, free rein may be given to it. But do not confuse the operation of the imagination with the operation of the pencil. Loss of simplicity does not necessarily follow when a design is enriched; it follows only when the design is falsely enriched, as when adventitious and impertinent products of ungoverned fancy interfere with the effect of some great and essential part. Adventitious features in a building should, like children, be seen and not heard.

Homogeneity is in these days more difficult to maintain because the prevailing habits of the time have prevented architects from closely following traditions which would compel homogeneity, while no new habits dependent upon the nature of the case have taken their places. Every structure has some few conditions so far beyond all others in importance that in expression all others should be subordinated to them and influenced by them. These conditions may seem at first contradictory, but they can always be reconciled, and rightly considered will impress upon each detail of the design an effect distinct and unavoidable. The whole matter is summed up, as in painting, in the necessity of keeping a true perspective, giving prominence to objects in proportion to their importance. Yet nothing about a house is too small for close attention—for frequent revision and re-study.

From: *John Wellborn Root: A Study of His Life and Work*, by Harriet Monroe. Boston: 1896, pages 65–75.

Character and Style

by

John Wellborn Root

Is it not time that the familiar architectural word "style" should be relegated to its proper meaning? As now used it has almost ceased to have significance even for architects themselves, while to the public at large the word has become a delusion. How often the architect of the day is compelled to strain his conscience in answering the familiar question as to the style of his designs, because he feels the necessity of calling by some traditional name designs often as unconventional as a chattering chimpanzee. For practical purposes, such phrases as "Grecian Doric," or "Roman Ionic," or any other names of the traditional styles have become impertinent, and are used only for lack of better terms.

The word "style," as generally used by the public, has, on the contrary, with all its varied applications a very comprehensive significance, and is rarely misused or misunderstood; to say that a woman, a dress, or a yacht has "style" is to convey an impression which is understood with moderate accuracy. Thus used the word carries a deeper meaning than mere adherence to given fashions, even if the latest; as in the case of many women who devote an energetic existence to the latest styles, yet are never accused by anyone of having "style." This quality has a wider sweep; it lies far beyond the creative power of a Worth or a L'Archevèque. It is inherent—a thing of the head and heart, not of the epidermis. It shines out from beneath a beggar's rags; it reveals itself in the touch of an inexperienced pianist, in the "handling" of an untrained artist, in the lines of a thatched cottage. We find that among the work of architects it is present in one building and absent in another. Often it characterizes an architect's smaller buildings and is absent in those more important, or vice-versa. In the progress of a design it frequently happens that a preliminary study will be full of "style" and the final design have not a bit of it.

Now, this common word "style" is manifestly not of the same signification as that used in architecture—as when we say that buildings are in the "Grecian Corinthian style," "the style of François Premier," or "the French Gothic style of the thirteenth century." With this special use of the word each one of us is presumably familiar, and I wish for a moment to call attention to "style" in its larger, fuller and more widely understood use.

And first let us note that so far as art is concerned, few created things have ever lived beyond the age of their creator that lacked this precise quality. Occasionally some titanic and monstrous mind will throw upon the world intellectual spawn which will live for ages because of the tremendous power and vitality which have been injected into it. But these phenomena are too infrequent to be worth discussing, and constitute only rare exceptions to a universal law.

Of all great works of art which have come down to us, spared by the tooth of time, we confess now what was confessed in each age before us—they have "style." This, in spite of the fact that the architectural style may be one we despise. Pierre de la Vallé probably had no warm admiration for that Gothic style which is built in the apse of Notre Dame de Paris; Christopher Wren certainly cared little for the similar style of old St. Paul's or Westminster Abbey, or the later Gothic designs of Oxford which he so mutilated. But I do not doubt that both architects would have admitted that the buildings which they did not admire had the kind of "style" we are discussing. Why was this? For a reason precisely similar to that which saves a gentleman of the old school from the ridicule of a gentleman of the new. You may feel that the manners of the *grande ècole* are out of key with our jaunty flippancy; but there can be no doubt that they fitted a different and perhaps better mode than ours, and in all essential things, all things of the heart, the two gentlemen are at one.

Thus, although Notre Dame de Paris and the Hotel de Ville are two buildings of different ages, as widely apart in manner as St. Louis and Henry IV, you will note how alike they are in certain respects. See the noble gravity with which in them large matters are treated; the sweet repose of manner in every-day affairs, the airily graceful and fantastic touch which enlivens lighter subjects. From the noble sweep of the centre door arch to the great griffins that from its tower-tops grin out over Paris, Notre Dame has this fine, gentlemanlike style. There are no solecisms. Everything is fitting; temperate when most exuberant, contained when most severe.

What is this fine style? How did these architects get it? How is it that all over the world—where the gleaming domes of Taj-Mahal sleep in the white sunshine; where gray pylons of Egypt enclose their depths of luminous shadow; where the pink pentalic columns of the Parthenon lie scattered on the Acropolis, bleaching like the bones of a dead demigod; where the dim, echoing aisles of Chartres filter from the sky its most heavenly rapture to pour it on the humbled worshiper—how is it that everywhere men have fixed in stone and wood and glass this quality, so subtle . . . it seems the . . . essence of art?

Any competent answer to this question will necessarily touch upon a field of ethics not confined to architecture alone, nor even to the arts alone, but pertaining to humanity itself. The arts, architecture among them, have been called polite. Perhaps in the earlier stages of this politeness architecture takes precedence of all others. Painting and sculpture began their career with no distinct debt to humanity; but architecture was, at its birth, shouldered with a large obligation, which it was in decency compelled to pay. Every house built to shelter man from the elements was a thing not to be avoided by its neighbors. It not only partially shut out from them grass and trees and sun and sky, but, by virtue of its very bigness and fixity, it became, whether a thing of beauty or not, a thing of prominence. This fact has made Mr. Garbett call architecture "the politeness of building."

Accepting this definition as sound, let us note some of the qualities which we find in a gentleman, as we understand the term, and see if they are not equally applicable to good buildings. These are: Repose, Refinement, Self-Containment, Sympathy, Discretion, Knowledge, Urbanity, Modesty.

Repose. Quietness of body and mind; not phlegmatism, but enforced quietness, as in the poise of a gladiator. The mind becomes finely receptive when held in this calmness of attitude.

Refinement. In which all things tend toward the loss of asperity, not loss of power nor of value; gaining in that smoothness of surface, that crystallineness of composition which give added currency and beauty to the thing refined.

Self-containment. Which avoids a too ready utterance of the momentary thought; which spares other people a swift infliction of all our knowledge; which inwardly debates before answering grave questions.

Sympathy. Which "puts yourself in his place"; which readily accepts a point of view; which quickly adjust itself to its environment;

which gives gravity for gravity, lightness for lightness, tears for tears, laughter for laughter.

Discretion. Which seeks always the fitting thing to do, thus supplementing sympathy; which holds its tongue when speech is unnecessary; which knows nothing when forgetfulness is a virtue.

Knowledge. The care of speech; the loving selection of words; the scrupulous nicety of grammar, the fullness of idea and illustration that decorates each subject touched.

Urbanity. As the name suggests, a quality begotten in cities; suavity; the faculty of avoiding friction; the knack of easily getting about in crowds of men; the attitude of deference to their weaknesses; the power, without creating offense, to ward off their aggression.

Modesty. Without which all other qualities may become offensive. Not affected modesty; not Uriah-Heepness; but the genuine self-esteem which, in justly valuing self, puts as well a just value on others, and thus confesses that self is small in many comparisons.

Now, what are these qualities in men that they are not in buildings? Their sum total makes a perfect gentleman. The sum total of their analogues makes a perfect building. As a man may lack some of them and still be a very good fellow, so from a building a number of these elements may be omitted and still the design not be utterly damned.

Let us now proceed to apply these qualities to a test of buildings.

As to repose. It seems at present heretic to say that it is the most essential of all qualities, but the fact remains that it is. The instinct of the world has decreed that all large things should be quiet or slow-moving, and that only little things like bees and butterflies may flutter. The world has also noted that all large things are soberly, even if richly, colored, and that in form all of their lines tend to the expression of the quality of repose.

Since, therefore, buildings are the largest things made by man, a deviation in them from this universal law is the most elemental of mistakes, increasing in enormity as the building considered increases in size. Both in this and other respects many things may be pardoned to a little house, or one without public significance, which becomes unpardonable in a larger or more important building.

I am aware that you may summon as apparent witnesses against me many of the notable buildings of the world, but even in these I think a close study will show that the principle is sound, and is carried out. As a matter of fact, so general a law as this always has within it a lesser principle which determines the exact application of the law.

and in this case the inner principle is simply this: What sentiment is the building designed to convey? Is it the restless aspiration of the soul after God, as embodied in the mediaeval cathedral? Is it the expression of the power and stability of a great corporation, as expressed in its office building? Evidently there must be very different treatment of the two classes of design, but it seems equally evident that both designs must consider the outer and elemental law to as great extent as is consistent with the expression of purpose.

Practical applications of this law a little reflection will show us, and it is worth while, therefore, to mention but a few. Probably nothing about a design is more expressive in this respect than the management of roof or cornice lines. In a small house, or one that is greatly varied in plan so that each of its parts is small, a very broken and even restless outline may be good. But even in this case, there should be sufficient allowance of quiet and unrelieved background to offset fully its whimsical features. In large and important buildings, however, especially those built for commercial purposes, I believe that experience will show simple sky-lines to be best, as best conducive to the quality of repose; and more than this, because a very broken sky-line is apt to suggest multiplicity of subdivision or function, and should, therefore, be coincident with these subdivisions or functions.

The value of plain surfaces in every building is not to be overestimated. Strive for them, and when the fates place at your disposal a good, generous sweep of masonry, accept it frankly and thank God. If this goodly surface come at the corners of your building, so much the better; for there can be no better guaranty that the house will "stay where it was put" than the presence in it of masses of simple masonry at its angles.

As to repose in color, you will know at once all that can be said by me, and will sympathize with the utter condemnation of the use of sharply conflicting colors in any structure of considerable size.

In general, our whims of all sorts, our fanciful vagaries, whether in color or form, may be put, perhaps safely, into small buildings, but if they go into large structures, they should be kept well subordinated to the general mass, whose largeness and dignity should be expressive of not only sober thought, but of the gravity becoming all great things.

Refinement is a quality whose importance will be at once apparent. Of late it has at times seemed obsolescent, but always in work which can never have permanent value. Refinement in architecture means not only the careful consideration of each detail in itself, but also the relation of each to its neighbors and to the whole. For what may be well enough in itself may be vulgar in juxtaposition with other things.

The laws by which refinement in a building is reached, would be most difficult to state; but apart from that close study which is necessary for each good element in a design, the mysterious thing called taste is of vast importance here; and the acquisition and cultivation of this is a matter to be constantly followed. In this pursuit not only is it wise to familiarize one's self with confessedly great architectural examples, but with all great art work. As much may be learned of color from one great canvas of Paul Veronese as from all the books on the subject ever written, and the study of the contours of Greek vases will do more to cultivate a niceness of taste in outline than many profiles purely architectural.

More than all others, however, the human form must remain the supreme school for the study of form and proportion in its most refined and significant expression. Here, as all artists have insisted, the methods of nature have their fullest revelation. This is the divinest design for any structure; this is the most pregnant essay on the much vexed questions of Proportion and Scale; here is a perfect solution of the relation of exterior expression to interior arrangement, and here is a demonstration of the fact that the utmost refinement may be combined with herculean strength. When fully expressed in architectural design, this refinement means all that it suggests in the human form itself. There is the same careful avoidance of useless features, the same perfect adjustment of each part to the function performed by it. Elephantine columns are not used to do the work of mice; necessary structural features are not emasculated by ornament too delicately wrought; purely decorative features are not so formed as to give a false suggestion of vital necessity.

Like the refinement of a man of the world, the refinement of a design will suggest itself through a thousand channels, sometimes through a direct appeal, sometimes through an indirect insinuation, sometimes through an effort to conceal some necessary weakness or misfortune, so as to spare needless pain to the observer. In all cases the quality has the true ring when it springs from soundness of purpose—from the heartfelt desire to please; and it becomes false and hollow in men and in buildings whenever it is an affectation.

Let us glance at the next attribute of a man or building of "style," Self-Containment.

Whenever we meet a man who impresses us as burning with the

wish to tell all he knows, let him be as graceful in speech, as wide in knowledge, as polite in manner as may be, we feel that he lacks a most essential element of "style." So with a building. Nothing is more offensive than those verbose and overdone designs which are not only mere *tours de force,* but which suggest the anxiety of the architect to tell all that he knows in one design. Very successful buildings have the quality of temperance, of self-containment. Even in the most exuberant French or Flemish Gothic the exuberance is a part of its age, and comes as a natural outgrowth from it. In good examples of these types there is no straining for effect, nor anything theatrical or merely declamatory. There is always the feeling that, however much the architect may have chosen to say, he has exhausted neither himself nor his subject, but kept in reserve a thousand strong images or quaint conceits for some future use.

In these days, when what we call "originality" is so much desired, self-containment is perhaps more difficult to attain than ever before. But we must learn it, distrusting the merit of any of our designs which seem labored to us, in which effort is made to express more than we really know, being assured that all over the building executed from such a design will be the painful traces of labor and sweat. In the varied solutions possible to a problem, the true labor to be expended is in first determining which one is best, then evolving it when it is found. The best solution will always be the simplest, and its full growth will follow with a directness and ease which suggest the budding of a flower rather than the forging of a columbiad.

Self-containment in the expression of a subject always means its thorough digestion. In conversation we may be pardoned if we occasionally think aloud, thus uttering many irrelevant or tentative remarks. Our buildings are much more serious things, for however much they may deserve oblivion, the fact that most of them remain standing after we are through with them prevents people from forgetting them. Every intemperate and hastily uttered thing about them remains to our discredit. We may not all succeed in doing original work, but each of us can do well considered work, expressive of that self-containment which thinks first and speaks afterwards.

Sympathy, another quality necessary in the gentleman, is also necessary in a building, and this means, of course, in an architect as well.

In each community there are certain tendencies of the people, certain peculiarities, full sympathy with which is essential to the successful designer. This is a point we are apt to neglect. Our work has too much of the transplanted look which comes from the absence of this active sentiment. Touched by the warmth and sunshine of an outgoing and vital sympathy, all styles of architecture become quickly acclimatized and characteristic. Yet it seems sometimes that one of our greatest efforts is to prevent this acclimatization by rigorous insistence upon mere traditions, too tenaciously holding to the dry canons of mere architectural style. This is altogether a mistake. A great type in architecture, like that of the Parthenon, becomes great not only because of its perfection as a solution of a given problem, but because in a hundred small respects it expresses the immediate influence of essentially local conditions.

This variation because of environment always comes about of itself in time, and this may be in spite of architects. No importation of Greek architects could save Roman work from swift differentiation from Greek work. Our attitude should therefore be one of readiness to accept and help forward the inevitable. By doing this we can insure that it will be the finer national characteristics, rather than the grosser, whose influence will be manifested.

Passing from this wider view, we must also note that sympathy is equally essential in considering the purpose of each building, and the idiosyncrasies of each owner. Many a most brilliant feature has been the outgrowth of what at first seemed in a client an idiotic whim; and many most successful buildings are so because they reveal on the part of the designer a point of view in warm sympathy with their intention. If the building is a warehouse, a dry-goods store, an office-building, or a hotel, the true points of view in designing them will be largely determined by these commercial considerations.

The architect occupies a position in this respect different from all other artists. He can never afford, even when the artistic expression of his design alone is considered, to neglect a single condition not only in the larger matters of climate, national characteristics, general purpose, etc., but also in matters apparently very trifling. I am confident that an architect designs a better grocery-store, if into his own professional view of the problem he will admit in all possible fullness the grocer's view. More than for all other artists does success for the architect depend on the activity and warmth of these sympathies.

But sympathy is a very dangerous thing without discretion. Sympathy leads us onward; discretion pulls us back. Without discretion architecture is like a machine without a governor.

Many houses suggest a clock in the act of striking twenty-four, or a locomotive driving-wheel whirling around on a slippery track. How many buildings do you know of in Chicago, against whose discretion no charge could be sustained? Of course, I do not mean the large class of tramp and bummer houses which, if justice had her way, would always be in the lock-up, on charges of "drunk and disorderly": I refer rather to houses of avowed morals, who profess not to stay out nights, and in whose daily and nightly life the latch-key has no place. In even these professedly good houses, how many skeletons dangle from the cornice, perch on the roof, hover about the doorways or crouch at the basement. What we need now more than anything else is "proper" houses, whose real discretion is what it professes to be. What would you think of a man who should wear his religion in the band of his hat, and yet get drunk, and not care enough about it to go home in a cab? This is exactly like the indiscretion of our houses. They are always doing indiscreet things. Columns, roofs, gables, balconies, are all over them, each loudly swearing it is what it pretends to be; and yet a blind man could see there is not a word of truth in it. In their anxiety to induce belief by volubility of protest, many of them look as if the source of their design had been a firework pinwheel, while some assert by their cumbrous features, by their heavy brows and wrinkled skins that they are great giants of houses, when it is evident that they are only wretched little pigmies.

Seriously, discretion is our crying need—the doing of the right thing in the right place and time. What discretion have we, when we assume in the prevalent craze that because a type of design is good for a house 100 feet wide and high, it is equally good for a dwelling 25 feet wide and 30 feet high? In other words, that the limbs of an elephant are good enough for a greyhound; or that nothing is so beautiful as the torso of the Medici Venus on the legs of the Farnese Hercules. This sort of thing is no more true in architecture than in any other art or in nature itself. As the fond mother said of her hopeful son's "swear word"—"It's worse than immoral—it's ungentlemanly."

Nor is it true discretion to assume that the same kind or scale of detail is equally good for all buildings. We don't sing Schubert's "Lorelei" on the floor of the board of trade, nor shout the price of grain in our music-rooms. And yet we spend a wealth of delicate ornament on our down-town edifices, and build our dwellings like Stonehenge. It would seem that ordinary discretion should teach us that the relation between dwellings and trade-palaces is the relation between an orchestra and a brass band. Whatever is to be spoken in a commercial building must be strongly and directly said. The very style of the ornament should be simple enough, and the scale large enough, to be easily comprehended. If not, if the unseeing eyes of busy men are daily saluted by delicate details, not only are the details wasted, but they are so far vulgarized as to become impotent to produce pleasure even when men have leisure to contemplate them. In the exercise of this discretion, let us consider each quality our building will express, making sure that its expression be appropriate, and that it be well adjusted to the mood of the spectator; not lowered down to his plane, but, although above the sordidness of his daily thought, sufficiently in recognition of it to escape total neglect. Our architecture will never live beyond our own lives until it loses much of its hap-hazard, hit-or-miss indiscretion.

Knowledge, if essential, is also obtainable. Genius is beyond most of us, knowledge is accessible to all of us; so that in this age of light, ignorance has become a crime. Occasionally we hear a certain kind of man deliver himself something after this fashion: "Knowledge is all very well if a man does not know too much." Then he will cite instances of college men who are starving on ten dollars a week, and of men like himself without education, who are "climbing to the top of the ladder." This sort of talk means nothing. Granting, for the moment, the point that starvation of the body is worse than starvation of the mind—that not to know mental hunger is to be well fed—it remains true that the college man is not necessarily better educated than his more successful critic. There are many men to whom ideas come freely and graphically through things, and with slowness and dimness through books. Viewed from what point you will, every man is distinctly the gainer by acquiring knowledge, and no man more than the architect. Every building bears the impress of the knowledge or ignorance of its designer, not of necessity in any one of its details, or even in the composition and adjustment of them all, but certainly in the subtle essence which we call "style." The profounder the knowledge, the fuller and richer the result.

It is valuable to know that architects of a certain age designed buildings after a certain fashion, and adapted to this fashion the various details of these buildings, but it is much more valuable to know the causes which lay back of these results. The mere facts, though significant, are bald and unproductive without their antecedent causes. To have mastered fully these causes is to be able to produce results analogous to those first produced—not in the dry and formal manner of the mere copyist, but with the fire and force of the original. No period of college or school training can do more for the architect than beget in him the sacred thirst of knowledge, which it should be his life work to gratify. Apart from the pleasure to be derived from consciousness of this knowledge, is the certainty that every design he makes will bear the impress of it. It may be in the selection of means to ends, it may be indicated only in certain turns of profiles, in certain delicate adjustments of parts, where a different treatment would have been only less good; it may be in still remoter ways; but everywhere will be shown the grasp, the copiousness of thought, the richness of apt illustration, born only of full knowledge. Just as in a critical essay by Matthew Arnold or James Russell Lowell, every sentence reveals the wealth of learning that lies back of it, so plainly does the architect reveal his knowledge in his work.

In the absorbing cares of an active life, those forms of knowledge whose bearing seems immediate, or as we say, "practical," will be most naturally acquired, but it is a misfortune to any architect, and an appreciable loss to his work, when he ceases to acquire that form of professional knowledge which is entirely literary, and which may be related to his profession only by some side-light shed from another art, which architecture may borrow. The so-called "practical" architect, who knows nothing of his art beyond what has been grafted into him by the surgery of dry practice, is passing away. Large and acute minds there are, in whose work you see the result of ripe wisdom and nice taste acquired by long experience and observation alone. These are not the men, however, who will deride that wideness of knowledge which is here commended. They are rather men who will point us to their earlier work as monuments, not to their glory, but perhaps to their shame or misfortune, and warn us to push with all vehemence our acquisition of the knowledge thus early denied to them. Our profession is rich enough to range and feed in during all our probable lives, without ever getting into our stomachs the indigestible food of "mere theory."

Urbanity is the next phase of politeness to which your attention is called.

If sympathy is fellow feeling, urbanity is the expression of readiness to extend sympathy even before it be asked. Time was when urbanity in a house was as unsuitable as a silk cap in a jousting tournament. The house was a castle, its owner its warrior defendant, and everybody outside it possible besiegers. But with the dawn of day after the long dark feudal night, the dwelling opened outward like a rose in the sun. Men like Jacques Coeur of Bruges built houses in which they delighted to express to all who passed the new-found peace and friendliness. In such houses was the frankest avowal of good fortune, the most charming confession of a desire to please. So that these newly blossomed dwellings had the native charm of a lovely *débutante* who delights that others shall admire her beauty.

Is not this the typical attitude of the nineteenth-century dwelling? Certainly no menace threatens our houses which stone walls can ward off. The brigand of to-day gains access wherever he can enter. We do not generally build our houses among people we don't speak to. Whence, therefore, the sudden growth among us of mediaeval castles, whose only lacking detail is a shriveled head thrust over the cornice on the end of a pike? Are we so badly put to it for ideas that we must not only borrow from the eleventh century but add to the mediaevalism of it? Surely if this sort of thing was good when men went about in steel, sword in hand, it is not good when men wear silk hats and smoke cigarettes. We may be aristocrats by instinct, but need we write over our doors, *'Odi profanum vulgus et arceo'?* In other words, should not our houses follow our personal example, if we be gentlemen, and doff their hats to their neighbors?

In my business hours I may perhaps be pardoned if I am sometimes brusque, and hence my business house may follow me in the expression of this. But am I equally pardonable if my churlishness is not only carried into my house, but is thrust upon the street offending my neighbors? Not so; the courtesy I expect I should extend, and the house in which I live should say plainly to those who can less escape the daily sight of it than of me, "Here lives a gentleman." This does not mean extravagance of ornament nor lavish outlay of money nor vulgar solicitation of notice. It is beyond and above these, and rather scorns than courts them. It is simple urbanity. It is the natural grace of a graceful society, to which every man in it owes allegiance.

And this allegiance suggests the last quality which we may consider —Modesty.

What man so great as to escape its obligation? what building? Today we expend our labor upon some carefully considered design. It is carried out, and becomes what we and perhaps the world call our masterpiece. This last creation, emanating from our highest powers, furnishes to some stronger contemporary just the suggestion he may have lacked, and forthwith our masterpiece is eclipsed, and no one is the wiser as to how it came about. Our work once done becomes the world's property, and is judged not by the impression of the moment but by criticism matured through long time—criticism in which often we become witnesses against ourselves.

The self-assertion of a man or of a design has in this calmly pronounced criticism no chance for favor nor for fame. All its cheapness and all its arrogance are revealed, and at last it stands forth a bragging humbug. Look at the splendid architecture of the second empire in France. Men of great talent created it. Millions were spent upon it. Why did it fall short of enduring fame? It is not modest, it protests too much; it claims too much. It has the cheap bluster of a hired bravo, and the false beauty of the street cocotte. We must learn to suspect in our designs all that directly demands admiration as its right. Ours should be rather the ambition to erect buildings which are said to "grow upon one." Not all of the buildings which have carried the world instantly by storm have held their place in its esteem. Most of them, in spite of pride and self-assertion, have fallen to their proper level. Fustian is always ephemeral, and brag is no more permanently effective in stone than in words.

All that has been said, all that might be said, only brings us back to well-known principles, and we find at last that the summits of a great profession are achieved only by a persistent course and hard climbing; by self-denial and steady self-analysis; by wide and catholic views and finely tempered taste. But we may be sure that our work will never rise higher than its source; that no great creation comes from a small man. Such qualities as we have considered do not get into the building except through its architect; so we see that a gentleman among buildings means a gentleman among architects. Remember it was not Michael Angelo who did the talebearing or indulged in the loud recrimination when St. Peter's was building.

From: *John Wellborn Root: A Study of His Life and Work,* by Harriet Monroe. Boston: 1896, pages 76–94.

The Naturalization of the House

by

John Burroughs

One of the greatest pleasures of life is to build a house for one's self. There is a peculiar satisfaction even in planting a tree from which you hope to eat the fruit or in the shade of which you hope to repose. But how much greater the pleasure in planting the roof-tree, the tree that bears the golden apples of home and hospitality, and under the protection of which you hope to pass the remainder of your days. My grandmother said the happiest day of her life was when she found herself mistress of a little log house in the woods. Grandfather and she had built it mainly with their own hands, and doubtless with as much eagerness and solicitude as the birds build their nests. It was made of birch and maple logs, the floor was of hewn logs, and its roof of black ash bark. But it was home and fireside, a few square feet of the great wild, inclement, inhospitable out-of-doors subdued and set about by four walls and made warm and redolent of human hearts. I notice how eager all men are in building their houses, how they linger about them or even about their proposed sites. When the cellar is being dug they want to take a hand in; the earth evidently looks a little different, a little more friendly and congenial, than other earth. When the foundation walls are up and the first floor rudely sketched by rough timbers, I see them walking pensively from one imaginary room to another, or sitting long and long, wrapped in sweet reverie, upon the naked joist. It is a favorite pastime to go there of a Sunday afternoon and linger fondly about: they take their friends or their neighbors and climb the skeleton stairs and look out of the vacant windows, and pass in and out of the just sketched door-ways. How long the house is a-finishing! The heart moves in long before the workmen move out. Will the mason and the painter and the plumber never be through?

When a new house is going up in my vicinity I find myself walking thitherward nearly every day to see how the work progresses. What pleasure to see the structure come into shape, and the architect's paper plans take form and substance in wood and stone! I like to see every piece fitted, every nail driven. I stand about till I am in the way of the carpenters, or masons. Another new roof to shelter somebody from the storms, another four walls to keep the great cosmic out-of-doors at bay!

Though there is pleasure in building our house, or in seeing our neighbor build, yet the old houses look the best. Disguise it as one will, the new house is more or less a wound upon nature, and time must elapse for the wound to heal. Then unless one builds with modesty and simplicity, and with a due regard to the fitness of things, his house will always be a wound, an object of offense upon the fair face of the landscape. Indeed, to build a house that shall not offend the wise eye, that shall not put Nature and all her gentle divinities to shame, is the great problem. In such matters, not to displease the eye is to please the heart.

Probably the most that is to be aimed at in doing domestic architecture is negative beauty, a condition of things which invites or suggests beauty to those who are capable of the sentiment, because a house, truly viewed, is but a setting, a background, and is not to be pushed to the front and made much of for its own sake. It is for shelter, for comfort, for health and hospitality, to eat in and sleep in, to be born in and to die in, and it is to accord in appearance with homely every-day usages, and with natural, universal objects and scenes. Indeed, is anything but negative beauty to be aimed at in the interior decorations as well? The hangings are but a background for the pictures and are to give tone and atmosphere to the rooms, while the whole interior is but a background for the human form, and for the domestic life to be lived there.

It may be observed that what we call beauty of nature is mainly negative beauty; that is, the mass, the huge rude background, made up of rocks, trees, hills, mountains, plains, water, etc., has not beauty as a positive quality, visible to all eyes, but affords the mind the conditions of beauty, namely: health, strength, fitness, etc., beauty being an experience of the beholder. Some things, on the other hand, as flowers, foliage, brilliant colors, sunsets, rainbows, water-falls, may be said to be beautiful in and of themselves; but how wearisome the world would be without the vast negative background upon which these things figure, and which provokes and stimulates the mind in a way the purely fair forms do not.

How we are drawn by that which retreats and hides itself, or gives only glimpses and half views! Hence the value of trees as a veil to an ugly ornamental house, and the admirable setting they form to the picturesque habitation I am contemplating. But the house the heart builds, whether it be cottage or villa, can stand the broad, open light without a screen of any kind. Its neutral gray or brown tints, its wide projections and deep shadows, its simple strong lines, its coarse open-air quality, its ample roof or roofs, blend it with the landscape wherever it stands. Such a house seems to retreat into itself, and invites the eye to follow. Its interior warmth and coziness penetrate the walls, and the eye gathers suggestions of them at every point.

We can miss almost anything else from a building rather than a look of repose. This it must have. Give it a look of repose, and all else shall be added. This is the supreme virtue in architecture. Go to the city, walk up and down the principal thoroughfares, and see what an effort many of the buildings make to stand up! What columns and arches they put forth where no columns or arches are needed! There is endless variety of form and line, great activity of iron and stone, when the eye demands simplicity and repose. No broad spaces, no neutral ground. The architect in his search for variety has made his façade bristle with meaningless forms. But now and then the eye is greeted by honest simplicity of structure. Look at that massive front yonder, built of granite blocks, simply one stone top of another from the ground to the roof, with no fuss or flutter about the openings in the walls. How easy, how simple, and what a look of dignity and repose! Probably the next time we come this way, they will have put hollow metal hoods over the windows, or otherwise marred the ease and dignity of that front.

Doubtless one main source of the pleasure we take in a brick or stone wall over one of wood is just in this element of simplicity and repose; the structure is visible; there is nothing intricate or difficult about it. It is one stone, or one brick top of another all the way up; the building makes no effort at all to stand up, but does so in the most natural and inevitable way in the world. In a wooden building the anatomy is more or less hidden; we do not see the sources of its strength. The same is true of a stuccoed or rough cast building; the eye sees nothing but smooth, expressionless surface.

One great objection to the Mansard roof in the country, now happily nearly gone out of date, is that it fails to give a look of repose. It fails also to give a look of protection. The roof of a building allies it to the open air, and carries the suggestion of shelter as no other part does, and to belittle it, or conceal it, or in any way take from the honest and direct purport of it as the shield, the main matter after all, is not to be allowed. In the city we see only the fronts, the façades of the houses, and the flat and Mansard are less offensive. But in the country, the house is individualized, stands defined, and every vital and necessary part is to be boldly and strongly treated. The Mansard gives to the country house a smart, dapper appearance, and the effect of being perched up, and looking about for compliments; such houses seem to be ready to make the military salute as you pass them. Whereas the steep, high roof gives the house a settled, brooding, introverted look. It also furnishes a sort of foil to the rest of the building.

What constitutes the charm to the eye of the old-fashioned country barn but its immense roof—a slope of gray shingle exposed to the weather like the side of a hill, and by its amplitude suggesting a bounty that warms the heart? Many of the old farm-houses, too, were modeled on the same generous scale, and at a distance little was visible but their great sloping roofs. They covered their inmates as a hen covereth her brood, and are touching pictures of the domestic spirit in its simpler forms.

What is a man's house but his nest, and why should it not be nest-like both outside and in—coarse, strong, negative in tone externally, and snug and well-feathered and modeled by the heart within? Why should he set it on a hill, when he can command a nook under the hill or on its side? Why should it look like an observatory, when it is a conservatory and dormitory?

The domestic spirit is quiet, informal, unceremonious, loves ease, privacy, low tones; loves the chimney-corner, the old arm-chair, the undress garb, homely cares, children, simple pleasures, etc.; and why should it, when it seeks to house itself from the weather, aim at the formal, the showy, the architectural, the external, the superfluous? Let state edifices look stately, but the private dwelling should express privacy and coziness.

Every man's house is in some sort an effigy of himself. It is not the snails and shell-fish alone that excrete their tenements, but man as well. When you seriously build a house, you make public proclamation of your taste and manners, or your want of these. If the domestic instinct is strong in you, and if you have humility and simplicity, they will show very plainly in your dwelling; if you have the opposite of these, false pride or a petty ambition, or coldness and exclusiveness, they will show also. A man seldom builds better than he knows, when he assumes to know anything about it.

I think that, on examination, it will be found that the main secret of the picturesqueness of more simple structures, like fences, bridges, sheds, log huts, etc., is that the *motive*, the principle of construction, is so open and obvious. No doubt much might be done to relieve the flatness of our pine-box houses by more frankness and boldness in this respect. If the eye could see more fully the necessities of the case, how the thing stood up and was held together, that it was not pasteboard, that it did not need to be anchored against the wind, etc., it would be a relief. Hence the lively pleasure we feel in what are called "timber-houses," and in every architectural device by which the anatomy, the real framework of the structure, inside or out, is allowed to show, or made to serve as ornament. The eye craves lines of strength, evidence of weight and stability. But in the wooden house, as usually treated, these lines are nearly all concealed, the ties and supports are carefully suppressed, and the eye must feed on the small, fine lines of the finish. When the mere outlines of the frame are indicated, so that the larger spaces appear as panels, it is a great help; or let any part of the internal economy show through, and the eye is interested, as the projection of the chimney-stack in brick or stone houses, or the separating of the upper from the main floor by a belt and slight projection, or by boldly projecting the chamber floor-joist, and letting one story overlap the other.

As I have already said, herein is the main reason of the picturesqueness of the stone house above all others. Every line is a line of strength and necessity. We see how the mass stands up; how it is bound and keyed and fortified. The construction is visible; the corners are locked by header and stretcher, and are towers of strength; the openings pierce the walls and reveal their cohesion; every stone is alive with purpose, and the whole affects one as a real triumph over Nature—so much form and proportion wrested from her grasp. There is power in stone, and in a less measure in brick; but wood must be boldly handled not to look frail or flat. Then unhewn stone has the negative beauty which is so desirable.

I say, therefore, build of stone by all means, if you have a natural taste to gratify, and the rockier your structure looks, the better. All things make friends with a stone house—the mosses and lichens, and vines and birds. It is kindred to the earth and the elements, and makes itself at home in any situation.

When I set out to look up a place in the country, I was chiefly intent on finding a few acres of good fruit land near a large stone-heap. While I was yet undecided about the land, the discovery of the stone-heap at a convenient distance, vast piles of square blocks of all sizes, wedged off the upright strata by the frost during uncounted ages, and all mottled and colored by the weather, made me hasten to close the bargain. The large country-seats in the neighborhood were mainly of brick or pine; only a few of the early settlers had availed themselves of this beautiful material that lay in such abundance handy to every man's back-door, and in those cases the stones were nearly buried in white mortar, as if they were something to be ashamed of. Truly, the besmeared, beplastered appearance of most stone houses is by no means a part of their beauty. Mortar plays a subordinate part in a structure, and the less we see of it, the better.

The proper way to treat the subject is this: as the work progresses, let the wall be got ready for pointing up, but never let the pointing be done, though your masons will be sorely grieved. Let the joints be made close, then scraped out, cut with the trowel, and while the mortar is yet green, sprinkled with sand. Instead, then, of a white band defining every stone, you have only sharp lines and seams here and there, which give the wall a rocky, natural appearance.

The point of union between the stones, according to my eye, should be a depression, a shadow, and not a raised joint. So that you have closeness and compactness, the face of your wall cannot be too broken or rough. When the rising or setting sun shines athwart it and brings out the shadows, how powerful and picturesque it looks! It is not in cut or hewn stone to express such majesty. I like the sills and lintels of undressed stone also,—"wild stone," as the old backwoodsman called them, untamed by the hammer or chisel. If the lintels are wide enough, a sort of hood many be formed over the openings by projecting them a few inches.

It seems to me that I built into my house every one of those superb autumn days which I spent in the woods getting out stone. I did not quarry the limestone ledge into blocks any more than I quarried the delicious weather into memories to adorn my walls. Every load that was sent home carried my heart and happiness with it. The jewels I had uncovered in the debris, or torn from the ledge in the morning, I saw in the jambs, or mounted high on the corners at night. Every day was filled with great events. The woods held unknown treasures. Those elder giants, frost and rain, had wrought industriously; now we would unearth from the leaf mould an ugly customer, a stone with a ragged quartz face, or cavernous, and set with rock crystals like great teeth, or else suggesting a battered and worm-eaten skull of some old stone dog. These I needed a sprinkling of for their quaintness, and to make the wall a true compendium of the locality. Then we would unexpectedly strike upon several loads of beautiful blocks all in a nest; or we would assault the ledge in a new place with wedge and bar, and rattle down headers and stretchers that surpassed any before. I had to be constantly on the lookout for corner stone, for mine is a house of seven corners, and on the strength and dignity of the corners the beauty of the wall largely depends. But when you bait your hook with your heart, the fish always bite. "The boss is as good as six men in the woods, getting out stone," flatteringly spoke up the master-mason. Certain it is that no such stone was found as when I headed the search. The men saw indifferently with their eyes; but I looked upon the ground with such desire that I saw what was beneath the moss and the leaves. With them it was hard labor at so much per day, with me it was a passionate pursuit; the enthusiasm of the chase venting itself with the bar and the hammer, and the day was too short for me to tire of the sport.

The stone was exceptionally fine, both in form and color. Sometimes it seemed as if we had struck upon the ruins of some ancient structure, the blocks were so regular and numerous. The ancient stonecutters, however, had shaped them all to a particular pattern, which was a little off the square, but in bringing them back with the modern pitching-tool the rock face was gained, which is the feature so desirable.

I like a live stone, one upon which time makes an impression, which in the open air assumes a certain tone and mellowness. The stone in my locality surpasses any I have ever seen in this respect. A warm gray is the ruling tint, and a wall built of this stone is of the color of the bole of the beech-tree, mottled, lively, and full of character.

What should a house of undressed stone be trimmed out with but unpainted wood? Oak, ash, cedar, cherry, maple—why import pine from Michigan or Maine when nearly all our woods contain plenty of these materials? And now that the planing mills are so abundant, and really do such admirable work, an ordinary-priced house may be trimmed out mainly in hard wood for nearly the same cost as with pine.

In my case I began at the stump; I viewed the trees before they were cut, and took a hand in sawing them down and hauling them to the mill. One bleak winter day I climbed to the top of a mountain to survey a large butternut which some hunters had told me of, and which now, one year later, I see about me in base and panel as I write. One thus gets a lively background of interest and reminiscence in his house from the start.

The natural color and grain of the wood give a richness and simplicity to an interior that no art can make up for. How the eye loves a genuine thing; how it delights in the nude beauty of the wood! A painted surface is a blank, meaningless surface; but the texture and figure of the wood is full of expression. It is the principle of construction again appearing in another field. How endless the variety of figures that appear even in one kind of wood, and, withal, how modest! The grainers do not imitate oak. They cannot. Their surface glares; their oak is only skin-deep; their figures put nature to shame.

Oak is the wood to start with in trimming a house. How clear and strong it looks! It is the master wood. When allowed to season in the log, it has a richness and ripeness of tone that are delicious. We have many kinds, as rock oak, black oak, red oak, white oak—all equally beautiful in their place. Red oak is the softest, and less liable to spring. By combining two different kinds, as red oak and white oak (white oak takes its name from the external color of the tree, and not from the color of the wood, which is dark amber color), a most pleasing effect is produced.

Butternut is the softest and most tractable of what are called hard woods, and its hue is eminently warm and mellow. Its figure is pointed and shooting—a sort of Gothic style in the grain. It makes admirable doors. Western butternut, which can usually be had in the Albany market, makes doors as light as pine, and as little liable to spring. The Western woods are all better than the Eastern for building purposes. They are lighter, coarser, easier worked. They grow easier and thriftier. The traveler through Northern Ohio and Indiana sees a wonderful crop of forest trees, tall, uniform, straight as candles, no knots, no gnarls—all clear, clean timber. The soil is deep and moist, and the trees grow rank and rapid. The chestnut, ash, and butternut grown here work like pine, besides being darker and richer in color than the same woods grown in leaner and more rocky soils. Western black ash is especially beautiful. In connection with our almost bone-white sugar maple for panels, it makes charming doors—just the thing for chambers, and scarcely more expensive than pine. Of our Eastern woods, red cedar is also good, with its pungent, moth-expelling odor, and should not be neglected. It soon fades, but it is very pleasing, with its hard, solid knots, even then. No doubt some wash might be applied that would preserve its color.

There is a species of birch growing upon our mountains that makes an admirable finish. It is usually called red or cherry birch, and it has a long wave or curl that is found in no other wood. It is very tough and refractory, and must be securely fastened. A black ash door, with maple or white pine panels set in a heavy frame of this red, wavy birch, is a most pleasing chamber finish. For a hard wood floor, in connection with oak or ash, it is to be preferred to cherry.

Growing alongside of the birch is the soft maple—the curly species —that must not be overlooked. It contains light wood and dark wood, as a fowl contains white meat and dark meat. It is not unusual to find a tree of this species, the heart of which will be a rich grayish brown, suggesting, by something in the tone and texture of it, the rarer shades of silk, while the outer part is white, and fine as ivory. I have seen a wainscoting composed of alternate strips of this light and dark wood from the same tree that was exquisite, and a great rarity.

The eye soon tires of sharp, violent contrasts. In general, that which is striking, or taking at first sight, is to be avoided in interior finishings or decorations, especially in the main or living rooms. In halls, a more pronounced style is permissible, and the contrast of walnut with pine, or maple, or oak is more endurable. What one wants in his living rooms is a quiet, warm tone, and the main secret of this is dark furniture and hangings, with a dash of color here and there, and floods of light,—big windows, and plenty of them. No room can be cheerful and inviting without plenty of light, and then, if the walls are light too, and the carpets showy, there is a flatness and garishness. The marble mantelpiece, with its senseless vases, and the marble-topped centre-table add the finishing touch of coldness and stiffness. Marble makes good tombstones, but it is an abomination in a house, either in furniture or in mantels.

There remains only to be added that after you have had the experience, after the house is finished and you have had a year or two to cool off in (it takes that long), you will probably feel a slight reaction. Or, it may be more than that; the scales may fall from your eyes, and you may see that it is not worth while after all to lay so much emphasis on the house, a place to shelter you from the elements, and that you have had only a different, but the same unworthy pride as the rest, as if anything was not good enough, and as if manhood was not sufficient to itself without these props.

You will have found, too, that with all your pains you have not built a house, nor can you build one, that just fills the eye and gives the same aesthetic pleasure as does the plain unpainted structure that took no thought of appearances, and that has not one stroke about it foreign to the necessities of the case.

Pride, when it is conscious of itself, is death to the nobly beautiful, whether in dress, manners, equipage, or house-building. The great monumental structures of the Old World show no pride or vanity, but on the contrary great humility and singleness of purpose. The Gothic cathedral does not try to look beautiful; it *is* beautiful from the start, and entirely serious. London Bridge is a heroic resolution in stone, and apparently has but one purpose, and that is to carry the paved street with all its surging masses safely over the river.

Unless, therefore, you have had the rare success of building without pride, your house will offend you by and by, and offend others.

Perhaps after one had graduated in this school and built four or five houses, he would have the courage to face the problem squarely, and build, much more plainly and unpretentiously, a low, nestling structure of undressed boards, or unhammered stone, and be content, like the oyster, with the roughest of shells without, so that he be sure of the mother-of-pearl within.

From: *Signs and Seasons,* by John Burroughs. Boston: 1886, pages 273–289.

Christian Science Church, Berkeley, California. Bernard Maybeck, architect.

Dodge House, Los Angeles, California. Irving Gill, architect. *Courtesy, Marvin Rand Associates.*

Gamble House, Pasadena, California. Greene Brothers, architects. *Courtesy, Greene and Greene Library.*

A. E. Bingham House, Santa Barbara, California. Bernard Maybeck, architect. *Courtesy, College of Environmental Design, University of California.*

Simplicity and Domestic Life

by

Gustav Stickley

. . . . We have endeavored to set forth as fully as possible the several parts which, taken together, go to make up the Craftsman idea of the kind of home environment that tends to result in wholesome living. We have shown the gradual growth of this idea, from the making of the first pieces of Craftsman furniture to the completed house which has in it all the elements of a permanently satisfying home. But we have left until the last the question of the right setting for such a home and the conditions under which the life that is lived in it could form the foundation for the fullest individual and social development.

There is no question now as to the reality of the world-wide movement in the direction of better things. We see everywhere efforts to reform social, political and industrial conditions; the desire to bring about better opportunities for all and to find some way of adjusting economic conditions so that the heart-breaking inequalities of our modern civilized life shall in some measure be done away with. But while we take the greatest interest in all efforts toward reform in any direction, we remain firm in the conviction that the root of all reform lies in the individual and that the life of the individual is shaped mainly by home surroundings and influences and by the kind of education that goes to make real men and women instead of grist for the commercial mill.

That the influence of the home is of the first importance in the shaping of character is a fact too well understood and too generally admitted to be offered here as a new idea. One need only turn to the pages of history to find abundant proof of the unerring action of Nature's law, for without exception the people whose lives are lived simply and wholesomely, in the open, and who have in a high degree the sense of the sacredness of the home, are the people who have made the greatest strides in the development of the race. When luxury enters in and a thousand artificial requirements come to be regarded as real needs, the nation is on the brink of degeneration. So often has the story repeated itself that he who runs may read its deep significance. In our own country, to which has fallen the heritage of all the older civilizations, the course has been swift, for we are yet close to the memory of the primitive pioneer days when the nation was building, and we have still the crudity as well as the vigor of youth. But so rapid and easy has been our development and so great our prosperity that even now we are in some respects very nearly in the same state as the older peoples who have passed the zenith of their power and are beginning to decline. In our own case, however, the saving grace lies in the fact that our taste for luxury and artificiality is not as yet deeply ingrained. We are intensely commercial, fond of all the good things of life, proud of our ability to "get there," and we yield the palm to none in the matter of owning anything that money can buy. But, fortunately, our pioneer days are not ended even now and we still have a goodly number of men and women who are helping to develop the country and make history merely by living simple natural lives close to the soil and full of the interest and pleasure which come for kinship with Nature and the kind of work that calls forth all their resources in the way of self-reliance and the power of initiative. Even in the rush and hurry of life in our busy cities we remember well the quality given to the growing nation by such men and women a generation or two ago and, in spite of the chaotic conditions brought about by our passion for money-getting, extravagance and show, we have still reason to believe that the dominant characteristics of the pioneer yet shape what are the salient qualities in American life.

To preserve these characteristics and to bring back to individual life and work the vigorous contructive spirit which during the last half-century has spent its activities in commercial and industrial expansion, is, in a nut-shell, the Craftsman idea. We need to straighten out our standards and to get rid of a lot of rubbish that we have accumulated along with our wealth and commercial supremacy. It is not that we are too energetic, but that in many ways we have wasted and misused our energy precisely as we have wasted and misused so many of our wonderful natural resources. All we really need is a change in our point of view toward life and a keener perception regarding the things that count and the things which merely burden us. This being the case, it would seem obvious that the place to begin a readjustment is in the home, for it is only natural that the relief from friction which would follow the ordering of our lives along more simple and reasonable lines would not only assure greater comfort, and therefore greater efficiency, to the workers of the nation, but would give the children a chance to grow up under conditions which would be conducive to a higher degree of mental, moral and physical efficiency.

Therefore we regard it as at least a step in the direction of bringing about better conditions when we try to plan and build houses which will simplify the work of home life and add to its wholesome joy and comfort. We have already made it plain to our readers that we do not believe in large houses with many rooms elaborately decorated and furnished, for the reason that these seem so essentially an outcome of the artificial conditions that lay such harassing burdens upon modern life and form such a serious menace to our ethical standards. Breeding as it does the spirit of extravagance and of discontent which in the end destroys all the sweetness of home life, the desire for luxury and show not only burdens beyond his strength the man who is ambitious to provide for his wife and children surroundings which are as good as the best, but taxes to the utmost the woman who is trying to keep up the appearances which she believes should belong to her station in life. Worst of all, it starts the children with standards which, in nine cases out of ten, utterly preclude the possibility of their beginning life on their own account in a simple and sensible way. Boys who are brought up in such homes are taught, by the silent influence of their early surroundings, to take it for granted that they must not marry until they are able to keep up an establishment of equal pretensions, and girls also take as a matter of course that marriage must mean something quite as luxurious as the home of their childhood or it is not a paying investment for their youth and beauty. Everyone who thinks at all deplores the kind of life that marks a man's face with the haggard lines of anxiety and makes him sharp and often unscrupulous in business, with no ambition beyond large profits and a rapid rise in the business world. Also we all realize regretfully the extravagance and uselessness of many of our women and admit that one of the gravest evils of our times is the light touch-and-go attitude toward marriage, which breaks up so many homes and makes the divorce courts in America a by-word to the world. But when we think into it a little more deeply, we have to acknowledge that such conditions are the logical outcome of our standards of living and that these standards are always shaped in the home.

That is why we have from the first planned houses that are based on the big fundamental principles of honesty, simplicity and usefulness,—the kind of houses that children will rejoice all their lives to remember as "home," and that give a sense of peace and comfort to the tired men who go back to them when the day's work is done. Because we believe that the healthiest and happiest life is that which maintains the closest relationship with out-of-doors, we have planned our houses with outdoor living rooms, dining rooms and sleeping rooms, and many windows to let in plenty of air and sunlight. . . . We have put into practical effect our conviction that a house, whatever its dimensions, should have plenty of free space unencumbered by unnecessary partitions or over-much furniture. Therefore we have made the general living rooms as large as possible and not too much separated one from the other. It seems to us much more friendly, homelike and comfortable to have one big living room into which one steps directly from the entrance door,—or from a small vestibule if the climate demands such a protection,—and to have this living room the place where all the business and pleasure of the common family life may be carried on. And we like it to have pleasant nooks and corners which give a comfortable sense of semi-privacy and yet are not in any way shut off from the larger life of the room. Such an arrangement has always seemed to us symbolic of the ideal conditions of social life. The big hospitable fireplace is almost a necessity, for the hearth-stone is always the center of true home life, and the very spirit of home seems to be lacking when a register or radiator tries ineffectually to take the place of a glowing grate or a crackling leaping fire of logs.

Then too we believe that the staircase, instead of being hidden away in a small hall or treated as a necessary evil, should be made one of the most beautiful and prominent features of the room because it forms a link between the social part of the house and the upper regions which belong to the inner and individual part of the family life. Equally symbolic is our purpose in making the dining room either almost or wholly a part of the living room, for to us it is a constant expression of the fine spirit of hospitality to have the dining room, in a way, open to all comers. Furthermore, such an arrangement is a strong and subtle influence in the direction of simpler living because entertainment under such conditions naturally grows less elaborate and more friendly—less alien to the regular life of the family and less a matter of social formality.

Take a house planned in this way, with a big living room made comfortable and homelike and beautiful with its great fireplace, open staircase, casement windows, built-in seats, cupboards, bookcases, sideboard and perhaps French doors opening out upon a porch which links the house with the garden; fill this room with soft rich restful color, based upon the mellow radiance of the wood tones and sparkling into the jeweled high-lights given forth by copper, brass, or embroideries; then contrast it in your own mind with a house which is cut up into vestibule, hall, reception room, parlor, library, dining room and den—each one a separate room, each one overcrowded with furniture, pictures and bric-a-brac—and judge for yourself whether or not home surroundings have any power to influence the family life and the development of character. If you will examine carefully the houses shown in this book, you will see that they all form varying expressions of the central idea we have just explained, although each one is modified to suit the individual taste and requirements of the owner. This is as it should be, for a house expresses character quite as vividly as does dress and the more intimate personal belongings, and no man or woman can step into a dwelling ready-made and decorated according to some other person's tastes and preferences without feeling a sense of strangeness that must be overcome before the house can be called a real home.

It will also be noticed in examining the plans of the Craftsman houses that we have paid particular attention to the convenient arrangement of the kitchen. In these days of difficulties with servants and of inadequate, inexperienced help, more and more women are, perforce, learning to depend upon themselves to keep the household machinery running smoothly. It is good that this should be so, for woman is above all things the homemaker and our grandmothers were not far wrong when they taught their daughters that a woman who could not keep house, and do it well, was not making of her life the success that could reasonably be expected of her, nor was she doing her whole duty by her family. The idea that housekeeping means drudgery is partly due to our fussy, artificial, overcrowded way of living and partly to our elaborate houses and to inconvenient arrangements. We believe in having the kitchen small, so that extra steps may be avoided, and fitted with every kind of convenience and comfort; with plenty of shelves and cupboards, open plumbing, the hooded range which carries off all odors of cooking, the refrigerator which can be filled from the outside—in fact, everything that tends to save time, strength and worry. In these days the cook is an uncertain quantity always and maids come and go like the seasons, so the wise woman keeps herself fully equipped to take up the work of her own house at a moment's notice, by being in such close touch with it all the time that she never lays down the reins of personal government. The Craftsman house is built for this kind of woman and we claim that it is in itself an incentive to the daughters of the house to take a genuine and pleasurable interest in household work and affairs, so that they in their turn will be fairly equipped as homemakers when the time comes for them to take up the more serious duties of life.

We have set forth the principles that rule the planning of the Craftsman house and have hinted at the kind of life that would naturally result from such an environment. But now comes one of the most important elements of the whole question—the surroundings of the home. We need hardly say that a house of the kind we have described belongs either in the open country or in a small village or town, where the dwellings do not elbow or crowd one another any more than the people do. We have planned houses for country living because we firmly believe that the country is the only place to live in. The city is all very well for business, for amusement and some formal entertainment—in fact for anything and everything that, by its nature, must be carried on outside of the home. But the home itself should be in some place where there is peace and quiet, plenty of room and the chance to establish a sense of intimate relationship with the hills and valleys, trees and brooks and all the things which tend to lessen the strain and worry of modern life by reminding us that after all we are one with Nature.

Also it is a fact that the type of mind which appreciates the value of having the right kind of home, and recognizes the right of growing children to the most natural and wholesome surroundings, is almost sure to feel the need of life in the open, where all the conditions of daily life may so easily be made sane and constructive instead of artificial and disintegrating. People who think enough about the influence of environment to put interest and care into the planning of a dwelling which shall express all that the word "home" means to them, are usually the people who like to have a personal acquaintance with every animal, tree and flower on the place. They appreciate the interest of planting things and seeing them grow, and enjoy to the fullest the exhilarating anxiety about crops that comes only to the man who planted them and means to use them to the best advantage. Then again, such people feel that half the zest of life would be gone if they were to miss the fulness of joy that each returning spring brings to those who watch eagerly for the new green of the grass and the blossoming of the trees. They feel that no summer resort can offer pleasures equal to that which they find in watching the full flowering of the year; in seeing how their own agricultural experiments turn out, and in triumphing over each success and each addition to the beauty of the place that is their own. Few of these people, too, would care to miss the sense of peace and fulfilment in autumn days, when the waning beauty of the year comes into such close kinship with the mellow ripeness of a well-spent life that has borne full fruit. And what child is there in the world who would spend the winter in the city when there are ice-covered brooks to skate on, the comfort of jolly evenings by the fire and the never-ending wonder of the snow? And all the year round there are the dumb creatures for whom we have no room or time in the city,—the younger brothers of humanity who submit so humbly to man's dominion and look so placidly to him for protection and sustenance.

From: *Craftsman Homes,* by Gustav Stickley. New York: 1909, pages 194–198.

The Post-Modern House

by

Joseph Hudnut

I have been thinking about those factory-built houses, pure products of technological research and manufacture, which are promised us as soon as a few remaining details of finance and distribution are worked out: houses pressed by giant machines out of plastics or chromium steel, pouring out of assembly lines by the tens of thousands, delivered anywhere in response to a telephone call, and upon delivery made ready for occupancy by the simple process of tightening a screw. I have been trying to capture one of these houses in my mind's eye; to construct there, not its form and features only but the life within it; to give it, if my readers will pardon me, a local habitation and a name.

I was assisted in this effort recently during an airplane trip to New York. As we left Boston we flew over a parking lot beside a baseball stadium and half an hour later, as we approached New York, over that immense parking area which lies back of Jones Beach. In each of these thousands of automobiles were ranged in herringbone patterns, all of them so far as we could see from the sky exactly alike—their forms, except for varying fancies in streamlining and nickel plate, being the perfect harvest of the technological mind unadulterated by art. It seemed to me that, parked in this way, these thousands of automobiles foreshadowed those future suburbs in which every family will have each its standardized mass-produced and movable shell, indistinguishable from those of its thousand neighbors except by a choice of paint and the (relative) ambitions of their owners to be housed in the latest model.

Now I am aware that uniformity in house design is for the greater part of mankind a condition which is often necessary and not always regrettable—a circumstance clearly illustrated by that cloudburst of Cape Cod cottages which is even now saturating our New England landscapes and which, it may be, is as distinct a forerunner of future standardizations in our houses as is the parked automobile. Just the same there is an important difference between these millions of wooden cottages and the more rigorous shapes of factory-built houses, a difference only obliquely related to materials and processes of manufacture. The factory-built house, as I imagine it, fails to furnish my mind with that totality of impression with which the word house (meaning a building occupied by a family) has always filled it: it leaves unexhibited that idea of home about which there cling so many nuances of thought and sentiment. My readers may count me a romanticist if they wish—and perhaps they can conceive of a home without romance?—but I do not discover in any one of the types of house prefigured in the published essays of technologists that *promise of happiness* which, in houses, is the important quality of all appearances.

My impression is obviously shared by a wide public—a circumstance which explains in part the persistence with which people, however enamored of science, cling to the familiar patterns of their houses. Among the soldiers who write letters to me there is, for example, one in Tokio who describes at some length, and not without eloquence, the many labor-saving devices, the new ideas in planning, the new materials, insulatings, and air-conditionings which are to beautify his new house. He ends his letter with the confident hope that these will not in any way change the design of the house which he expects me to build for him. He has in mind, if I have understood him correctly, a Cape Cod cottage which, upon being opened, will be seen to be a refrigerator-to-live-in; and I am by no means sure which of these requirements, assuming them to be inconsistent, is the more prescriptive. Having learned that I am an architect tinged with modernism, my soldier fears that I may be tempted to suspend his house from a tree or pivot it on a mast around which it can be made to revolve or perhaps give it the outward shape of an aluminum bean, and I take it that he is unwilling that my enthusiasm for a technological absolutism should carry me that far. He would like all the newest gadgets but would like these seasoned with that picture, sentiment, and symbol which, to one writing from Tokio, seem to be of equal importance. He would have mechanization but would not, in the phrase of a distinguished historian of art, allow mechanization to take command. I shouldn't be surprised to learn that his requirements reflect accurately those of the Army, the Navy, the Air Force, the WAC, and the WAVES.

Our soldiers are already sufficiently spoiled by compliments and yet I must admit that here is still another instance in which their prescience overleaps the judgments of science. Beneath the surface naïveté of my friend's letter there is expressed an idea which is of critical importance to architecture: a very ancient idea to be sure, but one which seems sometimes to be forgotten by architects. The total form and ordinance of our houses are not implied in the evolution of building techniques or concepts of planning. They do not proceed from these merely; they cannot be imagined wholly from these premises. In the hearts of the people at least they are relevant to something very far beyond science and the uses of science.

I wish to be understood in this matter. I am not excessively fond of Cape Cod cottages. In their native habitat these are quaint in form and charming in their forthrightness, and yet I find the type somewhat tedious now that it has been repeated four or five million times. I do wish that those contractors who spread their white nebulae of houses around our great cities might now and then tempt their market with some new form of sweetmeat. To speak frankly these represent a species of exploitation not more excusable than any other. Nevertheless it is a fact, patent to the most superficial observer, that millions of people find in these commutations of architecture compensations for an experience of which most of them are ignorant. They are the pale but necessary substitutes for the experience of an architecture in which emotional values are fused into technological values. Until we achieve that fusion Cape Cod cottages will take command.

Our architects are too often seduced by the novel enchantments of their techniques. I have known architects whose attitudes and ideals are not different from those of engineers; who find sufficient reward for their work in the intellectual satisfactions afforded by their inventions; who are quite indifferent to the formal consequences of their constructions—beauty being a flower which will spring unbidden from beneath their earnest feet. There are others who discover with such an excess of fervor the dramatic possibilities of concrete cantilevers and iron *piloti* that they forget to ask if these are in any way appropriate to the idea to be expressed. There are still others whose logic is so absolute that they will allow no felicity of form to go unexplained by economic necessity or technical virtuosity, nor will they permit any beauty to be enjoyed until justified as a consequence of the slide rule, and frequently her presence in their calculate halls will be acknowledged only after an argument.

Like a ministering angel the machine enters our house to give a new perspective and economy, a new range and efficiency, to the processes of daily living; to lengthen the hours of freedom; to dispel a thousand tyrannies of custom and prejudice, to lift mountains of drudgery from our shoulders. Like a herald from a young king newly-crowned the machine announces a new dynasty and welcomes us to its liberating authority. Like a first breath of April the machine purifies and invigorates. Architects are right to love the machine; they could not otherwise build a modern house.

We are right to love the machine but we must not permit it to extinguish the fire on our hearth. The shapes and relationships, the qualities and arrangements of color, light, textures, and the thousand other elements of building through which the human spirit makes itself known: these are the essential substance of a house, in no way incidental to patterns of economy or physical well-being. Through these our walls are made to reach out beyond utility to enclose the ethereal things without which a house is, in any real sense, a useless object. Through these they speak to us of security and peace, of intimate loyalties, love and the tender affection of children, of the romance for which our soldiers hunger, of an adventure relived a thousand times and forever new; nor is that too much to expect of a house.

There is a way of working, sometimes called art, which gives to things made by man qualities of form beyond those demanded by economic, social, or ethical expediency; a way of working which brings into harmony with ourselves some part of our environment created by us; which makes that environment, through education, a universal experience; which transforms the science of building into architecture.

If a dinner is to be served it is art which dresses the meat, determines the order of serving, prepares and arranges the table, establishes and directs the conventions of costume and conversation, and seasons the whole with that ceremony which, long before Lady Macbeth explained it to us, was the best of all possible sauces. If a story is to be told it is art which gives the events proportion and climax, fortifies them with contrast, tension, and the salient word, colors them with metaphor and allusion, and so makes them cognate and kindling to the heart. If a prayer is made, it is art which sets it to music, surrounds it with ancient observances, guards it under the solemn canopies of great cathedrals.

The shapes of all things made by man are determined by their functions, by the laws of materials and the laws of energies, by marketability (sometimes) and the terms of manufacture; but these shapes may also be determined by the need, more ancient and more imperious than your present techniques, for some assurance of importance and worth in those things which encompass humanity. That is true also of all forms of doing, of all patterns of work and conduct and pageantry. It is true of the house and of all that takes place in the house; for here among all the things made is that which presses most immediately upon the spirit—the symbol, the armor, and the hearth of a family. The temple itself grew from this root; and the House of God, which architecture celebrates with her most glorious gifts, is only the simulacrum and crowning affirmation of that spiritual knowledge which illumined first the life of the family and only afterwards the lives of men living in communities.

Here is that *shelter* which man shaped in the earth one hundred thousand years ago, the pit which became the wattle hut, the cave, the mound dwelling, the Sioux lodge, and the thousand other constructions with which our restless invention has since covered the earth; the *shelter* which in a million forms has accompanied man's long upward journey, his companion and shield and outer garment. Here is that *home* which first shaped and disciplined our emotions and over centuries formed and confirmed the habits and valuations upon which human society rests. Here is that *space* which man learned to refashion into patterns conformable to his spirit: the space which he made into architecture.

This theme, so lyrical in its essential nature, can be parodied by science. An excess of physiological realism, for example, can dissemble and disfigure the spirit quite as ingeniously as that excess of sugar which eclecticism in its popular aspect pours over the suburban house. A "fearless affirmation" of the functions of nutrition, dormation, education, procreation, and garbage disposal is quite as false a premise for design as that clutter of rambling roofs, huge chimneys, quaint dormers, that prim symmetry of shuttered window and overdoor fanlight, which form the more decorous disguise of Bronxville and Wellesley Hills; nor have I a firmer faith in the quaint language and high intentions of those sociologists who arrive at architecture through "an analytical study of environmental factors favorable to the living requirements of families considered as instruments of social continuity." I am even less persuaded by biologists: especially those who have created a vegetable humanity to be preserved or cooled or propagated in boxes created for those purposes. I mean those persons who make diagrams and action photographs showing the impact upon space made by a lady arranging a bouquet or a gentleman dressing for dinner or 3.81 children playing at kiss-in-the-ring and who then invite architects to fit their rooms around these "basic determinants." My requirements are somewhat more subtle than those of a ripe tomato or a caged hippopotamus, whatever may be the opinion of the Pierce Foundation.

We have developed in our day a new language of structural form. That language is capable of deep eloquence; and yet we use it too infrequently for the purposes of a language. Just as the historical styles of architecture are detached from modern technologies and by that detachment lose that vitality and vividness which might come from a direct reference to our times, so our new motives are detached from the idea to be expressed. They have their origin not in the idea but in problems of construction and in principles of planning. We have not yet learned to give them meanings sufficiently persuasive. They have often interesting aesthetic qualities, they arrest us by their novelty and their drama, but too often they have very little to say to us.

The architects of the Georgian tradition were as solicitous as we are of progress in the science of building. They designed their houses with the same care for practical use that they spent, for example, upon their coaches and their sailing ships; and yet their first consideration was for their way of life. When I visit the streets of Salem I am not so confident as are some of my colleagues that her architects suffered from a limited range of materials and structural methods. Standing in the midst of a culture alien to their quaint formalisms, these houses yet make known to me the idea they were meant to capture. I understand them as I might understand a song sung in a foreign tongue. We are too ready to mistake novelty for progress and progress for art. I tell my students that there were noble buildings before the invention of plywood. They listen indulgently but they do not believe me.

I sometimes think that we have to defend our houses against the new processes of construction and against the aesthetic forms which these engender. We must remind ourselves that techniques have a strictly limited value as elements of expression. Their competence lies in the way we use them. However they may intrigue us, they have no place in the design of a house unless they do indeed serve the purpose of the home and are congenial to its temper. When, as often happens, their only virtue is their show, their adventitious nature is soon realized; they are then as great an impediment to our melody as an excess of ornamentation. The mighty cantilever which projects my house over a kitchen yard or a waterfall; that flexible wall and stressed skin; these fanaticisms of glass brick; these strange hoverings of my house over the firm earth—these strike my eyes but not my heart. A master may at his peril use them; but for human nature's daily use we have still proportion, homely ordinance, quiet wall surfaces, good manners, common sense, and love. These also are excellent building materials.

The world will not ask architects to tell it that this is an age of invention, of new excitements and experiences and powers. The airplane, the radio, the V-bomb, and the giant works of engineering will give that assurance somewhat more persuasively than the most enormous of our contraptions. Beside the big top of industry our bearded lady will not long astonish the mob.

It should be understood that I do not despise the gifts of our new sciences; and certainly the architects of the 1920's made convincing demonstrations of the utility of these in an art of expression. They used structural inventions not for their own sake nor yet for the sake of economy and convenience merely, but as elements in a language. Functionalism was a secondary characteristic of their expressive art which had as its basic conception, so far as this is related to the home, a search for a form which should exhibit a contemporary phase of an ancient aspect of life. To this end new materials were used, old ones discarded; but the true reliance was not upon these but upon new and significant relationships among architectural elements—among which enclosed space was the prime medium, walls and roof being used as a means of establishing spatial compositions. To compose in prisms rather than in mass, to abolish the façade and deal in total form, to avoid the sense of enclosure, to admit to a precise and scrupulous structure no technique not consonant with the true culture of our day:

these were the important methods of an architecture never meant to be definitive or "international"—which offered rather a base from which a new progress might be possible, a principle which should have its peculiar countenance in every nation and in every clime. I should not venture here to restate a creed already so often stated had not a torrent of recent criticism distorted this architecture into a "cold and uncompromising functionalism," had it not been made the excuse for an arid materialism wholly alien to its intention.

We must rely not upon the wonder and drama of our inventions but upon the qualities, beyond wonder and beyond utility, which we can give them. Take, for example, *space*. Of all the inventions of modern architecture the new space is, it seems to me, the most likely to attain a deep eloquence. I mean by this not only that we have attained a new command of space but also a new quality of space. Our new structure and our new freedom in planning—a freedom made possible in part at least by the flat roof—has set us free to model space, to define it, to direct its flow and relationships; and at the same time these have given space an ethereal elegance unknown to the historic architectures. Our new structure permits almost every shape and relationship in this space. You may give it what proportion you please. With every change in height and width, in relation to the spaces which open from it, in the direction of the planes which enclose it, you give it a new expression. Modern space can be bent or curved; it can move or be static, rise or press downward, flow through glass walls to join the space of patio or garden, break into fragments around alcoves and galleries, filter through curtains or end abruptly against a stone wall. You may also give it balance and symmetrical rhythms.

If then we wish to express in this new architecture the idea of *home*, if we wish to say in this persuasive language that this idea accompanies, persistent and eloquent, the forward march of industry and the changing nature of society, we have in the different aspects of space alone a wide vocabulary for that purpose.

I have of course introduced this little dissertation on space in order to illustrate this resourcefulness. I did not intend a treatise. I might with equal relevance have mentioned light, which is certainly as felicitous a medium of modern design, or the new materials which offer so diversified a palette of texture and color, or the forms and energies of our new types of construction, or the relationships to site and to nature made possible by new principles of planning. There are also the arts of painting and sculpture, of furniture-making, of textiles, metalware, and ceramics—all of which are, or ought to be, harmonious accessories to architecture.

I have heard architects explain with formulas, calculation, diagram, and all manner of auricular language, the advantages of the glass wall—of wide areas of plate glass opening on a garden—when all that was necessary was to say that here is one of the loveliest ideas ever entertained by an architect. People who *feel* walls do not need to compute them; and people who are deaf to the rhythms of great squares of glass relieved by quiet areas of light-absorbing wall may as well resign the enjoyment of architecture. Because they are free of those "holes punched in a wall," of that balance and stiff formalism in window openings which proclaim the Georgian mode, because we can admit light where we please, we have in effect invented a new kind of light. We can direct light, control its intensity and its colorations; diffuse it over space, throw it in bright splashes against a wall, dissolve it and gather it up in quiet pools; and from those scientists who are at work on new fashions in artificial light we ought to expect not new efficiencies merely or new economies merely, but new radiances in living.

Space, structure, texture, light—these are less the elements of a technology than the elements of an art. They are the colors of the painter, the tones of the musician, the images out of which poets build their invisible architectures. Like color, tone, and image they are most serviceable when they are so used as to make known the grace and dignity of the spirit of man.

Of course I know that modern architecture must adjust its processes to the evolving pattern of industry, that building methods must attain an essential unity with all the other processes by which in this mechanized world materials are assembled and shaped for us. No doubt the wholesale nature of our constructions imposes upon us a monotony and banality beyond that achieved by past architectures—a condition not likely to be remedied by prefabrication—and no doubt our houses, as they conform more closely to our ever advancing technologies, will escape still further the control of art. Still more inimical to architecture will be those standardizations of thought and idea already widely established in our country; that assembly-line society which stamps men by the millions with mass attitudes and mass ecstasies. Our standards of judgment will be progressively formed by advertisement and the operations convenient to industry.

I shall not imagine for my future house a romantic owner, nor shall

I defend my client's preferences as those foibles and aberrations usually referred to as "human nature." No, he shall be a modern owner, a post-modern owner, if such a thing is conceivable. Free from all sentimentality or fantasy or caprice, his vision, his tastes, his habits of thought shall be those most necessary to a collective-industrial scheme of life; the world shall, if it pleases him, appear as a system of casual sequences transformed each day by the cumulative miracles of science. Even so he will claim for himself some inner experiences, free from outward control, unprofaned by the collective conscience. That opportunity, when the universe is socialized, mechanized, and standardized, will yet be discoverable in the home. Though his house is the most precise product of modern processes there will be entrenched within it this ancient loyalty invulnerable against the siege of our machines. It will be the architect's task, as it is today, to comprehend that loyalty—to comprehend it more firmly than anyone else—and, undefeated by all the armaments of industry, to bring it out in its true and beautiful character.

From: *Architecture and the Spirit of Man,* by Joseph Hudnut. Cambridge, Mass.: 1949, pages 108–119.

VI

Social Responsibilities

What is a House?

by

Charles Harris Whitaker

Since the war began, the British Government, under such financial and industrial pressure as never before befell a nation, has spent millions upon millions in building houses of all kinds for its workers. It is one of the most remarkable and deeply significant transformations wrought by War. While her vast industrial expansion and its accompanying congestion of workers are the undoubted causes of England's huge expenditure for better homes, the deeper significance may be found in her plans for carrying on this program as a measure of post-war prudence. War has raised the standard of the house in England for all time. It has given a new meaning to the word. . . .

With sound economic foresight, England determined to build permanent houses, except in cases where the emergency was so dire as to compel temporary expedients. She found that taking into account the expense of applying the utilities (streets, water, gas, sewage), the difference in cost between temporary and permanent houses was so little as to be negligible in her calculations. Rather than accept a questionable post-war salvage from temporary structures, with the inevitable temptation to continue their use as slums, she resolved to create a permanent national asset. Thus there have grown up in an incredibly short time whole new towns and villages which will not only remain after the war but which will compel a generally higher standard for workmen's homes—for permanency is only a part of the miracle.

Having come to this decision, it became necessary to ask what kind of houses to build, in other words, "What is a house?" During the last hundred years of industrial expansion the definition of a house has been sinking slowly to a level where it included almost everything which could claim walls and a roof. The percentage of unsanitary disease-breeding structures inhabited by men, women, and children in all the so-called civilized countries of the world has been a sad blot on their escutcheon. Without exception, all the great nations except the United States—even the newer lands of Australia and New Zealand are ahead of us—have recognized this condition and accepted the duty of attempting its amelioration by financial aid of different kinds, as a legitimate and just governmental function. It may be said without hesitation that the application of science and governmental aid to home-building for workmen in Germany was one of her vital steps in the great scheme of war preparedness. Her model villages have been cited the world over, while her coöperative home-building and land-owning associations, fostered by the government, have been studied with profit in all other countries. England had begun to deal with this question, of late years, so that when she was compelled to undertake an immediate industrial expansion which should outweigh and outshoot Germany's highly organized machine, the accompanying problem of house-building was not an entire novelty. She had dealt with it before. Her garden cities were among the pioneering movements of modern housing reform. All her communities have large powers in dealing with the question, and the model tenements of London, Liverpool, Glasgow, and other cities, though far from solving the question of "What is a house?" were long steps forward. Of profound significance is the fact that since war began, London has demolished acres of slums and erected model tenements thereon. In order to bring the rentals of these within reach of workmen, she has charged off the entire cost of the land against her more prosperous areas! . . .

In building her new towns and villages, England did not treat the house as an isolated factor. In the first place, she embodied in its design the traditions of that rural domestic architecture which has so much delighted the thousands of Americans who have roamed the English countryside. She arranged them, whether singly or in groups, to form a harmonious whole and to avoid the deadly monotony of straight streets lined with houses of one pattern, no one differing from any other and known only by a number, each possessing as much outward atmosphere of inviting appearance as a row of freight cars. Nothing has contributed more to the slowness with which we respond to questions of civic import than this deadly monotony. The man of means builds a home in which he may give expression to his tastes and inclinations. Slowly, but surely, this kind of domestic architecture has lifted itself out of the slough of the Victorian era and the slavish copying by architects too lazy or too ignorant to study their problems, and begun to claim a place as a distinctly national development of value. But this applies only to an infinitesimally small proportion of our house-building operations. In the main, our towns and cities, and even our rural districts, are made hideous by the multitude of tawdry houses and the ugliness of surroundings which that tawdriness inevitably breeds—bill-boards, dumps, shanties, with waste paper and refuse scattered in indiscriminate profusion. Slowly, but surely, we become accustomed to it; we tolerate it; we ignore it. But all unconsciously we never forget it, for we flee it as a plague. We flee it for the country when we can. We flee it for anything which offers a distraction. And when men, women, and children unconsciously begin to flee the neighborhood of their home, what chance has the community to develop civic, social, or even economic progress? Such flight is the unconscious surrender of a political ideal, the precursor of revolutions.

Yet against the ugliness of our miles and miles of desolate, monotonous streets, we can only point to the one-time picturesque quality of thousands of European communities by reminding ourselves that we have made progress in several important directions.

But why were we willing to accept advances in sanitation, comfort, convenience, with so little thought of the preservation of those other qualities of charm and picturesque attractiveness which we so much admire when we visit Europe, or still find untouched here and there in our own country? The answer involves a long study of our industrial and social transformations, wherein ruthless competition, unchecked by any community foresight, has raised land values unequally, destroyed them by the same ruthless method, and made highly speculative that which should of all things be permanent—realty values.

The full answer, taking cognizance of these things yet denying them their right to lower the standards of a nation by steadily reducing, first, the size of the lot, then the size of the house, then the size of the room, enunciates the warning that this ever more and more relentless compression also squeezes out the moral and physical values which are the only source of national progress.

In her wartime house-building, England has recognized this as a fundamental principle. Her houses have ample lot-room and a maximum of light and air. Instead of being monotonous they are as varied in their picturesque character as any of the ancient towns of England. These new villages are striking examples of what may be done when the size of lot and house and room—and their design and arrangement—are not arbitrarily and ruthlessly sacrificed to the financial limitations of private capital. And this is no indictment of the little-understood thing we call capital. It is an indictment of the community and of the nation which is so short-sighted as first to permit and then to compel, as a measure of business salvation to the owner, the erection of structures, houses, tenements, that quickly decline in value through deterioration, ultimately diminish the taxable value of the neighborhood in which they stand, and always lower the standards, moral and physical, of those who inhabit them.

This is the civic crime of the ages—the acceptance by the community of a business principle which every good business man would reject in his own business without the slightest hesitation. Against this condition, of what value are architects and building codes? Their efforts must be directed to cheapening the cost of construction, both by reduction in space area per family and by the use of the least expensive materials and methods of construction which will pass the code, either honestly or by connivance. Today we are in the grip of this inexorable condition; tomorrow, how long deferred we know not, we shall begin to emerge from it, or else one lesson of the war will be lost.

The building of houses is today a speculation. Whether a man builds with the hope of a profit through sale, or rise in value, or with the hope that he will not sustain a loss, does not matter. The speculative idea is there; it cannot be escaped. Worse than this, one man bent upon a speculation which promises large profits to him by taking advantage of the helpless community can erect a type of structure which will so damage a neighborhood as to force others to put their property to the same use. This is only a temporary expedient. In the end the community loses. It suffers the loss in taxable values which is the anxious consideration of the financial authorities of all our cities, and it suffers the moral loss of a descending rather than an ascending scale of life. It is idle to condemn speculative builders and so-called private capital for these practices. The fundamental fault, which must and will be corrected, is the neglect of the community to see that the longer it gives *carte blanche* to the individual to convert land values to his private gain by no matter what means, the larger will be the bill which the community will have to pay in undoing his misdeeds. This is becoming so increasingly evident that the zoning or districting law, which governs the character and occupancy of new structures in a city, is being applied in several of our American cities.

New York City welcomed it with open arms, as the only measure of conserving the city's taxable values, and giving any permanency to realty. It undoubtedly offers a large avenue of relief. European countries have applied it successfully, and while it may have a tendency temporarily to diminish the volume of building, in the end it encourages the erection of good buildings as a permanent rather than a speculative investment.

"What is a house?" It is the prime element of national growth. It is the soil whence springs that eagerness in the heart of every man for a home of his own. It is, after all, the physical attribute of life upon the possession or retention of which most of our energy is directed. Because of these things, it is the backbone of the nation. By the quality of its appearance, its convenience, its durability, one may infallibly determine the real degree of a nation's prosperity and civilization.

"What is a house?" It is not a solitary entity by any means. Let us not forget that. Just houses, no matter how well they answer our question, would not suffice. With houses go other things—good streets, for example (although our blind adherence to the old street idea wastes acres of land and involves costs of upkeep which are rapidly challenging attention), gas, water, light, fire protection (which ought to be needed less and less, rather than more and more), garbage removal —all of these things are indispensable in any modern community. But, in addition to these purely physical attributes, there must be provided opportunities for social recreation, for play, for the influences of the school, the drama, music, the dance, the arts in general. That is why England, in building thousands of homes for her workers (as Germany did before her), has had the foresight to build, wherever the existing community was incapable of meeting the need, schools, churches, halls, recreation grounds, laundries, and even public kitchens. There are large open areas for the children—and for grown-ups, too.

"Socialism," says somebody. "Fad," says another. "Paternalism," cries a third. But, mark this well, the least important thing about it is the name by which it is called. Those who live principally for the pleasure of hugging words to their bosom long after all spark of life has left the letters which they spell glibly over and over, may continue the pursuit of this childish pastime. Men who have sense enough to recognize human forces and currents—who know that the world is moved by these and that progress comes through them and not by the names they are called—such men will understand that England is putting her house in order by putting the houses of her people in order. In other words, she is getting ready to pay her debts by organizing her commerce and industry on new lines, far in advance of anything else (as Germany did before her). She is preparing for her reëntrance into world markets on a larger scale than before, for it is from those markets that all the nations must collect the money for paying their interest charges and debts. Such an economic measure will be precedent to the payment of national debts by all nations, ourselves included. And in the working out of that program, the house, as a giver of rest and contentment, source of satisfaction, emblem of true community growth, and forerunner of sound community values, will play a part which England seems to understand, at last.

Shall we learn?

In the great and wonderful epic of America we have been thrilled with the first coming of the pioneer. As he took his way westward into the depths of the wilderness, we have journeyed with him, breathless, in the great adventure. Is there not then a profound significance—a deep reproach—in the fact that where we once tingled with joy over the picture of the rude "home," the family "fireside," the welcoming "hearth-fire," the sheltering "roof-tree," we are now content to dismiss the picture from our minds and utter platitudes about "housing?" We even include it in our philanthropies and consign to the pathetic field of charity that which we once glorified as the very essence of our American spirit and courage—the quest of a home!

Bearing these things in mind let us glance at the Thirteenth Census, and particularly at the chapter entitled "Ownership of Homes," for here we are confronted with facts which seem to be a denial of one of the elements that once helped to make up our national ideal. For a whole century at least the United States was the goal of the landless and the houseless of all nations. . . . Mr. Roosevelt uttered a warning over the decline in the number of owned farms and the consequent increase in tenant-farmers. No one who has studied this question in the last decade has ignored its deep significance, but the same fact is equally patent when we study the house. Here, ownership by the occupant has declined in a far greater proportion than has farm ownership. The Census of 1910 tells the story. . . .

The figures for Alaska and Hawaii are of the greatest interest, because they reveal the swifter strides of the same transformative process of ownership in an earlier stage. The difference in the ten-year periods is marked by great descents. In the United States we note a slight increase in home ownership, other than farms, for the period from 1900 to 1910. This is traceable to the middle sections of the country and is probably due to economic causes connected with the first stages of industrial expansion.

As to the causes which have produced this result there can be but one general answer. Under our economic system we have denied the political and social ideal upon which the nation was founded. We have refuted democracy by beguiling ourselves with crude attempts to solve it in political terms, the while we gave ourselves unbridled license to exploit our land and all that it contained with no thought of what might be the ultimate effect upon ourselves as a nation and upon the democracy we professed to seek. The result we shall have to reckon with. Landlordism has steadily increased until we are in a fair way to actually repeat the very cycle from which men of other nations wished to escape by coming hither. It was an inevitable outcome of the individualism which has passed current for freedom, and constitutes a national acceptance of the doctrine that the whole welfare of the nation is subservient to the right of the individual to pursue his path as he pleases. We have struggled to curb this individualistic wilfulness by legislation, but without appreciable effect. War comes to us with a flaming warning.

In this struggle of mechanism against mechanism, victory will lie with the side which puts forth the greatest industrial energy. It is our discovery of the colossal need of ships and more ships, of guns and more guns, which also discovers to us the fact that our ability to manufacture is limited by the conditions under which workmen and their families live.

If we ask whether it is best, in any country, that the land and the buildings should be owned by a minority which inevitably grows smaller and smaller, we may safely answer that it has never yet yielded national stability. If, however, we assume, as so many do, that it is the unavoidable result of the struggle between men whose abilities are so unequal in carrying business, industry, and commerce, then we must admit that life consists merely of an endless and hopeless repetition of cycles, each with its débâcle and rebirth. But does the faith that these cannot and ought not to be prevented still claim so large a body of adherents, now that we are in the throes of the most violent convulsion the world has known—when we can see more clearly than ever before through eyes to which science has lent a new visionary power?

It is upon our answer to this question that the problem of building houses for workmen depends for the right solution, and it is this which also gives such emphasis to the importance of dealing rightly with the present dire emergency of shortage in houses and the consequent congestion to which so many thousands of our workers, with their wives and families, are condemned. War has made this so vital a question that we must now face it whether we will or not, but we cannot in any way find the right solution without asking ourselves these questions; they weave themselves into the figures in the Census with an insistence which almost implores us to find the answer.

Can it be true that the instinct for possessing a house has become a declining factor in our life? Has the acceptance of the rented substitute, in a steadily increasing measure over a long period of years, supplanted that desire to an extent which indicates its permanent passing? Do we admit that the "efficiency" of our life demands subservience, for the great majority, to a landlordism which cannot be escaped? Must we pursue to its cataclysmic end a system which decrees that the workman must relinquish his wish to own a home in order that he may conserve to himself the largest possible measure of economic freedom? The facts offer relentless evidence of the condition to which we have arrived, and the right solution of what we have pathetically termed the "industrial housing" problem depends utterly upon our resolve to study the problem with open minds and with all the facts squarely before us.

From: *The Housing Problem in War and in Peace,* by Charles Harris Whitaker, Frederick L. Ackerman, Richard S. Childs, Edith Elmer Wood. "The Journal of the American Institute of Architects Press," Washington: 1918, pages 3–8.

The Sad Story of American Housing

by

Henry Wright

Philadelphia, "city of brotherly love," has many fine traditions. The gridiron street system, laid down by William Penn, is not to be counted among them. As a city-planning method it constituted a mistaken experiment that has since ripened into a calamitous habit. The gridiron city plan brings about the narrow attenuated lot quite as directly as the shape of a pork chop is dependent on the ribs of the hog. In Philadelphia itself, these lots were occupied full width by closed rows of the "town house"; but not even the virtues of these closed rows, such as they were, remained when the gridiron crossed the Alleghanies and migrated over the national highway, or "overland," route into the Central West.

The most extensive and natural habitat of the gridiron street, with its attendant narrow lot and sunless side alley, has not been geographic but psychological, in the real-estate operator's mind. Here these three have been lodged as tenants by perpetual lease, salamanders never to be burnt out by even the hottest fire, or perhaps even as ineradicable grooves worn into the brain. To suggest that better methods were available has made no impression. To erect physical examples, in which the superiority of other methods has been successfully demonstrated, has as yet caused hardly a ripple. There remains, then, for us to examine the product of this speculative builder himself, to see whether the recent depression-sobered past has led him to develop anything *within* his narrow frame upon which we might predicate some kind of an advance, however halting, toward an adequate housing procedure.

The gridiron street pattern spread rapidly over almost the whole country during the period of rapid expansion and city building of the nineteenth century. The expansion followed the great avenues of commerce. Thus we find a brick town architecture, closely modelled on the seaboard cities in form and appearance, extending to Pittsburgh, and thence down the Ohio River to Cincinnati, to Louisville, and eventually to St. Louis on the upper Mississippi River. Other traditions than those brought over the mountains may have contributed in these new cities to the arrangement of the houses in detail. But in shape and general appearance the early houses of all these cities distinctly recall Philadelphia. The row principle in itself is not undesirable; in fact, row houses properly planned constitute the most hopeful form of low-cost single-family dwelling to be found here or in Europe. It is the tradition of the *narrow lot* with which we are concerned.

In the Pittsburgh area the practice of continuous row grouping was continued, and again at Wheeling. Even in the small town of Mount Pleasant, Ohio, near Wheeling, where land could scarcely at any time have been worth more than a few cents a square foot, houses on the main street were built in attached rows. In one case (here illustrated) an archway was placed at the end of the group to reach the rear yard, the house wall being carried up windowless on the property line.

But an important change took place when city building reached the more open plain of the Ohio Valley at Cincinnati. Here the town house met the impact of the pioneer spirit. The house was split from its neighbor by a narrow side yard—sometimes a mere passageway, sometimes faced by a few small windows. At St. Louis the precedent of Philadelphia is quite evident. But here the cleft between the houses divides them by only two feet—it is too narrow for passage except by alley cats, and is utilized for no window exposure; it is entirely meaningless, therefore, except as a vigorous expression of what our "rugged individualism" occasionally leads us to. Half a century has passed since this particular expression flourished; it has been discontinued on any large scale; but the fetish that inspired it has remained dominant throughout all the subsequent housing evolution.

Let us trace this evolution through a period of thirty years in the typical building construction of St. Louis. We shall find constant change, virtually devoid of any significant progress. From the town house characteristic of the 1870–1890 period we pass to the less stilted city house of 1890–1900. This latter is less rectangular, but it keeps to the narrow side yard. There is not yet a pressure from the rise of frontage costs that would explain such crowding.

At the turn of the century the increased complexities of street utilities have pushed up frontage costs to a point requiring more intensive use. The two-story house is evolved, with one family on each floor. This type is known generally as the "St. Louis flat," although it is by no means confined to St. Louis, since Chicago, for example, houses 375,000 families in this type of dwelling. The rectangular plan has to be lengthened, and the additional length emphasizes still more clearly the fissure-like character of the side yard.

For a decade the detached two-decker satisfied the demands of frontage economy. Then the unguided processes of rugged individualism, exemplified in neighborhoods of repetitive brick fronts, required a further contraction. The two-family unit was doubled along the party wall. This called for long dark interior halls and an exposure for most of the rooms on the narrow side yard. The arrangement of the rooms themselves in tandem, one behind the other, is an onerous one for purposes of housekeeping; yet it is the actual or at least the progenitive pattern of at least 70 per cent of the present housing in St. Louis, and of an even greater proportion in Chicago, to say nothing of Cleveland, Cincinnati, and Newark. The original Eastern row house was in itself fairly reasonable; it is the precedent which it established, of narrow-lot squeezing, which has done all the damage, having been accepted ever since as a necessary accompaniment of moderate-cost dwellings.

The fourth step in the evolution in these cities (the group now expanded by the inclusion of Kansas City and similar later communities) was to build up the double two-family flat to three stories. The tandem room arrangement was of course retained. The side yard remained narrow as before, and not only was its shadow deepened still further by the new floor, but, in the popular mode of the day, porches were added front and back as a still further discouragement to the feeble, smoky sunlight of these industrial cities. Nor was the situation relieved when the demands for larger dwelling space required the widening of the double unit, to gain a narrow extra room at the front and the rear. This process increased the distance in all the intermediate rooms from the inner wall to the window, which transmitted none too much light as it was.

The final decade has seen the expansion of the widened three-story double flat for service in the high-rent field. An interior court is introduced to form a U, with many of the rooms still ranged along the persistent narrow side-line courtyard. Chicago offers variations on these new atrocities, first by the introduction of the three-story detached flat (embracing about 170,000 dwellings), and then by closing up the front façade to give the effect of a nice continuous row, a procedure which just happens to cut off the already scanty circulation of air along the side courts.

Meanwhile, in many smaller cities the effort was successfully carried through to widen the standard lot. Forthwith an unguided public demand for the still more wasteful "bungalow" of one story filled up and overcrowded the lot in its new generous proportions. By 1930 even the builder himself realized that these bungalows looked somewhat awkward, jammed together. A movement then spread to camouflage the bungalow as a modest cottage. A high-pitch "cross gable" was turned across the front façade, to hide the huge mass of the house as it lumbered rearward, its main roof being kept invisible by virtue of a lower pitch. This ingenuity was cleverly manipulated in many Minneapolis examples, but botched in other cities. The ubiquitous front chimney, badly placed for living with, but easy to advertise, was also characteristic of this period.

Here at last was a spark of hope. Having once turned the roof, the builder might by some accident have hit on the corresponding expedient of rearranging the whole house. Having created the effect, he might have followed with the plain fact. At least he might have modified those extreme mistakes of form which had led him into the ultimate confession implied by his camouflage. But no, the spark of hope flickers and dies out. In 1929, 1930, 1931, we find the practical builder repeating the evolution that had already taken place in 1903, 1904, 1905. The causes and the effects are naïvely simple.

The bungalow is popular, therefore the accommodating realty effort, "striving to please," must retain it. Keeping an ear to the ground, "understanding and interpreting the public demand," is the admitted major accomplishment of the real-estate profession. But the bungalow, particularly in its crude narrow-lot form, happens to entail waste and expense which sooner or later register themselves as "sales resistance," something which, we regret, has never been countermanded by any Eighteenth Amendment. So the resourceful mind of the speculative builder invents the "investment bungalow," with an annex on the rear attic for a subtenant who pays part of the rent. Some sacrifice is appropriately required of the owning family on the first floor. The extra stairway needed for the new upper tenant crowds the living-room of the main unit forward into the erstwhile sun porch.

The next step for the practical mind is naturally to provide more space above for more rent, and the upper dwelling is consequently expanded into almost a full replica of that below. Almost, because the new two-family structure must still masquerade as a modest bungalow—for who wishes to admit his dependence on his neighbor (above) for the lion's share of his monthly costs? Very ingeniously the public is coddled into receiving this almost final step in the undoing of its bungalow ideal—very ingeniously deceptive in front, but brutally frank behind.

Finally the top story pushes itself out into a full replica of the story below—but still not quite. The effect must still be guarded by the "draping" of a false gambrel roof, which doesn't really fool any one, but makes a highly valued variation for each alternate unit in an endless row of equally dreary façades. But, prize of all! throughout this whole process the hardy resistance of the speculative builder's mind has preserved its integrity. Look down the line of these full-fledged two-flat dwellings of 1931. The "sun porch" appendage is still maintained in its distinguishing brick appliqué as the front half of the living-room, tied into the frame half of this room by the fake brick fireplace, at each side of which is the proverbial small window over the proverbial bookshelves; the get-up distinctly advertising the interior dishonesty by the fact that one window is in frame and the other in brick.

Need we introduce further evidence of the innate poverty of the whole ridiculous procedure? True enough, the public at first glance thinks it is getting the most house for its money if every available inch of the lot has something on it; but not even the general public insists on buying the largest suit of clothes in a store, or even insists any longer on the bulkiest furnace. When we consider such items as the construction wastes and the heat losses of our present-day, long, leaky barges, the calculation is less one of standards of sunlight or comfort than one of plain arithmetic; every ton of coal thrown out of the window decreases purchasing power, a part of which would have been available to the building industry. The public is ready to understand the comparative economics of the case whenever they are explained; but not so the builder. Housing progress in this country is impossible because of the inadequacy, amateurishness, and incapacity of those groups to whom it has been entrusted as a side-line to land merchandising and the mortgage business. It is time here as elsewhere for a distinctly "new deal."

We are not concerned, in this discussion, with land economics or finance as such. We are interested in them only in relation to housing. Hitherto they have pretty well buried housing.

If we stick strictly to the problem before us, determining that in some fashion or other housing must be accomplished, then from our standpoint it is a nuisance that so much of the "economics" of the land is entirely distinct from its useful employment.

Progressive housing, as practised both in this country and abroad, is based on the principle of compact districts developed to their fullest use in advance of any improvement of adjacent areas—such practice permits reasonable land development and specific planning. The general American practice, on the contrary, is one which permits vast areas around the city to be bought up years in advance of any possible use and held for ostensible "ripening." Figures covering the city of Grand Rapids, and assembled by Professor Ernest M. Fisher, of the University of Michigan, show a not unusual case. During twenty-two years, 1909–1931, covered by the study, approximately two lots were platted for every one used for building purposes. The whole number of lots used was only slightly greater than the number available and unused in 1909. "If utilization of lots should continue at the average rate prevailing between 1909 and 1931, it would require thirty-five years to absorb into use all of the lots which are now vacant."

This statement of fact is sufficient, without further deductions, to exhibit the wildness and the irresponsibility involved. This practice of speculative holding carries a triple menace. In the first place, it prevents the assembling, at a low price, of land needed by actual developers. In the second place, it has led our cities to the installation of expensive public services, far in advance of possible use; and, what is more important, in the third place, the city plans are deprived of any real or definite objective in terms of a specific region to be used in a special way. The street pattern has therefore had to be reduced to the lowest standardized plane a pattern of short blocks with an excessive number of cross streets requiring utilities and services. Thus we come upon the gridiron once more. No possibility has existed of foretelling which of the streets would be commercial and which entirely residential; and therefore *all* streets have been given the heavier construction necessary for commercial traffic.

The development of the land as a separate operation from building has entailed excessive charges for the separate items of subdividers' overhead, carrying charges until use, and profit. The number of fees and other contributions required to bring the separate organizations along the different divisions and stages of the work into some kind of alignment has already been described in the book "Housing America" by the editors of *Fortune*.

Through these costs, plus the high taxes involved in the cities' wasteful procedure, all existing moderate-intensity housing areas have been subjected to an immense burden which has forced their conversion to more intensive uses. The more intensive use, capitalized in turn as higher land value, has imposed multi-story buildings which put further heavy demands on streets and public services, so that the vicious circle is completed, with congestion everywhere and mounting public costs. The ironic result to the citizen who works in the central business district is that city expansion, despite its high cost, has been carried beyond the point of any convenience to him in terms of location.

As to the habits of land subdivision, we shall encounter again and again the vicious effect of habits formed, all of which rest on the single-family house. Since the first development of an outlying area is generally in terms of this single, free-standing house, land is platted in narrow, deep lots, and this constriction of the lot remains as a disadvantage to every further step. The history of the flat is essentially the history of a potentially superior building type thwarted at the outset by the single-family lot.

It has been shown in frequently published studies that of the average dollar expended for home purchase in the United States, approximately twenty-seven cents go into financing and promotion charges. This is more than is spent either for construction materials or for labor on the job, and considerably more than the average actual cost of the land and its improvement. This exorbitant cost of financing arises chiefly from our system of junior mortgages, with their large element of risk accompanied by higher rates of interest, plus discounts, commissions, and renewal fees. That the risks are real is attested by the widespread bankruptcy of second-mortgage houses, and by the difficulties of finding reputable sources of junior finance.

The first step in the cure of this situation lies in the improvement of the housing product as such. Improved planning in terms of stable communities will decrease the risks of vacancies and obsolescence to a point permitting conservative sources of money safely to enlarge the scope of first mortgages. Second mortgages, if any, may then be

Chatham Village, Pittsburgh, Pennsylvania. Ingham and Boyd, architects. Clarence S. Stein and Henry Wright, site planners and consultant architects. *Courtesy, Clarence S. Stein.*

Baldwin Hills Village, Los Angeles, California. Reginald D. Johnson and Wilson, Merrill and Alexander, associated architects. Clarence S. Stein, consulting architect. *Courtesy, Clarence S. Stein.*

stripped of most of their risk, and the amortization of all loans may be safely spread over materially longer periods than in present practice.

A desirable simplification would be for a larger proportion or all the mortgage money to come from a single source, a practice which can be justified for housing of demonstrated stability in use. Not even the most drastic economies achieved by skimping on construction costs could produce savings in rentals or in ownership charges equal to those to be derived from the slower rate of amortization resulting from stable financing.

The final goal in housing finance, however, is not merely that of improving mortgage rates, extending amortization periods, or simplifying the present complicated mess of senior, junior, and sub-junior mortgages, desirable though this might be. Large-scale housing should and must find its place as a primary investment which will attract permanent money, not temporary mortgage advances which must rapidly be withdrawn less because the undertaking is risky than because the lender has limited means. Such investment money should stand at least on a par with other public utility securities as a permanent stock subscription—negotiable as collateral, to be sure, but remaining in the general housing enterprise, as opposed to any particular housing project. The investment of such capital by the operating company in any particular housing unit would necessarily be protected by an adequate depreciation reserve, set aside regularly and specifically to offset probable reductions in current earning power from whatever cause. That is, it would take care of possible changes in surrounding conditions, making it possible to reduce rents, to allow for obsolescence or else to reduce it by undertaking alterations and renovations, and to permit complete restoration when necessary either in the same location or in another one. This would keep the capital continuously employed, without demanding the double drain on rentals for both depreciation and amortization which now is necessary in some degree even in large-scale projects, however well planned and managed.

As long as we remain dependent on mortgages, we are particularly handicapped by another bad financial habit, which consists in appraising projects on a wholesale basis. If gross cubage is to be the only measure, then a wasteful building not only escapes punishment but is often rewarded for its waste. Better planned, better built, and, most especially, better managed and protected projects should definitely be entitled to preferential treatment, both in priority of mortgages and in per cent covered by mortgage, although such preferment is seldom encountered today.

Quite another aspect of this subject has to do with the general extravagance and multiplicity of business charges assessed against house construction at every stage of production, from the subdivision of the raw land up to the trussing of the purchaser in his own shoestring. It might be considered going rather far to suggest that this sort of thing is respectable rather than racketeering, were it not that so many respectable agencies are implicated at some point in the process of building, mortgaging, advertising and selling. If there is any one best reason why investments in the field of "home" building have dried up, it lies in the practices connected with nearly every phase of production. The growing insistence that the first mortgage cover a lower per cent, and the demand for bonuses, arise directly out of the fact that those who supply mortgage money know too much about the inside workings of the system, and properly hesitate to loan more than the equivalent of the actual tangible assets. At the time when Sunnyside was built, there was a certain house in it that was offered at $8,300; one of the largest and most respectable agencies building in a competitive district offered an apparently equal house at $6,000. Equalizing the land value of the two houses by subtracting the extra cost in Sunnyside of improved vacant land, the Sunnyside house would come to $7,650. Yet the actual expenditures going into the complete building (all payments for labor, materials, equipment, fixtures, decoration and the like, and also building overhead) were only $2,450 for the competing house as against $5,212 for Sunnyside. Or, stated somewhat differently, the purchase price in the two cases represented *construction* costs as against *marketing* costs in very different proportions. For the $6,000 house, lot and improvements cost $675; landscaping $175; building complete $2,450; and then came a marketing overhead of $2,690, or about 45 per cent of the price. For the $8,300 cost, the same items were $1,325, $200, $5,212 and $1,563 respectively—that is, 61 per cent went into building and only 19 per cent into marketing overhead.

Have we now reached the point at which we can summarize what seems to be the present situation? We find that our cities not only suffer from slums but are riddled with blight throughout the great range of their supposedly middle-class construction. Such blight calls for rehabilitation before we can safely engage in any further irresponsible expansion. When we examine the housing types available for such rehabilitation, we find that we have an increasing proportion of group dwellings housing more than a single family; the single-family house is doomed to a permanent recession. These multi-family houses of ours—mostly flats, and only 5 per cent of them serviced apartments—have grown up under the hand of the speculative builder. We find them still struggling, as in 1900, with the narrow, single-family lot, or derivatives that are only slightly modified. We find the enterprise hampered by excessive holding of land for "ripening," by huge city outlays for service that cannot serve, by financial charges which represent in the main a measuring-rod of the chaos. We may now look about to see whether these normal processes of real-estate and speculative building are likely to improve. The answer, unfortunately but very positively, is "No."

From: *The Sad Story of American Housing*. In *Architecture*, Vol. LXVII. March 1933.

New Towns for New Purposes

by

Clarence S. Stein

To build a substantial setting for neighborhood and family life, rather than to control and regulate, requires a completely different kind of planning. That is why I intend to call it community development or *New Town Planning* to differentiate it from the procedure that is generally called city planning in America. There is actually an antithesis between the two procedures. The prime objective of one is to assist in the marketing and protection of property, of the other to create communities. The latter deals with the realities of living rather than with trading. The two are at cross-purposes: preserve and protect in contrast with devise and produce.

New Town planning is an integral part of a co-ordinated procedure for building communities that will be both contemporary and dynamic. Note:

Co-ordinated, not disorganized
Building, not delineating
Communities, not lots or streets
Contemporary, not obsolete
Dynamic, not static.

New Town planning is not a separate function; it is an integral part of a procedure that creates a complete, solid, living community. It is an essential link in the chain of related and interdependent processes that actually turn open country land into complete, vibrant towns—good places to live in.

City Planning is too often an afterthought; in other words it is no more than city patching. It is not the work of a creator, but of a surgeon called in too late to operate on a decaying carcass. Such city patching deals with *means* rather than ends. It creates superhighways, super-complicated intersections or other gargantuan minutiae while neglecting the causes and sources of congestion. Thus it often fans the flame instead of extinguishing the fire. It is so fully concerned with mechanical or engineering feats that it loses sight of the ultimate goal of planned development—better living.

The New Town planner requires a broad understanding of aims and objectives, and of all the related functions with which he must work to realize them. As his technical work is part of a larger process of creating a community background, that is to say of building, and not mapping or drawing, he must work as part of a team. . . .

The old type of city planning is merely one of a disorganized series of unrelated activities that produce chaotic cities, including land speculation, lot subdivision, skeleton highway plans, individual house plans, regulations, spotty location of public buildings, and ultimately rebuilding unrelated structures one after the other, when zoning inevitably surrenders to the greed of individual lot owners.

In all this the city planner plays but a minor role. It is not his detailed factual surveys, his traffic counts, his calculations of population growth, his clever graphs, his many colored diagrams of use and heights, nor his superbly presented reports that determine the ultimate form and substance of our cities. Look at the ugly, dangerous, irrational, chaotic messes we call cities: certainly these are not the result of a purposeful plan for good living or even for efficient industry and trade. The essential reality of these cities has not been conceived, devised, pre-determined.

This present kind of city planning does not deal with substantial realities; but with phantom cities, outlines of cities. It delineates bodiless skeletons instead of creating habitable, solid cities. Its subject is primarily a framework for saleable lots, not a community. It is concerned with separate and limited units: lots, individual houses, a single road, not community building. Because city planning outlines and regulates, and does not relate these units in a composed group or neighborhood, it must generalize. This requires stereotyped, conservative, easily classified, standardized objects; these are more easily marketed and regulated.

The present city form is not moulded by the planner. It is the random consequence of the separate and unrelated decisions of subdivider, municipal engineer, zoning board, speculative builder, aided and abetted by the FHA and the leading institutions.

Finally, the shape and appearance of things, and the relation of the parts that make the chaotic accidents called cities, are the summation of the haphazard, independent whims of a multitude of individuals. They ultimately determine the pattern for living by filling in the cubby-holes marketed by the subdivider; and for the individual there seems to be no alternative.

To fill in the form, the body, the reality of the town, city planning proceeds not by positive action but by negations. It restricts and regulates, and limits use, height and bulk by zoning laws.

These regulations are usually commonplace generalizations. They result in monotonous similarity of use, height, coverage and outline of neighboring buildings. Predetermined related variety of mass, height, and a common pooling of open spaces is found in our cities only in such exceptional large-scale unified developments as Rockefeller Center. This kind of purposeful organized design that produces architectural and civic beauty as well as better lighting and ventilation is never attainable by the old highway-framework-subdivision process of city planning, even with the addition of the best-intentioned and most expert zoning. Nor can the special community facilities be grouped in a serviceable or attractive manner by this type of wishful negation.

The kind of city planning of which I have just spoken was not helpful in creating the communities [I have] described. . . . It was foreign to their objectives: they would have been hampered, not aided, by its use. Experiments such as the Radburn Idea never could have been realized within the framework both legal and physical, that has circumscribed the city planners' thinking and activities. At Radburn we were able to work on a clear slate because we got there before the zoners and subdividers and the municipal highway engineers. Their immovable framework would have held up progress there and, afterward, at Chatham Village, the Greenbelt Towns and Baldwin Hills Village.

The full realization of the economic as well as the living advantages of the Radburn Plan cannot be attained by the ordinary piecemeal process of city planning for lot subdivision. It must be built in—houses, roads, walks, parks, gardens—and a definitely determined reality must be created that will fit a desired way of living long enough to pay off its capital, maintenance and operational costs. It must furthermore be arranged to allow the changes required to keep it in harmony with this changing world.

To attain the economies that the Radburn type of planning offers, the gambling chance of increased monetary values of a lot must be given up. If the less costly types of specialized means of communication, such as the cul-de-sac at Radburn or garage court at Baldwin Hills Village, are to be used, there is little opportunity of finding a better paying future use for an individual piece of property, for example, for a commercial purpose. Therefore zoning would be only reiteration. The future use is more purposefully and lastingly set by group buildings than by regulations open to constant change.

The green inner core of the superblock is the cheapest as well as the most satisfactory way of securing nearby verdant openness. But the unusual location of the inner block commons requires an unusual form of community organization or of legal framework to maintain and organize it.

In creating New Towns, planning and building go hand in hand. They must be united as two inseparable parts of one process. Just as architecture is concerned with the solid realities of structures, so New Town planners must deal in terms of three-dimensional actuality. As city architect or civic designer he must mould form and mass as well as predetermine city plan or outline. A beautiful and livable urban environment requires a comprehensive design embracing the site, the form, the mass and the detail of every building and the relation of each building to the whole site and neighboring structures—in short all the visual surroundings.

Civic design is foreign to the methods of the old city planning. It cannot be clamped within the confines of lots or of the conventional gridiron. It requires the unified design of a portion of the city at least large enough to form a complete visual picture. This picture the New Town planner must paint on a broad canvas, a canvas large enough to comprise all that the human eye can envisage at a time. The developments which are illustrated in this book have done this in different ways. In every case the landscape and the structures have been blended into a unified composition, with great foregrounds of lawns and related verdure, and the mass and color of buildings composing pleasantly together and with this background. In Baldwin Hills Village the long horizontal lines of the houses contrast with the rounded slopes of the surrounding hills; in Chatham Village the houses climb up the hills; and in Greenbelt the simple rows are arranged one above the other on the rising ground. In each one of them the great mass of spacious green around which they are set unifies and dominates the composition. At Radburn the broad lawns and spreading trees are the center of visual beauty just as much as they are the center of the community. It is this spaciousness that is the keynote of the wholesome, good living of these places. And the comprehensive views of grouped buildings are dependent on the openness of the central greens, around which each one is composed in a different way. Even the greens of Sunnyside, in spite of the more restricted gridiron frame, give a natural charm and beauty to the simple rows of brick buildings.

Going Places and Enjoying the Use of Places are quite distinct and different functions. What serves one is antagonistic to the other. Therefore a circulatory plan and a plan for a maximum practical and aesthetic use of the buildings and spaces of a city must be kept separate.

The same forms or means cannot serve the two at one time or at one place. Although they complement each other, they require different locations and forms, diametrically contrary in use. To co-ordinate these two is a basic problem of contemporary planned city development. That is the purpose of the Radburn type of plan.

Civic Design for inspiring delight, and City Traffic Planning for safe, easy, quick flow of modern traffic must be harmonized if a modern city is to be completely practical for circulation and use, and at the same time, full of beauty. Although these are by nature antagonistic, they must be integrated into a practical beauty. They will cripple or destroy each other unless they are functionally and spaciously separated and at the same time mutually serve each other.

Let us examine and compare the requirements of City Traffic Planning and Civic Design.

A City Traffic Plan requires for speed, safety and maximum steady flow:

1. Straight roads or long sweeps with clear visibility at crossings and of approaching traffic.
2. As few crossings as possible.
3. No access to or from buildings on primary roads.
4. Minimum visual distraction—the auto driver's attention should be kept on the road.

The objective of such planning is to allow vehicles to move from one place to another as safely, quickly, directly and easily as possible.

Civic Design, on the other hand, deals with the presentation of a city's buildings and open spaces so that they give the greatest pleasure and enjoyment. That each individual building should have beauty of form, mass and color is not sufficient.

The display of a building as part of civic design has much in common with display of the treasures in a well-designed museum. Buildings, like art objects, must be placed so that they will be observed, examined, appreciated and enjoyed. This is impossible in a formal monumental museum and equally so in a gridiron-patterned city.

The automobile has made obsolete the classical monumental type of city plan, dominated by highway axes leading from one important structure to another. Terminal vistas are not for the auto driver; he has not time to enjoy them while keeping on the move; and even if he did, his attention should not be distracted. In Edinburgh's Georgian "New Town" the man on horseback, or in a horse-drawn carriage, had an opportunity to observe and enjoy the street composition while approaching its terminal of church, monuments or government building. This met the requirements of the Eighteenth Century. But it is meaningless in a Twentieth-Century city. Vistas of dominant buildings there should be for leisurely enjoyment. Therefore they should face parks or public places from which vehicular traffic is excluded.

Even less appropriate to the needs of a contemporary New Town than the World's Fair kind of city plan is the typical gridiron plan, in which all buildings are filed away in cubby-holes at either side of a highway, so that one passes them by no matter how significant they may be. The architectural masterpieces might as well not exist for any citizen or visitor of a gridiron planned city. He passes good and bad alike, with merely a hasty glance to right or left. His mind and eye are on the traffic and the distant perspective. He is going somewhere—he has neither the time nor the desire for visual enjoyment. Before him, if he is in an automobile, he sees and observes only flashing green and red lights, traffic police and congested highway. If he is on foot his attention is concentrated on the danger of street crossings, while he battles with the crowds. A striking group of buildings or a monument terminating a busy highway would be wasted on either pedestrian or driver. But in the typical gridiron city neither walker nor motorist approaches a building or an architectural group of structures in an attractive setting. If he did see them the composition, no matter how attractive, would be lost on him. His attention is elsewhere. He is not in the spirit for beauty, grandeur, inspiration.

The setting in which interesting buildings or groups of buildings are to be viewed must be separated from the massed flow of machines or people. It is not enough for one to give them a passing glance and be momentarily attracted, one must remain long enough for the beauty to become part of one's consciousness. This is not possible in the midst of rushing activity. Peaceful surroundings, away from the movement and uproar of the streets, is the proper setting for civic design. Here buildings can be enjoyed in relation to open places or in natural surroundings, across water or gardens. One should be able to remain long and comfortably to discover varied beauties, as the light changes. One should approach the great monument or group reverently, slowly, by foot. And there should be several approaches, so that one can see it at various angles, in different compositions of landscape and architecture.

A New Town must remain contemporary for a very long period. Only thus can we afford it. It must last long enough to allow its original cost to be amortized. That on the face of it may seem impossible, for the main characteristic of the present time is change—change in our way of living, in our thinking, even our objectives; and above all in our technical facilities and ability to make changes.

New Towns must not only be the flowering of today's life and civilization, but they must have in them the seed of the future—or at least the facility of growing and changing to fit it. They must be dynamic. Therefore our New Towns, if they are not quickly to become our Old Towns, must be flexible. We must plan so as to limit the difficulties we now face in the redevelopment of our old cities, which require extravagant destruction and the rebuilding of vast areas.

To make this possible we need:

1. A community of completely integrated neighborhoods.
2. A minimum original investment in buildings or equipment which are costly to alter or replace.
3. Plentiful open space in which the community form and pattern can be set and developed.

The cause of blight in the old sections of cities is due largely to the fact that they were built not as the living-working place of an interrelated, interdependent community, but as a conglomeration of crowded, unrelated units or cells. These are so packed together that there is no room for the individual house or workplace to stretch, expand or change. There is no space in which the community form or pattern can be modified or reorganized without complete destruction.

If revision to meet gradual and continuous change is not to be wastefully extravagant, we need the smallest possible investment in big buildings with complicated mechanical equipment and therefore high first costs. It is practically impossible to amortize such investment in either skyscraper office or residential buildings before they are functionally obsolete, or before the congestion they foster blocks city transit and transportation and makes their servicing and use unbearably slow and costly.

Large sections of New York are now being rebuilt with massed, regimented apartment houses, both by the Municipal Housing Authority and by large insurance companies. This tendency is being followed in various other cities in America and even in Europe. Here the basic living requirement of easy access to adequate natural green surroundings is neglected. If the life of these buildings were figured less on the basis of structural and more on that of social obsolescence in a changing world, I think the policy would be different.

Spacious planning with large areas left open for future change is the surest method of preparing for flexible growth. That is one of the principal advantages of Green Cities, with great open space surrounding them as greenbelts and in the centers of superblocks. There is room for change and for the growth of present requirements without complete destruction and rebuilding.

Many elements of the existing communities tend to grow and to demand more space, without having adequate room for expansion. The present trend to build one-storey schools is an example. The increased acreage needs of play spaces for all ages is another. Additional community requirements, such as Health Centers, Nursery Schools, Youth Centers, are continually being recognized. As these new functions develop and need buildings, there should be room to place them in proper relation to other elements of the Neighborhood or District Center. Flexibility calls for, above all else, space more space than is needed to compass the original requirements.

Parking space for motor cars is the type of unforeseen change that requires flexible spaciousness. We now know that we must have immense parking space—far more than for building—if we are not to tie up all movement by filling our highways with parked cars. Yet old habits persist and many housing developments are still built with scant room for parking one car per family and no space for garaging.

These changes we have already seen. Others are sure to follow—for instance in transportation. If individual air traffic by helicopter or other means should replace or at least surpass the use of the automobile some day, nearby open areas either surrounding a town or neighborhood as green belts or in the middle of a superblock can be used advantageously to keep these towns contemporary.

The Unit of Design in New Towns is no longer each separate lot, street or building; it is a whole community: a co-ordinated entity. This means that the framework of the community and every detail down to the last house and the view from the windows must be conceived, planned and built as a related part of a great setting for convenient, wholesome, and beautiful contemporary living and working. In this way every house gains from its relation to the buildings around it. Beauty as well as convenience is produced by the rational relationship of the individual parts.

The planning of every house and every room in that house is part of the process which gives the superblock its ultimate shape and character. Thus, the size and specific requirements of inner green and private yard, of cul-de-sac or auto court, help mould the superblock in relation to good living in home, community and town.

As he plans, the New Town planner envisages the future home life of the individual and the family, and their life as part of the community. He sees it not only in terms of house and garden but in the grouping of houses in relation to each other so as to take the utmost advantage of sun and wind for every residence, and to open up pleasant, spacious and varied views from every house and, as far as possible, in every direction. He will in part be guided by the form and nature of the land, and how its trees and streams and rocks can best be used or preserved for the common use and enjoyment of the people who are going to form the community, and whose life, from birth to old age, will be moulded by the place.

New Town planning deals with the fundamental realities of living in a contemporary community, and, since we cannot foresee tomorrow's needs, it must take the future into account and allow for flexibility. The town plan must be moulded to the life people wish to lead, and to fit the special needs of the past. The form of the home and its surroundings and the whole city must fulfil the requirements and aspirations of those who are to live in them. What these needs and aspirations are the planner cannot learn from most books—certainly not from technical works that deal with merely spiritless forms. He generally cannot determine them by surveys of existing conditions and of past performance. That is more often the way to find out what not to do, because so much of the present-day form, structure, equipment and practice is outdated and obsolete, and unrelated to the needs of the day.

The planner cannot discover the needs of people merely by asking them what kinds of home and town or community they want to live in. They do not know beyond their experience. However, with their assistance—not their guidance—he must discover their requirements. He must explore patiently, realistically, imaginatively. He should live in the places he helps to create, as Raymond Unwin did at Hampstead Garden Suburb and Henry Wright did at Sunnyside and Radburn. If he does not become an active part of the community he should know the people and managers and storekeepers. He should visit them often and come to see the life there both through their eyes and his own. That is what I have tried to do, so that I might progress from one experience and experiment to the next, on the basis of the realities of living communities.

The guiding motive for the New Town planner in moulding the whole and its parts is this: he is creating a stage, a theater for the good life. Yes, the planner's work is in many ways surprisingly like that of the skilled scenic designer. Lee Simonson, who was trained as a painter, at first designed his sets as pictures that would surprise and delight the audience and draw their first applause. But, he has told me, he soon found that that did not serve the need throughout the play: the actors did not seem to fit into the place. So he carefully studied the text. In his mind's eye he followed each character as he would enter, move, stand and relate himself to other actors. He saw the life of the play, and as he followed this *it* set the stage; it determined the location of every door and piece of furniture. The shape of stage-set and the background became inevitable. The rest was easy.

That is just what the good planner does. He creates a setting in which people—the kind of people that will live there—will fit, where they will live a varied life, a convenient life, a beautiful life; where they will grow and change, and their surroundings can also change with them. The planner's subject, then, is man. It is his fellows and their reaction to their environment which he must study and understand.

I do not mean to suggest that taste and imagination and a feeling for good and great design in form and color are not essential requirements of community planner and architect. But they are not enough. New Town planning as well as architecture is an art, a great art, but it differs fundamentally from painting. The resulting work is not merely a form or pattern that the artist evolves out of his inner consciousness and projects on the canvas. Community planning starts not with aesthetic conception but with exploration, discovery, unveiling.

It facilitates growth and leaves a record of human ideals and purposes that may last beyond its time.

The Spirit in which the communities illustrated in this book were conceived, planned, developed, and in which most of them were operated, was that of exploration. From the days of Sunnyside to those of Baldwin Hills Village we have been in search of new or revised solutions of the setting for communities as well as for family and individual living. We have sought ways of bringing peaceful life in spacious green surroundings to ordinary people in this mechanical age. We have tried to simplify the complexity of needs and desire as contrasted with means, and thus to make changes, from the obsolete methods of the dead past, economically feasible.

Investigation and research has been an important guide in our progress. In this the economic study always paralleled the social or architectural, as illustrated by my studies for the Resettlement Administration and Henry Wright's analysis of building operations at Sunnyside.

It has been my experience that one can never accept a planning or architectural solution as final. Every problem seems to require fresh analysis, a new approach, a different angle. As soon as an idea has become formalized into a rule of procedure, and designers give up the adventurous search, the old solution seems to dry up and lose its quality and clarity.

Perhaps this tendency for ideas, that have bloomed, flowered and been accepted, to wither and petrify when given administrative sanction, has led me to be suspicious of all accepted formulas, even when I have sown the seed from which they grew. When an idea becomes conventional it is time to think it through again. Never-ending exploration and the charting of new ways is the life-force of the architect and the New Town planner, whose shield of battle should bear the simple device—a question mark.

From: *Toward New Towns for America,* by Clarence S. Stein. Public Administration Clearing House. Chicago: 1951, pages 198–207.

Towards a New Physical World

by

Catherine Bauer

By 1900 any fairly acute person might have realized that this matter of housing, in its largest sense as average human environment, was bound to be one of the pivotal questions of the twentieth century. It was not merely that the doctors and the sanitary inspectors, the reformers and the revolutionists, the progressive bureaucrats and the sentimental philanthropists, managed to agree at least that housing conditions were bad. Certain elementary but nevertheless fundamental changes in the general standard of demand were becoming apparent. After a full century, during which even the houses of the rich had been inconvenient, ugly and uncomfortable, there were vague stirrings of revolt. The "elements"—sun, air, cleanliness, order—were just beginning to come back over the threshold of consciousness.

Perhaps the best symbols of this new realism (and they were often hardly more than symbols) can be found in the typical suburban house of a "progressive" and fairly wealthy American of the period. A century had passed without any important changes in plan or equipment, and then quite suddenly what do we find? A white tiled bathroom, for one thing; a sleeping-porch for another; and finally, a "sun-parlor." The notion of "labor-saving" was also coming in: kitchens were to be "planned" to fit their functions. Moreover, there was a vague sort of idea, just gaining foothold, that "good taste" had something to do with simplicity. Some of the bric-a-brac and perhaps one set of curtains and one layer of carpet were dispensed with. I do not mean to imply that any of these things were achieved very *directly*, because people consciously and suddenly wanted sun and air and order in their lives. They have all been snobbisms to greater or less degree: and yet there *is* a qualitative difference between a snobbism about sunlight and a snobbism about useless objects.

In Europe there were not so many tiled bathrooms, perhaps, but the new desires and demands were just as apparent, and often rather wider in scope. Outdoor recreation, sports, "physical culture," and what a German sociologist called the "Back-to-the-land-Bewegung" were making large numbers of people dissatisfied with crowded tenements and dark, dirty cities. Perhaps no one has described this new attitude more accurately than Horsfall, when he was commenting on the changes which were going on in Germany at the turn of the century:

"Whatever improves the physical condition of a population, by causing its boys and girls, its men and women, to be taller, better-looking, and broader muscularly and nervously stronger and more vigorous, than they would otherwise be, and at the same time develops in them a healthy appreciation of health and strength and good looks, and a wholesome pride in possessing these advantages, necessarily does much towards giving desire for the conditions which are most favorable for the maintenance of health, strength and good looks, and distaste for the conditions which are unfavorable to their maintenance."

The proof of this, in so far as the "housing movement" in Europe is concerned, is that within fifty years it had developed from a simple little matter of providing a few philanthropic tenements for paupers to the problem of providing a decent living environment for everybody. There is nothing which shows the extent of public interest better than the growing number of associations, congresses, exhibitions, and publications which by 1910 is already too long to chronicle. From 1851 onward, every international exposition had its quota of "model" houses. The Paris Exhibition of 1900 had a complete block, including exhibits from Belgium, Switzerland, England, Germany, Holland, and France, just as "modern" for their time as the Stuttgart exhibition housing of 1927. Most important of all, these activities were no longer confined to social theorists: architects, engineers, and technicians were beginning to take part, however fruitlessly for the time being.

As early as 1850 there were forerunners of the modern promoters of "pre-fabrication," who saw the whole problem as a challenge to industrial and structural ingenuity alone. At the 1867 Paris Exposition a small house with an iron skeleton was given a medal. Shortly afterward, much attention was bestowed on a patent cement slab process invented by Mr. W. H. Lascelles, who received an award for designing an exhibition house in 1878 consisting of one large living-room and three rather constricted but nevertheless highly ingenious sleeping-alcoves which collapsed in the daytime. From the eighties onward, there is a whole series of standardized folding wooden houses, particularly from Scandinavia, usually complete with a diagram showing how neatly they could be fitted onto a horse-cart, jig-saw trimmings and all.

But it cannot be said that the really significant engineering-architecture of the time, of which Paxton's Crystal Palace of 1851 was the first important example and in some ways one of the masterpieces of the century, had any direct influence on the form and technique of housing until after the war. The tower of M. Eiffel looked down on the First International Housing Congress, and it may well have been the same sort of inspiration which led M. Cacheux, the engineer who was responsible for the model house exhibit, to betray such obvious pride in the dimensions and modernity of his "model" sewers and in the steam-laundry and drying equipment provided at Mulhouse. But there is no outward reflection in early housing of the structural audacity evident in the new iron and glass department stores, and in the remarkable experiments in reinforced concrete being conducted by M. Hennebique. M. Godin had covered his interior courts with glass roofs in the fifties, but actual window-areas in small dwellings underwent no particular change. (Indeed, the Tudor cottage designs submitted by Mr. Elsam in 1816 were probably more generous of light and air than almost any model housing of the century.) Albeit "ventilation" as a point of departure for ingenuity rather than sound planning was already well established. When "model" houses were still being built back-to-back, as they were at Mulhouse, there was often some complicated system of airducts, and the plans usually show such a whirlwind of breezy arrows that one instinctively turns to shut the window.

On the side of architectural form, there has been a fairly close relationship between the innovators and the housing movement almost from the beginning, although few very striking or ambitious experiments were made until after the war. Through Morris and some of his followers, above all through Raymond Unwin, the English Arts and Crafts Movement revived the decent tradition of brick craftsmanship and the simple cottage vernacular, which still mark the better part of English housing. (It should not be forgotten that even while the rage for degraded and pastiche "Queen Anne" was at its height, William Morris himself was lecturing eloquently against all forms of exterior ornament, and declaiming that even the ugly "brick box with a slate lid" of the utilitarian fifties was better than the jerry-built frippery of the nineties.)

But it was in Holland that the Romantic Movement left its most enduring mark. Berlage and his followers, influenced on the one hand by the mediaevalism of Morris and on the other by the freer and more original genius of the American, Frank Lloyd Wright, achieved the first real *vernacular* of modern architecture. That is, a "style" whose monuments were not to be found merely in isolated villas or public buildings, but in whole blocks and streets of "housing" and shops and offices, in plotting and planning, and within the dwelling of *l'homme moyen sensuel* as well as in those of the more advanced or Bohemian literati. This was particularly true in Amsterdam, where entire districts, including many low-cost workers' apartments put up with official assistance, and also palatial hotels and schools and bath-houses and bridges, bear witness to a fresh approach to a modern world, for the most part quite unified. Much of this was accomplished before the war, and largely determined the form of post-war housing in Holland. The same sort of rejuvenation (for there was no complete or revolutionary break with the past until much later) was going on in the Scandinavian countries, where the early co-operative housing has a sort of decent dignity difficult to discover in the model tenements of London or Paris or New York.

The Art Nouveau of Paris and Vienna had little direct effect at the time on housing forms, except in so far as it encouraged the use of new materials and a fresh approach in general. In Germany by 1900 there was already a pretty thorough break, at least among the younger architects, with that pompous and dreary neo-Baroque which had dominated the nineteenth-century cities. And the bristling Romanesque which one is led to call the Bismarck style, because so many of that gentleman's monuments are clothed in it, was fortunately short-lived. Hundreds of experiments followed: almost every city has its own assortment of pre-war "modern" buildings. And almost all of the innovators, among them many who were to guide the current of modern architecture into a more rational and unified stream after the war, were identified with the co-operative housing movement. Indeed, it was the modern architects themselves who took the lead in organizing most of those small suburban communities which were the best examples of pre-war German housing.

The Garden City Movement might well have been described in the section devoted to Utopias but for one thing. Namely, that Ebenezer Howard's idea has the remarkable distinction of having been concretely realized in two complete experiments and in many other partial ones.

Howard was neither a revolutionist, a millionaire suffering pangs of conscience, nor a modern architect. He was a short-hand writer. In Chicago in his youth he had seen the effects of the fire and had been led to think about the possibility of creating entirely new cities, whole and fresh from the bottom up and built according to a rational plan. In 1898 he published a little book called *Tomorrow* (later reissued as Garden Cities of Tomorrow) which outlined just such a project.

His idea was a simple one, not essentially very different from that of Buckingham and not nearly as radical in its social framework as that of Owen or Fourier. But the physical details were both original and eminently practical, and the convinced enthusiasm of Howard was equaled only by his common sense.

The easiest way to outline the principle involved is to quote the later definition of a Garden City. It is "a town designed for healthy living and industry; of a size that makes possible a full measure of social life, but not larger; surrounded by a rural belt; the whole of the land being in public ownership or held in trust for the community." No tiny isolated colony, then, but a complete working city whose estimated population was to be around thirty thousand. The diagrammatic scheme is circular, with a large central park containing also the principal public buildings and skirted by a main shopping street, with an outer circle of factories and the permanent green belt beyond. The city itself was to occupy one thousand acres and the agricultural belt five thousand. The railroad by-passes the town, meeting the circle at a tangent. By keeping the land in single ownership the possibility of speculation and overcrowding would be eliminated, and the increment of value created by the community in industrial and shop sites would be preserved for itself. Essentially, a thorough-going experiment in middle-class consumers' cooperation.[1]

[1] Theodor Fritsch, in *Die Stadt der Zukunft*, had expressed many of the same ideas a decade earlier. And the Archbishop of Canterbury at an official housing conference in 1884 had advocated a belt of common land to surround every town, beyond which all new development must take place.

In 1899 the Garden City Association was formed, and in 1901 it had thirteen hundred members. A site was procured in Hertfordshire, about forty minutes from London, and in 1903 the First Garden City, Limited, a limited dividend society, was organized and the building of Letchworth commenced. Today Letchworth has fifteen thousand inhabitants, pays the permitted five per cent on its stock, has one hundred and eleven factories and workshops, and is in every way a going concern. Its post-war successor, Welwyn Garden City, was started in 1920, has now about ten thousand population and something over fifty industries. Both towns have profited by the southward move of manufacturing in England, and have been able to draw relatively more new plants than have the neighboring cities. Howard's general principles, including the communal ownership of the land and the permanent green belt, have been carried through in both cases, and the garden cities have been a trying-ground for technical and planning improvements which influenced all of English post-war housing.

Both towns were fortunate in their makers. Letchworth was entirely planned by Barry Parker and Raymond Unwin, leaders and foremost practitioners of European town-planning in the past generation. Welwyn was planned by Louis de Soissons and various other architects. If the latter is at present the more attractive, due to a firmer architectural control of individual buildings and also to a somewhat more urbane central arrangement, the improvements in Welwyn grew naturally out of the experience at Letchworth and the better knowledge thus achieved. They are both disappointing if one is looking for architecture as modern as the plan conception. Only some of the Welwyn factories are really modern, the houses being for the most part various modifications, ordinarily simple and decent enough, of the traditional English cottage. They are built of brick, plain or stuccoed, and are usually grouped together.

Two important street-and-block planning principles, which have been largely followed in post-war English housing, were there developed. One was the idea, given wide circulation in Raymond Unwin's early pamphlet, *Nothing Gained by Over-crowding*, that very large blocks with a central common are actually more economical, if the land is reasonable in price, than the usual narrow By-Law block, due to the savings in street-pavement and utilities. The other was a further development of this, the super-block with indented dead-end streets, which insulates its residents from the traffic nuisance and also involves a maximum of economy in utilities and paving. One more feature of post-war English housing would hardly have been adopted if it had not been for the standards set up in the Garden Cities. Namely, the law which limits the number of houses to twelve per acre.

Letchworth and Welwyn remain the only Garden Cities, strictly speaking. However, their influence has been responsible for many partial suburban experiments. Here there can be no clear definition, as the phrase Garden Suburb or even Garden City has been applied, in any number of languages, to anything from a unit-planned strictly co-operative or public undertaking, with the land remaining in single ownership and at least a partial protective green belt, to a perfectly ordinary commercial front-foot-for-sale development. But such communities as Hampstead and Earswick, both largely designed by Unwin, and Hellerau near Dresden or Grünewald near Cologne—all built before the war—and also Radburn, New Jersey, and several post-war municipal developments in England, have a character and control unified enough to make their relation to the original idea a positive one. Almost every country has its Garden City Association, and the general principles and standards involved have exercised a very wide influence on all post-war housing policies, from the *Cité-Jardins* of the Seine to the more radically planned German communities.

The nineteenth century was a mining age. "Exploit and get out" was its slogan, and the methods of mining were applied, not merely to coal and iron, but, far more significantly, to forests and soils, to real estate and international markets, to wage labor and to consumers. The cities were built by the combined efforts of speculators, small and large, to mine congestion land-values. A whole system and ideology of house-production arose, which enabled the builder to "unload" as quickly as possible and escape with his profits.

But mining, by its very definition, is not a process which can be continued forever. Presently the end of the vein is in sight; the last frontier reached; the untended soil worked out; the exploited worker-consumer cannot buy any more; the jerry-built house and the inflated skyscraper no longer pay their taxes; the burden of palliatives and remedies—subways, policing, health measures, relief—become unbearable; the congested metropolis is bankrupt. And the whole paper scheme collapses—to be revived for another cycle of "prosperity" only by the ever more difficult discovery of new veins to work.

This state of things may or may not have been inevitable during the first century of the Industrial Revolution. In any case, it is fair to assume that the same psyche which accomplished the enormous changes in the productive pattern could not easily have set up the new system of values necessary to turn it to useful human purpose. The best revolutionaries are not ordinarily the best people to be entrusted with setting up a new order after the revolution has been accomplished.

But even from the beginning there were scientists who saw and protested against the waste and injustice and irrationality implicit in this scheme of things. The early Utopians; Marx and Engels; the anarchist geographers Kropotkin and Reclus; the sociologists Taine and Comte and Le Play; Ruskin and William Morris and Ebenezer Howard—they were all, in greater or less degree, scientific critics of an exploitive mining civilization. They saw the earth as a sum of resources, abundant but nevertheless limited in supply and location. And they saw human beings with certain needs and also with certain techniques for adapting resources to their needs. And most of them saw that mere restriction or even "conservation" would not be enough to transform a paper-and-profit economy of exploitation into a productive system based on permanent concrete values.

Indeed, everyone who confronted the housing problem squarely, even if he saw only one side of it, was forced into habits of thought which were not merely foreign to the current scheme of things, but were even subversive to it. This is why no judgment of the nineteenth century is complete unless it includes the houses and cities which that century created. For a social-economic system which in ordinary practice and on its own terms cannot provide a decent living environment is not a great civilization no matter what other things it can do; and conversely, a system which could provide good houses and workable cities would have something to be said for it no matter how outlandish its abstract deities might appear.

There was one scientist who gave a wholly new interpretation to this matter of human environment. Patrick Geddes, between the founding of Outlook Tower in Edinburgh in 1892 and his death in 1932, did work which entitles him to profound respect as a biologist, an economist, a sociologist, a geographer, a city-planner, and a philosopher. His great importance lies, not in any one narrow piece of specialization, but rather in the broad and consistent point of view with which he attacked any problem, from the plan of a city in India to the making of a metaphysical diagram. Probably not one piece of his thought could be made to fit neatly into any of the orthodox categories. "Simultaneous thinking" was one of his phrases, and it was his own method.

The importance of Geddes in the history of housing lies in the fact that he was the first person who really *placed* the housing problem within the larger physical and social framework of society. He saw a dwelling, not as a "model" something existing in a paper vacuum or at an International Exposition or set down in any available hold in the old pattern, nor yet as part of an idyllic and isolated community. He saw that people who live in a house require not merely private shelter but food and work and recreation and social life, and that this makes the house an inseparable part of the neighborhood, the surrounding open country and the region. Folk, Work, Place—Organism, Function, Environment—these were the three poles of his "simultaneous thinking." "For the biologist," he said, "life is process; life is reaction; and this two-fold, of environment in action upon organism, and of organism in reaction upon environment."

. . . If Geddes recognized and allowed for all the scientific physical and biological and social realities, he paid little heed to those abstractions which were almost the only realities of the paleotechnic world: paper "interests." Not because he was impractical or visionary; on the contrary, he saw that the old age was dead; that if the credits and debits were really added up, Megalopolis would not exist. That, granted the will and the desire, we have all the tools at hand ready to consolidate our scientific and technical gains into a civilization founded on real values; a "neotechnic" age as different from the paleotechnic nineteenth century as an automatic electrically driven plant is different from a cotton-mill of the sixties, or as the best modern housing developments are different from a speculative tenement district of the eighties.

From: *Modern Housing,* by Catherine Bauer. Boston: 1934, pages 106–116.

University of Virginia, Charlottesville, Virginia. Thomas Jefferson, architect.

VII

The Search for the Universal

The Language of Form

by

Claude Bragdon

With the echoes of distant battles in our ears and in the face of economic and industrial problems which clamor for solution, it may seem the height of futility to discuss mere matters of aesthetics. It is not so, however, any more than it is futile to forecast the harvest even while last year's stubble disappears before the plough. Outworn social orders go down before the cannon and sword in order that mankind may realize new ideals of beauty and beneficence already existent in the germ.

It is clear that "the old order changeth," not alone in the House of Life, but in the Palace of Art. Anarchy clamors at that door too. In painting, in music, and in the drama we are entered upon that phase in which the bolder spirits are rejecting alike the passing fashions and the forms sanctified by time, and are seeking new generalizations. Architecture, the least plastic of the arts, lags a little; but the great unrest has seized that also.

We observe a great confusion of ideas upon the whole subject of architecture, not alone on the part of the public, but in the profession itself. Eminent architects are found to differ widely in their opinions, and these differences find expression in their work. It is clear that there is no common agreement among them as to what constitutes excellence. If we apply only the criterion of everyday common-sense, it would appear that the modern architect has not grasped the modern problem. Let me try to prove to you that this is so.

First, the architect of today fails to think and work in terms of his place.

A proof of this failure is found in the unsuitability of many commonly used architectural forms and features to practical needs and to climatic and environic conditions. Cornices, made for the etching of strong shadows and for protection from a tropic sun, frown down from the skylines of our cloudy northern cities, where they gather dirt and soot in summer and in winter become traps for snow and ice. Arcades and colonnades, originally designed for shade and shelter, rob overstrained eyes of the precious light of day. Expensive and useless balustrades protect waste spaces of roof where people could not take their pleasure if they would.

Secondly, the architect fails to think and work in terms of his time.

A proof of this failure is found in the perfectly meaningless character of the architectural ornaments in common use: the acanthus scroll, the egg and tongue, the Greek fret and waterleaf, the festoon and wreath, a cartouche, a shield, a lion's head—echoes all of the past, not one eloquent of the present.

Thirdly, the architect fails to think and work in terms of his materials.

A proof of this failure is found in the common practice of substituting one material for another—wood for iron, terra-cotta for stone, stone for concrete, or vice versa—by reason of their differences in cost, without essential modification in design. One of the most important functions of architecture is thus violated—the showing forth of the splendor and beauty (be it a beauty of strength or of fragility) of different materials, making the most of the unique characteristics of each.

Now the beauty of terra-cotta, for example, is not less than that of stone, but it is different. Witness a Della Robbia lunette and a carved granite Egyptian bas-relief. Imagine the terra-cotta arcades of the Certosa of Pavia carved in stone. One would fairly ache at the thought of so much labor and feel a sort of terror at so great a weight so insufficiently supported. On the other hand, were the heavily rusticated street front of the Pitti Palace in Florence translated, without change, from stone to terra cotta, the result would be no less distressing, but for the opposite reason. There would be no charm of detail and texture to compensate for the splendid ponderosity of stone.

In the face of these facts, it will be well if we first of all find out exactly where we stand and what we are doing. Let us therefore try to get this clear without further loss of time.

Looking at the matter from the broadest possible point of view, it is evident that we dwell in a composite environment: that in which we find ourselves, Nature; and that which we make for ourselves, the product of industry and art. In this city of Chicago, for example, a wilderness of railroads, stockyards, houses, skyscrapers has obliterated the earlier wilderness of trees and swamp and prairie grass. Nothing so diametrically foreign to Nature as this gridiron plan and these rectilinear buildings could well be imagined. Man has himself essayed the role of creator and follows a different dream.

This has been the case more or less ever since the stern desire for mastery and the sweet disease of art disturbed the balance of Nature in men's souls. When we come to consider architecture through the world and down the ages, we find it bisected by a like inevitable duality: either it is *organic*, following the law of natural organisms; or it is *arranged*, according to some Euclidian ideal devised by proud-spirited man. In other words, it is either cultivated, like the flower; or it is cut, like the gem.

It is important that this fundamental difference in aim and method should be clearly perceived and thoroughly understood. This will be best accomplished by comparing and contrasting Gothic architecture, so-called, which is preeminently a striving toward a free organic expression of plan and construction, with Renaissance architecture, wherein predetermined canons of abstract beauty are imposed.

The popular conception of Gothic architecture is of a manner of building practiced throughout the north of Europe during the Middle Ages, the distinguishing characteristics of which were pointed arches, groined vaulting, buttressed walls, traceried windows, and the like. But if we study those principles of planning and construction which produced and determined the above-mentioned characteristics of the style, we might appropriately describe Gothic as a manner of building in which the form is everywhere determined by the function, changing as that changes. Renaissance architecture, on the other hand, represents an ideal in conformity with which the function is made to accommodate itself, to a certain extent, to forms and arrangements chosen less with a view to their exact suitability and expressiveness than to their innate beauty. In short, Gothic architecture is organic; Renaissance architecture is arranged.

These definitions, embodying the distinction noted, should not be taken to imply any disparagement of Renaissance architecture, that strained and triply refined medium through which some of the noblest strivings of the human spirit toward absolute beauty have achieved enduring realization. Arranged and organic architecture correspond to the two hemispheres of thought and feeling into which mankind is divided, the one pre-eminently intellectual, the other psychic. They represent fundamental differences of principle and ideal. . . .

In what, more specifically, do these differences consist? The basic one is that organic architecture, both in its forms and in the disposition of these forms, follows everywhere the line of the least resistance, achieving an effect of beauty mainly by reason of the fact that utility is the parent of beauty and that any increase in fitness is an increase in beauty.

In arranged architecture, on the other hand, this principle yields precedence to a metaphysical ideal of pure or abstract beauty, achieved by the employment of forms, rhythms, and arrangements, developed by a process of selection and survival, and having for that reason a less vital relation to the whole construction. . . .

Organic architecture does not reject any form or any arrangement developed by long use and of acknowledged beauty, so long as it, as well as another, tells a given story or accomplishes a given end. As soon as it becomes inexpressive or inefficient, however, by reason of changed conditions, it is modified or rejected, or a new one is created; whereas in arranged architecture, forms originally organic survive even after they have lost their *raison d'etre*. It was for this reason that the Romans employed the orders after they had developed the arch. To the devotee of arranged architecture, beauty is its own sufficient justification; to him who follows the organic ideal, as soon as a thing becomes false to the mind it ceases to be fair to the eye.

The spirit behind organic architecture is adroit, inventive, fertile, resourceful. It is economical of materials and means, even in its most sumptuous creations. It is most itself when engaged in attaining a given end in the simplest and most direct manner possible. It is given to short cuts and uses the tools and materials nearest to its hand. The great cathedrals are built of stones of easily manageable size, requiring no elaborate machinery. The spirit behind arranged architecture, on the other hand, disdains these considerations. There is a sublime arrogance in the way in which, to compass one of its grandiose effects, it spends money by millions and kills men like flies. The first seems to say to Nature: "Permit me, madam, to assist you; there is a final felicity which, with your permission, I shall add." And it does this quite in Nature's manner, without, so to speak, disturbing a hair of her head. The second says, rather, "I'll show you a trick worth two of that," and proceeds to obliterate the landscape and put something altogether different in its place. It is inconceivable, for example, that the Gothic builders would have converted a swamp into a pleasure garden, as Louis XIV, that prince of bromides, did at Versailles, at such enormous cost of lives and treasure. It is equally inconceivable that the architects of the Renaissance would have hung a church upon a crag, as the mediaeval builders did at Mont Saint Michel—without, at least, leveling and terracing the crag.

In all true Gothic there exists so intimate a relation between the interior arrangement and the exterior appearance—between the plan and the elevation—that from a study of the latter the former may with fair accuracy be read. The manner of construction rules the whole structure and declares itself at sight. In Renaissance architecture, even at its best, this by no means follows: the elevation, determined by considerations of grandeur, symmetry, proportion, is often only a mask. St. Paul's Cathedral, in London, is an example of this. The buttresses of the arches of the nave are concealed behind a curtain wall surmounted by a balustrade which stands, independent of any roof, high aloft in the air. The stone lantern which crowns the dome appears to be supported by it, but the visible dome is of wood, a falsework which conceals the truncated cone of brickwork which alone saves the lantern from tumbling into the center of the church. This mendacity of the Renaissance spirit is one of its distinguishing characteristics. The application to a wall of columns and entablature, arches and imposts, which support nothing, not even themselves, is one of its most common and most innocuous forms. Some of these artifices are quite justifiable from the standpoint of mere aesthetics, as I shall endeavor to show in my second lecture; but the true Gothicist will have none of them, his motto being, "Beauty is Truth; Truth, Beauty."

In arranged architecture, the various parts and details are assembled and combined by the sovereign good taste of the architect; in organic, they are melted and fused by the creative heat, the eagerness for self-expression. In whatever form it appears, organic architecture seems to spring up without effort, almost of its own volition, a natural outcropping of national and racial vitality. Men do not have to learn to understand it; they recognize themselves in it because they carry the clue to its meaning in their hearts. Arranged architecture, on the other hand, is the self-conscious embodiment of the pomp and the pride of life. Like Little Jack Horner, it seems to say, "What a great boy am I!"

It is not profitable to multiply these distinctions, for this might lead more to confusion than to clarity of mind. It is necessary only to remember that the real point of cleavage between organic and arranged architecture is the one first dwelt upon. In order to determine to which hemisphere of expression a given building belongs, it is necessary only to apply the acid test of Mr. Sullivan's formula and ask, "Does the form follow the function, or is the function made subservient to the form? Did the spirit build the house, or does the house confine the spirit?" If the first, it is organic; if the second, it is arranged.

Ponder this formula, then apply it. Strange truths emerge. It is plain from existing evidences, and from our knowledge of their psychology, that the Greeks built in the organic spirit, and that there is more real identity in principle between the Erechtheum, let us say, and the Saint Chapelle, than between the former and the most correctly classic building in all Paris. The Romans worked organically in the planning and construction of their vast and complicated basilicas, theaters, and baths; but they knew not where to stay their hand, and, seduced by a beauty which they did not comprehend, they meaninglessly applied the orders to their arch and vault construction—that is, they employed organic forms as mere ornament, after the virtue had flowed out of them by reason of a change of structural methods.

Turning the searchlight of our formula in different directions up and down the ages, we discern that the Church of Santa Sophia in Constantinople is organic, for the reason that it consists of a single consistent system of construction—that of the round arch and spherical vault—carried to its logical development, nowhere hidden, everywhere expressed. The Houses of Parliament in London, on the other hand, with a whole bagful of Gothic tricks, are nevertheless arranged architecture. They are this for the reason that the elaborately composed river façade gives no hint of what lies behind it, and the towers might have been in one place as well as another, or not at all, so far as any necessity is concerned. In other words, the element of inevitability is lacking, that sure index of the organic spirit. Called upon to create a Gothic design, Sir William Barry, the architect, could change the clothing of his idea, but not the complexion of his mind.

It is held by those who have intimate knowledge of the curious architecture of Japan that the Japanese built organically in the carrying of wood architecture to the highest logical development that the world has ever seen. That Mr. Cram should himself be the author of a delightful and scholarly treatise on Japanese architecture is an eloquent fact in this connection.

Coming again to the consideration of modern architecture here in America—barring a few thrice-blessed exceptions—it is certainly not organic, and to call it arranged would place it in the same category with the masterpieces of the Rennaissance, which would be to pay it a higher tribute than it deserves.

Let us consider the main features of this architecture, if on the face of chaos features can be discerned. To consider modern architecture from the standpoint of structure presents no difficulty. Every important building of today adheres to substantially one method of construction. Even a layman knows its characteristic features: a steel framework, floors and roof of hollow tile or reinforced concrete, and an outer covering of brick, stone, or terra-cotta, as the case may be. But when we come to consider the language in which the story is told to the beholder, there is the greatest confusion of tongues. Venetian palaces elbow French chateaux and Roman temples; pseudo-Gothic competes with neo-Greek, each masquerading as something other than it is—a Brobdingnagian saturnalia of vociferous unreason.

The cause of this discrepancy between the inner structure and its outward manifestation is not far to seek. The construction has been shaped by the living hand of necessity, and is therefore rational and logical; the outward expression is the result of the architect's "digging in the boneyard." There has been laid upon it the dead hand of the past. Free of this incumbus, the engineer has succeeded; subject to it, the architect has failed. That is, he has not seen that the new construction imperatively demanded a new space-language for its expression. By limiting himself to the great styles of the past and the forms developed by superseded methods of construction, he has shown himself impotent to create for this great age an architecture eloquent of it. This is the manner and measure of his failure, and it is grave.

Now it is true that architectural styles are not created merely by taking thought of the matter, but grow imperceptibly, new conditions modifying old traditions. Conservatism in architecture is therefore a good and necessary thing, but in times like the present, conservatism ceases to be a virtue. The architect who clings blindly to precedent in dealing with the unprecedented, as he is now constantly forced to do, is in the position of the boy who stood on the burning deck. This habitual attitude of looking backward at the past over the shoulder of the present, instead of fronting the future, has resulted for the architect in the atrophy of his creative faculty.

Of course, no architect can afford to dispense with a knowledge of his art as practiced throughout the world and down the ages. It is even well that he should train himself to think and work in terms of this style and of that, if only to learn that a style takes its form and characteristics from the materials and methods of construction employed, and its ornament from the racial and national psychology. From the history of architecture nothing is clearer than that a change of construction, or a change of consciousness, demands and finds fresh architectural forms for its expression. We of today use a kind of construction unknown to the ancients, and our psychology is different; yet we look about us in vain for a space-language which expresses both in terms of beauty. I use the term "space-language" because the time-language of today already exists or is in process of formation in the modern drama, the modern novel, and modern music—new art forms made to meet new needs of expression. The need is not less urgent for a new architectural language. It is bound to come in time. The question naturally arises: To which of the two hemispheres before mentioned will it belong; will it be organic or will it be arranged?

The answer to this question is probably involved in the answer to a more grave and vital question, one which the clouded and ambiguous aspect of the times cannot fail to suggest to every thoughtful mind. Putting aside all purely local and temporal issues, the great issue of the immediate future is between the forces of materialism, on the one hand, which work against the practical realization of human brotherhood, and those obscure spiritual forces which are working for it. If materialism triumphs—and materialism is as strongly intrenched in the hovel as in the mansion, in the church as in the market-place—architecture, however highly developed and perfected, will be the work of slaves for masters—*arranged* by master-minds. If, on the other hand, the spirit of democracy and of true brotherhood triumphs, architecture will become again *organic*, the ponderable expression of the truths of the spirit, wrought out in all humility and lovingness by those who are its subjects but not its slaves.

We are warranted in this conclusion by the history of art itself. Every organic architectural evolution followed in the wake of a religious impulse, and the ideal of brotherhood is the impulse which today moves men to those fervors and renunciations which have marked the religious manifestations of times past. If today we use, only to misuse, the architectural languages of the past, it is because materialism holds us and rules us; if tomorrow we are able to express ourselves in a language of new beauty, it will be the result of some fresh out-pouring of spiritual force, such as occurred long ago in

Egypt, later in Greece, in China following the introduction of Buddhism, and in Northern Europe during the two mystic centuries of the Middle Ages. Signs are not lacking that this change will come upon us too. The dense materiality of modern life is not necessarily an adverse factor; for of all paradoxes this is the most sublime, that good comes from evil, purity from corruption. The favorite food of epicures springs from the dunghill; the unspeakable saturnalia of Imperial Rome had issue in Christian saints and martyrs. Already may be noted presages of change. In the familiar warmed and lighted chamber of our everyday environment we sit snugly content, playing at what we call the game of life, when suddenly, just when we fancied we were safest, we are rapt out of ourselves into the infinite beatitude, as a fevered gambler might be summoned from his table by some beautiful, veiled woman, who leads him out into the cool, illimitable night.

After such an experience, life can never be the same. You who have dreamed are forced to follow your dream—to realize it, if you are an artist. From that day you are bound by an obligation which others do not and need not share. You can no longer dissipate your time and such talents as you possess in assimilating the popular taste in order to reproduce it. This would be a prostitution far more ignoble than that of the man who has never been thus elected to the service of beauty. To him, the fleshpots of the world, the price of a virtue which was never his; to you, the eternal quest, wherever it may lead.

Do not conceive of beauty in any narrow way, as limited to mere aesthetics. Seek out the things that thrill you and be sure that there is beauty in them, for the test of beauty is the measure of the joy it brings. Beauty is mystery and enchantment, the thing with star-dust on it. Learn to recognize the brush of its invisible wing, not alone in art galleries and concert halls, but in a face in a crowd, a song at twilight, moonrise, sunset; in the din and glare of cities as well as in the silence of great spaces; in the train taking its flight to the seaboard as well as in the crow taking its flight to the rooky wood.

Knowing not when nor in what questionable shape beauty may reveal itself, it behooves you to cultivate so wide a catholicity of taste that no manifestation, however strange and disturbing, may pass untested through the alembic of your mind. You should constantly strive to realize what I have called the organic ideal in the work of your hands, not permitting your personal power of invention to atrophy by continual copying of the work of others, no matter how beautiful nor how sanctioned by time that work may be. Of everything you should ask: first, is it sincere and expressive; second, is it beautiful *to you?*

Doubtless failure will crown your efforts more often than success. A pioneer and a precursor in a movement which, when all is said, may never move, the best that you can hope for is to labor at the foundation of a Palace of Art which will be reared, if it is reared at all, by other hands. Your reward will be that should the tide turn, while you live and work, from the ordered ideal to the organic, some part of the mighty current will flow through you, instead of tossing you relentlessly aside.

Because the word "Gothic" has been taken as the type of the art which is organic and "Renaissance" as a type of that which is arranged, there is still danger of misunderstanding. Comprehend clearly that in speaking of organic architecture I do not refer solely to the art as practiced during the Middle Ages; in speaking of Renaissance architecture I use it only as indicative of a habit of mind which is timeless. If we except the architecture of edifices of the established religion in which the Gothic style is traditional and therefore appropriate, nothing could be more absurd than the use by us of the mere externals of the medieval Gothic style. The forms of classic and Renaissance architecture are, of the two, on the whole more appropriate and amenable to modern needs and conditions; and if we are sticklers for precedent, they are better justified. The architecture of the future, whether arranged or organic, will probably resemble neither Gothic nor Renaissance. If it springs from deep within the soul, it will unfold new and unimagined beauties. If it is a product of the purely rational consciousness, it will consist of additions to, and modifications of, the architecture which we already have.

Because spirituality is the source of all beauty, arranged architecture proceeds from and succeeds organic. When the mystic spirit which produces organic architecture departs, the forms of its creating survive by reason of their beauty, but they are meaninglessly employed. All of the time-honored forms and arrangements of our so-called classic architecture were originally organic. Nothing could be more organic than the colonnade of a Grecian temple; nothing could be less so than the same colonnade with an iron stanchion buried in each column and the lintel held up by concealed steel beams.

Now, while it is necessary to draw these distinctions, and even to insist upon them, there is a higher synthesis in which they disappear.

Every masterpiece disdains and defies classification. If it succeeds, we know that whatever the means and methods, they can be only the right ones and are their own sufficient justification. As a matter of fact, every architectural masterpiece, whatever its style or period, is both organic and arranged. However artificial it may be, it obeys some organic law of the mind; however naturalistic, it is full of self-conscious artifice.

In art there is a demonic element which places it above and beyond all man-made classifications and categories. The true artist is guided by an over-soul, whether he acknowledges or whether he denies its sway.

The passive master lent his hand
To the vast soul that o'er him planned.

From: *Six Lectures on Architecture.* By R. A. Cram, Thomas Hastings, and Claude Bragdon. Chicago: 1917.

The Basis of Universalism

by

Lewis Mumford

Now there are two elements in every architecture, indeed in every esthetic or cultural expression. One of them is the local, the time-bound, that which adapts itself to special human capacities and circumstances, that belongs to a particular people and a particular soil and a particular set of economic and political institutions. Let us call this the regional element, though one must of course include in this term far more than the purely geographic characteristics. The other element is the universal: this element passes over boundaries and frontiers; it unites in a common bond people of the most diverse races and temperaments; it transcends the local, the limited, the partial. This universal element is what makes it possible for us to read Homer today, and to feel as sympathetic toward Odysseus as we do to a contemporary refugee who is buffeted from one country to another, or to enjoy the encounter of Nausicaa and Homer's battered hero, with perhaps even a little greater relish than one does the latest situation between a Hollywood actress and her male counterpart in a current motion picture. Without the existence of that universal element, which usually reaches its highest and widest expression in religion, mankind would still live only at the brute level of immediate impulses, sensations, habits; and there would be a deep unbridgeable gulf between the peoples of the earth.

Jefferson believed that the forms presented by classic architecture were of this universal and eternal nature. Though Jefferson was a patriotic American, a model of selfless devotion to his country, though he was a Virginian of the Virginians, the style that he sought to acclimate to his local soil was in fact neither American nor Virginian. His designs were conscious attempts to escape a provincialism which he openly despised; they were efforts to bring to America the "international style" of the eighteenth century. We now realize that part of Jefferson's fervor for the classic past was misplaced. He was taking the architecture of temples and palaces, quite exceptional buildings designed for special purposes connected with the religious cult and the political forms of ancient states; and he was attempting, as in the Richmond Capitol, to put these ancient forms to quite different purposes from those they had actually served: so far, I believe, he was mistaken. But Jefferson was right in thinking that there are universal principles, underlying an architecture, that must be sought out and understood; he was right in thinking that the best is none too good for one's own soil, and that if the best can only be found elsewhere the intelligent course is to import it and adapt it rather than to put up with the third-best and pretend that it is just as good. Jefferson was right, too, in thinking that the language a building spoke was as important as its practical offices: for in plan, in volume, in mass, and in detail, a building tells what was in the designer's mind; and it is important that the observers and users should be able to understand that language, and sufficiently moved by it to accept it as their own.

What Jefferson did not realize, merely because he was immersed in his own age and could not view it in perspective, is that two kinds of universal language were now being spoken in architecture: a dead language, that of the classics, and a live language, that of the machine. There were many institutions in the eighteenth century that had an underlying harmony with Roman civilization; slavery was one of them and despotism was another; but the power of the ancient world over the human imagination was already waning, and men were beginning to have a fresh confidence and pride, a fresh will to create, based not on the achievements of the past but on the possibilities of the future. This new order, founded upon mechanical invention and standardized production, upon the physical sciences and their applications, was not actually remote or foreign to Jefferson: he was too much a man of his own period to despise its comforts and conveniences. No one can do justice to Jefferson, either as a human personality or as an architect, who does not realize how much at home his mind was in the scientific and mechanical and rational order. He had no wish to make money out of it; but he accepted its preoccupations. It is not an accident that the McCormick reaper owes its ultimate invention to a train of thought started in Jefferson's mind while seated in a barber's chair to have his hair cut.

Unfortunately, Jefferson accepted the current notion that the mechanical and utilitarian are by nature unbeautiful; and that the architect must therefore endeavor to hide as far as possible the practical aspects of existence. In this complete separation of soul and body, he was a true disciple of Descartes. Like his English contemporaries, he concealed the practical offices of the farm and dissociated them from the house. This went so far as to have the kitchen at a distance from the house, in a separate building, with the food brought to the dining room by an underground passage. Such planning was tolerable only in a leisured society like that he enjoyed at Monticello. Jefferson's guests would sit down to dinner at four o'clock and not rise till seven, when the ladies, who had left when the table was cleared for wine, returned at seven with a tea tray.

Those who know Monticello even today will remember how his mechanical ingenuity and his practical scientific interests always threaten to break into his serene classic order. The ingenious cannonball calendar for telling the days of the week is hardly an esthetic embellishment to the front hall; and the sheltered weather vane in the porch, though a convenience for an owner who did not want to step out onto the lawn in inclement weather, was artful rather than artistic. All these mechanical improvements were fun; make no doubt of that. Some of them were really admirable, like the two-way dumb-waiter, which brought a full bottle of wine up from the cellar to the dining room, while the empty bottle was going down—or, with somewhat wider application, like the mechanism which opened or shut both doors of the drawing room when one pushed only one of them. A man who had an eye for such mechanical details was obviously living as intently in his own age as a Connecticut Yankee; he was not merely dreaming about the noble but defunct empire of Rome. But Jefferson unfortunately was not able, in terms of his philosophy, to accept the fact that the new universal forms provided by the machine needed a new soul: that these forms must be expressed in a fresh esthetic language. Where he could not conceal the mechanical elements he employed, he was unable to assimilate them into the esthetic design. That was a weakness. But it was an understandable weakness; for it took architects the better part of a century to awaken to the fact that in the machine modern man had created a new world: a world that cried to be understood, interpreted, and humanized.

Besides his interest in mechanical ingenuities, however, Jefferson was possessed by another passion for which his architectural faithfulness to the precedents of Greece and Rome gave no scope. That passion was a love for the New World itself: not merely a pride in its political government, but an intense scientific interest in its aboriginal background, in the native animals and plants, in the ways and customs of the Indians. He spared himself no effort to collect books about the New World and to assemble specimens, for the benefit of foreign naturalists, of its native species—sometimes at great cost to himself. A man who was as much possessed by American themes as Jefferson was could scarcely avoid making some allusion to them in architecture. Very possibly it was through Jefferson's influence that Latrobe chose to carve the capitals in the new capitol building with ears of corn, instead of acanthus leaves; but Jefferson went much farther, not in his architectural ornament, but in what he did to his classic structure after it had been erected. We tend to forget the actual appearance of the entrance hall of Monticello in Jefferson's lifetime. Let me describe it for you in the words of a young contemporary of Jefferson's, George Ticknor:

"You enter by a glass folding-door into a hall which reminds you of Fielding's 'Man of the Mountain' by the strange wealth of furniture on its walls. On one side hang the head and horns of an elk, a deer, a buffalo; another is covered with curiosities which Lewis and Clark found in their wild and perilous expedition. On the third . . . was the head of a mammoth, or as Cuvier calls it, a mastodon, containing the only *os frontis,* Mr. Jefferson tells me, that has yet been found. On the fourth side, in odd union with a fine painting of the Repentance of St. Peter, is an Indian map on leather of the southern waters of the Missouri and an Indian representation of a bloody battle handed down in their traditions. Through this hall—or rather museum—we passed to the dining room."

Now it was altogether fitting that these indigenous trophies and curiosities should have had a place in a house designed by a man as devoted to them as Jefferson was: they reflected a very vital concern in his life. What was disharmonious, what was in fact a little jarring, was that the structure itself had absolutely no relationship to this indigenous background. Plainly, there was no harmony of any kind between the two: the buffalo head and the mammoth's bones were, from the standpoint of the classic decoration, mere disfigurements—as savage and out of place as a German warrior, wrapped in bearskins, would have been in the streets of Rome in the time of the Antonines; or rather more so. In his architecture, Jefferson did not do justice to his pride in his native land; he did not create a background which fittingly embodied it, in contemporary terms. To a visitor, the hall looked like a mere museum. The native element appeared among these imported architectural forms as an intrusion: raw, barbarous, unassimilated. But in reality, it was the classic past that was the intruder; and it was contemporary America whose spirit cried to be represented in other forms than those of extinct mammoths.

Apparently, it was too early for Jefferson, too early perhaps for anyone, to absorb fully those lessons of the earth and sky and people of America to which Thoreau and Whitman turned themselves in the following generation: hence one of the deepest realities of Jefferson's life made its way into his home covertly—in the form of museum specimens, rather than by changes in the form of the building itself.

Yet though neither the mechanical nor the regional elements were integrated in the design of his structures, in other departments of building Jefferson was fully abreast with the demands of the opening age. This is clear if one examines the floor plans of Monticello. The plan of the second Monticello, the one Jefferson began to build after his return from Europe, by ruthlessly tearing down the existing building, derives directly from the Villa Rotunda designed by Palladio, which Jefferson greatly admired. But when one compares Jefferson's building with Palladio's, one discovers that his admiration did not lead to a blind copying of the Italian example: however genuine Jefferson's respect for the older master, the plan and the elevation were both brought into close conformity with the new needs. Palladio's plan for the Villa Rotunda is rigidly symmetrical: one element balances the other with mathematical precision. Except for the halls approaching the central unit, there is no special means of circulation between the rooms; and there is no differentiation of the rooms on the plan, according to their presumable use: every element is abstract, formalized, indifferent to everything but the outward effect. Such an abstract design is always at its best before the building has been spoiled by the presence of people—but it has no meaning for a house that is to be inhabited by a household where men and women eat and drink and talk and read and fall ill and are waited upon, and now are sociable or again want some quiet corner to which they may retire in completest solitude and privacy.

Jefferson's plan for Monticello, on the contrary, is already a modern plan: a plan which reflects the needs of the living and embodies those needs in well-organized space. The great drawing room of Monticello is on the axis of the hall; its bay projects onto the porch, and its ample windows embrace the view beyond. On the right, by the drawing room, are a dining room and beyond it a tea room; these rooms, which are different in size and shape and treatment, are separated by a passage from two bedrooms, placed side by side on the entrance side of the house. On the left side of the hall, as one enters, is a sitting room; this is connected with Jefferson's own room by a library, which has no counterpart in the divisions on the right side of the plan. Because of his desire to imitate classic models, Jefferson concealed the upper floor, which forms a mezzanine rather than a full floor, behind what looks to be a one-story facade: but even this close organization of the plan on a single level also marks Jefferson's plan as both modern and American—a prototype of the apartment, and the bungalow, if I may couple it with developments so remote from Jefferson's own intentions. The point that I would drive home to you here is that Jefferson, while searching for universal forms in his best work did not lose sight of the local and the particular: in Monticello one feels that every exposure, every outlook, every domestic arrangement has been studied and re-studied; that the house is based not merely on regional knowledge but on intimate domestic knowledge as well.

I do not propose to go over Jefferson's buildings and alterations one by one; for it is not by the mere bulk of his work that we can gauge his great qualities or understand how far he was able to solve the problem of meeting and expressing new needs, in a civilization whose building materials and methods of construction were still almost wholly traditional. By the time Jefferson retired from the Presidency, he was ready for the great work of his life; and it is on that great achievement and its meaning for us today that I wish now to direct your attention.

In every respect, the University of Virginia was the crowning episode in Jefferson's life: the seal of his conviction as a statesman and a political philosopher, the proof of his greatness as an architect. The University itself was one of his most persistent dreams; for he wished his native state, in his own words, to "give every citizen the information he needs for the transaction of his daily business . . . and, in general, to observe with intelligence and faithfulness all the social relations under which he shall be placed." We know that Jefferson, while a student at William and Mary, had come directly under the influence of three redoubtable tutors, who stood in the relation of friends, whilst he was still a student; and Jefferson, from the beginning, had it constantly in mind to create a series of buildings which would, by their very spacing and arrangement, favor the intimate kind of relation between professor and student by which he himself had profited.

Here we have, I think, one of the reasons for the imaginative sweep and formal clarity of Jefferson's design for the University. Almost all great works of art—I think one may safely generalize—have a long period of hidden gestation. They do not arise out of sudden and superficial demands that come from the outside; they are rather the mature working out of inner convictions and beliefs that the artist has long held, has mulled over, has perhaps sought to embody in preliminary essays. In short, the artist must live with his form, so that it becomes flesh of his flesh and bone of his bone, before he can start it on its independent career. Jefferson began his plans for the University with no formal structure, like the Maison Carrée, in his mind's eye: he began, rather, with the program of the new University, as a place in which professors and students would become partners in the exchange and pursuit of knowledge; and his problem was not to imitate a Greek temple or an Italian villa or even an Oxford college; but to find a fresh form which would mirror his purpose. In a letter to Governor Nicholas of Virginia, dated April 12, 1816, Jefferson wrote: "I would strongly recommend . . . instead of one immense building, to have a small one for every professorship, arranged at proper distances around a square, to admit of extensions, connected by a piazza, so that they may go dry from one school to another. The village form is preferable to a single great building for many reasons, particularly on account of fire, health, economy, peace, and quiet." Those were the words of a man who had a firm grip on every part of his problem.

The few precedents that existed in America did not hamper or guide Jefferson: the separate collegiate buildings of Harvard, Princeton, or William and Mary did not impress him: he made a clean departure from the current tradition. Nor was Jefferson influenced by the medieval quadrangles of Oxford, with their cloistered quiet and their carefully guarded enclosures. In the richness of his old age, his architectural thought had become purposeful and integrated, sure enough of its foundations to permit him to create a truly native form. Though he drew upon his architectural acquaintances like Dr. William Thornton and that excellent professional Benjamin Latrobe, what he sought were only specific suggestions for details: the main lines were already laid down in his mind. His letter to Dr. William Thornton, dated May 9, 1817, leaves no doubt as to this:

"We are commencing here," he wrote, "the establishment of a college. Instead of building a magnificent house which would exhaust all our funds, we propose to lay off a square of seven or eight hundred feet, in the outside of which we shall arrange separate pavilions, one for each professor and his scholars. Each pavilion will have a school room below and two rooms for the professor above, and between pavilion and pavilion a range of dormitories for the boys, one story high, giving to each a room 10 feet wide and 14 feet deep. The pavilions about 36 feet wide in front and 26 feet in depth . . . the whole of the pavilions to be united by a colonnade in front, of the height of the lower story of the pavilions." A few of these details underwent change: the distance between the rows was reduced from 800 to 200 feet, with both an esthetic and a social gain; and Jefferson, finding that not all professors were bachelors, had to provide bigger quarters for the professors' families, with four private rooms instead of two; but the main outlines of the scheme remained.

In designing the University Jefferson had the opportunity he had lacked in the Richmond State Capitol. Not merely was he constantly at hand to supervise the work, but he began with an adequate site, and from the beginning was able to control the use of the site no less than the individual designs of the buildings. Here again his common sense and imagination triumphed over his bias toward purely geometrical figures. As a lover of squared paper, he was inclined to favor the checkerboard plan in the design of cities; he had even thought of combating the plague of yellow fever by building cities on a literal checkerboard plan in which only the black squares would be used for building and the white ones left open, in turf and trees. When the ancient site of Babylon was rediscovered and its strictly rectangular plan was brought to light, Jefferson had hailed it as a model and thought it should serve as a precedent for Washington: indeed, he never fully reconciled himself to L'Enfant's starlike pattern of radial avenues which were superimposed on that design. Fortunately, not merely was Jefferson forced to narrow the space between the rows;

he was also forced to meet a drop in the land by building low transverse terraces. This slight irregularity, this modification of pure form to meet the exigencies of life, adds to the esthetic effectiveness of the plan itself.

If the palace of Versailles was one of the first examples of an open order of planning, in which the building stretched in a straight line, instead of making a quadrangle or a court, the University of Virginia buildings are the first, as far as I know, in which this kind of open plan was repeated in four parallel rows, of equal length. Here was a better suggestion for city planning than the suggestion for an open checkerboard, which Jefferson had made to Volney in 1805. This form of planning is what the Germans now call Zeilenbau, which merely means building in parallel rows open at the ends; and during recent years it has almost become a symbol of modern town planning, since, if the buildings are properly oriented, it permits the fullest exposure to sunlight and the freest exposure to the prevailing winds and the view. But Jefferson's open rows have a characteristic feature that most modern forms of Zeilenbau have not. The dormitories, instead of stretching in unbroken lines, are punctuated by the houses of the professors, which also contained the classrooms; or, on the further ranges, the students' rows are broken by the individual boarding houses, in which the students boarded. This interruption of the uniform facade is logical: it is functional; and it is aesthetic; in other words, it embodies Sir Henry Wotton's often quoted definition of the essentials of architecture: commodity, firmness, and delight. No one of these reasons alone would have been sufficient to make the rows the masterly architectural achievement that they are: it is the conjuncture of all three, and their perfect embodiment in the buildings themselves, that establish their success.

I would emphasize, even at the risk of being tedious, how much the beauty of the University of Virginia depends upon Jefferson's insight into the human needs that these buildings serve. That is obvious, for example, in the very intimate scale of the colonnades, with their succession of low arches; there is no effort to blow up this attractive architectural feature into monumental proportions. But it should be even more obvious when one sees how the principle of designing the college on a village pattern, rather than a palatial institutional one, leads naturally to breaking up both the professors' houses and the boarding houses into separate buildings.

Note how Jefferson avoided that characteristic monstrosity of our more recent American colleges, the huge dining hall; noisy, institutionalized, barracks-like. He provided, again in his own words, for "six hotels for dieting the students, with a single room in each for a refectory, and two rooms, a garden, and offices for the tenents." That introduces into the business of eating, a human, an intimate note; eating under these circumstances must have lent itself to conversation and friendship; and it probably lent itself likewise to a better sort of life for the people who cooked and served the food, and were by reason of the human scale, on more amiable terms with the boarders. As a member of a college building committee, I have fought to establish that principle in modern American practice; and though I have so far fought in vain, I am convinced that Jefferson was right, right both as an architect and as an educator; and that if we are interested in the whole process of education, we will pay as much attention to the conditions under which students eat, as we do to the conditions under which they take physical exercise; though it is the cultivation of the whole personality rather than the body alone that should be our main object in "dieting" the students.

The one place where Jefferson went wrong in the design of the University of Virginia was where he lost sight of his own fundamental principles, and as a result committed even an esthetic error. Jefferson, in his deference for high architectural authority, took over Latrobe's suggestion for a central domed building which should close up the axis and dominate the group. His original plans made no such provision: both ends of the rows left the landscape open to the eye. And though he had the good sense to transform Latrobe's proposed auditorium into a library, the scale and character of the building—the Rotunda—are entirely out of keeping with the village plan that Jefferson so wisely had in mind. Granting that a library building was a necessity, it would have been better sense and better architecture to have treated it as an integral part of the rest of the design; one can imagine a central stack room, with wings to serve the special departments of knowledge and provide more intimate reading and study alcoves—all conceived on the scale of the pavilions and dormitories, with such appropriate changes in windows and lighting as the storing and reading of books would naturally suggest. Such a building would have completed the design of the rows: whereas Jefferson's attempt to reproduce the Pantheon, despite its more modest scale, is entirely out of keeping both in design and in bulk with the modest buildings that were erected; neither in its original form, nor in McKim, Mead and White's reproduction, is it anything but an awkward overgrown structure, which mars the general picture and could not from the first, in the very nature of its composition, serve its own function adequately.

The library is the only real weakness, however, in the whole conception; in every other respect the design is a masterpiece. For if the plan and the general order were good, the execution of the details was no less admirable. Jefferson designed each of the professors' pavilions to be a replica, as far as possible, of some noble classic temple; in order that the students of architecture might have a model of the best taste of the past always before their eyes. Though his purpose here has ceased to be relevant, the actual effect is still charming: the variations he introduced in those buildings, now with a flat, now with a gabled roof, now with small, superimposed columns for the front porches, now with a full-scale temple portico, the austere ancient pattern sometimes broken in the balconies by a diamond pattern or a Chinese fret—all these variations on the central theme are music for the eye. The pavilions, again, lost some of that bleakness and gawkiness that the austere temple form sometimes has in the American landscape, by reason of the fact that they are supported by the low horizontal facades of the dormitories. The success of these buildings applies even to the smallest details. Consider his famous wall, with its undulating curves; this was an astonishing piece of virtuosity; for it is only one brick thick; and by laying a series of arches on the ground, as it were, he not only gave an interesting ripple of movement to what was otherwise just a barrier, but provided a sheltered, twice-warmed place for the more tender plantations.

In short, the University of Virginia was the marvelous embodiment of three great architectural essentials. The first was a well-conceived and well-translated program, based upon a fresh conception of the functions of a modern university. A good building serves as the physical and symbolic setting for a scheme of life: to build well, the first step is to understand the purposes, the motives, the habits, and the desires of those who are to be housed. Architecture, if it is to be anything better than scene painting, must be evolved from the inside out; and the architect much therefore begin, not with the land or the structure, but with the needs that the land or the structure are finally to satisfy. Unlike modern millionaires, who so often put up collegiate buildings for the pleasure of seeing their names on the facades, and who imagine that the more money they spend, the more highly their names will be edified, Jefferson began with certain definite convictions about the needs of students and scholars. Hence a certain modesty and economy of detail; hence a respect for human proportions. Although Jefferson spent freely when the need arose—I have told how he imported stonecutters from Italy to carve the capitals—there was no splurging in these buildings, if one perhaps excepts the unfortunate library. Jefferson had a carefully thought-out program; and he carried it through.

The second great architectural essential is that individual buildings should never be conceived as isolated units; they should always be conceived and executed as parts of the whole. Buildings exist in a landscape, in a village, or in a city; they are parts of a natural or an urban setting; they are elements in a whole. The individual unit must always be conceived and modified in terms of the whole. This cannot be done by architects who have their nose on the draughting board, and who, in their own conceit, have no regard for the principle of neighborliness and no interest in the surrounding works of nature or man.

A certain discipline, a certain restraint, even a certain sacrifice of private tastes and preferences is necessary if an individual is going to develop a positive character: people who do what they like, when and how they like, are not merely a nuisance to their neighbors, but they turn out to be weak characters, to boot. It is the same in architecture. The beauty of the University of Virginia buildings that Jefferson designed does not lie in any single detail; it does not lie in any single building; it does not even lie in any single row: it derives from the order and purpose that underlies the whole and creates a harmony, practical and esthetic, between its various parts. That is a lesson which the architects and builders largely forgot in the two generations that followed Jefferson's death. To pick up that tradition and reinstate it has been one of the main tasks of our own time, and it is one that is still only imperfectly performed.

The third great quality that Jefferson showed was his ability to modify details to meet a special situation, while holding to a rigorous and consistent plan. This is a quality that has special meaning for us today; for we are too often the helpless victims of the very mechanical order we have created. Now Jefferson was as much enamored as our most machine-minded contemporaries of regularity, of mathematical proportions, of mechanical accuracy; and his readiness to make departures from such order, when necessity arose, is one of the proofs of his mastership. Geometry satisfies a deep desire of the human mind: the desire for order, certainty, regularity, for form and stability in a world of flux. When this order is embodied in building, it satisfies the mind that man is for the moment on top and in control of the situation. But that victory of order always has its dangers, as the Greeks, who so well mastered geometry, were aware: the danger is that it may flout human needs, as completely as Procrustes did when he chopped off human legs in order to make his guests fit the beds they were to sleep in. Life without order is chaotic; but order without life is the end of everything, and eventually the end of order, too, since the purpose of order in building is to sustain human life. In the University of Virginia, Jefferson struck a balance between formal order and vital order, between the logic of building and the logic of life. And that is why this achievement of his ranks, not merely as one of the highest achievements of American architecture, but as one of the high points of architecture anywhere in the world in the nineteenth century. It dwarfs all of Jefferson's other buildings. It puts the works of his contemporaries and successors for the next fifty years distinctly into third rank. If Jefferson's achievement here had been studied by his successors with some of the reverence and love and understanding that it has belatedly received, the course of American architecture might have been appreciably changed; and changed, of course, for the better.

From: *The South in Architecture*, by Lewis Mumford. New York: 1941, pages 51–77.

The International Style

by

Henry-Russell Hitchcock, Jr., and Philip Johnson

> The light and airy systems of construction of the Gothic cathedrals, the freedom and slenderness of their supporting skeleton, afford, as it were, a presage of a style that began to develop in the nineteenth century, that of metallic architecture. With the use of metal, and of concrete reinforced by metal bars, modern builders could equal the most daring feats of Gothic architects without endangering the solidity of the structure. In the conflict that obtains between the two elements of construction, solidity and open space, everything seems to show that the principle of free spaces will prevail, that the palaces and houses of the future will be flooded with air and light. Thus the formula popularized by Gothic architecture has a great future before it. Following on the revival of Graeco-Roman architecture which prevailed from the sixteenth century to our own day, we shall see, with the full application of different materials, a yet more enduring rebirth of the Gothic style.
>
> SALAMON REINACH, *APOLLO*, 1904

Since the middle of the eighteenth century there have been recurrent attempts to achieve and to impose a controlling style in architecture such as existed in the earlier epochs of the past. The two chief of these attempts were the Classical Revival and the Mediaeval Revival. Out of the compromises between these two opposing schools and the difficulties of reconciling either sort of revivalism with the new needs and the new methods of construction of the day grew the stylistic confusion of the last hundred years.

The nineteenth century failed to create a style of architecture because it was unable to achieve a general discipline of structure and of design in the terms of the day. The revived "styles" were but a decorative garment to architecture, not the interior principles according to which it lived and grew. On the whole the development of engineering in building went on regardless of the Classical or Mediaeval architectural forms which were borrowed from the past. Thus the chaos of eclecticism served to give the very idea of style a bad name in the estimation of the first modern architects of the end of the nineteenth and the beginning of the twentieth century.

In the nineteenth century there was always not one style, but "styles," and the idea of "styles" implied a choice. The individualistic revolt of the first modern architects destroyed the prestige of the "styles," but it did not remove the implication that there was a possibility of choice between one aesthetic conception of design and another. In their reaction against revivalism these men sought rather to explore a great variety of free possibilities. The result, on the whole, added to the confusion of continuing eclecticism, although the new work possessed a general vitality which the later revivalists had quite lost. The revolt from stylistic discipline to extreme individualism at the beginning of the twentieth century was justified as the surest issue from an impasse of imitation and sterility. The individualists decried submission to fixed aesthetic principles as the imposition of a dead hand upon the living material of architecture, holding up the failure of the revivals as a proof that the very idea of style was an unhealthy delusion.

Today the strict issue of reviving the styles of the distant past is no longer one of serious consequence. But the peculiar traditions of imitation and modification of the styles of the past, which eclecticism inherited from the earlier Classical and Mediaeval Revivals, have not been easily forgotten. The influence of the past still most to be feared is that of the nineteenth century with its cheapening of the very idea of style. Modern architecture has nothing but the healthiest lessons to learn from the art of the further past, if that art be studied scientifically and not in a spirit of imitation. Now that it is possible to emulate the great styles of the past in their essence without imitating their surface, the problem of establishing one dominant style, which the nineteenth century set itself in terms of alternative revivals, is coming to a solution.

The idea of style, which began to degenerate when the revivals destroyed the disciplines of the Baroque, has become real and fertile again. Today a single new style has come into existence. The aesthetic conceptions on which its disciplines are based derive from the experimentation of the individualists. They and not the revivalists were the immediate masters of those who have created the new style. This contemporary style, which exists throughout the world, is unified and inclusive, not fragmentary and contradictory like so much of the production of the first generation of modern architects. In the last decade it has produced sufficient monuments of distinction to display its validity and its vitality. It may fairly be compared in significance with the styles of the past. In the handling of the problems of structure it is related to the Gothic, in the handling of the problems of design it is more akin to the Classical. In the pre-eminence given to the handling of function it is distinguished from both.

The unconscious and halting architectural developments of the nineteenth century, the confused and contradictory experimentation of the beginning of the twentieth, have been succeeded by a directed evolution. There is now a single body of discipline, fixed enough to integrate contemporary style as a reality and yet elastic enough to permit individual interpretation and to encourage general growth.

The idea of style as the frame of potential growth, rather than as a fixed and crushing mould, has developed with the recognition of underlying principles such as archaeologists discern in the great styles of the past. The principles are few and broad. They are not mere formulas of proportion such as distinguish the Doric from the Ionic order; they are fundamental, like the organic verticality of the Gothic or the rhythmical symmetry of the Baroque. There is, first, a new conception of architecture as volume rather than as mass. Secondly, regularity rather than axial symmetry serves as the chief means of ordering design. These two principles, with a third proscribing arbitrary applied decoration, mark the productions of the international style. This new style is not international in the sense that the production of one country is just like that of another. Nor is it so rigid that the work of various leaders is not clearly distinguishable. The international style has become evident and definable only gradually as different innovators throughout the world have successfully carried out parallel experiments.

In stating the general principles of the contemporary style, in analysing their derivation from structure and their modification by function, the appearance of a certain dogmatism can hardly be avoided. In opposition to those who claim that a new style of architecture is impossible or undesirable, it is necessary to stress the coherence of the results obtained within the range of possibilities thus far explored. For the international style already exists in the present; it is not merely something the future may hold in store. Architecture is always a set of actual monuments, not a vague corpus of theory.

The style of the twelfth and thirteenth centuries was the last before our own day to be created on the basis of a new type of construction. The break away from the High Gothic in the later Middle Ages was an aesthetic break without significant structural development. The Renaissance was a surface change of style generally coupled with actual regression in terms of structure. The Baroque and *a fortiori* the Romantic Age concerned themselves all but exclusively with problems of design. When a century ago new structural developments in the use of metal made their appearance they remained outside the art of architecture. The Crystal Palace at the London Exposition of 1851, Paxton's magnificent iron and glass construction, has far more in common with the architecture of our day than with that of its own. Ferroconcrete, to which the contemporary style owes so much, was invented in 1849. Yet it was at least fifty years before it first began to play a considerable part in architectural construction.

Metal had begun to be used incidentally in architecture before the end of the eighteenth century. Thenceforth it achieved a place of increasing importance, even in buildings of the most traditional design. Finally in the eighties it made possible the first skyscrapers. But on the whole the "arcades," the train sheds, the conservatories and the exhibition halls, of which the London Crystal Palace was the earliest and the finest, were adjuncts to, or substitutes for, conventional masonry buildings.

Behind the conventional story of nineteenth century revivals and eclecticism there are two further histories of architecture. One deals with the science of building alone. It traces the development of new engineering methods of construction and the gradual replacement of traditional masonry structure by successive innovations. The other history deals with the development of the art of architectural design regardless of specific imitations. Design was freed here and there from the control of the past. Some architects even sought novel forms and many aimed at a more direct expression of the new methods of construction. A new art of proportioning plane surfaces, a free study of silhouette, even a frank use of metal appear in the work of most of the leading nineteenth century architects. Soane in England, Schinkel and his followers in Germany, and Labrouste in France, were among these early precursors of modern architecture.

Within the Classical Revival there developed a new sense of design, purer and more rational than that of the Renaissance or the Baroque, yet not restricted merely to the purity and rationalism of the Greeks. Within the Mediaeval Revival there grew up a body of doctrine, based on the practice of the builders of the Middle Ages, which foreshadowed the theories of our own day. There is not much to change today in the passage that has been quoted from Salamon Reinach's *Apollo*. As late as 1904 it was possible to conceive of modern architecture chiefly as a sort of renaissance of the Gothic. Yet it should be stressed that the relation of the modern style to the Gothic is ideological rather than visual, a matter of principle rather than a matter of practice. In design, indeed, the leading modern architects aim at Greek serenity rather than Gothic aspiration.

In writing on modern architecture some few years ago it was possible to accept that the individualists of the end of the nineteenth century and the beginning of the twentieth, who first broke consciously with the nominal discipline of the revivals, established tentatively a *New Tradition*. It appeared then as a sort of style in which the greatest common denominator of the various revivals was preserved and fused with the new science of building. Today it seems more accurate to describe the work of the older generation of architects as half-modern. Each architect broke in his own way with the immediate past, each sought in his own direction the positive elements which have been combined in the last decade. But there was no real stylistic integration until after the War.

The industrial architecture of Peter Behrens in Germany in the years before the War was already extremely simplified and regular. The effect of volume began to replace the traditional effect of mass. Otto Wagner, a decade earlier in Vienna, cultivated qualities of lightness and developed the plane surfaces of his architecture for their own sake. The Belgian Van de Velde experimented with continuity of surface, making much use of curves. Berlage at Amsterdam based his compositions on geometry and handled both old and new materials with unusual straightforwardness. In the constructions of Perret in France the use of ferroconcrete led to a visible articulation of the supporting skeleton with the walls treated as mere screens between the posts. Thus in the different countries of Europe before the War the conceptions of the international style had come independently into existence. It remained for the younger generation to combine and crystallize the various aesthetic and technical results of the experimentation of their elders.

But it was in America that the promise of a new style appeared first and, up to the War, advanced most rapidly. Richardson in the seventies and eighties often went as far as did the next generation on the Continent in simplification of design and in direct expression of structure. Following him, Root and Sullivan deduced from steel skyscraper construction principles which have been modified but not essentially changed by later generations. Their work of the eighties and nineties in Chicago is still too little known. We have in America only a few commercial buildings of 1900 to compare with the radical steel and glass department stores of Europe; but these few are more notable than all the skyscrapers of the following twenty-five years.

In the first decades of the new century Frank Lloyd Wright continued brilliantly the work of the Chicago school in other fields of architecture. He introduced many innovations, particularly in domestic building, quite as important as those of the Art Nouveau and Jugendstil in France and Germany. His open planning broke the mould of the traditional house, to which Europe clung down to the War. He also was the first to conceive of architectural design in terms of planes existing freely in three dimensions rather than in terms of enclosed blocks. Wagner, Behrens and Perret lightened the solid massiveness of traditional architecture; Wright dynamited it.

While much of the innovation in Europe merely consisted in expressing more frankly new methods of construction within a framework of design still essentially Classical or Mediaeval, Wright from the beginning was radical in his aesthetic experimentation. One may regret the lack of continuity in his development and his unwillingness to absorb the innovations of his contemporaries and his juniors in Europe. But one cannot deny that among the architects of the older generation Wright made more contributions than any other. His consciously novel ornament may appear to lack even the vitality of the semi-traditional ornament of the first quarter of the century in Europe. Perret was, perhaps, a more important innovator in construction; Van de Velde showed a greater consistency and a purer taste in his aesthetic experiments. But Wright preserved better the balance between the mere expression of structure and the achievement of positive form.

There is, however, a definite breach between Wright and the

younger architects who created the contemporary style after the War. Ever since the days when he was Sullivan's discipline, Wright has remained an individualist. A rebel by temperament, he has refused even the disciplines of his own theories. Instead of developing some one of the manners which he has initiated, he has begun again and again with a different material or a different problem and arrived at a quite new manner. The new manner often enough contradicts some of the essential qualities of his previous work, qualities which European followers have emulated with distinction and used as the basis of further advance. In his refusal of the shackles of a fixed style he has created the illusion of infinite possible styles, like the mathematicians who have invented non-Euclidean geometries. His eternally young spirit rebels against the new style as vigorously as he rebelled against the "styles" of the nineteenth century.

Wright belongs to the international style no more than Behrens or Perret or Van de Velde. Some of these men have been ready to learn from their juniors. They have submitted in part to the disciplines of the international style. But their work is still marked by traces of the individualistic manners they achieved in their prime. Without their work the style could hardly have come into being. Yet their individualism and their relation to the past, for all its tenuousness, makes of them not so much the creators of a new style as the last representatives of Romanticism. They are more akin to the men of a hundred years ago than to the generation which has come to the fore since the War.

The continued existence of Romantic individualism is not a question of architecture alone. There is a dichotomy of the spirit more profound than any mere style can ever resolve. The case against individualism in architecture lies in the fact that Wright has been almost alone in America in achieving a distinguished architecture; while in Europe, and indeed in other parts of the world as well, an increasingly large group of architects work successfully within the disciplines of the new style.

There is a basic cleavage between the international style and the half-modern architecture of the beginning of the present century. We must not forget the debt that Le Corbusier, Gropius, Miës van der Rohe, Oud and the rest owe to the older men with whom they studied. We must not forget such exceptional monuments of the nineteenth century as the Crystal Palace. We must not dismiss as lacking historical significance the fine sense of proportion and the vigorous purity of the Classical Revival, or the splendid theories and the stupid practice of the Gothic Revival. Even the absurdities of Romantic artificial ruins and the linear and naturalistic ornament of 1900 have a place in the pedigree of the contemporary style. But the new style after ten years of existence and growth may now be studied for itself without continual reference to the immediate past.

There are certain times when a new period truly begins despite all the preparation that may be traced behind the event. Such a time came immediately after the War, when the international style came into being in France, in Holland, and in Germany. Indeed, if we follow the projects of the War years made by the Austrian Loos and the Italian Sant' Elia, it may appear that the new style was preparing on an even broader front. While the innovations of the half-moderns were individual and independent to the point of divergence, the innovations of their juniors were parallel and complementary, already informed by the coherent spirit of a style in the making.

It is particularly in the early work of three men, Walter Gropius in Germany, Oud in Holland, and Le Corbusier in France, that the various steps in the inception of the new style must be sought. These three with Miës van der Rohe in Germany remain the great leaders of modern architecture.

Gropius' factory at Alfeld, built just before the War, came nearer to an integration of the new style than any other edifice built before 1922. In industrial architecture the tradition of the styles of the past was not repressive, as many factories of the nineteenth century well illustrate. The need for using modern construction throughout and for serving function directly was peculiarly evident. Hence it was easier for Gropius to advance in this field beyond his master, Behrens, than it would have been in any other. The walls of the Alfeld factory are screens of glass with spandrels of metal at the floor levels. The crowning band of brickwork does not project beyond these screens. The purely mechanical elements are frankly handled and give interest to a design fundamentally so regular as to approach monotony. There is no applied ornamental decoration except the lettering. The organization of the parts of the complex structure is ordered by logic and consistency rather than by axial symmetry.

Yet there are traces still of the conceptions of traditional architecture. The glass screens are treated like projecting bays between the visible supports. These supports are sheathed with brick so that they appear like the last fragments of the solid masonry wall of the past. The entrance is symmetrical and heavy. For all its simplicity it is treated with a decorative emphasis. Gropius was not destined to achieve again so fine and so coherent a production in the contemporary style before the Bauhaus in 1926. There he profited from the intervening aesthetic experimentation of the Dutch Neoplasticists. The Bauhaus is something more than a mere development from the technical triumph of the Alfeld factory.

During the years of the War, Oud in Holland came into contact with the group of Dutch cubist painters led by Mondriaan and Van Doesburg, who called themselves Neoplasticists. Their positive influence on his work at first was negligible. Oud remained for a time still a disciple of Berlage, whose half-modern manner he had previously followed rather closely. He profited also by his study of the innovations of Wright, whose work was already better known in Europe than in America. Then he sought consciously to achieve a Neoplasticist architecture, and, from 1917 on, the influence of Berlage and Wright began to diminish. At the same time he found in concrete an adequate material for the expression of new conceptions of form. Oud's projects were increasingly simple, vigorous and geometrical. On the analogy of abstract painting he came to realize the aesthetic potentialities of planes in three dimensions with which Wright had already experimented. He reacted sharply against the picturesqueness of the other followers of Berlage and sought with almost Greek fervor to arrive at a scheme of proportions ever purer and more regular.

In his first housing projects carried out for the city of Rotterdam in 1918 and 1919 he did not advance as far as in his unexecuted projects. But at Oud-Mathenesse in 1921–22, although he was required to build the whole village in traditional materials and to continue the use of conventional roofs, the new style promised in his projects came into being. The avoidance of picturesqueness, the severe horizontality of the composition, the perfect simplicity and consistency which he achieved in executing a very complex project, all announced the conscious creation of a body of aesthetic disciplines.

Oud-Mathenesse exceeded Gropius' Alfeld factory in significance if not in impressiveness. Gropius made his innovations primarly in technics, Oud in design. He undoubtedly owed the initial impetus to the Neoplasticists, but his personal manner had freed itself from dependence on painting. The models Van Doesburg made of houses in the early twenties, in collaboration with other Neoplasticists, with their abstract play of volumes and bright colors, had their own direct influence in Germany.

But the man who first made the world aware that a new style was being born was Le Corbusier. As late as 1916, well after his technical and sociological theorizing had begun, his conceptions of design were still strongly marked by the Classical symmetry of his master Perret. His plans, however, were even more open than those of Wright. In his housing projects of the next few years he passed rapidly beyond his master Perret and beyond Behrens and Loos, with whom he had also come in contact. His *Citrohan* house model of 1921 was the thorough expression of a conception of architecture as radical technically as Gropius' factory and as novel aesthetically as Oud's village. The enormous window area and the terraces made possible by the use of ferroconcrete, together with the asymmetry of the composition, undoubtedly produced a design more thoroughly infused with a new spirit, more completely freed from the conventions of the past than any thus far projected.

The influence of Le Corbusier was the greater, the appearance of a new style the more remarked, because of the vehement propaganda which he contributed to the magazine *L'Esprit Nouveau*, 1920–1925. Since then, moreover, he has written a series of books effectively propagandizing his technical and aesthetic theories. In this way his name has become almost synonymous with the new architecture and it has been praised or condemned very largely in his person. But he was not, as we have seen, the only innovator nor was the style as it came generally into being after 1922 peculiarly his. He crystallized; he dramatized; but he was not alone in creating.

When in 1922 he built at Vaucresson his first house in the new style, he failed to equal the purity of design and the boldness of construction of the *Citrohan* project. But the houses that immediately followed this, one for the painter Ozenfant, and another for his parents outside Vevey, passed further beyond the transitional stage than anything that Oud or Gropius were to build for several more years. Ozenfant's sort of cubism, called Purism, had perhaps inspired Le Corbusier in his search for sources of formal inspiration for a new architecture. But on the whole Le Corbusier in these early years turned for precedent rather to steamships than to painting. Some of his early houses, such as that for the sculptor Miestchaninoff at Boulogne-sur-Seine, were definitely naval in feeling. But this marine phase was soon over like Oud's strictly Neoplasticist phase, or the Expressionist period in the work of the young architects of Germany. Various external influences helped to free architecture from the last remnants of a lingering traditionalism. The new style displayed its force in the rapidity with which it transmuted them beyond recognition.

Miës van der Rohe advanced toward the new style less rapidly at first than Gropius. Before the War he had simplified, clarified, and lightened the domestic style of Behrens to a point that suggests conscious inspiration from Schinkel and Persius. After the War in two projects for skyscrapers entirely of metal and glass he carried technical innovation even further than Gropius, further indeed than anyone has yet gone in practice. These buildings would have been pure volume, glazed cages supported from within, on a scale such as not even Paxton in the nineteenth century would have dreamed possible. However, in their form, with plans based on clustered circles or sharp angles, they were extravagantly Romantic and strongly marked by the contemporary wave of Expressionism in Germany.

It was in Miës' projects of 1922 that his true significance as an aesthetic innovator first appeared. In a design for a country house he broke with the conception of the wall as a continuous plane surrounding the plan and built up his composition of sections of intersecting planes. Thus he achieved, still with the use of supporting walls, a greater openness even than Le Corbusier with his ferroconcrete skeleton construction. Miës' sense of proportions remained as serene as before the War and even more pure. This project and the constructions of Oud and Le Corbusier in this year emphasize that it is just a decade ago that the new style came into existence.

The four leaders of modern architecture are Le Corbusier, Oud, Gropius and Miës van der Rohe. But others as well as they, Rietveld in Holland, Lurçat in France, even Mendelsohn in Germany, for all his lingering dalliance with Expressionism, took parallel steps of nearly equal importance in the years just after the War. The style did not spring from a single source but came into being generally. The writing of Oud and Gropius, and to a greater degree that of Le Corbusier, with the frequent publication of their projects of these years, carried the principles of the new style abroad. These projects have indeed become more famous than many executed buildings.

From the first there were also critics, who were not architects, to serve as publicists. Everyone who was interested in the creation of a modern architecture had to come to terms with the nascent style. The principles of the style that appeared already plainly by 1922 in the projects and the executed buildings of the leaders, still control today an ever increasing group of architects throughout the world.

In part the principles of the international style were from the first voiced in the manifestoes which were the order of the day. In part they have remained unconscious, so that even now it is far simpler to sense them than to explain them or to state them categorically. Many who appear to follow them, indeed, refuse to admit their validity. Some modern critics and groups of architects both in Europe and in America deny that the aesthetic element in architecture is important, or even that it exists. All aesthetic principles of style are to them meaningless and unreal. This new conception, that building is science and not art, developed as an exaggeration of the idea of functionalism.

In its most generally accepted form the idea of functionalism is sufficiently elastic. It derives its sanctions from both Greek and Gothic architecture, for in the temple as well as in the cathedral the aesthetic expression is based on structure and function. In all the original styles of the past the aesthetic is related to, even dependent on, the technical. The supporters of both the Classical Revival and the Mediaeval Revival in the nineteenth century were ready to defend much of their practice by functionalist arguments. The so-called rationalism of architects like Schinkel and Labrouste was a type of functionalism. It is vigorously advocated, moreover, in the archaeological criticism of Viollet-le-Duc and the ethical criticism of Pugin and Ruskin. Morris and his disciples brought this sort of functionalist theory down to our own day.

The doctrine of the contemporary anti-aesthetic functionalists is much more stringent. Its basis is economic rather than ethical or archaeological. Leading European critics, particularly Sigfried Giedion, claim with some justice that architecture has such immense practical problems to deal with in the modern world that aesthetic questions must take a secondary place in architectural criticism. Architects like Hannes Meyer go further. They claim that interest in proportions or in problems of design for their own sake is still an unfortunate remnant of nineteenth century ideology. For these men it is an absurdity to talk about the modern style in terms of aesthetics at all. If a building provides adequately, completely, and without compromise for its purpose, it is to them a good building, regardless of its appearance. Modern construction receives from them a straightforward expression; they use standardized parts whenever possible and they avoid ornament or unnecessary detail. Any elaboration of design, any unnecessary use of specially made parts, any applied decoration would add to the cost of the building. It is, however, nearly impossible to organize and execute a complicated building without making some choices not wholly determined by technics and economics. One may therefore refuse to admit that intentionally functionalist building is quite without a potential aesthetic element. Consciously or unconsciously the architect must make free choices before his design is completed. In these choices the European functionalists follow, rather than go against, the principles of the general contemporary style. Whether they admit it or not is beside the point.

In America also there are both architects and critics who consider architecture not an art, as it has been in the past, but merely a subordinate technic of industrial civilization. Aesthetic criticism of building appears to them nearly as meaningless as aesthetic criticism of road building. Their attitude has been to some extent a beneficial one in its effect on American building, even from the aesthetic point of view. Most European critics feel rightly that American engineers have always been far more successful with their technics than American architects with their aesthetics.

But to the American functionalists, unfortunately, design is a commodity like ornament. If the client insists, they still try to provide it in addition to the more tangible commodities which they believe rightly should come first. But they find one sort of design little better than another and are usually as ready to provide zigzag trimmings as rhythmical fenestration. For ornament can be added after the work is done and comes into no direct relation with the handling of function and structure. American modernism in design is usually as superficial as the revivalism which preceded it. Most American architects would regret the loss of applied ornament and imitative design. Such things serve to obscure the essential emptiness of skyscraper composition.

The European functionalists are primarily builders, and architects only unconsciously. This has its advantages even for architecture as an art. Critics should be articulate about problems of design; but architects whose training is more technical than intellectual, can afford to be unconscious of the aesthetic effects they produce. So, it may be assumed, were many of the great builders of the past. Since the works of the European functionalists usually fall within the limits of the international style, they may be claimed among its representatives. . . . . Naturally these doctrinaires achieve works of aesthetic distinction less often than some others who practice the art of architecture as assiduously as they pursue the science of building.

The American functionalists claim to be builders first. They are surely seldom architects in the fullest sense of the word. They are ready, as the European functionalists are not, to deface their building with bad architectural design if the client demands it. Nor can they claim for their skyscrapers and apartment houses the broad sociological justification that exists for the workers' housing, the schools and hospitals of Europe. On the whole, American factories, where the client expects no money to be spent on design, are better buildings and at least negatively purer in design than those constructions in which the architect is forced by circumstances to be more than an engineer. Technical developments, moreover, are rapidly forcing almost all commercial and industrial building into the mould of the international style.

It is not necessary to accept the contentions of the functionalists that there is no new style or even to consider their own work still another kind of architecture. While the older generation has continued faithful to individualism, a set of general aesthetic principles has come into use. While the functionalists continue to deny that the aesthetic element in architecture is important, more and more buildings are produced in which these principles are wisely and effectively followed without sacrifice of functional virtues.

From: *The International Style: Architecture Since 1922*, by Henry-Russell Hitchcock, Jr., and Philip Johnson. New York: 1932, pages 17-39. (Paperback reprint with new foreword, Norton, 1966)

The Example of Frank Lloyd Wright

by

Walter Curt Behrendt

Before Frank Lloyd Wright became Sullivan's pupil, he received the beginnings of professional training at the University of Wisconsin, where he attended an engineering course. Perhaps it is due to this realistic rather than formal education that, when he later became an architect, he was never benumbed by the academic dogma. From the start he preferred to be animated by the individual conditions of the problem at hand rather than to be confined to the general rules of the geometric law. To start from necessity, to proceed on the demands of service and efficiency, and not from random abstractions which escape from life: that was to the man sympathetic to the engineer an obligation as strong as self-evident.

With Wright's work the principle of organic structure recurred on a higher level. With him architecture, after having grown torpid through expressive occupation with the masterpieces of the past, turned decidedly to the rejuvenating sources of its strength: to Nature. But this new turn towards nature manifests itself not in an intentional naturalism, but in a new mode of thinking about the structure. In one of his earliest manifestoes, Wright declared: "Although for centuries our practice has been to turn from nature, seeking inspiration in books, adhering slavishly to dead formulas, her wealth of suggestion is inexhaustible, her riches greater than any man's desire. . . ." And he continues: "A sense of the organic in Nature is indispensable to an architect, and the knowledge of the relation of form to function is at the root of his practice."

These few sentences characterize clearly and comprehensively the spiritual standpoint, which shows, even in the formulation, a striking congruity with the principal belief of Goethe expressed in one of his

Essays on Art, when he said: "An universal knowledge of organic nature is necessary in order to understand and develop the artist through the labyrinth of his structure." Wright's reflection of nature is, conforming to the classic example of Goethe, of that creative kind, where "intuition itself becomes thinking, and thinking an intuition." It is directed upon the morphological, upon the problem of structure, and upon the laws of organic growth. From the study of nature and its formative laws, he gets a firm and definite conception for his architectural creation. He realizes "how form derives its structure from nature and from the character of the material and its conditions, exactly as a flower forms itself according to the law which lies in its seed." Subjecting the structure of building, with the severest logic, to the laws upon which all organic growth rests, he succeeded in reaching beyond the results that realistic architecture had hitherto achieved, deliberately based as it was on a one-sided rationalistic concept, and pushed on to forms of higher organic order. It was he who first brought the idea of organic structure defined in the striking formula of his master-teacher to realization: a new architectural form. And the sensuous effect of this form has evidently not suffered because the creative instinct was guided by a cognition derived from natural science. The result is not only convincing by its logic; it also gives delight through the manifold imaginativeness of the form. This form, stimulating by its fullness of nature and nearness to life, immediately appeals to intuition and feeling, enchanting the senses with the melody of its language and the expressive grace of its appearance.

One must consider the plans of Wright's buildings in detail in order to understand the change in the principle of structure and the working of the new law. The ground-plan shows itself freed from the rigid doctrine of geometric order. Mathematics, as is proper in the realm of art, has sunk from the commanding position as a determinant of the law of the form and structure to that of an auxiliary rôle: it has become a technical subsidiary science. With this new spirit in building, space has lost its architectural sovereignty. For it is not the aim in forming the structure to represent the geometric idea of space, but to create for the individual life, which unfolds itself within that space, an accurately adjusted shell. This explains the strange irregularity of these plans, which exhibit irregular contours with numerous projections, and also single rooms of various shapes with manifold juttings and recessions.

And with the conception of space the manner of arranging the rooms also changes. The plan is no longer a geometric distribution of rooms attached by a principle to a system of axes, but the rooms are arranged so that they complement each other in their services, forming in their totality a uniformly functioning whole. And in their connection, the rooms are so bound to one another, spliced like muscles, that by their inner tension they are brought into indissoluble cohesion. At first, this new method of joining the rooms was accomplished by arranging, as connecting links, short lobby-like passages between the main rooms, effecting an almost imperceptible flowing of the rooms into one another. Later, this method was felt to be too loose, and replaced by an interlacing of rooms, at times increased toward bold penetrations, so that it seems as though one room were evolving out of another. And the more the inner structure strengthened, the looser became its outer contour. The more the sureness in the mastery of the new laws increased, the freer and opener became the contours of the ground-plan. In the projects in which Wright has achieved the maturity of his style, the rooms are arranged around the nucleus of the chimney part, like leaves of a plant around their stem. Radiating as if from a power center, they reach out into the garden and the landscape, opening themselves to the light and the view on all sides.

In the same manner that the plan in all its parts forms an indissoluble whole, so, according to the law of organic growth, are the ground-plan and elevation inseparably united with one another. "An organic form," Wright has said, "grows its own structure out of conditions as a plant grows out of the soil: both unfold similarly from within." In this sense, the laws of organic planning find their continuation and completion in the external structure; and the manifold arrangement of the parts, the lively grouping of building masses, are to be viewed as the result of the inner logic of design, and not as a brilliant show-piece of a deliberately picturesque composition. As to these buildings, one had better avoid speaking of "composition" at all, since no less a man than Goethe has condemned this expression, in nature as well as in art, as degrading. "The organs do not compose themselves as if already previously finished," he said; "they develop themselves together and out of one another, to an existence which necessarily takes part in the whole." Wright's buildings are neither designed nor composed; they are built and created in three dimensions as coherent organisms. It is for that reason that his buildings have no definite main view or any real façade at all. As a plant viewed from any angle appears in its full beauty and always offers new charms, so the nature of these buildings can only be experienced by encircling them. Whatever the perspective may be to the building, it always offers new aspects, full of variety, and only in the succession of one upon the other is there disclosed the nature and meaning of the whole.

Speaking of the structure of these buildings, it is not by chance that one is, again and again, urged to a comparison with the world of plants. Like a plant, the building grows up from the earth to the light. Above a compact base unfolds a loosened bulk, developed into rich plastic form through the harmonic interplay of its necessary parts and through the extended fullness of its appropriate detail. And in the development of this detail any trace of a leaning upon historic examples has been eradicated. It is in its form entirely independent, and new, also, in the sense of being organic. "Form," Wright once said, "is made by function, but qualified by use. Therefore form changes with changing conditions. It is the aim of this new art of detail to develop every form to complete individuality, according to the individual conditions from which it grows and which, therefore, are studied with an incomparable degree of sensibility."

Here it becomes clear how the creative observation of nature turns into a new artistic vision. Take, for instance, the horizontal slabs boldly projected, that new motive which has been the most imitated in modern building: in these widely overhanging eaves, spreading themselves canopy-like over terraces and balconies, there seems to be plantlike existence translated into architectural form. Or again, look at the changing forms of the windows, their distribution, their arrangement in groups of rhythmic order, in which the law seems to repeat itself that determines the ranging and ranking of leaves. Notice the delicate relation between the building bulk and the detail: as the bulk rises higher from the ground it becomes looser and lighter, while the detail becomes more elaborate and more tenuous. Notice finally the new development of the roofs, which free themselves from the substructure through widely overhanging projections, and spread like lofty tree-tops, making the house with its loosened silhouette stand out against the horizon. There may creep in, at times, something too "motive-like"; there may occasionally be found in this new art of detail a relapse into compositional tendencies opposed to the command of artistic economy: the excess is easily attributable to the exuberant joy in the new vision, and considering the enrichment of form gained thereby, and its emotional effects, we will always feel our objections weakened.

It is quite within the sphere of this new vision that it also turns its special attention to the effects of light, and beyond this, also includes in the artistic calculation the air. Wright treats light as if it were a natural building material. The graduated interplay of light and shade is to him an artistic medium of expression. The broad shadows, cast by the wide eaves and roofs, shade off the plastic modeling, and the changing contrasts of light and dark underline the dynamics of the building groups. And similarly, the air is evaluated as an element of form, is drawn into the concept of building. Wright splits the building mass up, he loosens its volume, since he intermingles it with open air-space. With this inclusion of the air-space in the formation, there is accomplished an intimate connection of the inside with the outside, a new feature which from now on becomes the unmistakable characteristic of the modern house. "Wright," said one of his German critics, "is the first architect to whom the atmosphere is more than mere background to his works. He uses it, he calculates with it, again and again he tries to relate his work so finely with the atmosphere that both must seem indissolubly connected. His entire system of projecting flat roofs, the inclusion of air-space within the building, and the concentration of shadow, in contrast to the rows of loosened, almost light-drinking windows in the upper stories, serves unconsciously this goal. Almost everywhere he tries, with the most varied means, to create between the outer world and the building intermediate bodies, forming transitions and sympathetically and more fully molding the relation between the two, taking all harshness from the fusion."

The new relation to nature and to organic life, from which the fundamental ideas of Wright's art are derived, is finally revealed in the changed treatment of the material. Wright uses, as a rule, the material in the sense of its organic nature. For him the material is by nature a willing friend, and everything depends upon hewing out of it, through careful treatment, its essential peculiarity. Veneration for nature forbids him to destroy the natural grain of the wood; he never uses covering paint, but leaves the wood in its simple state, shows the chance work of its branching, or treats it at times with colored stains. In the same manner he turns to account the structure of plaster and of bricks, the surface glazing of ceramic tiles, the nature of stone, its jointing and its size, utilizing not only the physical but also the physiognomical properties of the material, in order to enhance the individualizing characteristics of his building. And never is there a casual, or even conflicting juxtaposition of materials: they are harmoniously connected with each other and organically joined in the sense of a natural common union.

This live feeling for materials is another reason why Wright's buildings fit so naturally in their surroundings. They are built into nature, almost bred into the life-space of their surrounding landscape. The majority of the country houses he built are on the wide plains of the Middle West, that solemn landscape consisting of luxuriant vegetation with ancient timber-lands, of gentle far-ranging hills and an endless horizon. The houses with their broad masses widely spread out, with their low proportions and the long horizontal lines of their roofs, follow these large contours of the landscape. Like dense thickets, rooted firmly in the earth, their low building-masses stretch out over the ground, always turning towards the light, following the natural tendencies of the site, adapting themselves pliantly to every fold of land, every elevation of ground, with far-stretched low walls framing the garden, trees and other vegetation of the surroundings and pulling them, as if with fangs, inward to the house.

The domestic buildings of Wright are like Japanese houses, so fitted into the landscape that the building almost imperceptibly blends with surrounding nature. The Japanese house manifests the same spirit of nature, the same tendency toward an organic structure. It also shows this intimate connection with the scene it is set in, this multiform arrangement of roofs meticulously calculated in its effects, and the careful treatment of materials according to their physical and physiognomical properties. It is not by chance that Wright's country houses recall the Japanese pattern. He was several times in Japan for long intervals (and in Tokio he even built a hotel which though one of his largest works is certainly not his best). The philosophy of a country where man merges in nature, and a civilization where art and life permeate each other so intimately, must have been especially favorable to his own conception of art. Wright's art is, in fact, similar to the Japanese, nature-like and rural; and it evidently loses its greatest values when it is diverted to projects of typical city building.

Wright's decided preference for low building corresponds to this pastoral character. He certainly knows the satisfaction of being able to build everything on the ground level, and he knows how to prize it, this "highest happiness of the architect": he has tasted it to the full in his own house Taliesin, which in its high perfection is to date his most mature work. In its organic structure and its intimate connection with nature, this house may justly take as its due the famous words of praise which Vasari coined for Raphael's Villa Farnesina: "Non murato, ma veramente nato."

Each house of Wright's is an individual organism, related in every detail to man, alive in itself, friendly to all life, and in complete harmony with nature, a growth. Always starting from the stern command of use, Wright tries to develop the form of the structure out of its functions; he tries to articulate the individual nature of each building, and to unfold this nature in its own world, in its own proper life-space, according to its immanent law. From this conception derives the stupendous manifoldness of his form, and the incomparable art of imbuing with character every part which marks the summit of his master.

Wright's work reevals a new conception of the idea of organic structure. The creative observation of nature which led him to that conception, and the stating of the morphological problem involved in it, is alone an achievement of extraordinary intellectuality. No less important is the architectural achievement with which the new idea of structure gained its artistic presentation. In it there is revealed the unfathomable strength of his intuition and the abundance of creative power with which he is gifted. From these extraordinary faculties there originated the inexhaustible richness of his form. His work is full of form, like nature herself whose laws are at the basis of his work. In every detail this law is evident, and yet the command of its necessity is followed with complete inner freedom. In the work itself the principle on which it is based has been completely absorbed, so that it constitutes not a demonstration but a work of art unfolding a new form of beauty. The form always binds itself to its law, but it yet remains free from any dogmatic inhibitions. It has been worked out with the most exacting care and with full technical conscientiousness. It makes copious use of modern building materials, of glass, iron and cement; it tries to utilize the new constructive possibilities in a functional way and to interpret their character in new architectural forms. It also makes use of the machine as a willing tool. And while so doing, it loses nothing of its lyrical charm, nothing of the impetuous boldness which completes the varying perspectives in their daring but always organic asymmetries.

A marginal note may be added. Jakob Burckhardt, the justly famous historian of Renaissance architecture, used to say that one must have money as well as luck and humor for the pleasure, so questionable to him, of creating an unsymmetric building. This pious prescription has been fulfilled for Wright in so far as he has almost always been able to build for the more affluent, who have placed at his command large, and even unusual, means. Thanks to this economic independence his forms have often been developed to a degree of lavishness that may very well represent the prosperity of their patrons, but has been to their creator rather a misfortune than an advantage. The abundance of means entices him into artistic effects, and to the degree to which these effects are sought for their own sake the work is removed from the principles on which it is based. Wright disposes of an abundance of fancy which is powerful enough to be the stock of a dozen architects. And this blossoming and luxuriant imagination, the strongest of his manifold talents, is also a danger. It undermines his artistic discipline, and sometimes lures him with its precious gifts into being unfaithful to his own theory, so that, as J. J. P. Oud remarked to the point, "Wright the artist renounces what Wright the prophet proclaims."

Wright's ornament, the product of his exuberant fancy, is like Sullivan's the most accidental and the most transitory part of his work: it proves that even he was confined to the limits of his generation. But leaving aside these rankly growing accessories, considering first the structure of his domestic buildings, and then studying the programmatic statements of his numerous manifestoes, one gets, indeed, a clear and thoroughly definite idea of the structural principles of modern building, which meanwhile have become international common property.

From: *Modern Building,* by Walter Curt Behrendt. New York: 1937, pages 129–138.

Composition in Modern Architecture

by

Matthew Nowicki

Much has been said and written about the "style" of the building movement of our time, but the problem of composition in architecture has, for the most part, been treated with reluctance or avoided altogether. If form is to be reduced to the automatic consequence of function, then a distrust of the problems of composition insofar as they are the problems of form is justified. Or again, where composition has become synonymous with academicism, its problems may be treated with suspicion by those who wish to stress the differences of our architecture from that of preceding periods.

Frank Lloyd Wright went one step further than his contemporaries when he said: " 'Form follows function' is but a statement of fact. When we say, 'Form and function are one,' only then do we take mere fact into the realm of creative thought." In other words, dependence of form on function would be replaced by interdependence of form and function. And if we accept the mutual dependence of form and function, then the problems of form in modern architecture might well be studied as are the problems of function.

Judging modern architecture on the merits of its form, Henry-Russell Hitchcock and Philip C. Johnson baptized it the "international style." Style in art and architecture means a number of striking similarities of form among works of a certain period that distinguishes

The Solomon R. Guggenheim Museum (Interior), New York. Frank Lloyd Wright, architect. *Courtesy, The Solomon R. Guggenheim Museum.*

Center for the Advanced Study in Behavioral Sciences, Inc., Stanford University; Palo Alto, California. Wurster, Bernardi and Emmons, Inc., architects. *Courtesy, Morley Baer.*

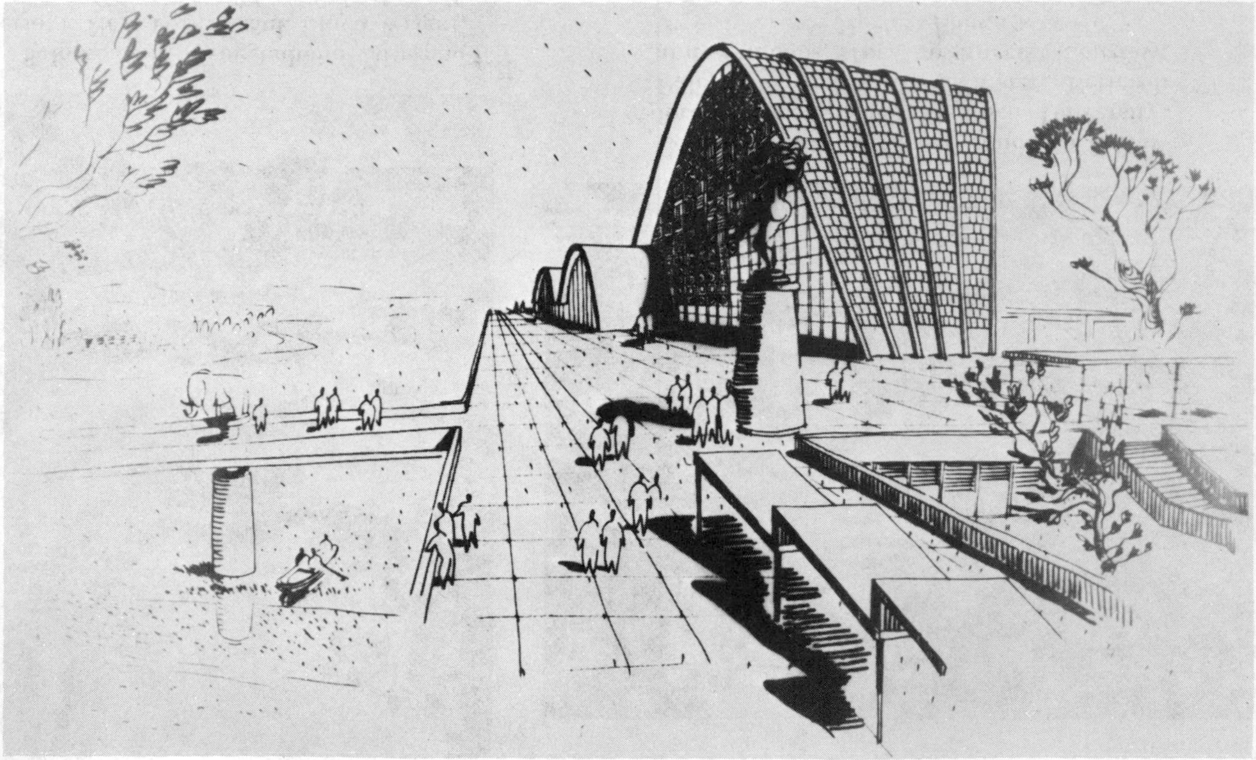

Sketch for the Capitol complex at Chandigarh, East Punjab, showing the assembly on the roof of the secretariat. Matthew Nowicki, architect. ***Courtesy, Albert Mayer.***

them from those of other times, and, although we may not like the word "style," it would be difficult to pretend that we do not notice those similarities in our day.

Humanism may well be considered the main principle of the new movement, even though functionalism was its official title. Man and his way of life became the main source of inspiration to a modern architect. Forgotten in the esthetic speculations of the nineteenth century, man, in the basic sense of individual and social character, again became the object of creative attention. Man presented two aspects. The first was the unchanging quality of the human individual: the size of his body, the length of his step and the speed of his walk—the same throughout ages—determine the unchanging factors of scale in architecture; his basic emotions, though changing in form of expression, are as old as the race itself. The second aspect deals with the constant change in human life and the differences that exist not only between generations but between men of different decades. Now this change is rapid and conspicuous, and it demands constant changes in architectural forms.

In direct application to architecture, these rapid changes of environment and technology are seen in the new materials available. The use of iron, steel and reinforced concrete is one source of the greatest revolution that has stirred architecture since the gothic period.

It is no accident that the new principles are already clearly expressed in Paxton's Crystal Palace of 1851. Skeleton construction, with its wide spanned-column layout and the cantilever, permitted a free treatment of plan to express the diversified functions of life. It also allowed for the interpenetration of free space and enclosed form which became one of the main features of the new style. In short, we may say that functionalism could not have developed its present shape if it had not been for the possibilities offered by construction.

Functionalism separated the traditional concept of a bearing wall into a structural element of column and a dividing element of screen, which now could be subjected to their own laws of composition. Construction and partition in a modern plan seem to symbolize the factors of stability and change in architecture. In a certain sense the first acquires an expression of classical discipline while the second becomes an element of romantic freedom. The eternal conflict of classicism and romanticism takes place here and can best be observed in the importance that some architects attach to the discipline of construction, while others subordinate construction to the organic expression of life.

Skeleton construction, despite its achievements, is probably still at the beginning of its possibilities. The use of new structural materials like aluminum, of new concepts of organization like prefabrication and of metal standardized forms for reinforced concrete will bring rich new shapes. Ceilings by Freyssinet in France and Wright's mushroom columns of the Johnson Wax factory in this country may well be considered the precursors of a future wave that will bring unpredicted solutions in form. How this may affect the esthetics of architecture, hitherto based for the most part on a rectangular discipline, still remains to be seen.

Humanism, functionalism and construction have been found to be the backbone of modern form. Esthetic judgment of the new shapes could not take place through the conventional method of comparison, since most of it was without direct precedent in architectural tradition. Therefore this judgment had to be based on the merits of the philosophy responsible for the form and the directness with which this philosophy was expressed in three dimensions.

"Less is more." This statement of Mies van der Rohe expresses one of the principles adopted by our period. Order and elimination seem to be the roots of the simplicity sought for by composition in contemporary architecture. But the latter, in contrast to the architecture of earlier periods, attempts to create an order of freedom instead of one of rigid subordination to a single dominating element. In illustration of these concepts, one might compare the static composition of St. Peter's in Rome (which with a slight stretch of imagination may resemble an outline of a mummy) with the balanced freedom of Le Corbusier's plan.

Though the old academic principle of bilateral symmetry has been replaced in modern composition by a free balance of parts, modern architecture does not reject the use of an abstract, geometrical discipline in plan or façade. Compositions on a large scale seem to demand a certain type of geometrical order that cannot be explained by simple interpretation of function. An important psychological factor of satisfaction and comfort lies in knowing what to expect from the whole by what one has experienced in the parts already seen. Regularity between certain elements of composition can aid in creating that unity which may be established only through a sensation of order.

Diversity is achieved by contrast within an ordered unity. Again a humanized explanation of this abstract approach is simple. Architecture should provide human comfort in the visual and psychological as well as in the strictly physical sense of the word, and understanding is part of psychological comfort. Established relations among the elements of a façade, for instance, though based on a geometrical principle, create an impression of order that is easy to understand and appreciate.

Order is the creation of an intellectual approach and unity based on order always has a classical flavor. Diversity is the expression of creative temperament, imagination and emotion and therefore is a factor of what we may call romanticism. Again the two forces exist side by side, one incomplete without the other, and we may conclude that the search for a balance between them is the objective of composition in modern architecture.

The possibilities offered by the new construction and by the free plan allow the inside of the building to be opened to the penetration of outside space. In modern composition mass is replaced by the conception of volume. The traditional wall pierced with windows and doors almost belongs to a past period: the transparent or opaque screen, fitted between floor and ceiling, is taking its place. A structural brick wall used today in small architectural problems is often employed with the same feeling of screen principle. The predominant construction of a given period influences the shapes adopted by one less typical for the same time, and thus contemporary brick architecture follows the esthetics characteristic for the column and screen principle.

Relations between notes in music, colors in painting and elements of space in architecture bring pleasure if they satisfy man's instinct of proportion.

There is probably no way to establish rules of good proportion as there is no way to establish rules of beauty, but every period in architecture seems to develop a predilection for certain proportions. In ancient Egypt the element of cult introduced the sacred triangle. Humanism in Greece was based on proportions governing relations among parts of the human body, and the golden section was the result. The abstract simplicity of a square appealed to architects of other times: both the gothic cathedrals and the arches of triumph of the late renaissance are examples of architecture subordinated to this discipline.

Based as it was on the purity of functionalism and the principle of expressing on the exterior a plan evolved from the inside, the modern period could not govern its form by any preconceived geometric rule. It therefore claims that the choice of proportions is a personal and emotional, rather than an intellectual one. Nevertheless it is interesting to note new attempts to introduce into architectural composition factors more stable than individual temperament. "Modulor" of Le Corbusier, a measure to control relations of elements, is the best example of this approach and is evolved from the proportions of the human body.

Since previous techniques had resulted for the most part in a vertical accent, it was some time before modern construction, with its wide spans and the new cantilever, was able to introduce a sympathy for a strong horizontal expression. But now a liking for a wide horizontal shape, related to the rest of the composition through a module, seems to be the principal characteristic of proportion in contemporary architecture.

As every period has its own feeling for proportion, so it has for scale. By scale in composition, we understand the size of an element of this composition—in other words, the size of a unit by the repetition or other use of which the composition is formed. In this way the scale of a building is partly independent of its size. In fact, some of the structures of Palladio in Vicenza, for example, though only some fifty feet high, have a much greater scale than a New York skyscraper fifty stories high, a fact accounted for by the tremendous difference in the size of the respective elements of composition. Just as proportion establishes relations among divisions of space, so scale establishes relations between man and space, so that, properly used, scale can become one of the factors of humanism in architecture.

Humanism, as we have stated, is basic in modern architecture, and man's comfort applies to his psychological relations to space as well as to his physical convenience within it. A great contrast between the size of man and the size of a basic element of composition may provoke many emotions but not a feeling of comfort and well-being, and modern architecture, with its insistence on small scale, is only too conscious of this.

In terms of functionalism, a larger interior must be expressed as frankly as a small one, and a unit planned for crowds should have a different scale from one planned for an individual, so that the scale of modern architecture must allow for a certain flexibility. This raises the controversial problem of monumentality which was, by its opponents, usually linked to the Greek or Roman column, a decorative dome covering a pompous interior, the inconvenience of outside stairs, etc. Monumentality does not in fact depend on any form but is a problem of scale. The humanistic ideal of individual freedom and comfort adopted by our architecture and expressed in its sympathy to the small-scale treatment should influence also the resolution of the monumental problem, just as the large scale of the baroque influenced every small programme of the period. This would seem to eliminate monumentality from modern architecture; but monumentality, in the sense of a contrast between architecture of exceptional importance and the size of an individual, has its true and eternal qualities of which man should not be deprived. Within the realm of its favorite scale, modern architecture should no doubt distinguish a variety of treatments that will be appropriate to the expression of its diversified contents.

Subordinated to order, proportion and scale are the problems of detail and ornament. The detail of today seems to be a direct issue of mass production and standardization. Its uniformity is probably more pronounced than in any other time when it usually was more of an individual problem in esthetics.

In the present use of detail, one must not forget that modern architecture began by a complete elimination of it. Its reappearance, which has been coming gradually, is due both to technical and esthetic reasons. A detail expresses, if only symbolically, the richness and refinement of form, and in its maturity every movement in architecture should express these qualities by the use of detail.

Detail often develops into an ornament that poses a problem of its own today. Modern architecture, committed to the spirit of purity and of freedom, seems to look longingly in its search for the richness of form at the forbidden fruit of ornament. An architect of today hesitates to design an ornament but welcomes into his composition fresco, mosaics, tiles, brick or stone, treating them all as decorative textures, free and independent of architectural rhythm. The concept of a free plan seems to have as a corresponding element the concept of a free ornament.

Architecture may be considered a science, a profession, a craft, a hobby, a way of life and many other things, but it is also an art. All art has its roots in nature and in life, but we realize by now that its purpose is not accurate representation but discovery of underlying truth.

"Exactitude is not truth"—this sentence of Matisse's is beyond any misunderstanding. Exactitude is not the truth in architecture any more than in any other art. Truth in composition is not the exact disclosure of the inside functions of the building on its exterior, nor is it the frank expression of its construction. Both functionalism and construction must be ordered by the truth of unity and the diversity within it; in other words by the basic laws of the universe, the expression of which man calls beauty.

Not until this fact is established in the minds of our architects will there be a reason to study contemporary composition. But it would seem that our period is now ready for this study and ready to submit objects for its criticism—modern buildings rising out of the experience of our times.

From: *Composition in Modern Architecture,* by Matthew Nowicki. "The Magazine of Art," New York: March, 1949, pages 108–111.

Function and Form

by

Matthew Nowicki

I suspect that I will no longer provoke you as much as I should by opening these remarks on the origins and trends of modern architecture with a statement that sometime ago our design became a style. No matter how ingeniously we dodge the unpleasant issue, it comes at us with full force in thousands of creations of the contemporary designer. A style, with all the restrictions, disciplines, limitations and blessings that we usually associate with the term. A style in the similarities between designs differing basically in the purpose of their use and destination, subordinating to its demands a refrigerator or a motor car, a factory or a museum. A style which perhaps follows sales, quoting Edgar Kaufmann, just as form followed function in the words of Greenough and the Renaissance architecture followed its antique models in the work of Palladio. A style as pronounced, as defined, more limited perhaps, and as legitimate for our times as the style of Renaissance had been in its days.

In the growing maturity and self-consciousness of our century, we cannot avoid the recognition of this fact, and we have to realize what it stands for. We can no longer avoid this term "style" simply because it brings to our minds unpleasant memories. We cannot keep on pretending that we solve our problems without a precedent in form.

We have to realize that in the overwhelming majority of modern design form follows *form* and not *function*. And even when a form results from a functional analysis, this analysis follows a pattern that leads to a discovery of the same function, whether in a factory or a museum. Approached in a certain way an answer to every architectural problem is a flexible space with no reason why one flexible space should be different from another, and many practical reasons why they should be alike.

In saying all this, I am not an advocate of a diversity in design for its own sake. Such a diversity is just confirming the rule of regimentation that always is the result of a style. The more one attempts to escape one's period, the more part of it one becomes. The constructive diversity that provides strength to an expanding and virile civilization comes through a creative sensitivity to the eternally changing circumstance where "every opportunity stands alone."

This sensitivity is the main source of something for which I have no better word than freshness. Freshness is a physical part of youth, and youth disappears with time. This is the law of life true equally in the case of an individual or a civilization. Freshness can be preserved if the source of it depends not on the physical state of being young, but on the consciousness of its origin. Some individuals preserve this creative freshness in their maturity. Those are the great artists. Some civilizations preserve this freshness for ages and then become great cultures. For although maturity aims at perfection and the stride for perfection must end with an unchanging standard of classical excellence, the consciousness of the source of freshness can provide a magnified scope to this stride. The magnitude of this scope is the measure of ambitions and strength of a civilization, and the prophecy of its future achievements.

Thinking in terms of the contemporary, or should I say modern, period of design, we realize by now that it has passed its early youth. The experiments with form, of the new space concept, the playfulness with the machine to live in, the machine to look at or the machine to touch, in architecture, painting and sculpture are more remote from us than the time alone would indicate. There was a freshness in those youthful days of the aesthetic revolution, a physical freshness of a beginning. There was a diversity in those days of forms that grew without a direct precedent in form.

I speak of architecture because it incorporates the full field of design. In its changes we can discover those that affected the interior design, the industrial design, problems of organized landscape and others, with or without a separate name. And, it is these changes of the architectural concept that I propose to analyze with the aim of establishing our present position in their chain. From the analysis of these changes I will not develop any law of analogy, nor will I make predictions on what will be the coming change. I propose to define our present position because this is our strategic point of departure for the investigation of the full field of opportunity that lies within our period. To define our present stage, I shall try to trace it to its origins.

It seems to me that the beginning of modern architecture has its roots in the domestic structure of the late Renaissance. It was then that the problem of human comfort was rediscovered. Functionalism in terms of the importance of good living was introduced along with a number of technical gadgets of which the stove in Fontainbleau was probably a vanguard. Architecture descended from its pedestal of heroism and rapidly started to grow human and even bourgeois. In France after the death of Louis XIV, the despotic "Roi soleil" the private residence "building boom" produced a plan in which areas of different use were defined and located with regard to one another. The plan of this new type differed from its predecessor where a sequence of rectangular round oval and otherwise shaped interiors had a changing use, and one ate, slept or entertained in any one of them, according to a passing or a more permanent fancy. This change was not the beginning of functionalism, as architecture always had to satisfy a function, but the beginning of its modern interpretation. Resigning from heroism, architecture diminished its scale becoming cut to the size of an ordinary man. A good illustration of this change is the comparison between the Palace of Versailles and the Petit Trianon.

In the change of the predominant scale and the introduction of the problems of comfort, we can find the beginning of our architecture. These changes, essential as they were, could not alone produce the new form. Other factors were to complete the picture of the final change. One of them was expressed in 1825 by the German architect, Schinkel, after his visit to the industrialized Manchester in his famous question, "Why not a new style." The eternal desire of change was responsible for violent shifts of attitude to form through the 19th century. To illustrate this violence and its extremes, I would like to quote two striking and not very well known examples. In the early years of the century, a French archeologist proposed a system of destroying the Gothic cathedrals, considered in the days of the Empire as edifices of barbarism. Cutting a groove at the base of the limestone columns, then surrounding them with piles of wood and setting fire to them was suggested. The archeologist was convinced that under this treatment the unsavory structure would crumble "in less than ten minutes" relieving civilization of its shameful presence.

A few decades later Ruskin, paving the way for the Pre-Raphaelite movement, wrote in his "Modern Painters" that no public funds should be spent to purchase paintings later than Raphael, as the spirit of art was confined to the medieval period and replaced later by a superficial technology of a craft. Out of these shifts of sympathies came the consciousness that some basic change in the eclectic sequence is indispensable. This was the psychological background to what we call the "modern" form. And although we shudder at the word style, Schinkel's search for its new expression contributed to the birth of modern architecture, perhaps as much as any other factor. No new form of architecture could have been created without a new structure, and the psychological receptiveness had to wait for its fulfillment until the structural possibilities ripened.

The middle of the last century with Paxton's Crystal Palace—its modular re-erection on a new site, its space concept of openness, created a new era. The following use of cast iron then ferroconcrete and steel created the spine of the new frame structure from those days on dominant in modern building. Independence of the partitioning wall from the frame created the free plan and, thus, all elements of the new architecture were present at the beginning of our century.

What would have been the characteristics of modern architecture should it follow the direction of those early days? Its form influenced strongly by the expression of the structure would have been intricate and detailed. The logical development of the skeleton would accentuate the delicate ribs dividing areas of the building into supporting and supported members. The resulting form would perhaps acquire the lightness and openness of lacework filled with translucent or opaque screen. In its final stage the screen would probably be replaced with a secondary skeleton filling the lacework with more lacework.

This is the way the Gothic skeleton developed with its stained glass window and this was the road explored by Paxton, Labrouste, Eiffel and their contemporaries. Modern architecture instead chose a road different in every respect from these expectations. To understand this change of destiny we have to make a digression. Architecture with its social, economic and technical complexities never was in the lead of aesthetic changes. As a rule it followed other media of art. The changes of taste in the XIX century, mentioned before, affected architecture very profoundly but they resulted from factors remote to the problems of building or design.

The great change introduced by the Renaissance can be quoted here as a striking example of the same problem. At the rebirth of the classical idiom the medieval Gothic structure reached the climax of its growth. The future life and growth of this structure was interrupted by an aesthetic wave unrelated to the technics of architecture. No structural competition to the Gothic building was offered by the new style. The building methods of the Renaissance were crude when compared to the advanced standard of the medieval mason. The change in architecture followed the changing aesthetic of the period and the responsibility and credit for this change should rest with its men of letters. In this way Petrarch and Dante fathered the architecture of the Renaissance.

A somewhat similar thing happened to modern architecture. This time the change of taste was inspired by the painters and not by the men of letters. The broad and open manner of Cezanne, the architectonic painting of synthetic Cubism introduced a new taste for the purity and simplicity of form. The development of the structural skeleton mentioned before could not be molded into the new aesthetic. The problems of structure and materials became secondary in a period preoccupied with the aesthetics of form. One has the impression that for an architect of the early twenties construction was the necessary evil. Architecture became "idealized" and "dematerialized." Colorful planes meeting at the corners of the cube emphasized the lack of material thickness. Structural detail was eliminated conforming to the demands of purity and the idealized structure reacted badly to time and weather. A column in this architecture became simply a cylinder surrounded by planes, a vertical among horizontals. The contrast of this juxtaposition had to be achieved to the satisfaction of the intellect so that no shape was created without a function which it should express and serve. But to create the shape a function was created or conveniently over-emphasized. Here my thoughts wander to those two massive cylinders dividing the steps of Le Corbusier's Salvation Army Paris building. Although emphasized more than any other structural element of the building they function as ventilation shafts and maybe even now, if technically obsolete, might have lost their functional meaning preserving the compositional importance. This architecture of the "international style" romantically disposed to the over-impressive technology developed a notion which I shall call *functional exactitude.* The truth of architecture was considered as the exact expression of every function. When building became technically obsolete and therefore no longer ideally serving those changing functions it was to be removed and replaced by a more efficient one.

The concept of functional exactitude found a source of decorative qualities in the inventive interpretation of human life and movement. One might say that this architecture became the decoration of function. The period of functional exactitude looked for its inspiration towards the physical function. The psychological one was not considered in its philosophy. The concept of controlled environment resulted and the main purpose of architecture was to control *physical* environment to the *physical* satisfaction of the user. Let us see what happened later.

The recent changes in modern architecture are perhaps as basic as those separating the nineteen twenties from their predecessors. True that we share our vocabulary with this period of yesterday but the same words have for us a different and often a basically opposite meaning. We also speak of functionalism but then it meant the exactitude and now it means the flexibility. Those are two opposite concepts. In our thoughts priority often is given to the psychological and not the physical human function. The concept of a short lived structure removed with the rapid change of technology is replaced by a notion of architecture that will be our contribution to the life of future generations. Le Corbusier introduces a measure on which this contribution can be composed, the "modulor" with its mystery of the golden section. This measure of good proportion is most significant for the change of values. No longer the measure of functional space, no longer the measure of time, but a measure of beauty. Whatever the validity of such a measure may be it is interesting to notice that in the sequence of "time, space and architecture" the emphasis is shifting towards the last word in terms of the mystery of its art. The free plan is replaced by the modular plan. Again these are two opposite notions. A module is the most rigid discipline to which a plan can be subjected. A modular plan in reality is the opposite of a free plan. We are no longer preoccupied with the proximities of related functions but with the nature of space that leads from one function to another. It is no longer "how quickly to get there" but "how to get there," that matters most in our plans. It seems that from a quantitative period we have jumped into a qualitative one.

These changes are not always conscious nor pronounced to the degree pointed out in my remarks. It is an irresistible temptation to express those changes in the most striking manner. But, in order to be objective one has to realize that a dividing line between periods can never be geometrically defined. This division can better be compared to a wide ribbon which separates and joins at the same time like a gray belt between fields of black and white.

With respect to the main channels of human creation namely the invention and the discovery, one might say that our present period is also different from the yesterday. The discovery of formal symbol of the unchanging laws of the universe seems to replace the invention of the form without a precedent. The eternal story of gravitation is again consciously contemplated. We are aware that the form of the discovery has to change but the object of it remains the same; over and over discovered in many ways.

Along with these elements of philosophy we also react in a different way to the techniques of our craft. Architecture discovered its own medium of creation and the difference between this medium and the others. Picasso writing recently about his "blue period" of 1912 and several later years said that he discovered late the difference between sculpture and painting. Maturity brings a "sense of medium" and mature architecture in the same way discovered the difference between painting and the art of organizing accessible space. As a result we rely in our expression on the potentialities of materials and structures almost picking up the trend of the XIX century. This interest in structure and material may discover within the building medium decorative qualities of ornament much too involved for the purist of yesterday. The symbolic meaning of a support became rediscovered and a steel column is used frankly as a symbol of structure even when it is not part of the structure itself. The period of functional exactitude expressed its mysterious longings for ornament in the decoration of function.

This period of functional flexibility expresses them in the decoration of structure. Art tends not only to discover the truth but to exaggerate and finally to distort it. *And, maybe in this distortion lies the essence of art.*

I have described our stage of the modern design as a style. Will this style repeat the sad story of other styles becoming an addition to the repertoire of a future eclecticism? The life and the decline of cultures follows an organic pattern which seems to be inevitable. But span of life of a culture and its rebirth into another rests in the hands of the people responsible for its creation. Where is the future of modern design?

It seems to me that it depends on the constant effort of approaching every problem with the consciousness that there is no single way of solving it. "Art una-species mille." This battle cry of the Renaissance should be repeated again and again. Art may be one but there are a thousand species. We must face the dangers of the crystallizing style not negating its existence but trying to enrich its scope by opening new roads for investigation and future refinements.

"Form follows function" may no longer satisfy ambitions aroused when form becomes judged for its universal values, but sensitivity to the minute exigencies of life remains the source of creative invention leading through the elimination of "exactitudes" to the more important and more general truth which equals beauty.

From: *Origins and Trends in Modern Architecture,* by Matthew Nowicki. "The Magazine of Art," New York: November, 1951, pages 273–279.

Biographical Sketches

FREDERICK LEE ACKERMAN (1878–1950) was born in up-state New York, and practiced in New York City, but lived heart and soul on the island of Nantucket, where the old spirit of independence, self-reliance, and craftsmanship, which he loved, still kept a foothold. He was perhaps, with Grosvenor Atterbury and John Irwin Bright, the first important architect, after Louis Sullivan, to be fully alive to the social responsibilities—and the economic conditioning—of architecture. The work he did in awakening an interest in constructive housing, first as investigator, then as practitioner with the United States Shipping Board, was in every way exemplary. His later work in Sunnyside Gardens and Radburn, and for the New York Housing Authority, maintained this social interest. Coming under the influence of Thorstein Veblen, Ackerman became skeptical of the possibilities of sound architecture without a profound reorientation of industrial society; and in some of his best essays, like the present one on craftsmen and machines, he went into the conflict he was constantly aware of between the "instinct of workmanship" and the "theory of business enterprise." Though Ackerman's intelligence led him to accept the machine unconditionally, his heart was in an earlier age: so much so that when he designed colonial houses for a middle class subdivision at Manhasset, L. I. he insisted that the gutters should be wood, not metal, as in true colonial dwellings. Esthetically, he never caught up with the Chicago school, though toward the end of his life he designed a wholly air-conditioned apartment house with sealed glass windows. But his sardonic, skeptical, challenging, almost eighteenth century mind left a mark on all who came close to him.

DANKMAR ADLER (1844–1900) was born near Eisenach in Germany, but was brought by his widowed father to Detroit, in 1854, and got his education in Detroit and Ann Arbor. He failed to pass the entrance examinations for the University of Michigan, but an aptitude for drawing led his father to place him under John Schaefer, a Detroit architect. In 1861 his father became rabbi of a Chicago congregation—the same for which Adler and Sullivan were to build a new synagogue in 1892—and Dankmar followed him to that city, only to enlist a little later in the Illinois Light Artillery. He participated in some of the major engagements of the war, and was wounded. Detailed toward the end as draftsman in the Topographical Engineer's office, he obtained valuable engineering experience. In 1871 Adler formed an architectural partnership with Edward Burling, but in 1879, he set up for himself, and very shortly after took in Louis Sullivan, first as draftsman, then full partner. As designer of the Central Music Hall in 1879 Adler got experience both in interior construction and in acoustics that served him well on one of the great masterpieces of the new firm, Adler and Sullivan, the Auditorium. His talents were in perfect complement to Sullivan's, though from the beginning he seems to have given the younger man a free hand in design. Their partnership, unfortunately for both men, was dissolved in 1895. Adler's modest personality, his sense of civic responsibility, his immense grasp of practical detail, his theoretic interest in the dominant technical problems of his day, all combined to make him an exemplary figure in his profession; and perhaps only Frank Lloyd Wright, who observed both men at first hand, has fully done justice to his contribution to the great partnership. (But see Hugh Morrison's biography of Sullivan, with its appendix on Adler.)

CATHERINE BAUER [Mrs. William Wurster] (1905–1964), the daughter of the New Jersey Highway Commissioner, Jacob L. Bauer, who initiated the modern superhighways that by-pass major towns, expressed an early interest in architecture, but left the architectural school at Cornell to pursue more general studies at Vassar. Her concern with architecture took a more social turn through her association from 1930 with the Regional Planning Association of America group; and after a period of study in Berlin in 1930, she returned to America to win the Fortune prize in Industrial Design in 1931 by writing an essay on the significance of modern architecture, mainly in Germany. During the next few years, she made a series of planning studies with Mr. Clarence S. Stein, and did further research on housing. In 1934 she published *Modern Housing*, a classic study of the origins and methods and purposes of modern workers' housing —a book at once sound in its scholarship, brilliant in its historical interpretations, and challenging in its hard-headed realism. *Modern Housing* established Miss Bauer as an authority in this field; and her later work in the Federal Housing Authority, as administrator, as co-drafter of housing legislation, and as propagandist for public housing generally on democratic lines has given her a unique place in the whole movement. Besides visiting lectureships at various universities, she taught at Harvard University and, from 1950 to her death, in the Department of City and Regional Planning at the University of California (Berkeley). No one did more to make plain the necessity for political intelligence and responsibility, in translating ideal programs into concrete projects. Through Catherine Bauer's becoming a housing specialist, architecture lost a brilliant critic, as her present contribution bears witness.

WALTER CURT BEHRENDT (1884–1945) was born in Alsace, studied architecture at Berlin and Munich, and became Doctor of Engineering in Architecture with a thesis on the Block as the Unit of City Design. With his highly developed critical sense, he became aware of a lack of creativeness in his own designs and courageously decided to devote himself to the administrative problems connected with architecture. From 1912 onward he served successively in the Prussian Ministry of Public Buildings, the Ministry of Public Health, Department of Housing and City Planning (1919–1926) and as technical adviser to the Ministry of Finance, in charge of Prussian public buildings, from 1927 to 1933. In these offices he helped shape public policy not merely in housing and city development but in the regional projects for the Ruhr District, Greater Hamburg, and Middle Germany. As a critic, he came at first under the influence of an older contemporary, Karl Scheffler. For long a regular contributor on architecture to the Frankfurter Zeitung, in 1925 he became the editor of Die Form, the organ of the Deutscher Werkbund. Deprived of his governmental post in 1933, he came to America in 1934, as visiting lecturer in Housing and City Planning at Dartmouth College, and except for a period as Technical Director of the City Planning Association at Buffalo, 1937–1941, his main work was at Dartmouth College, which made him a professor in 1941, in recognition of his brilliant gifts as teacher. No modern critic could, perhaps, boast such a combination of fundamental professional training, practical experience, and mature critical judgement, based on the widest sort of humanistic study, as Behrendt possessed. His early book, published in 1920 but written before the first World War, on "the battle over style in the arts and crafts and in architecture," was a fundamental document, which should long ago have been translated into English; and though as early as 1927 he published a little book on *The Victory of the New Building Style*, in which he hailed the new movement, he always remained a judicious and discerning critic of the actual performances of modern architects. His book, *Modern Building*, 1937, is the best single text on the whole movement, at once succinct and comprehensive, with historical perspective and a rich insight into the nature of our age and its social as well as its architectural problems. Through his early death at Hanover, New Hampshire, in 1945, America lost a rare citizen, who loved her land and her folkways, and who demanded the best of his students, so that they might serve her well.

CLAUDE BRAGDON (1866–1947) was one of the few architects in the East whose work and thought, between 1890 and 1930, showed any real sympathy with the new architecture of the Chicago school. Bragdon lived part of his life in Rochester, New York, an industrial community whose greatest venture had been the popularization of the Kodak. The only large opportunity Bragdon apparently had there was the design of the New York Central Railroad Station, conventional in its exterior, though still quite handsome, with its sombre brown brick interior and vaulted ceiling. Bragdon's opportunity for creativity came mainly in his work as stage designer in New York, during the nineteen-twenties and thirties. By reason of his contacts with Louis Sullivan and his natural sympathy with all that pertained to the life of our democracy, he became the chief link in writing, apart from Sullivan and Wright, with the architectural critics of an earlier period. Because he took the work seriously and published a series of books on architecture, Bragdon's influence was greater than that of perhaps the only other architect who might be mentioned in the same breath, Irving Pond, whose chatty comments, "From Foreign Shores" were once a monthly feature of the Journal of the A.I.A. Perhaps Bragdon's own philosophy would have had a greater impact on his contemporaries had not his architectural theories been intermingled with Theosophy—the central interest of his life—and a four dimensional theory of ornament. His esthetic principles, still more his perceptions, were robust enough to do justice to Renaissance humanism as well as to Gothic constructivism: so that here he was

Dankmar Adler

Catherine Bauer. *Photograph by Carol Baldwin.*

Walter Curt Behrendt

John Burroughs

Andrew Jackson Downing

a sounder critic than Geoffrey Scott. His best book on architecture is probably his *Architecture and Democracy* (1919).

JOHN BURROUGHS (1837–1921) was born in Roxbury, in Delaware County, New York, and in 1873 established himself on a farm near Esopus, close to the Hudson. In one sense, he was a continuator of Whitman, whom he met in 1863, and of Thoreau, another amateur naturalist, whose occasional errors he sometimes primly corrected. Burroughs' essays on nature began to appear in The Atlantic Monthly in 1865, and his reputation came chiefly from the long succession of essays and books he wrote in this field. He thus provided the background in the popular mind for the landscape painters and illustrators and landscape architects, and the exponents of the new cottage architecture; and doubtless helped to acclimate their works to the Amercan scene. Was there perhaps some relation between the increasing love of nature, in its wilder moods, and the growing possibility of comfort in the midst of nature, in houses whose central heating apparatus kept water from freezing in the pitcher overnight, and whose indoor toilets eased some of the strain of outdoor living, when the day was over? At all events, a love for the rough, the primitive, the elemental, came into architecture during Burroughs' heyday; so that the new houses looked more shaggy and earthbound than, say, a seventeenth century dwelling in Dedham or Hingham. Burroughs' work helped carry into architecture, as an integral part of domestic form, those indigenous aspects that hung merely as trophies on the walls of Jefferson's Monticello. In many ways the present essay outlines the kind of house, in material and in mood, that Frank Lloyd Wright was to carry to perfection during the next generation.

ANDREW JACKSON DOWNING (1815–1852) was a horticulturist before he practiced architecture, like Joseph Paxton, his greater British contemporary. While the Hudson River school was establishing the first truly American tradition of landscape painting, Downing, who was born at Newburgh on the West bank of the Hudson, was performing the same function in landscape gardening and in architecture. Though his style, like that of the painters, was derivative from the naturalistic gardeners of the eighteenth century in Britain, something more authentically native, more deeply individualized, would almost surely have come out of it, as it did in the case of his one-time pupil, Olmstėd. In 1841 Downing published his first book, *The Theory and Practise of Landscape Gardening;* and the success of this work was so decisive that he turned out a series of similar books on architecture, while in 1846 he became editor of The Horticulturist, then published at Albany, though his own home was at Newburgh. Commissions flowed into his office, and in 1851 he was selected to lay out the grounds of the White House, the Capitol, and the Smithsonian Institution. The work performed by Downing, in encouraging appreciation of native varieties of plants and trees, and in getting his countrymen to humanize and enjoy the natural setting of their houses, paved the way for the more original work of Frederick Law Olmsted, and for the more truly indigenous architecture introduced by H. H. Richardson, W. R. Emerson, and their contemporaries in the eighteen-eighties. He gave people pride in the land, and a feeling for all the esthetic possibilities that nature offers even to the least trained and tutored. But for his early death, which took place the same year as Greenough's, his influence on modern form might have been invigorating, as he reached the confidence of maturity.

SIGFRIED GIEDION (1888-1968) was from the first one of the leading philosophers and critics of the modern movement that stems from Le Corbusier, though in his own thinking he went far beyond the limitations of its original expression. A citizen of Zurich, he had the stimulus of a distinguished group of modern architects, including Karl and Werner Moser; and he took an active part in the organization of the C.I.A.M. His most important work, however, dates from his lectures as Charles Eliot Norton Professor at Harvard. These lectures, which became the foundation for his distinguished book, *Space, Time and Architecture,* immediately put him in the first rank of architectural historians, as much for the daring of his hypotheses as for the sound scholarship that underlay his demonstrations. Though his later book, *Mechanization Takes Command,* is not confined to building, it throws many important sidelights on this field, and that part of it which is based on a firsthand study of American documents in technics makes it likewise a valuable contribution to the history of American culture. In both technics and architecture he demonstrated how much important material American scholars have either taken for granted or lacked the ability to uncover or the insight to interpret; as witness the present essay on Balloon Frame construction.

HORATIO GREENOUGH (1805–1852) though he spent half his life as an expatriate in Rome, was a character deep in "the American grain." While he was a student at Harvard, he made the design for the Bunker Hill Monument; but in 1825, before finishing his college course, he went forth to Florence. Though he had bold ideas as to subject matter and treatment—his Washington embarrassed his countrymen by showing a splendid torso, naked like that of a Roman Emperor—his ability as a sculptor was less remarkable than his independence and originality as a thinker. He called himself, in the title of the book he published in 1852, a Yankee Stone-Cutter; and with less education he might indeed have been a carver of figureheads in Salem or Portland. But he was above all the ingenious thinking Yankee, looking upon the world as if all things might perhaps start fresh again in his generation; and he was the first thinker anywhere, as far as I know, to interpret the meaning of biological and mechanical functions in terms of esthetics. No one had a better understanding than Greenough of what Claude Bragdon later called "the beautiful necessity." This artist's vigorous, uncompromising ideas, gaining in clarity by contrast with the immemorial past he confronted in

Sigfried Giedion. *Courtesy, Harvard University.*

Horatio Greenough

Henry-Russell Hitchcock. ***Courtesy, Smith College.***

Joseph Hudnut

Rome, deeply impressed Emerson; and had Greenough not died of a brain fever shortly after his return to America, he might have gone even further in his esthetic thinking. As it is, his esthetic doctrines built the ideological foundations of functionalism, and constitute with Tolstoy's *What is Art,* and Ruskin's passage On the Nature of the Gothic, one of the few masterpieces of esthetic criticism of the nineteenth century.

HENRY-RUSSELL HITCHCOCK (1903–) has been a notable pioneer both as critic and historian, beginning with the distinguished essays on modern architecture he first published in Hound and Horn. Born in Boston and graduated from Harvard in 1924, his early book on *Modern Architecture* made a valuable distinction between the "new pioneer" and the "new traditionalist" and did much to provide a sound outline for a history of the modern movement, a work mainly carried on during the next two decades by Pevsner and Giedion. As a pioneer work in interpreting the modern movement it still has more than historical importance. The essay on the International Style, though perhaps historically more significant, lacks the rounded quality of Hitchcock's book. Strangely enough, his biographical study of Richardson (1936) does better with Richardson's early years than with the more modern elements in his work: so it is not surprising that he has exploited his specific gift for historical scholarship by writing what may well turn out to be a classic work on Victorian architecture, some of which has already appeared in the Architectural Review. His first monograph on Frank Lloyd Wright was published in Paris in 1928. In 1942 he supplanted that essay, written on the narrow platform of the "new pioneers," with his comprehensive study, *In the Nature of Materials: 1887–1941: The Buildings of Frank Lloyd Wright.* This is outstanding work, done with breadth, sympathy, and exactitude. In 1945–1946 he was a Guggenheim Fellow. He has taught at Smith, Yale, Cambridge, and Harvard.

JOSEPH HUDNUT (1886–1968) was born in Michigan and was graduated from the Department of Engineering in the University of Michigan. His career alternated between architectural offices and teaching; and his teaching posts included a directorship of the School of Fine Arts in the University of Virginia, in 1923–1926, and a professorship of the History of Architecture at Columbia University. As Dean at Columbia University for a year, and later as Dean of the new Graduate School of Design at Harvard, he won a special distinction as being one of the first of the leaders trained in traditional architecture to recognize the importance and value of the modern movement; likewise the necessity, which followed from this, to revamp the architectural school's curriculum and to restaff it with men trained in the contemporary idiom. He brought Walter Gropius to Harvard as senior professor, welcomed Marcel Breuer and Martin Wagner, and campaigned valiantly on behalf of a modern design for the National Gallery of Art Competition in Washington. As an active administrator Dean Hudnut smoothed the way of modern architecture in American architectural schools, where it had never penetrated even during the heyday in Chicago; but he became increasingly concerned, as a historian and a humanist, for enduring traditional values which, instead of being translated into modern forms, have sometimes been totally forgotten by the younger architects, for whom the past is merely "a bucket of ashes." With a witty and felicitous pen, he opposed both pious dogmatism and humorless rigidity, as exhibited by one wing of modern architecture. The upshot of his efforts, so far from undermining the modern movement, should be to provide it with a firm basis of historical understanding and self-respect.

JAMES JACKSON JARVES (1818–1888) might be called the American Ruskin, but of course a Ruskin manqué. But if his writings lack Ruskin's magnificent strokes of genius they also happily lack his petulant caprices and foolish dogmatisms. Goaded as a youth by illness and impaired eyesight, Jarves travelled widely, in California, Mexico, Central America, and the Hawaiian Islands; and founded the first weekly newspaper in the Islands. Returning home in 1848, he went on to Europe where, with a keen eye for esthetic excellence and a pre-Raphaelite bias, he gathered the admirable collection that now is housed in Yale University. Like his essays on art and architecture, Jarves's collection was long stupidly undervalued, though it stands incomparably higher, considering the circumstances that attended its assemblage, than the blundering plunder of the great financiers who, very belatedly, followed him. His eclectic taste acted perhaps as a brake upon his originality; but though no one need read *Art Hints* or *The Art Idea*, unless he is intensely interested in the culture of the period, there is much that is challenging in Jarves's books, and the very format in which they were printed, their red bindings with paper labels, set them apart. Not the least proof of his capacity as a pioneer is the fact that he published *A Glimpse of the Art of Japan* in 1876—one of the first of a series of books, including Fennollosa's outstanding work, that acclimated Japanese forms to the modern world. Along with the fact that an authentic Japanese house was built in Rhode Island in the eighties by a returned missionary—though presently it burned down—Jarves's work helps explain this influence in American architecture. His observations on architecture speak for themselves; but their date should be underscored. He stands midway between Greenough and Montgomery Schuyler. If he sometimes rouses a hope for more originality than he shows, we should nevertheless be grateful for his range and his balance. Mrs. Edith Wharton supposedly used Jarves in her picture of a pre-Raphaelite rebel of the fifties in False Dawn. He was decorated in Hawaii with the order of Kamehemeha I. Our own republic did not, at any point, treat him so handsomely.

PHILIP JOHNSON (1906–) was born in Cleveland, Ohio, came into architecture first as a talented amateur, interested in the arts, and then as a Harvard-trained architect in his own right. In the first capacity he helped organize the first show of

James Jackson Jarves

Philip Johnson. *Photograph by Homer Page.*

Benton Mackaye. *Photograph by Kenneth S. Warren.*

Lewis Mumford. *Courtesy, National Film Board, Canada.*

Modern Architecture in America, and has been partly responsible for the interest the Modern Museum has shown in this department ever since. Originally Johnson did much to popularize the conceptions of the International Style, particularly the austerities and rigidities of Mies van der Rohe, as in his once-famous guest house in Connecticut, a transparent shell. But after his monograph on van der Rohe (1949) and his collaboration on the Seagram Building in New York, he turned to a freer if no less frigid esthetic expression, as in his work at New York City's Lincoln Center and elsewhere. His early association with Henry Russell Hitchcock, and his later directorship of the Department of Architecture of the Museum of Modern Art from 1949 to 1954, did much to establish the fashionable appreciation of modern architectural forms out of which his own work has grown.

BENTON MACKAYE (1879–), though born in New York City, a son of the redoubtable Steele MacKaye, the actor, is the most veritable of New England Yankees; and his true life began with his schooldays at Shirley Center, Massachusetts, a classic small specimen of the old New England Village, duly presented in the film called *The City*. Graduating from Harvard College in 1901, influenced by the great geologist Nathaniel Southgate Shaler, MacKaye became a forester and ranged over the whole country in his professional pursuits. As one of Gifford Pinchot's men, he helped draft a bill for the conservation of the Natural Resources of Alaska, and in 1917 planned a forest community for war veterans for Louis Post, in the Department of Labor. MacKaye published his now famous proposal for the Appalachian Trail in the Journal of the American Institute of Architects in 1921: a Eutopian idea which in less than a generation has become a solid reality, with marked trails, and at many points overnight cabins, from Maine to Georgia. As a charter member of the Regional Planning Association of America, MacKaye's thought helped to shape that of the group of architects and planners who sought to deal, not with houses alone, but with the whole environment, as re-shaped by man. He was mainly responsible for the Regional Planning number of the Survey Graphic (May 1925). MacKaye's classic but long-neglected study of regional planning, *The New Exploration* (1928) was republished in paperback (1962) by the University of Illinois Press. His work links our generation to the great pioneers of humanistic ecology and conservation, Powell, Marsh, and Thoreau.

LEWIS MUMFORD (1895–), in his capacity as architectural critic, may be looked upon as one of the few continuators of Montgomery Schuyler; and there is even a slight thread of connection in the fact that Herbert Croly, who had begun his literary life as an editor of Schuyler's paper, the Architectural Record, was one of the editors who as early as 1921 opened the pages of his magazine, The New Republic, to Mumford's writings upon modern architecture. Encouraged by Charles Harris Whitaker, the Editor of the Journal of the A.I.A., his first essays on architecture appeared in that journal in 1920. In 1923 he offered perhaps the first course on the history of American architecture at the New School for Social Research; and when no one came, he turned his course into a book, *Sticks and Stones* (1924). Lacking Schuyler's thorough grounding in architectural history and construction, Mumford's early work was mainly a social and esthetic interpretation. Though his historical studies have been incidental, his pioneering work in *The Brown Decades,* reinterpreting Olmsted and Roebling, re-establishing Richardson, pointing out the significance of Gill and Maybeck and the Chicago school, opened the way for more specialized scholarship. From 1931 to 1962 he contributed regular architectural criticism to *The New Yorker*; and his major articles have appeared in two paperbacks, *From the Ground Up* (1956) and *The Highway and the City* (1963). Still other studies of buildings and cities were gathered together in *The South in Architecture* (1941), *City Development* (1945), and *The Urban Prospect* (1968). But Mumford's most influential contributions in this field are *The Culture of Cities* (1938) and *The City in History* (1961), works that gave him a worldwide reputation. Though not an architect, Mumford is an honorary member of the leading architectural and city-planning institutes of the English-speaking countries; and among his many honors received the Royal Gold Medal from the R.I.B.A.

MATTHEW NOWICKI (1910–1950) was born in Chita, near the Siberian border of China, the son of a father who was active in politics as a leader in the Agrarian Party. After being graduated from the architectural school of the Warsaw Polytechnic his genius swiftly blossomed, and he won a series of prizes in competitions, which gave him the opportunity to travel widely, to France, and Italy, to Greece and Egypt and to Brazil, before the German assault in 1939 found him serving as an artillery lieutenant on the front. During the occupation of Warsaw, he continued his study and teaching in architectural and townplanning, and after participating in the ill-fated insurrection, he became in 1945, as soon as Warsaw was liberated, the chief of the planners who visualized and planned the future reconstruction of Warsaw. Given the opportunity to visit the United States in 1947, he toured the country as a member of the United Nations' site finding committee. After that, he served as a consultant on the Board of Design Consultants and took part, though not without many misgivings, in the design of the resultant structures. Appointed senior professor of Architecture at the reorganized School of Design at North Carolina State College in Raleigh, his outstanding capacities as a teacher and leader were not lost on his students. Because of his great human gifts, he had no difficulty in establishing good relations with the local community, and during his second year there, in association with the Raleigh architect, William Henley Deitrick, he got the opportunity to design a succession of buildings, beginning with the grandstand for the State Fair—with the State Library and Museum as the next job in prospect. At this juncture, working in collaboration with Albert Mayer on the townplanning of the new capital of the East Punjab, he went to India during the summer of

Matthew Nowicki

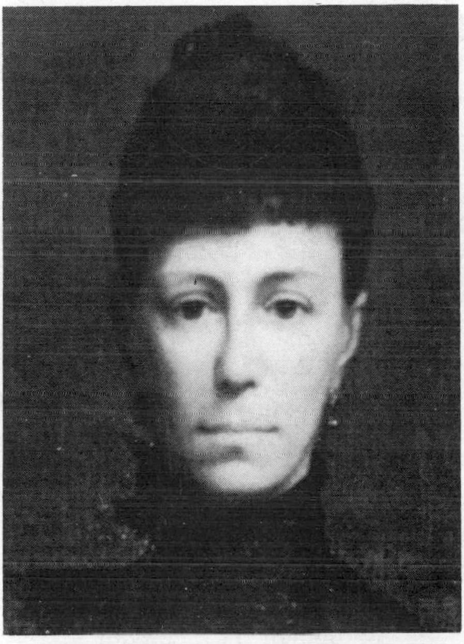

Mariana Griswold van Rensselaer

John Wellborn Root

Montgomery Schuyler

1950. He met his death in an airplane accident on his way home from Cairo late that August. That Indian trip, which turned out so tragic, might well have opened a further phase in his own architectural development, for his quick intuitions absorbed on a rapid trip through the country those elements of richness and heightened feeling that had been left out of the discipline of the modern architect; and his marvellous sketches for the Capitol are ripe with that unfulfilled promise. Wholly dedicated to his art, he breathed it and lived it and thought about it almost every hour of his life. Fortunately, he left behind a few manuscripts of his recent lectures and talks, essays that in some small measure reveal the quality of his thought. A monograph on his work will presently be announced.

MARIANA GRISWOLD VAN RENSSELAER [Mrs. Schuyler van Rensselaer] (1851–1935) came of the same Dutch-English stock as Melville, Whitman, and Montgomery Schuyler, and like Schuyler she was a writer with a wider range than architecture; indeed, after the nineties, most of her writing consisted of stories and verses. As an advanced woman of her day, she appreciated the work of Henry Hobson Richardson, and her treatment of him is not merely the first fullfledged monograph on the work of an architect to be written in America, but an outstandingly good critical biography in its own right. She was too near Richardson in time, when she wrote the biography, to see his work in full perspective; hence her over-emphasis on the more conventional part of his career, and her failure to give sufficient attention to his departures—whose full significance could in fact only be interpreted later, in terms of what they led to. Her architectural criticisms appeared frequently in the Century Magazine; but after Richardson, she succumbed to the general drift toward eclecticism with the emphasis on McKim Mead and White's Renaissance; so her architectural criticism, though copious, did not do for the layman what Montgomery Schuyler was doing for the professional in interpreting and supporting the innovators. For all that, Mrs. Van Rensselaer was a pioneer whose work deserves inclusion in this broad panorama; and her fine essay on the architect and the client neatly complements that of John Root. It is remarkable that the second biography of an architect, that of Root, was also written by a woman: his sister-in-law, Harriet Monroe, known to a later generation as the editor of Poetry: A Magazine of Verse.

JOHN WELLBORN ROOT (1850–1891), born in Lumpkin, Georgia, settled in Chicago in the seventies, and learned his profession largely in the school of practice. He established a partnership in the eighties with Daniel Burnham, and from that time on, with a variety of jobs pouring into their busy office, he matured rapidly as a designer. As with Sullivan before 1890, his major work was done with fundamentally masonry forms, not as with Major Jenney or Holabird and Roche, with the new form of skyscraper construction. With an imagination almost as rich and exuberant as Sullivan's, his early buildings were sometimes effusive in their ornament and in archaic formal elements like gables and oriels; but with a sensible, self-confident business enterpriser as client, Root abandoned ornament and created a masterpiece of clean masonry and glass, the Monadnock Building, with its uniform brick front, its projecting bays, its subtly modeled base and "cornice" derived from—but not imitative of—historic Egyptian examples. Root had been designated as chief designer of the World's Fair of 1893 and had he lived to carry out the project, he and Sullivan might between them have averted that relapse into eclectic "good taste" which the Eastern architects, reacting against Richardson and over-enamored of the historic fleshpots of Paris and Rome, brought to Chicago. Again like Sullivan and Wright, Root's active mind played with the philosophical and social foundations of his art; but unfortunately his lucubrations on architecture are for the most part buried in a book that is itself generally inaccessible, the monograph his sister-in-law Harriet Monroe wrote on his life and work. A more self-conscious generation, building on the present readings, may republish more extensively Root's writings on his art.

MONTGOMERY SCHUYLER (1843–1914) was the first full-fledged critic of architecture in America, and for his soundness, if not his originality, he must still be counted the best. A newspaper man by profession, one of the group of young writers who gathered about Manton Marble on the New York World, he joined the New York Times in 1883 and retired from it only in 1907. Before he helped found the Architectural Record in 1891, he had made architecture, in particular American architecture, his own. His early criticisms were gathered together in his *American Architecture*, 1892; but apart from his monographs on a group of Chicago architects, the most significant of which is on Adler and Sullivan—first published in the Architectural Record and then bound together in a little pamphlet—his later essays have never been collected. Affected by Ruskin and Viollet-le-Duc, Schuyler preached a return to construction, as the source of a truly modern architecture. To a contemporary, reviewing *American Architecture* in the Architectural Record, Mr. Schuyler was "unfortunately troubled with a point of view, and, unfortunately again, this point of view is a moral one." The statement was accurate, but the implication was fatuous; for who can be a critic without a point of view, or a great critic without a profound moral sense? What Schuyler actually stood for is best stated in his own words to the National Association of Builders in 1891: "The real radical defect of modern architecture in general, if not of American architecture in particular, is the estrangement between architecture and building—between the poetry and the prose of the art of building, which can never be disjoined without injury to both." That was true in Montgomery Schuyler's time; and it still holds.

CLARENCE S. STEIN (1882–) was born in Rochester, New York, and studied at Columbia University and the Ecole des Beaux Arts in Paris, at first with the thought of becoming an interior decorator. Returning to New York in 1911, he in time became chief designer in the office of Bertram Grosvenor Goodhue. As a citizen, he grew interested in the housing problems of New York and after 1920 became active on the committee of Community Planning in the American Institute of Architects, in which group he succeeded John Irwin Bright, another social-minded architect of Philadelphia, as Chairman. Through his political skill and social insight, Stein became the natural leader of the new movement for the better housing of the lower income groups, and helped bring about the formation in 1923 of the New York State Housing and Regional Planning Commission, of which he became director. At the same time, in 1923, he launched the Regional Planning Association of America, and, with Henry Wright, was architect and planner for the City Housing Corporation, which began building Sunnyside Gardens in 1924 and Radburn, N. J., in 1928. He himself has told the story of these and later experiments in social architecture and planning in his recent *New Towns for America,* from which the present chapter is taken. Though large scale public housing proceeded during the thirties largely without calling upon his services, except for the Greenbelt towns, he served as consultant for Greenbelt and for Baldwin Hills Village, the two outstanding planning projects of the period. In 1951 he became chief consultant on planning for the Alcan's new town of Kittamac. His present position in America corresponds to that of Sir Raymond Unwin in England, an older contemporary whose work he carried further.

WILLIAM AIKEN STARRETT (1877–1932) was born on a Kansas farm. His father was a builder and his five brothers all became builders. Too late to participate in the first adventurous days of steel-frame construction in Chicago, he nevertheless devoted himself with zeal to his profession and in 1919 became Vice-President of a distinguished construction company, George A. Fuller and Company. His own professional work took him to Japan where he introduced steel framed earthquake resisting structures, and he lived just long enough to work on the plans for the tallest building produced in his time, the Empire State Building. Like another engineer of his period, D. B. Steinman, who wrote the classic history of the building of the Brooklyn Bridge, Colonel Starrett addressed himself to the history of the skyscraper, thus setting an example that should be more widely followed by industrial leaders, who would find the ancient annals and records of their industries far more exciting to explore than most of the trivial diversions that occupy their declining years. Though as historian Starrett does not stand on the level of a Giedion, it is good to have this bit of skyscraper history presented by an engineer who knew by experience and practice of what he spoke.

GUSTAV STICKLEY (1858–1942) was one of the handful of American designers who carried on in America the tradition of the Arts and Crafts movement that William Morris had founded in England. Born in Wisconsin, at twelve Stickley learned the stone mason's craft from his father and by the age of seventeen received a journeyman's wages. Later, he worked in a chair-factory belonging to an uncle, who was a follower of

Ruskin's, and four years later took over the factory. In 1884 he moved to Binghamton, New York, with the factory and sought deliberately to revive the traditions of handicraft. One of the first to appreciate and revive the Windsor chair, Stickley began in 1900 to produce furniture after his own design. In the handsomely designed pages of The Craftsman, he also continued the typographical traditions of that movement, particularly in the early numbers; and he gave expression to the social philosophy of Morris, Tolstoi, and Kropotkin, which formed the moral humus in which that fresh growth took place. As editor of The Craftsman he published critical articles on Art Nouveau and important articles on the work of the new leaders in house design and town planning, including Barry Parker, Unwin, Baillie, Scott, Voysey, and others. Louis Sullivan contributed to The Craftsman during the half generation when it flourished; and here the works of the Brothers Greene and Irving Gill were appreciatively reviewed. As leader of the Craftsman Movement, Stickley's most immediate success was with Craftsman-furniture; for it was he who acclimatized the "mission style," with its sturdy oak members, its unpartable mortise-and-tenon joints, its leather coverings: the first designs that put California esthetically on the modern map. Though the forms were overcrude and clumsy, with none of the finesse of Gimson's and Heal's contemporary work in England, some of this furniture still survives in college dormitories: a staggering proof of sound craftsmanship. Stickley's second feat was to direct middle class housing toward the bungalow, that early one-story predecessor of the "ranch house"; and again, though the form was often blatantly ugly, it led directly to more simple and rationalized construction of today—or would have had it not been for the impact between 1915 and 1935 of genteel revivalism.

LOUIS HENRI SULLIVAN (1856–1924) is one of the hardest figures to place in American architecture, though his distinction and his creativity are indisputable. A graduate of the Massachusetts Institute of Technology, he studied in the office of that powerful masculine mind, Frank Furness of Philadelphia, an architect of forthright if disordered originality, and at the Beaux Arts in Paris, before he settled in Chicago. There he came under the immediate influence of the brilliant group of technicians, esthetically undertrained but bold in experiment, who began to evolve the new skyscraper; and he had before him the robust example of the mature Richardson, whose work Sullivan not only admired but at times—in the Walker Warehouse—openly but unsuccessfully followed. Becoming a partner of Adler in 1883, at the age of twenty-four, Sullivan's rise as designer was perhaps too rapid and may account for the withering contempt in which he held his fellow workers, beginning with his own draftsmen. As an architect Sullivan's work grew to self-consciousness through his criticism; and as a castigator of the insincere, the basely imitative, the fraudulent, he was without peer, though when confronted with a great work like the Marshall Field building he could be generous in appreciation. Sullivan's *Kindergarten Chats,* which had a long underground reputation

Clarence S. Stein

Louis Henri Sullivan

Henry David Thoreau

Calvert Vaux

before being republished, in 1935 and in 1944, show him at his best and his worst: the Wagnerian prose is often perfervid and bombastic; his attitude toward his interlocutor, a student, is unpleasantly superior and over-authoritative; nuggets of pure gold in criticism and in interpretation are often buried in rhetorical mud. His *Autobiography of an Idea* holds perhaps the best of his writings; and the student who seeks to come close to him would do well to begin with this work.

HENRY DAVID THOREAU (1807–1862) grows in stature and significance with the years: like fern in springtime, tightly curled during his short life, the large fronds have now unfolded and show the true dimensions of his thought. His contemporaries foolishly patronized him or ignored him for the very things that now give him his great importance. Even before our civilization had let mechanism ride over us and over-ride us, Thoreau knew the value of personal integrity and the need for stripping life close to the bone, so that our true values and needs should not be encumbered by fictitious ones. When he turned to architecture proper, he was under the spell of current taste, as witness the summer house he and Alcott built in Emerson's absence from his home; and he openly thought the lean Cape Cod houses, which now seem so fitly regional, a little unsatisfactory. But from his central philosophy, this New England stoic, this classically educated Natty Bumpo, projected the essential spirit of the new building, with its emphasis on the natural, the direct, and the simple: indeed, he even described the kind of living in one large unspecialized room, uniting all household activities, that has become—without any conscious debt or discipleship—the mark of many modern homes. Long before the science of ecology had taken form, Thoreau was a practicing ecologist; and in his explorations of the primeval American environment he included men, as well as trees and birds and animals, as objects of investigation, and looked with equal interest on the wind-driven sand and beach grass of Cape Cod and the tangled forests of Maine. In all, he was a surveyor and assayer of the natural landscape, sampling it in all its variety, discerning its varied possibilities at different seasons of the year, measuring its potential rewards for the human spirit. Though an outstanding individualist, bristling with a hedgehog's sense of privacy, Thoreau likewise had the old New England sense of civic responsibility: witness his refusal to pay taxes to an immoral government, that sponsored slavery and the imperialist land-stealing of the Mexican war: witness his sturdy abolitionism, his participation in the underground railroad, his defense of John Brown; and not least, his sense that the citizen of the American commonwealth was not less entitled to access to primeval nature, by right of common ownership, than the old kings of England with their vast hunting domains. Indeed, it was Thoreau himself who first conceived the need for the public reservation of great areas of the wilderness as natural parks; and a large part of the practical work of a later generation, under people like Major John Wesley Powell and Frederick Law Olmsted, was but a carrying out of his ideas into action. Thoreau's love for the primeval environment has helped turn the tide against the ruthless spoliation of our natural background. If Walden Pond is now hopelessly overcrowded in summer, there are other primitive areas that will be better reclaimed because of Thoreau's reflections there.

CALVERT VAUX (1824–1895) has hardly yet received a full measure of appreciation for his contributions to American architecture: indeed the *Dictionary of American Biography* makes no mention of Vaux's architecture except in reference to Olmsted. But as an architect he created such a sound and even experimental structure as the original unit of the Metropolitan Museum of Art, and such a handsome example of straightforward stone construction, antedating Richardson's free style as the Museum of Natural History, showing only traces of Adam's "baronial Gothic." As such, he deserves our respect, and the contribution he made to Olmsted's self-conscious development in the days of their partnership should not be under-rated. Born in London, educated at the Tailor's School, and articled as pupil in the office of L. H. Cottingham, he was chosen by Andrew Jackson Downing on a visit in 1850 to assist him in his work at Newburgh and did so until Downing's death. Like Latrobe, Vaux had a fresh sense of the possibilities a new country offers to new forms, and like a later English designer, Ernest Wilby (once the chief designer for Albert Kahn, Inc.), he made his own fresh contribution.

CHARLES HARRIS WHITAKER (1872–1938), born in Rhode Island, was the son of a New England machinist and hydraulic engineer; and as a lad used to go along with his father when he installed machinery in mills throughout the region. Beginning as a student of the piano, he went to Berlin a little later than Alfred Stieglitz, only to become, not a musician, but a crack billiard player. His subsequent education, desultory but varied, was partly spent in an architect's office. It culiminated in his becoming a writer of great charm and individuality whose contributions to The Freeman in the early nineteen-twenties were distinguished: at the same time, he became in 1913 editor of the Journal of the American Institute of Architects and remained so until 1928. Between 1915 and 1925 he made the Journal the organ of the new social tradition in architecture, picking up the thread here at the moment that The Craftsman, going out of existence, dropped it. Whitaker was one of the few men of his generation in the East who understood the importance of Louis Sullivan; though his own taste was toward the traditional and rural values of his boyhood. His approach to architecture was colored by an appreciation of the part played by economic decisions and by a distrust of the commercial and the venal motives that had ruined so many promising careers; and for long he pinned his faith for improvement upon the introduction of the Single Tax. "The future of this or of any other country," he wrote in the Journal in 1913, "is in truth more dependent upon 'country planning' than upon city planning." In the Journal of the A.I.A. he brought together the new leaders of social architecture, Ackerman, Bigger, Bright, Stein, and Wright. Besides editing the definitive

Monograph on B. G. Goodhue, he published *From Rameses to Rockefeller* in 1935; a popular and personal interpretation of the history of architecture. But some of his best writing unfortunately remains in manuscript that is still unpublished.

FRANK LLOYD WRIGHT (1869–1959) was outstanding as the most original and creative architect of the last century. For sheer fertility and abundance of fresh designs, he was without rival, perhaps, among architects of any time or place. The very munificence of his powers in a time of transition like the present has kept some of his best work from having the stability and lastingness that a less demonstrative genius, coming in a more firmly knitted society at a less destructive epoch in history, might have produced. After almost completing his course at The School of Engineering at the University of Wisconsin in 1887 he went to Chicago and in remarkably short order became Adler and Sullivan's chief designer. In 1892 he opened his own office. In the early period of his professional life, Wright's own ample powers were enhanced by the confidence and daring of his contemporaries in the Chicago school; but in the middle period that followed, from 1900 to 1930, he was almost the only architect in America sufficiently strong in principle and conviction to stand firm against the spirit of timid eclecticism, pious archaicism, and snivelling compromise. But because of the hostility to original works of modern art shown by business leaders during this period, some of Wright's most important work suffered by neglect or destruction: witness Midway Gardens, in Chicago. Whether in times of neglect or in times of appreciation, Frank Lloyd Wright constituted an army of one: a David capable of conquering, not only the Goliath of modern industrialism, but the whole army of embattled Philistines that stand behind that over-armored giant. Certainly, in none of the arts has America produced a figure of more indisputable originality than Wright, or more deeply colored by his native soil and the folkways of the genial, cornfed, land-enveloped, sky-open Middle West, the land that nourished his literary contemporaries, Carl Sandburg, Theodore Dreiser, Sherwood Anderson, Edgar Lee Masters, and one greater than they, Abraham Lincoln himself, before them. More consciously if not more willingly than his contemporaries in Chicago, he embraced the machine; at the same time, since his main work lay in the design of dwelling houses, not skyscrapers, he kept non-commercial values more constantly in view, and sought to weave into a unified fabric the mechanical, the regional, and the human. Contrary to popular superstition, he worked in a relatively sympathetic environment, at least as concerns his clients, and had, till his departure to Tokyo, an abundance of commissions: so it is absurd to suggest that his work did not gain recognition here till the German monograph on his work appeared in 1910. The true interpretation, I think, is that his work, which flourished in America despite his convention-flouting forms and methods, had from the beginning a universal appeal: all the more because the spiritual influence of the Orient, particularly Japan, played upon his imagination. Wright's writings, though less copious and less brilliant than his architecture, show a high degree of self-consciousness; and his series of essays in the Architectural Record, "On the Nature of Materials," perhaps best give the measure of his talents and the underlying motive of his work. His lectures on the Machine marked his own bold departure from the retrospective note of the current Arts and Crafts movement of the eighteen-nineties. Like old Hokusai, some of Wright's most original and daring work was done after reaching three-score and ten: a period of abundant opportunity that has proved a veritable second youth. Rejected by both traditionalists and "International Stylists" in the nineteen-twenties as an "old-timer," Wright upset that judgment by proving the constructive pioneer whose technical audacity, in the Johnson Wax Factory and whose esthetic audacity in "Falling Water," make much of the work of the so-called International Stylists seem costive and constrained. Wright's later projects, culminating in the Guggenheim Museum in New York, brought his career to a dazzling and breath-taking close.

HENRY WRIGHT (1878–1936) was born in the East and studied architecture at the University of Pennsylvania, but settled down as a landscape architect in St. Louis and for a time worked in the office of Harland Bartholomew. His skill as a site planner was developed in work on subdivisions, by preference on difficult and almost unusable sites such as Brentwood and Forest Ridge, near Forest Park in St. Louis. In 1918 he joined the U. S. Shipping Board as a planner, working under Mr. Robert D. Kohn, and in 1923, he settled in New York to take part in the practical work of the City Housing Corporation and the intellectual activities of the Regional Planning Association of America. In addition to his major influence in the planning of Sunnyside Gardens and Radburn, he wrote extensive articles on the subject of planning, culminating in his book on *Re-Housing Urban America*. Like Stein, Ackerman, and Bigger, with whom he served in the middle twenties on the Committee on Community Planning of the American Institute of Architects, he was a severe critic of American zoning policies with its segregated residential districts, and their social and esthetic monotony; and his conception of planning was always three-dimensional. Sojourning in Germany in 1932, he came abreast of modern architectural design, as he found it in Berlin, Frankfort-am-Main and Zurich, and when he started a summer school of his own at his farm in Mt. Olive, New Jersey, he drew around him some of the best of the young architects and planners, working in the new idiom. His most consummate work as planner was perhaps his site planning of Chatham Village, in Pittsburgh, the older part with Stein, the latter part alone. In 1933 he founded, with Albert Mayer and Lewis Mumford, the Housing Study Guild, which did much to help train the new generation of planners; and the same year he served as housing consultant for the Public Works Administration. In 1935 he became the planner of the aborted greenbelt town, Greenbrook, and was still working on the plan when he died in 1936. Not the least important task performed by Wright was as educator, drawing people from various university departments into

Frank Lloyd Wright

Henry Wright

cooperative relations for the better service of the art of planning; and the promise of his work during his final years as professor at Columbia University only made more acute the loss through his too early death. Though Wright's creativeness lay in the realm of ideas more than of formal design, his fertile mind and his firm grasp of practical detail made him the outstanding American planner of his generation. For evidence see his *Re-Housing Urban America* (1935) and Clarence S. Stein's *New Towns for America* (1951). Nor must one overlook the very real contribution he made in the realm of regional planning, as director of planning for the Housing and Regional Planning Commission of the State of New York, which culminated in his final report in 1926 on a Plan for the State of New York: a work of outstanding importance. The failure to mention it in the later comprehensive conspectus of regional planning published by the National Resources Board was one of those curious Freudian errors that future historians of the movement have an obligation to rectify.

JOSEPH WARREN YOST (1842?–1923) born near Clarington, Ohio, was called from obscurity by the discovery of his article on modern constructional forms, nestling next to one by Dankmar Adler, better known, in the *Proceedings* of the American Institute of Architects. To Arthur Holden belongs the credit for finding this article and recognizing its worth, even as thanks for recognizing the importance of Adler's present contribution must be given to Frank Lloyd Wright. About Joseph Yost himself there are few surviving accounts. Reared on a farm, he attended Harlem College in 1864, and Mt. Union College from 1866 to 1868; then he studied mechanics, civil engineering, and architecture, finally beginning practice as an architect in 1870 in Bellaire, Ohio. His early work included Court Houses, High Schools, and Children's Homes, all presumably technically simple structures. In 1882 he moved his office to Columbus, Ohio, and thus became one of that interesting galaxy of provincial worthies, men of talent, character, and potentially greater distinction, about whom Mr. James Thurber has so lovingly written in The New Yorker. Perhaps Yost's most delicate if not most important task was the enlargement of the Capitol at Columbus—itself surely the finest building of its kind before the Nebraska State Capitol. In 1891 Yost entered into a brief partnership, Yost and Packard; and in 1900 moved to New York to form the firm of D'Oench and Yost. It is a source of wonder that a man of such a limited background should at such an early date have made this excellent analysis of the fundamental problems of modern design.

Credits

"Form and Function" by Horatio Greenough from *A Memorial of Horatio Greenough* by Henry T. Tuckerman, published by G. P. PUTNAM'S SONS.

"Towards the Organic" by Louis Henri Sullivan from *Kindergarten Chats* by Louis Henri Sullivan. Latest revised edition, WITTENBORN SCHULTZ, INC., 1947.

"Frederick Law Olmsted's Contribution" by Lewis Mumford from *The Brown Decades,* copyright 1931, by Lewis Mumford. Reprinted by permission of HARCOURT, BRACE AND COMPANY, INC.

"The Regionalism of Richardson" by Lewis Mumford from *The South in Architecture,* copyright 1941, by Lewis Mumford. Reprinted by permission of HARCOURT, BRACE AND COMPANY, INC.

"Nature as Architect" by Frank Lloyd Wright from *Frank Lloyd Wright on Architecture* edited by Frederick L. Gutheim, copyright 1941 by DUELL, SLOAN AND PEARCE, INC. Reprinted by permission of the publishers.

"Environment as a Natural Resource" by Benton Mac Kaye from *The New Exploration,* copyright 1928, by Benton Mac Kaye. Reprinted by permission of the author.

"The Art and Craft of the Machine" by Frank Lloyd Wright from *Modern Architecture,* copyright 1931, by Frank Lloyd Wright. Reprinted by permission of PRINCETON UNIVERSITY PRESS and the author.

"The Balloon Frame and Industrialization" by Sigfried Giedion from *Space, Time and Architecture—The Growth of a New Tradition* by Sigfried Giedion, copyright 1949, by HARVARD UNIVERSITY PRESS. Reprinted by permission of the publishers.

"The First Skyscraper" by Colonel W. A. Starrett from *Skyscrapers and the Men Who Built Them* by Colonel W. A. Starrett, copyright 1928 by CHARLES SCRIBNER'S SONS. Reprinted by permission of the publishers.

"The Post-Modern House" by Joseph Hudnut from *Architecture and the Spirit of Man* by Joseph Hudnut, copyright 1949 by HARVARD UNIVERSITY PRESS. Reprinted by permission of the publishers.

"New Towns for New Purposes" by Clarence S. Stein, from *New Towns for America* by Clarence S. Stein. Reprinted by permission of the author, THE UNIVERSITY PRESS OF LIVERPOOL, Liverpool, England, and Public Administration Service, Western Hemisphere Agent for The University Press of Liverpool.

"Towards a New Physical World" by Catherine Bauer, from *Modern Housing*, copyright 1934, by Catherine Bauer. Reprinted by permission of HOUGHTON MIFFLIN COMPANY.

"The Basis of Universalism" by Lewis Mumford. From *The South in Architecture*, copyright 1941, by Lewis Mumford. Reprinted by permission of HARCOURT BRACE AND COMPANY, INC.

"The International Style" by Henry-Russell Hitchcock, Jr., and Philip Johnson. From *The International Style: Architecture Since 1922* by Henry-Russell Hitchcock, Jr., and Philip Johnson, 1932. Reprinted by permission of THE MUSEUM OF MODERN ART, New York.

"The Example of Frank Lloyd Wright" by Walter Curt Behrendt. From *Modern Building, Its Nature, Problems and Forms* by Walter Curt Behrendt, copyright, 1937, by HARCOURT BRACE AND COMPANY, INC. Reprinted by permission of the publishers.

"Composition in Modern Architecture" by Matthew Nowicki. Reprinted by permission of THE MAGAZINE OF ART.

"Function and Form" by Matthew Nowicki (formerly titled "Origins and Trends in Modern Architecture"). Reprinted by permission of THE MAGAZINE OF ART and THE NORTH CAROLINA STATE SCHOOL OF DESIGN STUDENT PUBLICATIONS.

Index

A

A (Continued)

A (Continued)

B

B (Continued)

C

C (Continued)

C (Continued)

C (Continued)

D

E

F

F (Continued)

G

G (Continued)

H

H (Continued)

H (Continued)

I

J

K

L

L (Continued)

M

M (Continued)

N

N (Continued)

O

O (Continued)

P

P (Continued)

R

R (Continued)

S

S (Continued)

S (Continued)

S (Continued)

T

U

U (Continued)

V

W

W (Continued)

Y

Z

A CATALOGUE OF SELECTED DOVER BOOKS IN ALL FIELDS OF INTEREST

THE ART DECO STYLE, ed. by Theodore Menten. Furniture, jewelry, metalwork, ceramics, fabrics, lighting fixtures, interior decors, exteriors, graphics from pure French sources. Best sampling around. Over 400 photographs. 183pp. 8³/₈ x 11¼. 22824-X Pa. $4.00

THE GENTLEMAN AND CABINET MAKER'S DIRECTOR, Thomas Chippendale. Full reprint, 1762 style book, most influential of all time; chairs, tables, sofas, mirrors, cabinets, etc. 200 plates, plus 24 photographs of surviving pieces. 249pp. 9⁷/₈ x 12¾. 21601-2 Pa. $6.00

PINE FURNITURE OF EARLY NEW ENGLAND, Russell H. Kettell. Basic book. Thorough historical text, plus 200 illustrations of boxes, highboys, candlesticks, desks, etc. 477pp. 7⁷/₈ x 10¾. 20145-7 Clothbd. $12.50

ORIENTAL RUGS, ANTIQUE AND MODERN, Walter A. Hawley. Persia, Turkey, Caucasus, Central Asia, China, other traditions. Best general survey of all aspects: styles and periods, manufacture, uses, symbols and their interpretation, and identification. 96 illustrations, 11 in color. 320pp. 6¹/₈ x 9¼. 22366-3 Pa. $5.00

DECORATIVE ANTIQUE IRONWORK, Henry R. d'Allemagne. Photographs of 4500 iron artifacts from world's finest collection, Rouen. Hinges, locks, candelabra, weapons, lighting devices, clocks, tools, from Roman times to mid-19th century. Nothing else comparable to it. 420pp. 9 x 12. 22082-6 Pa. $8.50

THE COMPLETE BOOK OF DOLL MAKING AND COLLECTING, Catherine Christopher. Instructions, patterns for dozens of dolls, from rag doll on up to elaborate, historically accurate figures. Mould faces, sew clothing, make doll houses, etc. Also collecting information. Many illustrations. 288pp. 6 x 9. 22066-4 Pa. $3.00

ANTIQUE PAPER DOLLS: 1915-1920, edited by Arnold Arnold. 7 antique cut-out dolls and 24 costumes from 1915-1920, selected by Arnold Arnold from his collection of rare children's books and entertainments, all in full color. 32pp. 9¼ x 12¼. 23176-3 Pa. $2.00

ANTIQUE PAPER DOLLS: THE EDWARDIAN ERA, Epinal. Full-color reproductions of two historic series of paper dolls that show clothing styles in 1908 and at the beginning of the First World War. 8 two-sided, stand-up dolls and 32 complete, two-sided costumes. Full instructions for assembling included. 32pp. 9¼ x 12¼. 23175-5 Pa. $2.00

A HISTORY OF COSTUME, Carl Köhler, Emma von Sichardt. Egypt, Babylon, Greece up through 19th century Europe; based on surviving pieces, art works, etc. Full text and 595 illustrations, including many clear, measured patterns for reproducing historic costume. Practical. 464pp. 21030-8 Pa. $4.00

EARLY AMERICAN LOCOMOTIVES, John H. White, Jr. Finest locomotive engravings from late 19th century: historical (1804-1874), main-line (after 1870), special, foreign, etc. 147 plates. 200pp. 11³/₈ x 8¼. 22772-3 Pa. $3.50

VISUAL ILLUSIONS: THEIR CAUSES, CHARACTERISTICS, AND APPLICATIONS, Matthew Luckiesh. Thorough description and discussion of optical illusion, geometric and perspective, particularly; size and shape distortions, illusions of color, of motion; natural illusions; use of illusion in art and magic, industry, etc. Most useful today with op art, also for classical art. Scores of effects illustrated. Introduction by William H. Ittleson. 100 illustrations. xxi + 252pp.
21530-X Paperbound $2.50

A HANDBOOK OF ANATOMY FOR ART STUDENTS, Arthur Thomson. Thorough, virtually exhaustive coverage of skeletal structure, musculature, etc. Full text, supplemented by anatomical diagrams and drawings and by photographs of undraped figures. Unique in its comparison of male and female forms, pointing out differences of contour, texture, form. 211 figures, 40 drawings, 86 photographs. xx + 459pp. 5⅜ x 8⅜. 21163-0 Paperbound $5.00

150 MASTERPIECES OF DRAWING, Selected by Anthony Toney. Full page reproductions of drawings from the early 16th to the end of the 18th century, all beautifully reproduced: Rembrandt, Michelangelo, Dürer, Fragonard, Urs, Graf, Wouwerman, many others. First-rate browsing book, model book for artists. xviii + 150pp. 8⅜ x 11¼. 21032-4 Paperbound $4.00

THE LATER WORK OF AUBREY BEARDSLEY, Aubrey Beardsley. Exotic, erotic, ironic masterpieces in full maturity: Comedy Ballet, Venus and Tannhauser, Pierrot, Lysistrata, Rape of the Lock, Savoy material, Ali Baba, Volpone, etc. This material revolutionized the art world, and is still powerful, fresh, brilliant. With *The Early Work*, all Beardsley's finest work. 174 plates, 2 in color. xiv + 176pp. 8⅛ x 11.
21817-1 Paperbound $4.00

DRAWINGS OF REMBRANDT, Rembrandt van Rijn. Complete reproduction of fabulously rare edition by Lippmann and Hofstede de Groot, completely reedited, updated, improved by Prof. Seymour Slive, Fogg Museum. Portraits, Biblical sketches, landscapes, Oriental types, nudes, episodes from classical mythology All Rembrandt's fertile genius. Also selection of drawings by his pupils and followers. "Stunning volumes," *Saturday Review*. 550 illustrations. lxxviii + 552pp. 9⅛ x 12¼. 21485-0, 21486-9 Two volumes, Paperbound $12.00

THE DISASTERS OF WAR, Francisco Goya. One of the masterpieces of Western civilization—83 etchings that record Goya's shattering, bitter reaction to the Napoleonic war that swept through Spain after the insurrection of 1808 and to war in general. Reprint of the first edition, with three additional plates from Boston's Museum of Fine Arts. All plates facsimile size. Introduction by Philip Hofer, Fogg Museum. v + 97pp. 9⅜ x 8¼. 21872-4 Paperbound $3.00

GRAPHIC WORKS OF ODILON REDON. Largest collection of Redon's graphic works ever assembled: 172 lithographs, 28 etchings and engravings, 9 drawings. These include some of his most famous works. All the plates from *Odilon Redon: oeuvre graphique complet*, plus additional plates. New introduction and caption translations by Alfred Werner. 209 illustrations. xxvii + 209pp. 9⅛ x 12¼.
21966-8 Paperbound $6.00

HOW TO SOLVE CHESS PROBLEMS, Kenneth S. Howard. Practical suggestions on problem solving for very beginners. 58 two-move problems, 46 3-movers, 8 4-movers for practice, plus hints. 171pp. 20748-X Pa. $2.00

A GUIDE TO FAIRY CHESS, Anthony Dickins. 3-D chess, 4-D chess, chess on a cylindrical board, reflecting pieces that bounce off edges, cooperative chess, retrograde chess, maximummers, much more. Most based on work of great Dawson. Full handbook, 100 problems. 66pp. 7⅞ x 10¾. 22687-5 Pa. $2.00

WIN AT BACKGAMMON, Millard Hopper. Best opening moves, running game, blocking game, back game, tables of odds, etc. Hopper makes the game clear enough for anyone to play, and win. 43 diagrams. 111pp. 22894-0 Pa. $1.50

BIDDING A BRIDGE HAND, Terence Reese. Master player "thinks out loud" the binding of 75 hands that defy point count systems. Organized by bidding problem—no-fit situations, overbidding, underbidding, cueing your defense, etc. 254pp. EBE 22830-4 Pa. $3.00

THE PRECISION BIDDING SYSTEM IN BRIDGE, C.C. Wei, edited by Alan Truscott. Inventor of precision bidding presents average hands and hands from actual play, including games from 1969 Bermuda Bowl where system emerged. 114 exercises. 116pp. 21171-1 Pa. $1.75

LEARN MAGIC, Henry Hay. 20 simple, easy-to-follow lessons on magic for the new magician: illusions, card tricks, silks, sleights of hand, coin manipulations, escapes, and more —all with a minimum amount of equipment. Final chapter explains the great stage illusions. 92 illustrations. 285pp. 21238-6 Pa. $2.95

THE NEW MAGICIAN'S MANUAL, Walter B. Gibson. Step-by-step instructions and clear illustrations guide the novice in mastering 36 tricks; much equipment supplied on 16 pages of cut-out materials. 36 additional tricks. 64 illustrations. 159pp. 6⅝ x 10. 23113-5 Pa. $3.00

PROFESSIONAL MAGIC FOR AMATEURS, Walter B. Gibson. 50 easy, effective tricks used by professionals —cards, string, tumblers, handkerchiefs, mental magic, etc. 63 illustrations. 223pp. 23012-0 Pa. $2.50

CARD MANIPULATIONS, Jean Hugard. Very rich collection of manipulations; has taught thousands of fine magicians tricks that are really workable, eye-catching. Easily followed, serious work. Over 200 illustrations. 163pp. 20539-8 Pa. $2.00

ABBOTT'S ENCYCLOPEDIA OF ROPE TRICKS FOR MAGICIANS, Stewart James. Complete reference book for amateur and professional magicians containing more than 150 tricks involving knots, penetrations, cut and restored rope, etc. 510 illustrations. Reprint of 3rd edition. 400pp. 23206-9 Pa. $3.50

THE SECRETS OF HOUDINI, J.C. Cannell. Classic study of Houdini's incredible magic, exposing closely-kept professional secrets and revealing, in general terms, the whole art of stage magic. 67 illustrations. 279pp. 22913-0 Pa. $2.50

HOUDINI ON MAGIC, Harold Houdini. Edited by Walter Gibson, Morris N. Young. How he escaped; exposés of fake spiritualists; instructions for eye-catching tricks; other fascinating material by and about greatest magician. 155 illustrations. 280pp. 20384-0 Pa. $2.75

HANDBOOK OF THE NUTRITIONAL CONTENTS OF FOOD, U.S. Dept. of Agriculture. Largest, most detailed source of food nutrition information ever prepared. Two mammoth tables: one measuring nutrients in 100 grams of edible portion; the other, in edible portion of 1 pound as purchased. Originally titled Composition of Foods. 190pp. 9 x 12. 21342-0 Pa. $4.00

COMPLETE GUIDE TO HOME CANNING, PRESERVING AND FREEZING, U.S. Dept. of Agriculture. Seven basic manuals with full instructions for jams and jellies; pickles and relishes; canning fruits, vegetables, meat; freezing anything. Really good recipes, exact instructions for optimal results. Save a fortune in food. 156 illustrations. 214pp. 6⅛ x 9¼. 22911-4 Pa. $2.50

THE BREAD TRAY, Louis P. De Gouy. Nearly every bread the cook could buy or make: bread sticks of Italy, fruit breads of Greece, glazed rolls of Vienna, everything from corn pone to croissants. Over 500 recipes altogether. including buns, rolls, muffins, scones, and more. 463pp. 23000-7 Pa. $3.50

CREATIVE HAMBURGER COOKERY, Louis P. De Gouy. 182 unusual recipes for casseroles, meat loaves and hamburgers that turn inexpensive ground meat into memorable main dishes: Arizona chili burgers, burger tamale pie, burger stew, burger corn loaf, burger wine loaf, and more. 120pp. 23001-5 Pa. $1.75

LONG ISLAND SEAFOOD COOKBOOK, J. George Frederick and Jean Joyce. Probably the best American seafood cookbook. Hundreds of recipes. 40 gourmet sauces, 123 recipes using oysters alone! All varieties of fish and seafood amply represented. 324pp. 22677-8 Pa. $3.50

THE EPICUREAN: A COMPLETE TREATISE OF ANALYTICAL AND PRACTICAL STUDIES IN THE CULINARY ART, Charles Ranhofer. Great modern classic. 3,500 recipes from master chef of Delmonico's, turn-of-the-century America's best restaurant. Also explained, many techniques known only to professional chefs. 775 illustrations. 1183pp. 6⅝ x 10. 22680-8 Clothbd. $22.50

THE AMERICAN WINE COOK BOOK, Ted Hatch. Over 700 recipes: old favorites livened up with wine plus many more: Czech fish soup, quince soup, sauce Perigueux, shrimp shortcake, filets Stroganoff, cordon bleu goulash, jambonneau, wine fruit cake, more. 314pp. 22796-0 Pa. $2.50

DELICIOUS VEGETARIAN COOKING, Ivan Baker. Close to 500 delicious and varied recipes: soups, main course dishes (pea, bean, lentil, cheese, vegetable, pasta, and egg dishes), savories, stews, whole-wheat breads and cakes, more. 168pp. USO 22834-7 Pa. $1.75

EAST O' THE SUN AND WEST O' THE MOON, George W. Dasent. Considered the best of all translations of these Norwegian folk tales, this collection has been enjoyed by generations of children (and folklorists too). Includes True and Untrue, Why the Sea is Salt, East O' the Sun and West O' the Moon, Why the Bear is Stumpy-Tailed, Boots and the Troll, The Cock and the Hen, Rich Peter the Pedlar, and 52 more. The only edition with all 59 tales. 77 illustrations by Erik Werenskiold and Theodor Kittelsen. xv + 418pp. 22521-6 Paperbound **$4.00**

GOOPS AND HOW TO BE THEM, Gelett Burgess. Classic of tongue-in-cheek humor, masquerading as etiquette book. 87 verses, twice as many cartoons, show mischievous Goops as they demonstrate to children virtues of table manners, neatness, courtesy, etc. Favorite for generations. viii + 88pp. 6½ x 9¼. 22233-0 Paperbound **$2.00**

ALICE'S ADVENTURES UNDER GROUND, Lewis Carroll. The first version, quite different from the final *Alice in Wonderland,* printed out by Carroll himself with his own illustrations. Complete facsimile of the "million dollar" manuscript Carroll gave to Alice Liddell in 1864. Introduction by Martin Gardner. viii + 96pp. Title and dedication pages in color. 21482-6 Paperbound **$1.50**

THE BROWNIES, THEIR BOOK, Palmer Cox. Small as mice, cunning as foxes, exuberant and full of mischief, the Brownies go to the zoo, toy shop, seashore, circus, etc., in 24 verse adventures and 266 illustrations. Long a favorite, since their first appearance in St. Nicholas Magazine. xi + 144pp. 6⅝ x 9¼. 21265-3 Paperbound **$2.50**

SONGS OF CHILDHOOD, Walter De La Mare. Published (under the pseudonym Walter Ramal) when De La Mare was only 29, this charming collection has long been a favorite children's book. A facsimile of the first edition in paper, the 47 poems capture the simplicity of the nursery rhyme and the ballad, including such lyrics as I Met Eve, Tartary, The Silver Penny. vii + 106pp. (USO) 21972-0 Paperbound **$2.00**

THE COMPLETE NONSENSE OF EDWARD LEAR, Edward Lear. The finest 19th-century humorist-cartoonist in full: all nonsense limericks, zany alphabets, Owl and Pussycat, songs, nonsense botany, and more than 500 illustrations by Lear himself. Edited by Holbrook Jackson. xxix + 287pp. (USO) 20167-8 Paperbound **$3.00**

BILLY WHISKERS: THE AUTOBIOGRAPHY OF A GOAT, Frances Trego Montgomery. A favorite of children since the early 20th century, here are the escapades of that rambunctious, irresistible and mischievous goat—Billy Whiskers. Much in the spirit of *Peck's Bad Boy,* this is a book that children never tire of reading or hearing. All the original familiar illustrations by W. H. Fry are included: 6 color plates, 18 black and white drawings. 159pp. 22345-0 Paperbound **$2.75**

MOTHER GOOSE MELODIES. Faithful republication of the fabulously rare Munroe and Francis "copyright 1833" Boston edition—the most important Mother Goose collection, usually referred to as the "original." Familiar rhymes plus many rare ones, with wonderful old woodcut illustrations. Edited by E. F. Bleiler. 128pp. 4½ x 6⅜. 22577-1 Paperbound **$1.50**

CATALOGUE OF DOVER BOOKS

[illegible] Watts. [illegible] Buddhism [illegible] meditation, control of [illegible] [illegible] pp. [illegible]

[illegible] Persian Mysticism [illegible] 1324 [illegible]

The [illegible] translation, edited by [illegible] Catholics and Protestants. [illegible] 22232-0 [illegible]

[illegible] 8 illustrations. [illegible]

[illegible] Dervish [illegible] Knight. [illegible] 21861-1 [illegible]

[illegible] Martin [illegible] [illegible] 20839-[illegible]

[illegible] 54 illustrations [illegible] 20405-[illegible]

[illegible]

[illegible] 22770-1 [illegible]

[illegible] Dept. [illegible] Dover Publications, Inc., 180 Varick St., N.Y., N.Y. 10014. Dover publishes more than 150 [illegible]